Becoming Male in the Middle Ages

THE NEW MIDDLE AGES
VOLUME 4
GARLAND REFERENCE LIBRARY OF THE HUMANITIES
VOLUME 2066

THE NEW MIDDLE AGES

BONNIE WHEELER
Series Editor

The New Middle Ages is dedicated to transdisciplinary studies of medieval cultures, with particular emphasis on women's history and feminist and gender analyses. The series includes both scholarly monographs and essay collections.

Clothes Make the Man: Female Cross Dressing in Medieval Europe
by Valerie R. Hotchkiss

Medieval Mothering
edited by John Carmi Parsons and Bonnie Wheeler

Fresh Verdicts on Joan of Arc
edited by Bonnie Wheeler and Charles T. Wood

Becoming Male in the Middle Ages
edited by Jeffrey Jerome Cohen and Bonnie Wheeler

Becoming Male in the Middle Ages

EDITED BY
JEFFREY JEROME COHEN
BONNIE WHEELER

GARLAND PUBLISHING, INC.
NEW YORK AND LONDON
2000

First paperback edition published in 2000 by
Garland Publishing Inc.
A Member of the Taylor & Francis Group
19 Union Square West
New York, NY 10003

10 9 8 7 6 5 4 3 2 1

Library of Congress Cataloging-in-Publication Data

Becoming male in the middle ages / edited by Jeffrey Jerome Cohen and Bonnie Wheeler.
p. cm. — (Garland reference library of the humanities ; v. 2066. The new Middle Ages ; v. 4)
Includes bibliographical references.
ISBN 0-8153-3770-1 (alk. paper)
1. Masculinity (Psychology)—History. 2. Civilization, Medieval. 3. Men in literature. I. Cohen, Jeffrey Jerome. II. Wheeler, Bonnie. III. Series: Garland reference library of the humanities ; v. 2066. IV. Series: Garland reference library of the humanities. New Middle Ages ; vol. 4.
HQ1088.B43 1997
305.31'09—dc21 97-1520
CIP

Cover illustration of *40 Martyrs of Sebaste* courtesy of
Dumbarton Oaks, Washington, DC © 1996.

Printed on acid-free, 250-year-life paper
Manufactured in the United States of America

CONTENTS

BECOMING AND UNBECOMING

Jeffrey Jerome Cohen and Bonnie Wheeler

"What then is the real state of affairs?"
Claude Lévi-Strauss[1]

THEATRE

This story takes place more than fifty years ago, in one of "the lower-priced restaurants in the south of France."[2] A man enters the crowded little place, which is full of similar men who have come alone after work for their evening meal. No one recognizes anyone else here: the men are united in their anonymity. The waitress motions for him to take a seat at one of the numerous small tables, directly across from someone already awaiting his dinner. The two exchange awkward glances, perhaps a tight smile, then look away to see what is taking the food so long to arrive. They feel "both alone and together," for they are strangers at a place-setting for intimacy. An "almost imperceptible anxiety" arises (59).

At last the waitress drops plates of meat and vegetables in front of them, and they silently examine each other's repast to ensure that neither has been favored with a larger portion. The wine arrives in two dirty carafes, each holding a glassful of sour red. The man who was seated at the table first reaches for his carafe. Making nothing of the fact that his holds a slightly more generous portion, he pours the entire contents into his tablemate's glass. The recipient smiles, reaches for his own container, and returns the favor. They raise their wine to each other and sip. The ice has been broken once the exchange has transpired, and a lively conversation follows:

> This is the fleeting but difficult situation resolved by the exchange of wine. It is an assertion of good grace which does away with the mutual uncertainty. It substitutes a social relationship for a spatial juxtaposition. (59)

Throughout the restaurant the scene is repeated as strangers fill the glasses of those with whom, by chance, they share a table and a meal. The simple dinner is transformed from mere sustenance to a cultural event, a metamorphosis precipitated through the catalyst of exchange.

This happy little vignette occurs not in some recent piece of cinema imported from France, but early in Claude Lévi-Strauss' monumental anthropological work, *The Elementary Structures of Kinship*. The scene functions as a point of origin for Lévi-Strauss: he uses the narrative of the restaurant table both to theorize and illustrate his thesis that culture comes into being the moment men establish relationships through a rule-bound transfer of women. This exchange requires the prohibition of incest, which in turn generates those regulations that produce the family, the clan, the tribe. Primitive groups of men, meeting by chance as they wandered their scattered territories, must have felt as awkward as two strangers sharing a single restaurant table; they exchange women as the rural Frenchmen exchange wine, a social relation is established, and culture receives its structuration. The laws of exogamy and endogamy (the juridical network which regulates sexuality) organize a system of culture from the chaos of nature.

The doubled story is full of transubstantiations: working-class men become "individuals of primitive bands" (60), southern France becomes universal prehistory, wine becomes the feminine body. Chez Lévi-Strauss, the possibility of a woman seated at the table is unthinkable. Woman is definitionally a "mystery" in the exchange system; her voice and agency are wholly excluded from this masculine economy.[3] Unthinkable here, too, is that the men will converse with each other prior to the gesture that breaks the ice; verbalization would be an exchange outside of this system which is materialized through the commodification of women's bodies-as-wine. And perhaps it takes art-house cinema imported from France to imagine a world in which the two strangers might quickly leave the restaurant for the nearby hotel, even before the wine is consumed. The exchange at the table, like the exchange between the primitive groups, is regulated by strict prohibitions that organize the whole proceeding into an economy of bodies, genders, and identities constitutive of what Gayle Rubin labels the heterosexual matrix.[4] The traffic in women distributes culturally coherent sexualities to women and men like a well-oiled machine.

This coldly mechanical model of identity construction is also the site of a disturbing violence. The French psychoanalyst Jacques Lacan, who relied heavily upon Lévi-Strauss's structural anthropology, is infamous for his assertion "*La femme n'existe pas*" ("Woman does not exist"). Lacan is here provocative rather than mistaken: within the confines of the exchange model of cultural formation, "woman" is reduced to functional matter whose value resides only its social imprint. She is a semi-mystical "rich food," like wine; she exists not *as* woman, but only in order to enable systematicity in human relations. Man, in this model, is the sole locus of power and agency; (imaginary) woman becomes a "symptom" of (universal) man.

At least, that's how it appears at first glance. But a certain claustrophobia inheres in this system, even as it articulates the supposedly more copious space of the masculine. Perhaps it is the fact that the model's structure seems to have congealed into place so long ago (whenever those primitive tribes were wandering the open spaces of the young earth, sharing an "almost imperceptible anxiety" and then exchanging women to alleviate it). Or perhaps the asphyxiatic feel derives from the model's impossible timelessness: as on the primitive savanna, so in southern France. Its reductive reliance on simple gender binaries adds to its disturbing totalitarianism. Perhaps also the model commits violence to all gendered identities by robbing them of true relationality, movement, possibility: this structural anthropology hardens the process of *becoming* into a simple prescription for *being* that eradicates the complexities of sexuality by freezing it, under a severe and universal law, into a system unnuanced and unmalleable. The kinds of masculinity and femininity that the exchange matrix constructs pass themselves off as inevitable, as universal, but as we have begun to see, they might be culturally contingent, limited, and local.

Perhaps the drama of identity is not always to be played in the same universal theatre, with the same roles, the same stage, the same script.

FACTORY

When, seven years after its initial publication, Eve Kosofsky Sedgwick returned to her book *Between Men* to write a new preface, she was struck by its dual purpose: this "complicating, antiseparationist, and antihomophobic" contribution to feminism was also meant as a challenge to some of its most revered paradigms, especially those which neatly aligned "feminism" with "the female," as if the relation between those two terms was transparent and unproblematic.[5] Relying heavily on Lévi-Strauss' exchange model as triangulated through René Girard's theory of mimetic desire, Sedgwick argued that identity is a field across which gender is plotted asymmetrically but relationally, and is therefore subject to disruption by the identities and possibilities it excludes. The effect of her investigation was to announce, loudly, that the study of the construction of masculinity is a necessary feminist enterprise. That she has been labeled the "queen of gay studies" is a direct effect of her intervention into feminism.[6] Yet the royal title flattens the complex implications of her arguments by straightjacketing them to a single, new discipline created in part to contain them.

Thanks to feminist theorists like Sedgwick and Butler, masculine and feminine are both now seen as multiple sites for the production of cultural meaning. If *la femme* does not exist, neither does *l'homme*, at least not as a monolithic and atemporal structure for "being in the world." Sedgwick and (especially) Butler argue for a "performative" or "citational" model of gender, in which "there is no nature, only the effects of nature: denaturalization or naturalization."[7] Gender becomes not a biological fact but a cultural production.[8] Butler positions her critique of dominant identity manufacture from the abjected margins of the heterosexual matrix—the place to which those queer bodies excluded by the system are banished, to dwell in illegibility, incoherence, illegality. If these outlawed sexualities can be demonstrated to be necessary to the production of all identities, then the process as a whole can be challenged through disidentifications that contest and reconfigure cultural norms.[9] Butler aims to expose the contingency of the whole system, its non-necessity, the dangerous possibility of pushing it to run otherwise.

Theorizing gender does not sublime the body's solidity to melt, suddenly, into air. The conceptual categories "man" and "woman" have profoundly material effects on the production of human subjects, and theorizing gender (femininities, masculinities, and all the possibilities these terms exclude) only historicizes the process of this sedimentation. The challenge, however, is to begin to see sexuality and its categories not simply as system-bound surfaces permanently encoded by the social process that produced their coherence, but as virtualities, bodies, and affects in motion that are always crossing lines, always becoming deterritorialized and reterritorialized, always becoming something other than an immobile and eternal self-same. Gender is a culturally specific process of becoming. It is a kind of alchemy: perhaps it has a stated *telos* (the "purity" of frozen being, of exactly coinciding with the static "gold" of a gender ideal), but in fact it is all about impurity and phantasmatic "refinement," explosions of like and unlike, matter warring against matter, multiple transubstantiations, equations that map trajectories of perpetual motion rather than models that trace the contours of closed and lifeless systems.

BECOMING MEDIEVAL

We intend the present volume to be a contribution to this alchemical history of how gender is materialized over time and through place. Specifically, we are interested here in how masculinity—which has for too long functioned as the universal category of being—can be unpacked and reapproached through the eclectic toolbox which the confluence of medieval studies, feminism, gender theory, and cultural studies provides.

No progress narrative will be offered here. It is not the responsibility of the past to account for the present, nor to determine the future. Although we are interested in the cultural specificity of becoming male in the Middle Ages, we do not insist that masculinities have a singular origin here or elsewhere in history; for origins are always elsewhere, in some anxious "primitive tribes" or a similar, retroactively posited fantasy field. Nor shall we insist upon a *telos*: we ignore the complexity of identities when we read them backwards from some fixed, unambiguous endpoint. We are more interested in mapping the movements of gender, in respecting the imperfection inherent in becoming-as-process. We ought to account for the ways in which the Middle Ages have been rendered a point of origin in metanarratives of history (so that, for example, it becomes the field of alterity for modernity as explicated by those scholars who used to study the Renaissance but now work in the Early Modern Period). We need not construct such narratives ourselves—only critical genealogies, only engagements with processes of transformation and sedimentation, rather than with frozen narratives of being. As for history, so for masculinity: it is not very useful to explore gender in terms of its stability and "pre-given" materiality; better to engage the unending process of its becoming, its stabilization, its materialization.

Of the "Middle" Ages we might ask, "middle" to what? Clearly one answer is to detail the evolutionary narrative that renders the medieval period middle to the birth of the west in classical Greece and Rome and that culminates in the appearance of a modern age, already approaching the senescence of postmodernity. A more challenging conceptualization, however, would embrace the middleness of the Middle Ages and insist upon its *absolute status as middle to nothing*. Divorced from a *telos* (modernity, which has never had anything but contempt for the medieval) and freed from the dictative power of a simple origin (freed, that is, from simple filiation, as if inheritance were destiny), the Middle Ages becomes a geometric line: that which passes through and connects two points, but is defined as the movement across and beyond those points rather than the flat space contained between them. A line is simultaneously pure middle and pure movement. A line is an infinity of becoming, curving into space.

To map these lines of flight is not to insist that masculinity or the Middle Ages are *all* things, which would reduce both to nothing at all. The medieval and the masculine have their specificities, their affects, their relational significations; but they are terms (bodies, *corpora*) that are always on the move. That mobility is the very complexity that structuralist and post-structuralist systematization denies. The heterosexual matrix as articulated through Lévi-Strauss' principles of exchange and universal prohibition finds its counterpart in the historical narrative that grids time into a system which functions through the principles of difference and linear cause and effect. Both models produce categories that function as natural and discrete, as if they were the bedrock of the Real. But bedrock is typically produced through sedimentation, and sedimentation is in turn produced by monolithic systems that arrest arcs of becoming into categories of being by plotting them, repeatedly, against the twin axes of (stable, unchanging, linear) space and time. Point A to Point B is then rendered a progress narrative, a pilgrimage, rather than a trajectory or geometric line. The past congeals as the prescriptive foundation of the present; the Middle Ages is the wayside inn where humanity paused briefly before continuing to the Canterbury of whatever end-point we are writing from.

But bedrock, no matter how firmly stratified, can be broken. Even Chaucer's *Canterbury Tales*, that infinitely dilating narrative framed but in no way contained by the artificial book-ends of London and Canterbury, contains a middle that is all motion, and a vision of pilgrimage that does not end at the bones of a long-dead martyr. Of this world between worlds which we inhabit, Egeus declares over the body of trampled Arcite, "we been pilgrymes, passynge to and fro."[10] An extraordinary pilgrimage that is simultaneously *towards* and *from*, a journey without *telos* or simple origin, a journey of pure movement, pure encounter, pure becoming.[11]

Like Augustine before him, Chaucer is among those medieval thinkers who grapple with such *middle*-ness, such interactivity of subject with object, of stability with persistent "conversions" of identity, space, and time. Our narratives of "gender" are just as malleable (culture-driven but self-defining) as our inherited stories of time and space. This position, shared by the contributors to this present collection of essays, asserts that gender, like time and space, is continually negotiated, continually in the act of becoming. These essays take medieval representations of masculinities as their collective subject, but it is not the object of these essays to define authoritatively "masculinity," "masculinities," or even "medieval masculinities." It would be inappropriate to propose inflexible definitions, since the usual manner of defining such things requires rigid assumptions about origins or *tele*. Eschewing originary fantasies and teleological outcomes, we are interested instead in trajectories of gender, in how ideas and ideologies of masculinity were regarded and elaborated in the Middle Ages. These essays catch moments in which we can observe masculinity in performance and masculinity as performance. The collection interrogates ways in which masculinity is written on the body, through the body, and by the mind into culture. Gender performances mark not only private but also cultural constructs of power and powerlessness, and frequently reveal individual and collective anxieties about identity boundaries, about the Other in terms of sex, status, race, and religion.

The project of this collection is historical as well as provocative: some struggles and displays of men *qua* men are here reclaimed and recuperated into historical discourse, but in no case is masculinity a category granted transhistorical hegemony. Our enterprise does not purport to be comprehensive or exhaustive. We begin (Smith, Kruger) and end (Uebel) with essays that theorize medieval masculinities. The other essays are arranged by the chronology of their subject matter. Different orderings that evoke new prismatic patterns will, we hope, suggest themselves to the reader.

Vance Smith's nuanced essay, "Body Doubles: Producing the Masculine *Corpus*," argues that representations and projections of the masculine body, both as microcosm and macrocosm, often root medieval political, scientific, and religious discourse. The material body's "primary function" is perceived in a reciprocal economy, a joint labor of material procreation and politics, since "producing the male body is often regarded in the Middle Ages as being the same thing as producing the world.... [M]an, in fact, produces the body of the world." Smith holds medieval materiality and medieval transcendence in counterpoint—alchemy, for example, identifies plenitude and "preservation of the body politic" with the alembic of the male body distilling sperm. Quintessential virility, as sperm was thought to be, restores and balances the male body just as the male body restores and preserves the body politic. Steven Kruger also highlights theories of the masculine body, in his case locating a "certain disturbance of gender" displayed in the conflicted Christian discourse about the "heresies" of Islam and Judaism: is becoming Christian, he asks, equivalent to becoming male?

Allen Frantzen reminds us that masculinity is a mark not only of the man, but of the boy. His study of Anglo-Saxon penitentials amply demonstrates facts known to medievalists but often suppressed by modernists: the medieval world produced a substantial discourse about sexuality, the sexuality of boys, and sexual discipline. Sexual suppression is relentlessly advocated (in penitentials that by their very existence testify to probable sexual conduct) so that boys, "already constructed as men," would adopt approved gender roles and learn to be appropriately "male." The Latin *Waltharius* renders problematic the very notions of appropriate maleness it constructs, argues David Townsend in a subtle reading of that epic, since its ironic strategies lead readers to resist its portrayal of heroic masculinity—in which "the price of phallic potency is amputation."

Issues of sexual mutilation and gendered subjectivity converge in the three subsequent essays, each of which refracts a different aspect of the notorious Abelard's insistent projection of his own masculinity, especially in his *Historia calamitatum* and his correspondence with Heloise. Martin Irvine analyzes Abelard's post-castration epistolary and philosophic discourse in terms of Abelard's project of "remasculating himself with new imagined objects of wholeness." In Irvine's view, Abelard "clearly advanced a performative model of masculinity." Irvine uses twelfth-century castration narratives as a cultural compass for situating Abelard's strategies within "a network of social values and anxieties." In her analysis of Abelard's confessional strategies, Bonnie Wheeler argues instead that Abelard, with Heloise's complicity, consistently represents himself as fully masculine. Sundering sexuality from gender, Abelard constructs masculinity as intellectual performance and (in a brilliant inversion of expectation) he *essentializes* his gender, not his bodily sexuality. Reviewing some tantalizing materials, psychoanalyst Yves Ferroul examines the nature of Abelard's castration (what actually was excised?), his claustration (why/how is his post-castration choice of monastic life "naturalized"?), and the subsequent cultural reception of both his castration and his claustration.

The spiritual rather than physical eunuch is Elliot Wolfson's subject in his study of thirteenth-century Jewish mystics and the ascetic ideal. In the kabbalistic tradition, heterosexual eros and homoeroticism are transposed in cycles of divine autoeroticism, and, as Wolfson concludes, attitudes toward gender had a "profound impact on the nature of the mystic's experience with God." Wolfson investigates those "shifting gender valences implied by...chain[s] of desire," since the "ultimate goal of the mystic's interpretive efforts is the union of the masculine and feminine aspects of the divine, but this union results in the restoration of the latter to the former." The ascetic ideal requires the integration of masculine and feminine.

What happens when that possibility is denied? In an historical overview, Ruth Mazo Karras considers some consequences "of the exclusion of women from the universities" of late medieval Europe: that early institutional decision, as Karras shows, had profound results not only on scholarship but also on identity formation, among them that "universities were not primarily training scholars; they were training men." Intellectually bonded by a misogynistic curriculum, the masculine identity of this elite was socialized by highly privileged, widely tolerated rituals of male conviviality, symbolically marked by drunken rowdiness.

In literature as in life, masculinity is revealed and released through differing symbols and actions. In *La Chanson de Roland*, for example, Charlemagne expresses his physical prowess when he assuages his grief for Roland by wreaking vengeance on cultural/religious "others," but Charlemagne himself often lacks control of events or decisions. His masculinity is most often symbolized by his silent stroking of his long beard, a code that poignantly renders masculinity as the quiet (when not passive) endurance of life's complex pain. But his is not the only manifestation of masculinity privileged in *La Chanson*. The masculine performance of *fiers* (fear-inspiring as well as powerful) Roland is summarized in his refusal to sound Olifant. Roland's extremity—admittedly dangerous, violent, and verging on monstrosity—marks one endpoint of masculine display. Medieval literary discourse often literalizes this gendered extremity through problematic presentations of monsters, and two essays in this collection explore the relation between becoming male and becoming monstrous. Leslie Dunton-Downer's analysis of linguistic dualism and oppositionalism in Marie de France's *Bisclavret* foregrounds connections between violence and maleness through the figure of the *lai*'s sympathetic werewolf. This werewolf provokes one to confront all linguistic devising of ontological status (human/animal, past/present, feminine/masculine) as potential obstruction and deformation. Jeffrey Jerome Cohen examines related ontological issues in his analysis of monstrosity, bodily plasticity, and masculinity in the late Middle English verse romance *Sir Gowther*. That romance, like *Bisclavret*, presents "familializing" imprints, and Cohen tracks "the genealogy of Oedipal configuration," animated by a "complex process of intersubjective embodiment," to argue "that gender is constructed and that bodies are sexed in culturally specific ways." Thus he rejects static Freudian/Lacanian depictions of the unconscious as inevitably repetitive theatre; instead (in the mode of Deleuze and Guattari) he adopts the model of the unconscious as factory, marked by discontinuities and flux.

The two subsequent essays use queer theory to interrogate the "reproduction of masculine authority" in two of Chaucer's *Canterbury Tales*. The carnivalesque fabliau of *The Miller's Tale*, argues Glenn Burger, "queers the heteronormative sexual politics" of (especially) *The Knight's Tale*. Although the "masculinist, dominating gaze" reasserts itself and bodily discipline is enforced in *The Miller's*

Tale, readers are invited to choose both temporary release from this domination and "the 'humiliation' of the tale's category confusion": one is challenged "to 'see' via the nether eye." Robert Sturges, in "The Pardoner, Veiled and Unveiled," demonstrates that the Pardoner's veils, like the Pardoner himself, simultaneously conceal and reveal multivalent "figure[s] of fluid gender."

Gender fluidity also interests Ad Putter in the following essay, "Transvestite Knights in Medieval Life and Literature." Here, as in Sturges's reading of Chaucer's Pardoner, gender performance is mirrored and amplified by clothing. Putter studies literal and literary cross-dressers—especially those knights who embody hypermasculine ideology for chivalric culture—to argue that knightly transvestism reinforces rather than challenges gender norms. Considering costume, gender, and sexual orientation from the vantage point of the late fifteenth-century drama *Mankind*, Garrett Epp interrogates cultural commonplaces about sodomy and effeminacy. In the play, male decoration, stigmatized as an effeminate superfluity, signifies corruption, but effeminacy is not however equated with "any particular sexual role or orientation." Though *Mankind* "treats sodomy as the end to which effeminacy leads," the moral interlude evokes a "perverse dynamic" in which masculine and feminine, like good and evil, are "transgressively reinscribed over [each] other." In this dynamic, homoerotic desire gains "visible representation—a name, and a costume." In this same late medieval theatrical context, Claire Sponsler looks at issues of gender and lower-class identity formation through the use of transvestism and blackface in "men's seasonal ceremonials known as mummings and morris dances." These rituals, "sites of cultural alterity," both internalized and repressed imagined threats from cultural others, and in doing so, they "did not just feature laboring-class men, they *produced* them."

James Goldstein moves us toward the volume's boundaries as he historicizes Judith Butler's theory of performativity in his brief biographical analysis of the "pivotal" Scottish writer Sir David Lindsay of the Mount. He investigates varying dimensions of Lindsay's preoccupation with the male body (especially the heteronormative and patriarchal body of the king) and with sodomy. Though gender performance is mobile and particular, individuals (like Lindsay) and cultures tend to totalize an approved ideal of masculinity. Goldstein shows that studies of the fluctuations in prohibitions and taboos about masculine sexuality and behavior can help historians to recuperate shifting views of masculinity, of male bodies that matter. In the final essay, Michael Uebel situates, synthesizes, and spacializes the volume's central project: What is "the historical formation of men's desire to become?"

The "becoming medieval" of this subsection is meant to suggest the "becoming male" of this collection's title. To become medieval is to approach the Middle Ages in all its fullness and to acknowledge that *both* bodies will be changed by the encounter. This is the second collection of essays to appear on the subject of medieval masculinities.[12] In her introduction to her own collection, Clare A. Lees insists that "*Medieval Masculinities* is timely above all precisely because it constitutes a challenge to those contemporary theories of sex, gender, and patriarchy that gesture toward but cannot adequately deal with the study of the past" (xix). It is impossible to disagree. But Lees' point can be pushed even further: what is at stake in this encounter with medieval masculinities is the very pastness of the past, its placement in a temporal category that declares the past has already done its work, that we who study it merely trace its pre-effects to posit cause. To take the absolute middleness—the absolute motion—of the Middle Ages seriously is to declare that the time-object under scrutiny is not going to stay in its place, but has already become entangled in a complicated and multiple process of becoming that provokes the authors collected in this book to write and map, that provokes the readers of this book to encounter again the medieval body in a meeting that could uncannily change both. The Middle Ages have a power, and it is not the tyrannical power of the past to determine the present through some dull progress narrative or evolutionary tree. The power of the Middle Ages is the fact that it is middle to nothing, that it does not end, that we encounter its processes of becoming only through a dangerous becoming-process of our own.

BECOMING MALE

By now it will be clear that the title of this collection of essays is intended to be polysemous, relational, and oppositional. Despite these multiple possibilities, the title also has a specificity. "Becoming" suggests critical genealogy, process in motion, and an encounter that involves subject, object, and innocent bystander in its alchemical ignitions. The noun "male" which follows the title's gerund indicates that masculinity is only one identity term among the many that gender a subject. "Becoming male" suggests that the production of gender is not to be conflated with the "fact" of anatomy. Biology is not irrelevant, but making a boy out of a body born with a penis is a cultural process just as complicated and life-long as "girling" a body declared female on the basis of her vagina.

The collection is called "becoming male" rather than "becoming gendered" because to suggest that the construction of sex is commensurable across genders is to collapse sexual difference entirely. Were we to start with the assumption that the boy is "boyed" and the girl is "girled" identically, the study of masculinities would be the same as the study of a universal, and we already know the violence that collapse into univocality commits. Male and female are not simple binaries, but multiplicities that are simultaneously relational and oppositional. To insist that to study one is the same as to study the other is absurdly masculinist. To insist that medieval masculinities must be encountered in their mobile specificities, to suggest that the study of masculinities might necessitate critical work "independent and asymmetrical"[13] from feminist theory and queer studies, and to acknowledge nonetheless that feminism, queer theory, and gay and lesbian studies have allowed the very possibility of asking these kinds of questions here and now, is to evoke both the danger and the rewards of theorizing the medieval male body.

NOTES

1. *The Elementary Structures of Kinship* [*Les Structures élémentaires de la Parenté*], tr. James Harle Bell, John Richard von Sturmer, and Rodney Needham (Boston: Beacon Press, 1969), p. 7.

2. Lévi-Strauss, p. 58. Further references are marked by page numbers.

3. See Luce Irigaray, "When the Goods Get Together," in *New French Feminisms*, ed. Elaine Marks and Isabelle de Courtivron (New York: Schocken, 1981), pp. 107–11.

4. Gayle Rubin, "The Traffic in Women: Notes on the 'Political Economy' of Sex," in *Toward an Anthropology of Women*, ed. Rayna R. Reiter (New York: Monthly Review Press, 1975). Judith Butler argues that a prohibition of homosexuality rather than of incest is primary to the Lévi-Strauss account of the genesis of this matrix; see *Gender Trouble: Feminism*

and the Subversion of Identity (New York: Routledge, 1990), especially pp. 35–43.

5. Eve Kosofsky Sedgwick, *Between Men: English Literature and Male Homosocial Desire* (New York: Columbia University Press, 1985), pp. vii–x.

6. "The soft-spoken queen of gay studies" is the title bestowed upon Sedgwick by no less an authority than *Rolling Stone*, at least according to the blurb on the back cover of her collection of essays *Tendencies* (Durham, NC: Duke University Press, 1993).

7. The quotation is taken from Jacques Derrida's *Donner le Temps*. It is used as an epigraph to the introduction of Judith Butler's *Bodies That Matter: On the Discursive Limits of 'Sex'* (New York: Routledge, 1993), p. 1.

8. Even matter loses its stability, its fixity, becoming not a "site or surface," as Butler notes in *Bodies That Matter*, pp. 9–10:

> [but] a process of materialization that stabilizes over time to produce the effect of boundary, fixity, and surface we call matter. That matter has to be materialized has, I think, to be thought in relation to the productive and, indeed, materializing effects of power in the Foucaultian sense. Thus the question is no longer, How is gender constituted as and through a certain interpretation of sex? (a question that leaves the 'matter' of sex untheorized), but rather, Through what regulatory norm is sex itself materialized?

9. See *Bodies That Matter*, pp. 3–4 and pp. 223–42.

10. "The Knight's Tale," l. 2848, *The Riverside Chaucer*, 3rd ed., Larry D. Benson, gen. ed. (Boston: Houghton Mifflin, 1987).

11. Medieval theorists themselves, particularly neo-Aristotelian scholastics, often think fixedly about both origin and *telos*.

12. The first was *Medieval Masculinities: Regarding Men in the Middle Ages*, ed. Clare A. Lees (Minneapolis: University of Minnesota Press, 1994). See also the *Interscripta* hypertext article "Medieval Masculinities: Heroism, Sanctity, and Gender" (http://www.georgetown.edu/labyrinth/e-center/interscripta/mm.html) and the version of the same piece published as "The Armour of an Alienating Identity," *Arthuriana* 6.4 (Winter 1996). Two recent, important collections cross-pollinate gender and medieval studies: *Feminist Approaches to the Body in Medieval Literature*, ed. Linda Lomperis and Sarah Stanbury (Philadelphia: University of Pennsylvania Press, 1993); and *Premodern Sexualities*, ed. Louise Fradenburg and Carla Freccero (New York: Routledge, 1995).

13. The quotation is from Michael Uebel's review of *Medieval Masculinities*. Masculinity, he writes, is too often posited "as the defining quality of men, of their social and historical experiences of self and other, rather than as one coordinate of their identity that exists in a constant dialectical relation with other coordinates." See *Arthuriana* 5.4 (Winter 1995): 109–111. See also Robert S. Sturges' important review of the book, "Medieval Masculinity (Singular)" in the *Lesbian and Gay Studies Newsletter* 22.1 (March 1995), 26–27, which argues for the importance of sexuality in the exploration of masculinities.

Becoming Male in the Middle Ages

BODY DOUBLES:

PRODUCING THE MASCULINE *Corpus*

D. Vance Smith

This survey of idealized images of the medieval male body suggests that they are neither as stable nor as abstract as they seem, since they must both transcend and exemplify matter.

The king is not the only man in the Middle Ages who has two bodies. From Christ himself came the notion that a man could inhabit one physical body yet signify another abstract, powerful corpus. While this paradox is one of the central features of Christianity, Ernst Kantorowicz has shown how the nature of the abstract corpus was also appropriated by political discourse. Originally referring to the divine nature of Christ and to the sacrament of the altar, the term *corpus mysticum* became increasingly politicized, eventually applying to both the body politic of the church and the secular realm.[1] But even though, as Kantorowicz argues, discourses on the relation between the physical and the abstract bodies, the *corpus verum* and the *corpus mysticum*, produce a powerful and coherent group of writings that explains how physical and political bodies can be conjoined in the person of the king, the persistence and monumentality of such efforts attests that the conjunction is not an effortless or even a natural one. The work of inscribing the *corpus mysticum* is complex because it is a profound critique of the way masculine bodily representation is conceived of in the Middle Ages. I would like to suggest not only that the medieval masculine body is imagined as an abstract body, but that its abstraction is the consequence of discourses concerning the materiality of the masculine body itself. The notion of an abstract corpus appears in medieval writers who discuss the involvement of men in the earthiest of activities: the labor of preserving the physical body.

For Vincent of Beauvais, the soul, and not the body, is created in the image of God; yet the male body "indicat" the soul because of its upright stature.[2] This simultaneous denial of the male body's signifying potential and affirmation of it as an index of both spirituality and political power—of *dominium*—is a paradox found throughout the Middle Ages. In a number of writers, the male body takes on two forms: on the one hand, the material body, which is subject to the mutability, degeneration, and corruptibility of all matter; on the other hand, a figurative body that seemingly transcends these problems, suggesting the coherence of all matter and a masculinity that transcends materiality. These two ways of looking at the male body's involvement in the world are not necessarily contradictory, although they have everything to do with the male body's implication in production, itself both a curse and a principle of survival.

The complex dynamics of representing the male body in the Middle Ages are in no small measure due to the responsibility of production and labor given to the male body. Labor and the marks of labor are the double aspects of the curse God placed on the male body: Adam will eat his bread in sweat until he returns to the earth of which he is made, says God (Genesis 3: 9). The relation between work and signifying work is self-sustaining, just as the male body must be. As Jean-Joseph Goux puts it, following Engels, labor and technology are "*unnatural generative* forces, which allow those who have through them renounced the body of the nurturing mother earth to be naturalized anew in the land of transformed matter."[3] The natural demands that Adam's body makes signal his fallen state, his alienation from the plenitude of the paradisiacal "primitive" economy (Marx's term). And as he labors to satisfy those demands, the sweat that appears on his brow signifies both the body's implacable materiality and his failure to satisfy it fully. Parodying the natural plenitude of Eden, the body must continually transform material to sustain itself, while those very efforts remind it of its naturalness. Sweat is the sign of labor so necessary that its effects appear as a natural, corporeal, sign. The most insidious effect of the curse is that fundamentally unnatural activities now appear to be not only vitally necessary, but essentially natural. For Gilbert Crispin, an abbot at Westminster in the twelfth century, this is the fundamental condition of a man's life: "ad laborem nascebatur homo, ad laborem moriebatur" (man was born to labor, and to labor he died).[4] On a more practical level, Peter of Padua's treatise on physiognomy associates men with production, pointing out that they are "long-suffering at the tasks of labor."[5] Most of the other virtues associated with men in Peter's treatise have to do with stability and permanence, qualities that often appear in conjunction with references to the productivity of the male body. What sets it apart from the female body is its involvement in the productivity of the external world. This is precisely the distinction that Vincent of Beauvais makes between men and women: "viro extrinseca poena imponitur. Cum ei dicitur, *Maledicta terra in opere tuo*. Mulieri vero intrinsica…cum dicitur, *Multiplicato aerumnas tuas*" (external hardship is imposed on the man: as it is said of him, 'Cursed [will be] the earth in your labor.' Internal [hardship is imposed] on the woman; as it says, 'I will multiply your labors.')[6] As we will see, the male body's involvement in the world external to itself has two consequences: because its labor is never finished, it means that it is forever accountable to the larger world, but it also means that the body is unceasingly projected onto the larger world.

The medieval male body, in other words, is caught between production and representation. It stands, in many ways, for the larger world; but it is also responsible, in part, for producing and maintaining that world. The failures of the world itself can be attributed to the failures of the male body. When Adam sinned, as Vincent of Beauvais suggests, all matter was affected: "In hominis ergo lapsu omnia elementa detrimentum sustinuerunt, nam ante terra spinas & tribulos non proferebat, Aer iste non tantae crassitudinis, sed purus erat. Sic etiam Sol & Luna & sydera coeli detrimentum sustinuerunt luminis sui" (With the fall of man all elements sustained damage, for before that happened the earth did not bring forth thorns and thorn-bushes, the air then was not as thick, but was pure. The sun and moon and heavenly bodies likewise suffered a decrease in their light).[7] The male body's four complexions do not just represent the four elements. They are the four elements, and maintaining their proper proportions is a work of bodily and cosmographical fashioning.[8] For some medieval writers, the masculine body is literally a balancing act. The body of Adam, according to Guillaume of Conches, was made of clay comprised of a perfect balance of the elements.[9] John Gower's use of the age-old *minor est mundus homo* trope[10] in the *Confessio amantis* shows the agon involved in maintaining the body: "It may first preve upon a man;/ The which, for his complexioun/ Is mad upon divisioun/ Of cold, of hot, of moist, of drye...the contraire of his astat/ Stant evermore i[n] such debat,/ Til that o part be overcome,/ Ther may no final pes be nome."[11] Like the world, the male body is a *discordia concors* that resists resolution, and that requires continual exertion.

As we see here, producing the male body is often regarded in the Middle Ages as being the same thing as producing the world. For Bartholomaeus Anglicus, the male body's balance of complexions serves a propaedeutic function. Because the male's *sensus discretio* is finer than the female's and because his bodily complexion is superior, he is also given greater *potestas* and *dominatio*.[12] The configurations of the male body are projected onto the larger world; mastery of the humors is translated into a mastery of human affairs. As we shall see later, the *minor mundus* trope is not just a statement of a correspondence between man and the universe; it also describes the configuration of the world in the form of the male body.

Such concepts of the male body as a signifying organism work against other powerful and more demeaning representations of the body. They render insignificant the contingencies, fluctuations, and failures of the particular body. Illustrations of the male body in medical treatises, even in discussions of the most undignified aspects of corporeal existence, show him as a macrocosmic giant, spilling over the bounds of the text, signifying more than physical dimensions, or at least more than the physical dimensions of the individual body. Examples from divergent sciences include the Spanish zodiacal man, a male body configured as the Zodiac, with its penis compared to Scorpio and a fifteenth-century illustrated Bartholomaeus Anglicus that shows the male body as the conjunction of the four elements.[13] Like the Christ of the Aachen Gospels, the male body in a thirteenth-century medical treatise, the so-called "vein man," is superimposed over the accompanying text and spills over the margins, more than its frame can contain, larger than the *materia* in which it is embodied.[14]

The medieval male body can be both an insignificant and undesirable mass of matter and the site of a signifying process that, paradoxically, makes the body significant by purging it of its materiality. Value is attached to a male body that becomes more than its matter. Alchemy imagines an idealized male body that is what Marx might have called the "universal equivalent" of mutable essences, an abstract product from which all elemental impurities have been extracted, but a product against which the value of all subordinate products can be gauged.[15] The anonymous translator of John de Rupescissa's *Liber de quintessentie* calls the alchemical quintessence "mannys heuen," an incorruptible distillation of the elements that make up the body and that, like the "heuene of oure lord god," work to conserve its constituent elements: "This is oure quinta essencia. þat is to seie, mannys heuene, þat god made to þe conseruacioun of þe 4 qualitees of mannys body. riȝt as he made his heuene to þe conseruacioun of al þe world."[16] This transcendent figuration of the male body is related to the common medieval notion that the sperm is the purified substance of the whole body.[17] The transcendent quintessence can be used to infuse into the real body the virility it lacks: administered with "brennynge watir" the quintessence causes the "coward man" to "lese al maner drede and feyntnesse of herte."[18] This idealized essence of the male body is not a phenomenon of merely the physical sciences: military and political leaders are warned to guard its secret closely. The restoration of the male body is, therefore, the same project as the preservation of the body politic. Alchemy's medicinal effects restore the primitive elemental balance of the body,[19] reproducing its virility. As the translation of the *Liber de quintessentie* says, *aurum potabile* (Chaucer's Physician's "gold in physick") heals old men who are "feble in kynde," restoring them to their "firste strenk[þ]is of ȝong[þ]e in [þ]e same degree [þ]at is in al kynde."[20]

What is restored, in other words, is more than the virility of the male body: it is true *potentia*, an originary plenitude that is signified by the male body. The mnemonic and contemplative equivalent of this is the lesson of the microcosmic body, compactly expressed by Gower: "minor est mundus homo....Est homo qui mundus de iure suo sibi mundum/ Subdit, et in melius dirigit inde status" (man is a lesser world...the man who is true to principle subjects the world to himself and guides its condition for the better).[21] Since Plato's *Phaedrus*, indeed, the male body has been a signifying organism, distilling, as language does, into the seed that carries its potential. Medieval medicine conceived of the male body as a kind of alembic, continually producing purified, less material, versions of itself.[22]

Like language, the male body points toward a transcendental signifier that seems to differ ontologically and epistemologically from itself. As Giles of Rome argued, following Aristotle, the sperm contains something of the divine virtue, placing it above matter itself; Aquinas defined the seed as "the recipient of the power of the heavenly bodies."[23] The male seed is a distilled quintessence of the matter of the male body but a quintessence that is significant because it does not fully participate in the sterility and formlessness of matter. It is however still pulled ineluctably toward the material. In the male body, according to the *Timaeus*, the presence of the sperm itself provokes a desire to reproduce matter, a "love for procreation."[24] The contradictory impulses that govern the male body's relation to the material are not unlike the paradoxes that govern language, which also seeks to signify beyond itself by supplementing its material presence. In Socrates' comparison of language to a seed in the *Phaedrus*, both the farmer and rhetorician who are concerned with producing things that endure stand in a different relation to the material world than those who are merely concerned with pleasure. The serious producer ensures that his seeds are planted in "suitable" soil and tended carefully; those concerned merely with entertainment, says Socrates, will write "'in water' with pen and ink, sowing words which can neither speak for themselves nor teach the truth adequately."[25] When the seed, the potential of matter, is situated with the right material and cultivated carefully, it flourishes, acquiring significance. When it is committed to the flux of the material world, with no care for its material position, it neither adds to the repository of the material world nor comes to mean anything.

The production of matter, in other words, is accompanied by the production of significance: the body is an agglutination of signifiers. The male body is regulated by a set of non-material constraints that determine its primary function to be the production of more matter, the principle of fecundity. As Derrida points out, citing the *Laws,* when the male body conforms to the principles of procreation, there is "a marked unity between *logos* and *nomos.*" As we will see, it is because sodomy is regarded as a sterile practice that it is condemned by many medieval writers. The *Laws* talk about "restricting procreative intercourse to its natural function by abstention from congress with our own sex, with its...wasting of the seed of life on a stony and rocky soil, where it will never take root and bear its natural fruit, and equal abstention from any female field whence you would desire no harvest."[26] It is, paradoxically, because the male body is thought to transcend matter that it is implicated in an act of continual production, an extension of its own materiality.

Even when the male body points toward a vanishing point of matter, it is still marked with a desire to produce. In the alchemical movement of distillation and purifaction, the male body seeks its universal equivalent, the abstract value that allows it to be subjected to exchange. As we have seen, the quintessence and the male body are subsumed into the same abstract value. The liquid form of the quintessence, *aurum potabile*, is valuable because of what it does for the body: its value seems to derive from its restorative power. But that pragmatic value is effortlessly translated into the idea of economic value in general. Precisely this slippage is the point of the joke in Chaucer's description of the Physician: "gold in physick is a cordial,/ Therefore he lovede gold in special."[27]

Perhaps the clearest account of the body's subjection to the flows of monetary representation, and of its concomitant disappearance into semiotic flux, is in Lydgate's petitionary *Letter to Gloucester*. Beginning with the image of an anthropomorphized purse that is racked by a laxative and "made slendre by a consumpcioun,"[28] the poem focuses more on the kinesis of monetary use than on the stability offered by capital or patronage. Figures of ebb and flow permeate the poem: even the Customs are metaphorically affected by the ebbing of fortune. The conjunction of the body and the State is one we will return to in a moment: both are placed in jeopardy by their subjection to the flows of capital. It may be that jeopardy to the body occurs because it is constructed in much the same way as are the figures of monetary exchange. By the end of the brief poem the medicinal has been subsumed by the economic: *aurum potabile* is no longer a quasi-mystical panacea but a liquefied infusion of capital: "In quynt-essence best restauracioun/ With siluer plate."(47–48) The remedy for old age or for the exhaustion of the purse is not the solidity of coin but the abstract form of money:

> A drye tisyk makith oold men ful feynt;
> Reediest weye to renewe ther corage,
> Is a fressh dragge, of no spycis mente,
> But of a briht plate, enpreentyd with coinage. (53–56)

It is the act of imprinting, and not the qualities of any physical substance, that meets the demands of impecunious purse and declining man.

At one level the male body and the monetary object merge. According to medieval economic theory, money is regulated and forced into significance when coins are imprinted by the royal mint, usually with an image of the king's body. This act has its equivalent at the inception of every body: according to a number of neoplatonists, the body came into being when the "shapeless" matter of the feminine was imprinted with masculine form, "as in a mint."[29] The body on the coin helps to stabilize what is uncertain and transitive, but the flow of capital is also important to the stability of the *corpus politicum*. The king's body does not signify adequately if it does not circulate: Edward III, for instance, was forced to issue several versions of the gold noble before continental markets began to distribute it widely.

Like currency, the male body signifies only an idealized kind of production. Apparently stable and immutable, the body also depends on a metaphoric or transferrential circulation, on the appropriation of signifiers that create a new syntagmatic dimension. The body is the site of both political and contemplative discourse without being its subject. The medieval male body is frequently allied with currency because the function of money, too, is the signification of production, an infinitely deferred return to matter. The myth of superfluous material that could be produced in one place and transported to another by the medium of coin underpins theories of medieval exchange, justifying potential transgressions against prohibitions on usury and so-called "sterile" profit. The vast body of warnings against the making of sterile profit, the multiplication of money without external intervention, also deserves a closer look because it shows how the abstract corpus that is implied by the circulation of money is related to the abstract corpus implied by the *homo economicus*.

In the Middle Ages, misappropriations of money and of the male body are often linked. The short-circuiting of production is a sin against the body itself, whether it takes the particular forms of usury or sodomy, both sins that transgress against representations of production. Usury is prohibited by canon law because, as writers from Thomas Aquinas on point out, it rests on a disruption of the link between labor and its sign—money.[30] Whatever profit there is in a usurious loan comes from the labor invested by the debtor (as Roland of Cremona says, *de denariis et labore hominum qui inde laborant* [from the coins and labor of the men who labor thereby]), not the creditor.[31] The usurer engages in an unnatural act whenever he expects a profit. This transgression against nature is defined as a refusal to obey the divine precept to engage in labor that we have already discussed. As Thomas of Chobham says, "the usurer seeks to profit without any labor even while asleep, which is against the precept of the Lord, who says, 'In labour and the sweat of thy face shalt thou eat bread.'"[32] Focusing more on the dubious nature of the usurer's "product," Hugh of St. Cher echoes the language of condemnation against alchemy in arguing that usury is forbidden because it "transmutes species unnaturally, turning silver into gold and gold into corn."[33] Like alchemists, usurers transgress natural laws because they produce objects that lack the essential features of what they purport to be.

One of the principal objections to usury is that it produces fruit from money, which is essentially sterile.[34] This abdication of labor with the expectation of refining, transmuting, and reproducing bodies is, paradoxically, shadowed by reminders that sterile labor, a kind of work that only masquerades as work, compromises the distinctiveness of the body. In usury, especially, a number of medieval writers saw a tendency that ultimately robbed the body of meaning because it avoided the obligations of labor. Usury is a sin "without measure or bound" that leads, especially in popular warnings against the practice, to a collapse of the body or even the confusion and loss of identity. The cupidinous appropriation of a loan, usury helps to materialize (or, perhaps more accurately, to pervert) what is implicit in the act of borrowing. Standard etymological definitions of the loan or *mutuum* claim that its name comes from the passage of what is mine (*meum*) to what is yours (*tuum*).[35] The usurer's money can take on the qualities of the usurer's body, devouring itself and matter similar to it: Caesarius of Heisterbach, for instance, recounts the story of a Cistercian monastery's money devoured in a coffer by a usurer's money. When the coffer was opened, none of the money remained.[36] Condemnations of usury suggest that usurers are punished by losing altogether their one alienable property—the body.

The usurer's refusal to manage the material world in accordance with the divine injunction to labor means that his body loses some of its masculine or human distinctiveness, tending to become literally bestial. Lester Little has called attention to a figure he identifies with avarice in the margin of British Library Add. 29253, fol. 41v., which shows a "hybrid man defecating coins into a bowl held by an ape."[37] Usurers and their beneficiaries are afflicted with leprosy and St. Anthony's fire in an exemplum from the *Tabula exemplorum*.[38] Several exempla describe the usurer's body being torn by wild animals or even supplanted by them. In one exemplum, a usurer's grave is opened to reveal two toads. After death, the usurer's body lost its resting place: it is often expelled from the grave itself. These exempla may echo the injunction in the *Decretals* forbidding the usurer's body from being given a Christian burial.[39] In such cases, the body becomes superfluous matter, the meaningless detritus of a life spent avoiding the obligations of production.

Cantos 12–17 of Dante's *Inferno* concern, in large part, men like the usurers and sodomites who have avoided the injunction to labor and produce; and figures of bestiality dominate the section. The first figure Dante encounters after Virgil's discussion of the divine injunction to labor (11.107–08) is the Minotaur; in the remainder of these cantos they also encounter the Harpies with birds' wings and "visi umani" (13.13), and Geryon, the image of Fraud itself, who has the face "d'uom giusto," but the body of a serpent, the paws of a beast, and the sting of a scorpion (17.10–27). Perhaps not uncoincidentally, the beasts that Dante may have modeled Geryon after are devourers of human flesh.[40] While these figures represent the degeneration into bestiality of those who practice fraud, they frame even more specific consequences for the bodies of men—especially those of the usurers and sodomites—who have performed only the simulacrum of labor.

The poem's earliest readers seem to read this particular kind of fraud as the strongest thematic link in this group of cantos. Perhaps following Dante's own linking of usury and sodomy by naming them according to the most notorious sites at which they were practiced ("Soddoma e Caorsa"), they treat these two groups as complementary pairs. As Boccaccio says, in using the names of cities, Dante describes the "due spezie d'uomini li quali offendono o fanno violenza a Dio nelle cose sue" (two kinds of men who offend or commit violence against God with their things).[41] While the pun on "cose" with reference to the sodomites is probably not incidental, what is most important here is the way in which sodomites and usurers are related through their use and misappropriation of the material world. As we have seen, usurers are faulted in part because they make fertile what should "naturally" be infertile; sodomites are faulted, according to a number of medieval writers, because they make infertile what should be fertile, misappropriating the "natural" urge to reproduce.[42]

The things that the usurers appropriate are, in a sense, not really things. Money in medieval economic theory is a *medium* or *mezzo*, merely a sign of material, not material itself.[43] By making it the object of their production, usurers mistake a sign of the thing, or of things in general, for the thing itself. In the *Inferno*, their bodies become things that lack the meaning usually invested in the male body. They lack all distinction, possessing bodies that have become literally effaced. Dante is unable to recognize a single one of them until he realizes that the purses hanging about their necks depict their coats of arms. Because they have invested in signs during life rather than engaging in the work of maintaining the body, their bodies no longer signify their identities. The metonymy of the familial sign supplants the whole body, which becomes a redundant piece of matter.

While the sodomites are not accused of mistaking sign for matter, they fail, in the *Inferno*, at the duties of production that maintain the body by failing to become involved in the work of reproducing the body. Remigio of Florence's treatise on usury, which uses sodomy to represent transgressions against natural law in general, argues that every being "naturaliter appetit conservare speciem suam" (naturally wishes to preserve its kind).[44] Impeded in sodomites, Remigio says, this impulse is important for conserving both *ens* and *substantia*, both the abstract quality of life and the body itself. But even apart from these considerations, Remigio argues, sodomites impede natural inclinations because they fail to observe the natural constraints of matter. According to him, their sexual practices do not amount to a tenable mode of corporeal activity (although Peter of Abano does suggest that the *consuetudo* of sodomy might amount to something like what Joan Cadden calls a "new nature," despite his condemnation of that *consuetudo*).[45] What prevents homosexuality from becoming a mode of masculinity, for Remigio, is the principle that binds all matter: "ea que sunt contra naturam non possunt per consuetudinem fieri, sicut lapis numquam assuescit ferri sursum nec ignis deorsum" (things that are contrary to nature cannot come about by habit, just as a stone never becomes assimilated with (accustomed to) iron and fire).[46] The place that kinds of matter inhabit in the material world is a feature of their intrinsic properties. The male body, despite its implication in almost the entire material world, is no different. It inhabits a material and ideological place, and when that place is disturbed, so is the potential that is manifested in the body or acted on by the body.

The bodies of the sodomites in Dante are condemned never to rest in one place, to become perpetual *loci* for action. Prevented from resting for even a *punto*, their bodies parody the possibility of becoming, a possibility that both Peter of Abano and Remigio of Florence hint at. Literally displaced, they are doomed forever to represent activity without a purpose, movement without becoming. Where Dante had faulted the usurers earlier because they "altra via tiene," (11.109) he represents the sodomites as inhabiting a place that is literally untenable. The male body is no longer a signifying *corpus* that collates the world, dominating it by laboring in it and by mapping it according to some of the principles that regulate that body; it becomes forced into meaningless activity.

In this series of cantos that records the dissolution of the bonds between the signifying male body and its world, there is, however, one reminder of the powerful way in which the body makes the world coherent. Dante does not find out until the canto just before he meets Brunetto Latini that an important feature of the geography of Hell—its rivers—are actually comprised of the tears that issue out of a fissure in the statue of a "gran veglio" that stands on Crete. This figure, too, is a symbol of degeneration, made up of a mixture of materials, from a gold head to a clay foot. Yet even its representations of the fallen state of humanity help to configure the world. While the devolution of materials in the body of the statue recalls both Nebuchadnezzar's dream and the Ovidian myth of the Golden Age, the statue's most obvious flaw, the fissure that runs the length of the body, ultimately is the source of the rivers that bound Hell. One of these, Lethe, is also one of the rivers that appears in the earthly paradise of the *Purgatorio* and which obliterates the traces of sin. It restores the original integrity of the world, and the original integrity of the body, whose only traces remain the statue's head of gold. The earthly paradise represents the return of the body to its primal unity with nature at the time of the Golden Age, to "l'umana radice" (28.141), before even the time when labor was forced on the male body: the earth is in a state of constant fruition (28.143). The economy of the *gran veglio*'s body returns to it its original significance by means of the very fault that compromised its significance.

Although in several ways it represents the source of infernal misery, the figure of the *gran veglio* also stands for the literal and metaphorical ways in which the male body organizes the world despite its imperfections. The poem's earliest readers recognize the *gran veglio* as a manifestation of the *minor mundus est homo* trope. Pietro Alighieri sees in the deterioration of metals that make up the body an allegory of the ages of man and the world.[47] Benvenuto, too, calls attention to the similarity of the passage of age in both domains but treats the similarity as something more significant and more actively produced than a mere isomorph: "homo appellatur a philosophis minor mundus quia nihil est fere in ipso mundo quod non rapiatur ab homine ipso" (man is called by philosophers a lesser world, because hardly anything exists in this world that is not seized from man himself).[48] The bodies of man and of the world do not just happen to be similar: man, in fact, produces the body of the world. Man not only provides a tablet onto which a significant world can be inscribed but also produces a world that becomes significant. The natural world in which the male body must labor, in other words, cannot be represented without the intervention of the male body. The correspondence between large and little worlds is more than a natural pattern; it is the consequence of the curse placed on Adam's body. Just as the male body must be constantly regulated, just as its physiological well-being is the result of a series of acts of somatic regulation, the body of the world itself is subject to the activities of production. That production is what literally and figuratively shapes it. The presence that the male body maintains in the larger material world is both natural and artificial, as Boccaccio's allegorizing of the mountain under which the *gran veglio* is standing suggests: it represents the "moltitudine di terra acumulata o dalla natura delle cose o dall'artificio degli uomini" (great quantity of earth accumulated either by the nature of things or by the skill of men).[49] By creating, on the one hand, the isomorph we have been tracing—the correspondences between man and world—writings about medieval masculinity create identities that appear natural because of the complexity and scope of those similarities. On the other hand, by disclosing the extent to which either the "minor" or "major" bodies of man involve constant acts of fashioning, representations of the medieval male body echo the paradox of the primal curse placed on it. Its very nature is bound up in artifice. It does not exist independently of nature, yet that very labor makes the body seem overwhelmingly natural, its abstract dominance a seemingly natural thing.

NOTES

1. Ernst Kantorowicz, *The King's Two Bodies: A Study in Medieval Political Theology* (Princeton: Princeton UP, 1957), pp. 193–232.

2. Vincent of Beauvais, *Speculum quadruplex; sive, Speculum maius. Speculum naturale*, 3 vols. (Graz, 1624) 1: col. 2215.

3. Jean-Joseph Goux, *Symbolic Economies after Marx and Freud*, trans. Jennifer Curtiss Gage (Ithaca: Cornell UP, 1990), p. 215.

4. *Patrologia Latina*, J.-P. Migne, ed., 220 vols. (Paris, 1844) 159: col. 1021.

5. Peter of Padua, *Liber compilationis physionomie*, MS lat. 16089, Bibliotheque Nationale, f. 99r. Cited in Joan Cadden, *Meanings of Sex Difference in the Middle Ages: Medicine, Science, and Culture* (Cambridge: Cambridge UP, 1988).

6. Vincent of Beauvais, *Speculum naturale,* Bk. 30, cap. 85, col. 2279.

7. Ibid.

8. Bodily fashioning can be linked to a specifically masculine generative principle that applies also to the *polis* and the cosmos. Bernardus Silvestris's *Cosmographia* portrays the urge of reproduction as a continual struggle: "The phallus wars against Lachesis and carefully rejoins the vital threads severed by the hands of the Fates. Blood sent forth from the seat of the brain flows down to the loins, bearing the image of the shining sperm. Artful Nature molds and shapes the fluid, that in conceiving it may reproduce the forms of ancestors. The nature of the universe outlives itself, for it flows back into itself, and so survives and is nourished by its very flowing away." Bernardus Silvestris, *Cosmographia*, Winthrop Wetherbee, trans. (New York: Columbia UP, 1973), p. 126. Dynastic continuity is assured by the Aristotelian principle that a "virtus activa," as Aquinas calls it (*Summa* I, q. 119, art. I, resp. 2), is transmitted in the seed from father to son. See Kantorowicz, *Two Bodies*, pp. 314–336.

9. Guillaume de Conches, *Philosophia*, ed. and trans. Gregor Maurach with Heidemarie Telle (Pretoria: University of South Africa, 1980) Bk. I, ch.13 sect. 4305, pp. 38–40. Cited in Cadden, *Meanings of Sex Difference,* p. 74 n. 50.

10. John Gower, *The Complete Works of John Gower*, 4 vols., G.C. Macaulay, ed., vol. 4. *The Latin Works* (Oxford: Clarendon, 1902) *Vox clamantis*, 7.8.

11. Gower, *Confessio amantis*, ibid., vol. 2. *Prologue* 974–82.

12. Bartholomaeus Anglicus, *De proprietatibus rerum.*, Georgius Bartholdus Posanus, ed. (Frankfurt, 1601; rep., Frankfurt am Main: Minerva, 1964), Bk. VI, ch. xii, p. 244.

13. MS Esp. 30, Bibliothèque Nationale de France; MS Fr. 135, Bibliothèque Nationale de France, fol. 91.

14. MS Ashmole 399, Bodleian Library, Oxford, fol. 18r.

15. Material designated as the sign of the universal equivalent no longer has a syntagmatic relation to other material: "The universal equivalent form is a form of value in general…if a commodity be found to have assumed the universal equivalent form…this is only because it has been excluded from the rest of all other commodities as their equivalent." Karl Marx, *Capital: A Critique of Political Economy*, Samuel Moore and Edward Aveling, trans. (New York: Modern Library, 1906), pp. 79–81.

16. *The Book of Quinte Essence*, F.J. Furnivall, ed. (London: EETS, 1866), pp. 2–3.

17. See, for instance, William of Conches' definition: "Sperm is thus the seed of the man, composed of the purest substance of all parts of the body." *Dragmaticon philosophiae* (Strasbourg, 1567), pp. 236–7. Cited in Danielle Jacquart and Claude Thomasset, *Sexuality and Medicine in the Middle Ages* (Princeton: Princeton UP, 1988), p. 54.

18. *The Book of Quinte Essence*, p. 23.

19. See Roger Bacon, *In libro sex scientarum*, *Opera hactenus inedita*, A.G. Little and E. Withington, ed. (1928), 9:183–184.

20. *The Book of Quinte Essence*, p. 1.

21. Gower, *Vox clamantis*, Bk. 7, chap. 8, ll. 645–48.

22. See Jacquart and Thomasset, *Sexuality and Medicine in the Middle Ages*, pp. 49–86. The *Liber de quintessentie*, in fact, represents the alembic as a male body, in a passage that recalls medical writers on the formation of sperm from the natural heat of the male body: "[th]is is a wonderful instrument [th]at [th]at [th]ing [th]at by vertues of fier ascendith and distillith wi[th]inne [th]e vessel. [th]er canales brachiales. [th]at is, by pipis lich to armis, be bore a3en, and eftsoones ascendith, and eft descendith contynuely day and ny3t til [th]e brennynge water heuenly be turned into quintam essenciam," p. 4.

23. Giles of Rome, *De formatione corporis humani in utero* (Venice, 1523), p. 55. Cited in Jacquart and Thomasset, *Sexuality and Medicine in the Middle Ages*, p. 57, p. 59.

24. Plato, *Timaeus*, *The Dialogues of Plato*, B. Jowett, trans., 2 vols. (New York: Random House, 1937) 2: 67. See also Constantinus Africanus,

Constantini liber de coitu, ed. E. Montero Cartelle (Santiago de Compostela: University of Santiago de Compostela, 1983).

25. Plato, *Phaedra*. In *The Dialogues of Plato*. 1: 279.

26. *Laws* VIII, 838e–839b. Cited in Jacques Derrida, *Dissemination*, Barbara Jordan, trans. (Chicago: U of Chicago P, 1981), pp. 152–153.

27. Geoffrey Chaucer, "The General Prologue," 443–444, in *The Riverside Chaucer*, 3rd ed., Larry D. Benson, gen. ed. (Boston: Houghton Mifflin, 1987).

28. John Lydgate, "Letter to Gloucester," *The Minor Poems of John Lydgate*, 2 vols. (London: EETS, 1934). *Part II: Secular Poems*, Henry Noble MacCracken, ed., p. 15.

29. See Macrobius's commentary on Scipio's dream. *Commentarii in somnium scipionis*, Jacob Willis, ed. (Leipzig: B. G. Teubner, 1970), I, 6, 63. For a discussion of the problems in the Platonic notion of "female" matter, see Judith Butler, *Bodies That Matter: The Discursive Limits of 'Sex'* (New York: Routledge, 1993), pp. 27–55; and Goux, "Sexual Difference and History," in *Symbolic Economies*, pp. 213–244.

30. Odd Langholm, *Economics in the Medieval Schools: Wealth, Exchange, Value, Money and Usury according to the Paris Theological Tradition 1200–1350* (Leiden: Brill, 1992), p. 244, p. 338.

31. Langholm, *Economics*, p. 95.

32. Thomas of Chobham, *Summa confessorum*, F. Broomfield, ed., *Analecta medievalia namurcensia* 25 (Paris, 1968), 7.6, 11, 1: 504–5. Cited in Langholm, *Economics*, p. 56.

33. Hugh of St. Cher, *In Lucam*, *Opera Omnia*, vol. 6 (Lyon, 1645) 35. Cited in Langholm, *Economics*, p. 104.

34. "It is contrary to nature that inanimate objects should breed, but in usury money breeds money," in Langholm, *Economics*, p. 464.

35. Langholm, *Economics*, p. 48.

36. Caesarius of Heisterbach, *Dialogus miraculorum*, Joseph Strange, ed. (Cologne, 1851) 1.108. *Distinctio secunda: De contritione*, cap. 34. Cited in Jacques le Goff, "The Usurer and Purgatory," *The Dawn of Modern Banking* (New Haven: Yale UP, 1979), pp. 37–38.

37. Lester K. Little, "Pride Goes Before Avarice: Social Change and the Vices in Latin Christendom," *American Historical Review* 76 (1971): 38.

38. Le Goff, "The Usurer and Purgatory," p. 38, n. 42.

39. Gregory IX, *Decretales, corpus iuris canonici*, Aemilius Friedberg, ed. (Graz, 1955), 1: 812.

40. See Pliny, *Historia naturalis* VIII, 30; Albertus Magnus, *De animalibus* Lib. XXII, TR. ii, cap. I; Brunetto Latini, *Tresor* V, ch. 59.

41. Giovanni Boccaccio, *Esposizioni sopra la Comedia di Dante*, Giorgio Paduan, ed., in *Tutte le opere di Giovanni Boccaccio*, Vittore Branca, ed. (Arnoldo Mondadoni: Gennaio, 1965) 6:545.

42. Cf. Peter of Abano, *Expositio problematum Aristotelis*. Fol. 70 v. Cited in Cadden, *Meanings of Sex Difference,* p. 216.

43. See, for example, Henry of Ghent, *Quodlibet VI*, in *Opera omnia*, R. Macken, ed. (Leiden: Brill, 1979) 10:210; *L'ottimo commento della Divina commedia*, A. Torri, ed. (Pisa, 1827) 1: *Inf.* 11.106–11.

44. Remigio of Florence, *De peccato usurae*, ed. Ovidio Capitani, *Studi medievali* 6.2 (1965): 614.

45. Cadden, *Meanings of Sex Difference,* p. 216.

46. Remigio, *De peccato usurae*, 614.

47. Pietro Alighieri, *Il Commentarium*, Roberto Della Vedova and Maria Teresa Silvotti, eds. (Florence : L. S. Olschki, 1978), *Inf.* 14.103–114.

48. Benvenuto da Imola, *Comentum super Dantis Aldigherij comoediam*, Jacobo Philippo Lacaita, ed. (Florence : G. Barbera, 1887) *Inf.* 14.103–105.

49. Boccaccio, *Esposizioni*, 658. Karl Marx, too, argues that it is, paradoxically, the natural that is produced in labor: "The chief objective condition of labour itself appears not as the *product* of labour, but occurs as *nature*." *Pre–Capitalist Economic Formations*, Jack Cohen, trans. (New York: International Publishers, 1964), p. 81.

BECOMING CHRISTIAN, BECOMING MALE?

Steven F. Kruger

This essay examines intersections and dissonances between medieval discourses of gender and of religious/racial difference, suggesting that religious conversion did not necessarily entail a parallel conversion of gender identity.

Gender was a crucial term in medieval Christian constructions of religious otherness. "Heretical" movements within Christianity were often depicted as appealing particularly to women; John of Salisbury claimed, for instance, that Arnold of Brescia "built up a faction known as the heretical sect of the Lombards...[who] found their chief supporters among pious women."[1] A women's religious movement like the Beguines was particularly likely to be viewed as heterodox,[2] and accusations of women leading unorthodox religious lives often arose from concern over the subversion of gender hierarchy. Thus, in *The Book of Margery Kempe*, the Mayor of Leicester charges Kempe with wanting "to lure away our wives from us, and lead them off with you"; certain women more domestically inclined—that is, more properly "feminine"—than Kempe come "running out of their houses with their distaffs, crying to the people, 'Burn this false heretic'"; certain men call her a Lollard, and others instruct her to "give up this life that you lead, and go and spin, and card wool, as other women do."[3] Clearly, Kempe's suspected "heresy" and her violation of "properly" gendered behavior depend upon each other.

Islam and Judaism were closely connected to each other in medieval Christian imaginations, and each was strongly affiliated with "heresy": indeed, Islam was often treated as a Christian "heresy" and Judaism often linked to "heretical" conspiracies.[4] From a Christian perspective, both these alternative religious traditions involved, like "heresy," a certain disturbance of gender. By virtue of circumcision, Jewish and Muslim men displayed a lack of masculinity on their bodies.[5] Classical Roman law associated circumcision with castration,[6] and some early Christians saw circumcision, not always disapprovingly, as occasioning a loss of virile sexual energy; thus, for Origen, the prophets' "acceptance of circumcision showed…that [they] accepted the discipline of sexual restraint, since circumcision signified a commitment to cut off the lusts of the flesh."[7] While "devirilization" might in some ways be a Christian desideratum, as Origen's own taking on of castration clearly suggests, in medieval Christian depictions of contemporary Jewish and Muslim men (and not the prophets), it most often served the purposes of stigmatization. The association of eunuchry with "the East"—not just Islam but also the "schismatic" Christianity of Byzantium—performed a certain hopeful emasculation of threatening forces on the borders of Western Europe.[8] In reporting that the Greek emperor had commanded each family in his realm to make one of its daughters a prostitute and one of its sons a eunuch, Guibert of Nogent made clear his view that castration enervated and devirilized not just the individual but the nation: "[the emperor thus] rendered the bodies of [these] males weak and effeminate, their virile powers taken away, [and] those qualities useful for the practice of warfare may no longer be possessed; indeed, as the finishing touch to the damage done, future offspring is cut off in those men, by whose increase they might have been able to hope for aid against their enemies."[9] Even when literal castration or the mark of circumcision was not explicitly at issue, Western European Christian discourses tended to construct Muslim and Jewish men as failing to live up to "masculine" ideals in the public realm, and specifically in the realm of warfare. Louise Mirrer concludes that, in Castilian epic and ballad, Muslim men were depicted as "defeated, docile, and often 'unmanly'" and "Jewish men…frequently accorded the sexual and status identity of the powerless."[10] Marco Polo comments that "Christians are far more valiant than Saracens."[11] And Jews were rarely associated with martial prowess, in large part because they were often legally prohibited from bearing arms.[12]

In depictions of Jews, circumcision served as a particularly fertile site for the construction of gender difference, a construction that tended to conflate lack of Jewish "virility" with a deep threat to Christian "masculinity." In the 1494 confession forced from the Jews of Tyrnau, "the wound of circumcision" entails, on the one hand, a lack in Jewish gender and sexuality and, on the other, a compensatory violence directed against the unwounded bodies of Christians:

> Firstly, they were convinced by the judgment of their ancestors that the blood of a Christian was a good remedy for the alleviation of the wound of circumcision. Secondly, they were of opinion that this blood, put into food, is very efficacious for the awakening of mutual love. Thirdly, they had discovered, as men and women among them suffered equally from menstruation that the blood of a Christian is a specific medicine for it, when drunk. Fourthly, they had an ancient but secret ordinance by which they are under obligation to shed Christian blood in honor of God in daily sacrifices in some spot or other; they said it had happened in this way that the lot for the present year had fallen on the Tyrnau Jews.[13]

That circumcision made Jewish men less sexually attractive to women, a circumstance that would make necessary the artificial "awakening of mutual love," was expressed, for instance, by Peter Abelard: "the sign of circumcision seems so abhorrent to the Gentiles that if we [Jews] were to seek their women, the women would in no way give their consent, believing that the truncating of this member is the height of foulness, and detesting the divine sign of holiness as an idolatry."[14] Further, that Jewish men experienced a "bloody flux," in Caesarius of Heisterbach affiliated with their crucifixion of Christ and in many writers identified with menstruation, was a commonplace.[15] The association of a "feminizing" deficiency in Jewish men's bodies with the originary moment of Jewish violence against Christ was part of a complex economy that bound the "degenerate" body of the Jewish man to attacks on Christian bodies, both the supposed murder of Christians for their blood and the desecrations of the host that represented a continued attack on Christ's own body.[16] Jewish violence was in particular imagined as threatening Christian "masculinity." Thus, as James Shapiro points out, ritual murder accusations, particularly in England, often sketched a "sequence of criminal acts beginning with abduction and circumcision and ending with crucifixion and cannibalism."[17] Jews at Norwich in the 1230s were prosecuted for kidnapping and circumcising (though not killing) a five-year-old boy who may have been the son of a converted Jew.[18] And D'Blossiers Tovey points out, in his eighteenth-century *Anglia Judaica*, that "the *first*

Indictment that appears any where upon *Record*, against a *Jew*" was against "one *Bonefand* a *Jew* of *Bedford*...not for *Circumcising*, but *totally* cutting off the Privy Member of one *Richard*, the Nephew of *Robert de Sutton*."[19]

The medieval Christian "feminization" of religious others operated in a variety of other ways as well. Jews were frequently associated with female prostitutes, and brothels and "Jewries" were often located side-by-side; just as prostitutes satisfied certain disavowed sexual needs for Christian communities, Jews, in their assigned role as "usurers," satisfied certain disavowed economic needs.[20] Those politically supporting Jews, or those thought to be not vigilant enough in guarding against them, themselves became the object of gendered aspersions. Thus, Matthew Paris notes that "a certain most wicked and merciless Jew," acting in a royal investigation of Jewish economic crimes, "reproached without fail Christians who were grieving over and bewailing the sufferings of the Jews and called the royal bailiffs lukewarm and effeminate"; here, the Jewish enemy of Jews is also, complicatedly, cast as the "feminizing" attacker of Christians.[21] And the Jewish community as a whole might be "feminized." In Caesarius of Heisterbach, through the cleverness of a Christian clerk who has had sex with and impregnated a Jewish virgin, a Jewish community is led to expect the birth of its Messiah; the vanity of that wish, and of Jewish belief more generally, is demonstrated at the Messiah's birth: "The hour came in which the unhappy one should be delivered, and there ensued the usual pain, groans and cries. At last she brought forth an infant, not indeed the Messiah, but a daughter" (1.106). The "feminized" people, Jews who passed up their chance to recognize the "true" Messiah, can here bring forth only a weak (female) parody of Christ.

Given the "feminization" of Jewish and Muslim men in Western European Christian discourses, we might expect to find a corresponding "masculinization" of Muslim and Jewish women, and in at least some texts this is the case. In Chaucer's *Man of Law's Tale*, the sultaness is a "Virago," "Semyrame the secounde," "serpent under femynynytee," and "feyned womman."[22] There are at least some social historical indications that, in certain parts of Europe, Jewish women were more involved in public life than Christian women;[23] Christians may have seen this as indicating a subversion of gender distinctions, both a "masculinization" of properly "feminine" behavior and a "feminizing" arrogation of male authority to women. On the other hand, however, we may find Muslim and Jewish women depicted as particularly "feminine"—beautiful and seductive. Thus, in Boccaccio's story of Alatiel, the daughter of the sultan (*Decameron* 2.7)—a story that might be read as a parody of the type of tale recorded in Chaucer's *Man of Law's Tale*—Alatiel is "according to everybody who had set eyes on her, ... the most beautiful woman to be found anywhere on earth"; she arouses lust in a long series of men, and she satisfies that lust.[24] When finally she is returned to the man originally meant to be her husband, "despite the fact that eight separate men had made love to her on thousands of different occasions, she entered his bed as a virgin and convinced him that it was really so."[25] Here, the religiously other woman is seen in particularly corporealized and sexualized terms, and this is also the case of Jewish women in two of Caesarius of Heisterbach's narratives (ii.23–24). These women are "like many of [their] race, ... very beautiful" (1.102), and they attract the attention of "young [Christian] clerks" who fall in love with them and by whom they are seduced (1.102, 104–5). The sexualized depiction of Jewish and Muslim women is not inconsistent with the general "feminization" and corporealization of Judaism and Islam. In Caesarius, the Jewish women's desire for Christian men also reconfirms stereotypes about the sexual unattractiveness of (circumcised) Jewish men. But something beyond the "feminization" of Judaism is also happening in Caesarius: in the first of his stories, the Jewish woman ultimately comes to "be born again in the grace of baptism," marrying the Christian clerk (who thus "lose[s] all hope of ecclesiastical preferment"), but ultimately, along with her husband, taking vows in the Cistercian order (1.104). Further, in the two stories (ii.25–26) that directly follow his accounts of sexually attractive Jewish women, Caesarius depicts two other Jewish women who are chaste and who become, "by the providence of God, imbued with the Christian faith" (1.107; compare 1.109). Here, Jewish women, unlike the obdurate men of their "race," seem particularly susceptible to Christianity's "truth." Perhaps this too represents a sort of gender reversal: where in Christianity it is the "fathers" of the Church who most strongly recognize and speak its truths, here it is daughters who, despite a certain carnality associated with their femaleness and

Jewishness, come to recognize spiritual truth and break the yoke of "the infidel father" (1.107).[26]

***

Clearly there is much rich medieval material in which gender and religious otherness are complexly interlinked, and a fuller study of that material, beyond the scope of this essay, is needed. Here, in furthering that larger project, I will address a question that I believe can be widely revealing about medieval categories of identity and their interimplication. Given that Muslim and Jewish men are depicted as not just religiously, doctrinally or spiritually, different from Christian men, but as different in their gendered bodies, what happens when those men convert, when they *become* Christian men?[27] Medieval Christian ideas of Jewishness or Muslimness involve more than what, in the strictest sense, we would call *religious* difference; those ideas, in focusing attention on qualities thought to be based in biology, in the "nature" of bodies, move into what, at least in terms of modern identity categories, we would call a *racial* realm, a realm that, at least in the modern West, is generally thought to be intractable to change.[28] As Shapiro suggests, in relation to the early-modern idea that upon conversion Jews lost their "natural" foul smell (the *foetor judaicus*),

> It was one thing to claim that Jews were, as John Foxe and others put it, aromatized by their conversion; it was quite another to figure out what happened to their racial otherness when they converted and entered or tried to enter a Christian commonwealth. The complications raised by conversion disturbed English commentators, some of whom offered vague theories of racial assimilation to explain away the problem. Richard Baxter, for example, proposed that once converted, the Jews 'would be no Jews immediately in a religious sense nor within sixty to eighty years in a natural sense.'[29]

To state my own question more pointedly, when Jewish or Muslim men converted to Christianity, what was thought to happen to their gendered bodies? Insofar as conversion experience was conceived as effecting a complete reorganization of the self—that is, insofar as Jewishness or Muslimness was fully effaced in the convert—that experience should have entailed not just a religious realignment but a process of "masculinization," a loss of "abnormal" gender features, a regendering simultaneous with the realignment of belief and of moral stance. Can we find such gender conversion in medieval texts? How susceptible to transformation are those embodied traits that, for medieval Christians, seem integral to the differentiation of "true believers" and "infidels"?

On the one hand, it is not unlikely that such a transformation would have been thought possible in the Middle Ages, where a "one-sex model" provided at least one available understanding of the physiological relation between maleness and femaleness. Thomas Laqueur cites various medieval and Renaissance accounts in which "Bodies actually seem to slip from their sexual anchorage."[30] On the other hand, given Christian models of conversion that date back to the early Church—models in which conversion entails the renunciation of worldly power, family ties, and sexuality—one can imagine a certain strong resistance to the idea of conversion as entailing a bodily "masculinization." As in Chaucer's *Second Nun's Tale*, traditional Christian conversion is most often a "demasculinizing" movement out of the world. Valerian and his brother Tiburce, in converting to Christianity, submit themselves to Cecilia's superior spiritual authority; the gender hierarchy of Cecilia and Valerian's marriage is reversed. And in a world where the Church has yet to gain political power, the move into Christianity also involves a forfeiture of public, "masculine" authority: Valerian and Tiburce, rightfully part of the Roman ruling class, become, as converts, subject to legal action, "torment" (VIII.373, 376), and martyrdom.

Though such a model of conversion remains central within Christianity (see, for instance, the Franciscan conversion accounts included in *The Little Flowers of St. Francis*),[31] by the High and Late Middle Ages the social reality around conversion had changed significantly. The Western Church was no longer a persecuted, powerless agent, and while converts like the early Franciscans who moved, *within* Christianity, from secular, and perhaps socially powerful, positions to embrace a spiritual life might still be understood through the model of conversion developed in the early Church, the situation was significantly different for converts from *outside* Christianity who, in embracing the hegemonic religion of the West, potentially empowered themselves, moving out of positions of social and political marginality. Indeed, as the history of the Franciscan order shows, too vigorous an embracing of poverty, too stark a renunciation of worldly power, too strong a movement out of the realm of "masculine" authority, could come to be viewed with suspicion, even as "heretical," because potentially critical of the Church and its real power.

A medieval Jewish or Muslim man converting to Christianity thus necessarily found himself in a vexed position in relation to the question of gender. Conversion for the "feminized" Jew or Muslim seems to call for "masculinization," a loss of those gendered qualities used, in Christian constructions, to denigrate religious others, to keep them other. But the most common Christian models of conversion entail quite a different sort of movement, away from "masculine" roles and power. It is not, then, surprising that what we most often find in medieval accounts of conversion is not a straightforward rectification of gender but its further problematizing: conversion most often entails a "gender trouble" that circulates around the figure of the convert.

Think, for instance, of the ways in which the two situations of conversion depicted in Chaucer's *Man of Law's Tale* are intimately, complicatedly, and perhaps contradictorily tied up with questions of gender. In each instance, a non-Christian ruler—the Muslim sultan, the pagan King Alla—converts to Christianity, and in each case the conversion is closely linked to his marrying the Christian Constance (II.225-26, II.683–93). The association of marriage with conversion here might be read in a variety of ways: as "feminizing" the sultan, who surrenders his own religious tradition not out of any conviction of Christianity's superiority but in order to facilitate his marriage (Alla on the other hand converts before there is any indication that he plans to marry Constance); as "masculinizing" the sultan, who through conversion and marriage becomes the son-in-law of the Roman emperor, forging an important homosocial alliance with Western Europe; as "feminizing" Alla, who chooses not only to submit himself to a foreign religious tradition but to ally himself with a destitute woman who (seemingly) has no important family or political connections. Significantly, in each case, the conversion and marriage are strongly opposed by the male ruler's *mother*; the defense of Islam and of paganism, as these are abandoned by men, falls to women, and in each case a woman who is distinctly "mannysh" (II.782). This action is readable in two contradictory ways. On the one hand, perhaps the "masculine" authority that the sultaness and Donegild display reveals a certain gender disorder inherent to Islam and paganism, traditions where power is revealed as resting, inappropriately, from the perspective of the Christian text, with matriarchs rather than patriarchs. Or perhaps the disruption of gender is to be thought of not as inherent to these religious traditions but rather as consequential on the movement of conversion: the decision to abandon the native religious tradition undermines gender hierarchy. I think that both these possibilities function in Chaucer's tale: non-Christian religions are always already sites of gender disruption but so too are the movements of conversion in which those religions are left behind for Christianity.

For the sultan, certainly, conversion, rather than providing the opportunity to escape a "feminized" religion, leads to the loss of "masculine" power. He, all the "converted" "Surryens" (II.435), and all the "Cristen folk" (II.416) accompanying Constance to the wedding feast (except Constance herself) are massacred, and they meet their deaths in a particularly unvaliant way—"al tohewe and stiked at the bord" (II.430), subjected to the power of "This olde Sowdanesse, cursed krone" (II.432). Of course, the sultaness, as representative of the old religion, and not the conversion itself, is "responsible" for what happens to the sultan and his men, but one might still read the figure of the intransigent *mother* here as representing some inherent, genetic, Muslim intractability to full religious transformation. The sultan may want to become a Christian, but something in the "feminized," gender-disordered family, realm, and religious tradition that he tries to leave behind will not allow his departure.

Alla's movement into Christianity, despite his mother Donegild's resistance, is, by contrast, more successful. He responds to his mother's treacherous activities, her undermining of his authority, with a strong reconsolidation of power, violently eliminating Donegild and thus those aspects of his prior, pagan life that she may represent: "Th'effect is this: that Alla, out of drede, / His mooder slow—that may men pleynly rede— / For that she traitour was to hire ligeance. / Thus endeth olde Donegild, with meschance!" (II.893–96). But though the narrator's final exclamation here indicates approval of Alla's violence, the movement of conversion does not end with the violent reassertion of "masculine" power. In terms of the traditional model of Christian conversion as a movement away from the world, into humility, Alla's entrance into Christianity is problematic, and it is not completed by the "masculine" violence he directs against his mother and his mother's religion. A countermovement of "repentance" and pilgrimage (II.988–94), in which he submits to the higher authority of the Church—he "putte hym in the Popes ordinaunce / In heigh and logh, and Jhesu Crist bisoghte / Foryeve his wikked werkes that he wroghte" (II.992–94)—is necessary before he can be reunited with Constance and his son Maurice, and before he can return to England as a true Christian monarch. But Alla perhaps is never an unproblematic figure; once fully Christianized, he quickly dies, and Constance returns to Rome, to "hir fader" (II.1152) the emperor, to the heart of a patriarchal Christianity left behind in her (missionary) journeys into Islam and paganism but finally fully reentered. And Maurice—unlike his father, born into Christianity; raised alone by the unambiguously Christian, even saintly, Constance—is destined to be made "Emperour...by the Pope" (II.1121–22); unlike his father, he can "lyve cristenly" (II.1122) with little difficulty.

***

In texts by Jewish men who converted to Christianity, the "femininity" of the Jewish body is less evident than it is in traditions of anti-Semitic Christian writing. This is perhaps unsurprising. Jewish male converts may not have experienced their gender as labile; they may have felt themselves to be equally "masculine" before and after their religious transformation. Given, however, that the sense of Jewish gender difference was so strong in the Christian culture that converts entered, gender and the question of bodily difference must have been important issues, and points of anxiety, for new converts. Indeed, we might suppose that a certain *avoidance* of the body in the texts of converts was itself a response to anxiety about gender and the gendered body. From Paul's epistles on, Jewishness was identified with carnality and, in the realm of interpretation, with a literalizing (mis)reading of texts; Christianity, in contrast, was spiritualized, and allegorical reading, a recognition of texts' "real" truths, identified as a peculiarly Christian process.[32] Further, as Carolyn Dinshaw has shown in her discussion of medieval "sexual poetics," the same opposition was gendered: the "Pauline model of reading would mean to discard altogether the mode of woman as central, naked truth of the text, to rigorously pass through the text's female body on the way to its spirit—its male spirit, as Ambrose and others suggest."[33] Not to talk overmuch about body was perhaps one means by which the convert could demonstrate that he had overcome Jewish carnality, literality, and "femininity."

As I have argued elsewhere about Hermann of Cologne, a convert from Judaism to Christianity and author of the *Opusculum de conversione sua*, the main movement of Christianization involves learning to read allegorically, learning to leave behind a literalizing, "Jewish" understanding of texts for a spiritualizing, Christian one.[34] Such a process is, as Dinshaw's work suggests, always also gendered: as Hermann learns to read as a Christian, he is also learning to read in a "masculine" fashion. Indeed, in Hermann's autobiographical account, one of the main impediments to conversion, one of the Jewish "seductions" that makes him hesitate in embracing Christianity, is a carnal and female one: he is held back from his growing understanding of Christian "truth" by "concupiscentias," "carnis voluptate" [pleasure of the flesh], and "carnis delectationem" [delight of the flesh] when he agrees to marry a Jewish woman.[35]

Literal and allegorical reading, and the gendered implications of these, are similarly central to the early twelfth-century *Dialogue* between a Jew and a Christian written by the Spanish convert Petrus Alphonsi.[36] While not an account of conversion but rather a dispute over the competing religious and scriptural claims of Christianity, Judaism, and Islam, the fact of Peter's conversion is central to the *Dialogue*: the two interlocutors are "Petrus" and "Moyses," and as Peter makes explicit, Moses is the name that he himself had before baptism ("nomen quod ante baptismum habueram" [538]). The debate thus becomes one between pre- and post-conversion selves, dramatizing the different ways in which the unconverted Jew and the Christian convert understand Scripture, the spirit, God, and the world.

Throughout, the difference between the two is precisely one of understanding. Peter describes his own conversion as allowing a new kind of seeing, the removal of an obfuscating "veil" that he describes in terms evocative of medieval theories of allegoresis: "Omnipotens suo nos Spiritu inspiravit, et ad viae rectae semitam direxit, tenuem prius oculorum albuginem, et post grave corrupti animi velamentum removens" [The omnipotent one inspired us with his spirit, and directed us into the path of a straight life, removing first the thin white film covering the eyes and afterwards the heavy veil of the corrupt soul] (536). Moses, and Jews more generally, err particularly in how they read the biblical law, an error that the Christian Peter himself can now "see" and must demonstrate to Moses—"video eos [Judaeos] solam legis superficiem attendere, et litteram non spiritualiter, sed carnaliter exponere, unde maximo decepti sunt errore" (I see that they [Jews] attend to only the surface of the law and expound the letter not spiritually but carnally, whence they have been deceived by the greatest error, 540). Indeed, the first, and longest, chapter of the *Dialogue* is devoted to showing that "Judaei verba prophetarum carnaliter intelligunt, et ea falso exponunt" [the Jews understand the words of the prophets carnally and expound them falsely] (541), and the opposition between literal/Jewish and spiritual/Christian reading repeatedly recurs.[37]

The *Dialogue* thus thematizes the differences between Jewish and Christian modes of understanding, and in its debate structure—where Moses repeatedly voices erroneous positions in order to be corrected by Peter—it also dramatizes those differences. The debate is quite clearly set up as a "masculine" contest, metaphorized as a battle between two armed opponents. Moses proposes that "uterque in alternae rationis *campo* discurramus" [each of us run about on the *field* of dialogic reason] (539; emphasis mine); soon after, setting the terms for using Hebrew scripture in the argument, Peter expresses his desire ("multum cupio") "tuo...gladio occidere te" [to strike you down with your own sword] (539). It quickly becomes clear, however, that only one of the two "combatants" has a truly "masculine" understanding of things, that the "sword" of reason and wisdom—qualities that, in the opening prayer of the *Dialogue*, Peter sees as distinguishing man ("homo") from the animals (535)—belongs only to the Christian. Though Moses *is* enlightened in various ways as the debate proceeds, admitting over and over again the truth of Peter's positions—"Magnae caecitatis velamen de pectore meo educens, veritatis lucernam clarissime infudisti, quare digna a Deo compensetur retributio tibi" [You have poured out the light of truth most clearly, drawing forth the veil of great blindness from my breast; for which, may a worthy payment be weighed out to you by God] (546)—when the *Dialogue* closes, Peter must still pray for Moses' conversion, and the "illumination" that would bring (671-72).[38]

Though Moses is Peter before his conversion, the *Dialogue* interestingly chooses not to bring us to the moment when Jew becomes Christian. The two religious positionings remain separate, and this allows for a starker posing of Judaism against Christianity. Even after Peter has persuaded him that many Jewish beliefs are in error, Moses shows himself not quite to "get it," expressing surprise that, given his recognition of Jewish error, Peter has chosen to embrace Christianity rather than *Islam.* Moses' error here makes it necessary for Peter to demonstrate that Islam is even more debased—more corporeal and "feminized"—than Judaism; thus, for instance, he comments on how Islam emphasizes "extrinsic" rather than "intrinsic" purity, and he makes clear that the "extrinsic" is to be associated with the "feminine": "Munditia autem de ablutione membrorum pertinebat cultoribus stellae Veneris, qui volentes eam orare, ad modum feminae se aptabant" [The purity of washing one's limbs, however, belonged to the worshippers of the star, Venus, who, wishing to worship her, conformed themselves to the manner of a woman] (602). Moses, in his impulse to move from Judaism to Islam rather than to Christianity, shows himself to be still immersed in Jewish corporeal, and specifically "feminine," misreading.

Attracted to the bodiliness of Islam rather than the spirituality of Christianity, Moses, even as he recognizes the errors of Jewish corporeality, is still a Jew, and Peter can—even toward the end of the debate, when Moses has approached most closely to a Christian positioning—repeatedly berate him, and his people, for stupidity: "Stultissime omnium, O Moyses" [Most foolish of all, O Moses] (636; compare 645); "Non est gens in toto mundo stolidior vobis" [There is not a nation in the whole world more obtuse than you] (637). On the field of intellectual battle, there is no real contest between Christian and Jew. Indeed, Jewish arguments belong not to the "human" realm of true reason and wisdom (535) nor to the "masculine" realm of the "campus" (539) but to an infantilized and "feminized" realm: "de eo (i.e., Deo) tales protulere sententias, quae non aliud nisi verba videntur jocantium in scholis puerorum, vel nentium in plateis mulierum" [they brought forth such statements concerning him (i.e., God), that these seemed not other than the words of boys jesting in the schools, or of women spinning in the streets] (540). This is not just a momentary comparison, but is later reiterated verbatim, and self-consciously: "Hoc itaque est quod tibi superius dixi, verba doctorum vestrorum non aliud videri quam verba jocantium in scholis puerorum, vel nentium in plateis mulierum" [And thus this is as I said to you above: that the words of your doctors seem not other than the words of boys jesting in the schools, or of women spinning in the streets] (567).

Of course, the disparagement of Jewish positions as "feminine" and irrational, and hence perhaps not fully "human," presents a certain danger for Peter himself. It is, after all, a former Jew who writes the *Dialogue*, and who argues with, and creates, a Jewish interlocutor who is also himself. Peter anxiously positions his post-conversion self in such a way as to "masculinize" it: the Peter of the debate is identified with spiritual (masculine/Christian) reading; he is in control in the dialogue, repeatedly defeating Moses on the field of battle; he is hyper-rational and hyper-intellectual, introducing into the debate a variety of abstruse philosophical and scientific topics—the geography of the earth (543–47), the physiology of "ira" and of crying (549–50), philosophical proofs for the existence of God the Creator (555)—uncommon in religious polemic, and clearly intended to impress the reader with the extent of Peter's intellectual capital. It is, I would suggest, the feared remnants of Jewishness—including perhaps especially the remnants of Jewish gender difference—that necessitate such demonstrations of intellectual prowess. Once a Jew, Peter is now able to stand opposed to his former self; he can defeat that self on the field of reasoned battle. But that former self never disappears, is never transformed; Moses remains present throughout—"stolid," making the arguments of women—a reminder of Peter's Jewishness that, at least in this text, is never effaced.

NOTES

1. Quoted in R.I. Moore, *The Origins of European Dissent* (Oxford: Basil Blackwell, 1985 [1977]), p. 126.

2. See R.W. Southern's discussion of the Beguines of Cologne, *Western Society and the Church in the Middle Ages* (Harmondsworth: Penguin, 1970), pp. 319-31. For an overview of the literature on "the swelling numbers of women attracted to both orthodox and heterodox movements in the twelfth to the fourteenth centuries," see Caroline Walker Bynum, *Jesus as Mother: Studies in the Spirituality of the High Middle Ages* (Berkeley, Los Angeles, and London: University of California Press, 1982), pp. 182-83, n. 33. And for a recent treatment of the Beguine movement, see Joanna

Ziegler, "Reality as Imitation: The Role of Religious Imagery Among the Beguines of the Low Countries," in *Maps of Flesh and Light: The Religious Experience of Medieval Women Mystics,* ed. Ulrike Wiethaus (Syracuse: Syracuse University Press, 1993), pp. 112-26.

3. *The Book of Margery Kempe*, trans. B.A. Windeatt (London: Penguin, 1985), pp. 153, 168; also see p. 172.

4. For the conflation of Judaism and Islam, see, for instance, the Towneley Herod play, where Herod is described as "the heynd kyng...of Iury" "By grace of Mahowne" (*The Townely Plays*, 2 vols., ed. Martin Stevens and A.C. Cawley, E.E.T.S., S.S., pp. 13–14 [Oxford: Oxford University Press, 1994], 16.14-16); or the Croxton *Play of the Sacrament* (in *Medieval Drama*, ed. David Bevington [Boston: Houghton Mifflin, 1975]), where the Jewish merchant Jonathas invokes "almighty Machomet" (149); or William Dunbar's "The Fenyeit Freir of Tungland" (in *The Poems of William Dunbar*, ed. W. Mackay Mackenzie [London: Faber and Faber, 1932]), where a "Turk of Tartary" (5) is described also as a "jow" (31). For the conflation of Jews and Muslims in a very different (legal) context, see *Jews and Saracens in the Consilia of Oldradus de Ponte*, ed. and trans. Norman Zacour (Toronto: Pontifical Institute of Mediaeval Studies, 1990), esp. pp. 21–22. On the depiction of Islam as a Christian "heresy," see Norman Daniel, *Islam and the West: The Making of an Image*, revised ed. (Oxford: Oneworld, 1993 [1960]), pp. 209–13; Daniel, *The Arabs and Mediaeval Europe*, 2nd ed. (London and New York: Longman, 1979 [1975]), pp. 246, 249–52; and R.W. Southern, *Western Views of Islam in the Middle Ages* (Cambridge, Mass.: Harvard University Press, 1962), pp. 38–39. For a particularly rich and suggestive discussion of accusations against Jews that linked them to Muslims, to heretics, and to lepers, see the first two chapters in Carlo Ginzburg, *Ecstasies: Deciphering the Witches' Sabbath*, trans. Raymond Rosenthal (New York: Pantheon, 1991 [1989]).

5. James Shapiro, *Shakespeare and the Jews* (New York: Columbia University Press, 1996), has recently examined the significance of circumcision, including the affiliations of circumcision with emasculation, in Elizabethan culture; see especially pp. 113–30. For earlier consideration of some of the issues about Jewish and Muslim bodies, gender, and sexuality raised in the present essay, see Steven F. Kruger, "The Bodies of Jews in the Late Middle Ages," in *The Idea of Medieval Literature: New Essays on Chaucer and Medieval Culture in Honor of Donald R. Howard*, ed. James M. Dean and Christian K. Zacher (Newark: University of Delaware Press; London and Toronto: Associated University Presses, 1992), pp. 301–23; "Racial/Religious and Sexual Queerness in the Middle Ages," *Medieval Feminist Newsletter*, no. 16 (Fall 1993): 32–36; and "Conversion and Medieval Sexual, Religious, and Racial Categories," in *Constructing Medieval Sexuality*, ed. Karma Lochrie, Peggy McCracken, and James Schultz (Minneapolis and London: University of Minnesota Press, forthcoming).

6. Mark R. Cohen, *Under Crescent and Cross: The Jews in the Middle Ages* (Princeton: Princeton University Press, 1994), p. 35.

7. Quoted in James A. Brundage, *Law, Sex, and Christian Society in Medieval Europe* (Chicago and London: The University of Chicago Press, 1987), p. 66. Certain traditions within Judaism explain circumcision in a similar way; see, most notably, Moses Maimonides, *The Guide for the Perplexed,* 2nd ed., trans. M. Friedländer (New York: Dover, 1956 [1904]), III.49 (p. 378): "As regards circumcision, I think that one of its objects is to limit sexual intercourse, and to weaken the organ of generation as far as possible, and thus cause man to be moderate." Daniel Boyarin, "'This We Know to Be the Carnal Israel': Circumcision and the Erotic Life of God and Israel," *Critical Inquiry* 18 (1992): 474–505, notes this passage (pp. 486–87 n. 37), comparing Maimonides' position to a similar reading of circumcision in Philo (pp. 485–87). He points out as well that the traditional circumcision ceremony involves addressing the circumcised boy with the second-person *feminine* pronoun (p. 496); as Boyarin suggests, "circumcision is understood...as feminizing the male" (p. 495; and see the more extensive discussion, pp. 494–97).

8. For a brief overview of the "extremely important function" of eunuchs "in the Byzantine state" (p. 16), see Vern L. Bullough, "Formation of Medieval Ideals: Christian Theory and Christian Practice," in *Sexual Practices and the Medieval Church*, ed.Vern L. Bullough and James Brundage (Buffalo: Prometheus Books, 1982), pp. 16–17.

9. Guibert of Nogent, *Gesta Dei per Francos*, in *Receuil des historiens des croisades, Historiens occidentaux*, vol. 4, L'Academie des Inscriptions et Belles-Lettres (Paris: Imprimerie Nationale, 1879), pp. 113–263, at 133. The original text reads: "edicto celebri, de pluribus universorum filiabus unam per omne imperium suum prostitui juberet, et fisco proprio lucrum foedissimae passionis inferret. Nec minus illud, quod de pluribus filiis unum eunuchizari, data praecepti auctoritate, mandaverit: et corpora marium ademptis virilibus enervia ac effeminata reddiderit, quae usibus militiae jam non habeantur utilia; immo ad detrimenti cumulum, abscidatur in ipsis propago futura, cujus incrementis sperari valerent contra hostes auxilia."

10. Louise Mirrer, "Representing 'Other' Men: Muslims, Jews, and Masculine Ideals in Medieval Castilian Epic and Ballad," in *Medieval Masculinities: Regarding Men in the Middle Ages*, ed. Clare A. Lees, with Thelma Fenster and Jo Ann McNamara (Minneapolis: University of Minnesota Press, 1994), pp. 169–86; the citation is at 173. Salo Wittmayer Baron, *A Social and Religious History of the Jews*, 2nd ed., 18 vols. (New York: Columbia University Press, 1952–1983), observes that, in a later period in Spanish literature, Cervantes spoke of the Jews "as the *gente afeminada*" (11.54); that "With many Spanish authors the diminutive, *judihuelo*, stood for both a little Jewish boy and a coward" (11.54); and that "In his

Reprobación del amor mundano o Carbacho, written in 1438, Alphonso Martínez de Toledo, 'archpriest' of Talavera, on several occasions uses the term *judío* as a synonym for *coward* or *cowardly*, placing Jews on a par with women and priests" (11.341–42, n. 3).

11. Marco Polo, *The Travels*, trans. Ronald Latham (Harmondsworth: Penguin, 1958), p. 306.

12. See Baron, *Social and Religious History*, 11.154, 11.342 n. 3, and Cohen, *Under Crescent and Cross*, pp. 35, 47. Baron notes that "The popular mind saw no conflict between...allegations of Jewish proneness to violence and the growingly accepted view that Jews were effeminate and cowardly, a view which doubtless gained in currency with the spreading prohibitions for Jews to bear arms. Even in Spain, where Jews often continued to conduct themselves as *hidalgos*, denigration of Jewish courage was even applied to the sixteenth-century *conversos*" (11.154). One might in fact argue that the very idea of a Jewish "proneness to violence," and of a strong Muslim military threat to Europe, necessitated emasculating depictions of Jewish and Muslim men. For an examination of how, in a very different context, male bodies are constructed as simultaneously threatening and debilitated, see Steven F. Kruger, *AIDS Narratives: Gender and Sexuality, Fiction and Science* (New York: Garland, 1996), chapter 2.

13. Quoted in Joshua Trachtenberg, *The Devil and the Jews: The Medieval Conception of the Jew and Its Relation to Modern Anti-Semitism* (Philadelphia: The Jewish Publication Society of America, 1983 [1943]), p. 149.

14. Peter Abelard, *A Dialogue of a Philosopher with a Jew, and a Christian*, trans. Pierre J. Payer (Toronto: Pontifical Institute of Mediaeval Studies, 1979), p. 47. A similar idea persists into the Renaissance and is expressed, for instance, by Thomas Browne, who argues in *Pseudodoxia Epidemica* that "Jewish women 'desire copulation' with Christians 'rather than [with men of] their own nation, and affect Christian carnality above circumcised venery'" (quoted in Shapiro, *Shakespeare and the Jews*, p. 37).

15. See Caesarius of Heisterbach, *The Dialogue on Miracles*, 2 vols., trans. H. von E. Scott and C.C. Swinton Bland (London: George Routledge and Sons, 1929), 1.102; further references to Caesarius will be indicated parenthetically in my text. Jewish male bodily deficiency here provides the opportunity for a Jewish woman to escape the watchful eye of her father and have sex with a Christian clerk since, "on the night of the Friday before your Easter...the Jews are said to labour under a sickness called the bloody flux, with which they are so much occupied, that they can scarcely pay attention to anything else at that time." Sander Gilman, *Jewish Self-Hatred: Anti-Semitism and the Hidden Language of the Jews* (Baltimore and London: The Johns Hopkins University Press, 1986), identifies Thomas of Cantimpré as the first to present a "'scientific' statement of the phenomenon" of Jewish male menstruation (p. 74). On belief in this phenomenon, see also

Trachtenberg, *The Devil and the Jews*, pp. 50, 149, 228, n. 27 (Trachtenberg discusses the more general belief that Jews suffered diseases of bleeding [pp. 50–51], and he places that belief in relation to the blood accusations made against Jews [pp. 140–55]); Léon Poliakov, *Histoire de l'anti-semitisme: Du Christ aux juifs de cour*, vol. 1 (Paris: Calmann-Lévy, 1955),p. 160; Baron, *Social and Religious History*, 11.153–54; and Shapiro, *Shakespeare and the Jews*, pp. 37–38, 241–42, n. 116. Shapiro also notes, in Renaissance writers, the idea that "Jewish men were sometimes capable of breast-feeding": "Samuel Purchas writes that 'if you believe their *Gemara* (can you choose?), a poor Jew having buried his wife and not able to hire a nurse for his child had his own breasts miraculously filled with milk, and became nurse himself.' Purchas also cites a Midrashic tradition regarding the Book of Esther that the orphaned Esther had been breast-fed by Mordechai" (p. 38).

16. The problem that the circumcision of Christ's own body posed in relation to denigrations of the circumcised bodies of medieval Jews—an association of Christ's perfect body with the debased, "feminized" bodies of Jews—was partly solved by depictions that made the circumcision a prefiguration of the crucifixion, one more Jewish attack on Christ's divinized humanity, and an attack thus affiliated with Christ's salvific submission to violence. For one depiction of Christ's circumcision as Jewish attack, see Ruth Mellinkoff, *Outcasts: Signs of Otherness in Northern European Art of the Late Middle Ages*, 2 vols. (Berkeley, Los Angeles, and Oxford: University of California Press, 1993), plate II.23, and the discussion at 1.43 and 1.106–7.

17. Shapiro, *Shakespeare and the Jews*, p. 102. Shapiro discusses both medieval and Renaissance instances (pp. 100–111). As he notes, "the one feature of the myth of ritual murder most peculiar to English versions (it was nowhere near as central to accusations made elsewhere in Europe) was that Jews circumcised their young male victims" (p. 111).

18. V.D. Lipman, *The Jews of Medieval Norwich* (London: The Jewish Historical Society of England, 1967), pp. 59–62.

19. D'Blossiers Tovey, *Anglia Judaica: Or the History and Antiquities of the Jews of England* (Oxford, 1738; rpt. New York: Burt Franklin, 1967), pp. 65–66. As Tovey points out, "*Bonefand* pleaded *not guilty*, and was very honourably acquitted" (p. 65; emphasis in original). Tovey dates the accusation to the fourth year of the reign of King John (1199–1216).

20. See Baron, *Social and Religious History*, 11.86. A direct connection between Jewish "usury" and female prostitution was made in the Renaissance (see Shapiro, *Shakespeare and the Jews*, pp. 99–100 and p. 256 n. 38), and medieval economic accusations against Jews were importantly wrapped up with gender constructions. See, for instance, Matthew Paris's comment on the crime of coin-clipping: "Moreover it was said and discovered that the coins were being circumcised by circumcised people and infidel Jews who, because of the heavy royal taxes, were reduced to begging.

Other crimes, too, were said to have originated with them" (*Chronicles of Matthew Paris: Monastic Life in the Thirteenth Century*, ed. and trans. Richard Vaughan [Gloucester: Alan Sutton; New York: St. Martin's Press, 1986 [1984]], p. 95). The association of circumcision and debasement of currency persisted at least until the eighteenth century: "In brave Edward's days they (the Jews) were caught in a gin, / For clipping our coin, now to add sin to sin, / As they've got all our pelf, they'd be clipping our skin. / Those foes to the pork of old England" (quoted in Shapiro, *Shakespeare and the Jews*, p. 210). Note further the association, in William Langland's *Piers Plowman*, of a debased coin, the "Loscheborw" (17.72, 17.82, 17.168), with "leccherye and oþer lustes of synne" (17.79) and with a Muhammad whom Langland depicts as a Christian "heretic": "Me fynde wel þat Macometh was a man ycristened / And a cardinal of court, a gret clerk withalle, / And pursuede to haue be pope, prince of holy chirche. / Ac for he was lyk a Lossheborw y leue oure lord hym lette" (17.165–69); I quote the text from *Piers Plowman by William Langland: An Edition of the C-Text*, ed. Derek Pearsall (Berkeley and Los Angeles: University of California Press, 1978).

21. Matthew Paris, *Chronicles*, p. 215.

22.Geoffrey Chaucer, *The Riverside Chaucer*, 3rd ed., Larry D. Benson, gen. ed. (Boston: Houghton Mifflin, 1987), II.359–62; subsequent references to Chaucer (fragment and line numbers) will be given parenthetically in my text. On the medieval Semiramis—a female usurper of properly male authority—see Irene Samuel, "Semiramis in the Middle Ages: The History of a Legend," *Medievalia et Humanistica* 2 (1944): 32–44, and Johnstone Parr, "Chaucer's Semiramis," *Chaucer Review* 5 (1970): 57–61.

23. See, for instance, Michael Adler, *Jews of Medieval England* (London: The Jewish Historical Society of England, 1939), 17–42.

24. Giovanni Boccaccio, *The Decameron*, G.H. McWilliam, trans. (Harmondsworth: Penguin, 1972), pp. 169–91; the quotation is at p. 170.

25. Boccaccio, p. 191.

26. Also see Shapiro's suggestion that, in the Renaissance, "conversion is not quite the same for Jewish women as it is for Jewish men": "In the world of fiction, the marriage and conversion of Jewish women usually go hand in hand....In contrast, Jewish men who convert to Christianity are never married off to Christian women. And where Jewish women are always depicted as young and desirable, male Jewish converts are invariably old and impotent, condemned to remain unwed and at the periphery of the Christian community....To early modern Englishmen, the fantasy of Christian men marrying converting Jewesses was far more appealing than the idea of Jewish men, even converted ones, marrying Christian women" (*Shakespeare and the Jews*, p. 132).

27. I address a similar question in "Conversion and Medieval Sexual, Religious, and Racial Categories," but there I focus on questions of sexuality rather than gender.

28. For the suggestion, however, that the Middle Ages at least sometimes thought biological and racial differences as "convertible," see my "Conversion and Medieval Sexual, Religious, and Racial Categories."

29. Shapiro, *Shakespeare and the Jews*, pp. 170–71. On the idea of the *foetor judaicus*, see further Trachtenberg, *The Devil and the Jews*, pp. 47–50.

30. Thomas Laqueur, *Making Sex: Body and Gender from the Greeks to Freud* (Cambridge, Mass., and London: Harvard University Press, 1990), p. 124. Laqueur's argument has been controversial. I would suggest that, while the "one-sex model" was not necessarily dominant in all discursive realms throughout the Middle Ages, it was a widely available model. For a fuller discussion of medieval medical models of sex, see Danielle Jacquart and Claude Thomasset, *Sexuality and Medicine in the Middle Ages*, trans. Matthew Adamson (Princeton: Princeton University Press, 1988 [1985]).

31. *The Little Flowers of St. Francis*, trans. Raphael Brown (Garden City, NY: Image Books, 1958).

32. See Boyarin, "'This We Know to Be the Carnal Israel,'" for a recent discussion of the origins of this formulation.

33. Carolyn Dinshaw, *Chaucer's Sexual Poetics* (Madison and London: The University of Wisconsin Press, 1989), p. 22. The work of Caroline Walker Bynum has problematized, in our reading of medieval culture, a simple identification of body with femaleness and soul or spirit with maleness; see, most recently, *The Resurrection of the Body in Western Christianity, 200–1336* (New York: Columbia University Press, 1995). Still, I believe that a series of analogical dichotomies—body/spirit, female/male, Jewish/Christian—underpins certain crucial medieval understandings.

34. Steven F. Kruger, *Dreaming in the Middle Ages* (Cambridge: Cambridge University Press, 1992), pp. 154–65.

35. Hermann of Cologne, *Opusculum de conversione sua*, ed. Gerlinde Niemeyer, Monumenta Germaniae Historica, Quellen zur Geistesgeschichte des Mittelalters, 4 (Weimar: Hermann Böhlaus Nachfolger, 1963), pp. 101–3. I discuss this episode at somewhat greater length in "Conversion and Medieval Sexual, Religious, and Racial Categories."

36. Petrus Alphonsi, *Dialogi*, PL 157: 535–672; subsequent citations are given parenthetically in my text. For information on Peter's life and work, and for further bibliography, see Bernhard Blumenkranz, "Jüdische und christliche Konvertiten im jüdisch-christlichen Religionsgespräch des Mittelalters," in *Judentum im Mittelalter: Beiträge zum christlich-jüdischer Gespräch*, ed. Paul Wilpert (Berlin: Walter de Gruyter, 1966), pp. 264–82, esp. pp. 272–75; and Jeremy Cohen, "The Mentality of the Medieval Jewish

Apostate," in *Jewish Apostasy in the Modern World*, ed. Todd M. Endelman (New York and London: Holmes and Meier, 1987), pp. 20–47, esp. pp. 23–29.

37. For some of the most striking instances of the opposition between Jewish and Christian modes of reading, see cols. 553–54, 596 (where Peter refers explicitly to Pauline doctrine), 611–12, 615, 627, 630, 631–32, 666–68. But these are only particularly striking instances; the opposition is in fact prominent throughout the text.

38. The first four chapters and the last three chapters of the *Dialogue* all end with Peter praying for Moses' enlightenment and conversion. The fifth chapter also ends with Peter voicing a prayer, though here it is for his own freedom from Jewish error and for the capacity to complete his (Christian) argument aright (col. 606). There are twelve chapters in all; chapters 6–9 do not end with the formulaic prayer.

WHERE THE BOYS ARE: CHILDREN AND SEX IN THE ANGLO-SAXON PENITENTIALS

Allen J. Frantzen

This essay examines the Anglo-Saxon penitentials, a significant but neglected source of information on regulations concerning both homosexual and heterosexual acts associated with children.

One of the many valuable contributions of penitentials to our knowledge of medieval culture is the attention they give to acts, sexual and otherwise, involving children.[1] My aim in this essay is to examine references to children in the Anglo-Saxon penitentials, a topic which has scarcely been discussed. Most of the regulations concerning girls or boys of various ages are not sexual. Of the canons that pertain to sexual acts, many focus on young males and their interactions with each other and with grown men rather than with females of any age. The emphasis on boys is not peculiar to Anglo-Saxon culture; Vern L. Bullough shows that concern with the sexuality of boys, familiar in studies of ancient Greece, spans the period from late Rome to the twelfth century and beyond.[2] It is apparent that most of the regulations concerning boys derive from penitentials written for Irish monasteries. Although they include regulations for monks and nuns, the Anglo-Saxon penitentials are not monastic documents. It is not safe to assume that their regulation of children's sexual acts concerns the laity as well as the religious of Anglo-Saxon society. It is likely, in the case of boys at least, that boys in the monastery—oblates—are the focus of the canons, but it is possible that the penitentials' regulations also refer more widely to sexual acts of boys who were outside monastic communities.

After discussing some theoretical contexts for evaluating children's sexual activity, I will categorize the penitential canons concerning children, examining in detail those that describe both heterosexual and homosexual acts. I propose that such regulations tell us where the boys are in two senses—not only where, seen as sexual actors, boys are to be found but also where they are located in the spectrum of sexual behavior that defines medieval ideas of the masculine and feminine.

All these regulations, especially those that concern sexual acts, correspond to the requirements of what I will hypothetically describe as the "sex-gender" system, a shorthand construct that I will use to describe the code of sexual conduct and its relation to the heteronormative standards to which Anglo-Saxon men, women, boys, and girls were held. The boundaries of the system are most apparent when they are violated—for example, by cross-dressing or other acts in which men appear not to be manly or women, womanly. An outline of the "sex-gender" system of medieval Norse culture can be seen in the work of Carol J. Clover, who places the "moveable" categories of "woman" and "man" along a continuum of behavior measured not by biological sex but by "powerlessness, and the lack or loss of volition."[3] The penitentials are only partial testimony to the "sex-gender" system of Anglo-Saxon England, a discourse which engaged many kinds of texts (and, of course, other evidence as well). Nor is the evidence of the penitentials unproblematic, as I have stressed elsewhere.[4] But they exist in several manuscripts, translate far older Latin sources, conform to secular laws on most issues, and are supported by frequent calls for confession and penance in other sources. It seems reasonable to assume that they correspond in some way to the social and sexual standards of the late Anglo-Saxon Church.

THEORETICAL CONTEXTS

Discussions of medieval childhood must take note of the value attached to children in Scripture. "Whoever receives me, receives not me but the One who sent me," Christ said to the Apostles. The context points to the significance of children:

> So he sat down, called the Twelve, and said to them, 'If anyone wants to be first, he must make himself last of all and servant of all.' Then he took a child, set him in front of them, and put his arm round him. 'Whoever receives a child like this in my name,' he said,

'receives me, and whoever receives me, receives not me but the One who sent me.' (Mark 9: 35–39)[5]

Just as his father was present in him, Christ himself claimed to be present in children. The child, therefore, cannot be said merely to be a child. In reference to Christ teaching in the Temple, Milton wrote that "The childhood shows the man / As morning shows the day"; Wordsworth's claim for the unity of his days is even better known: "The Child is the father of the Man."[6] Because the medieval child was understood as representing the adult he or she would become, the child's life was divided into phases marking the emergence of adult status. Various ninth-century Latin penitentials attributed to Bede and Egbert list them: "infans, puer, juvenis, adulescens, aetate, senex."[7] In comparable Anglo-Saxon texts, unfortunately, this list is reduced to a simple requirement that the priest know whether the sinner who confesses is young or old ("hu geong he sig oþþe hu eald").[8] But elsewhere the penitentials mark age boundaries between childhood and adulthood that determine the child's ability to accept responsibility for his or her own actions.

Although historians dispute Philippe Ariès' claims that medieval children were little more than miniature adults and that medieval childhood was neglected and not understood as a distinct phase of life, his work is still influential.[9] Outlining some errors in Ariès' methodology, Janet L. Nelson has traced some of the ways in which medieval children, far from being neglected, symbolically served adult purposes. "Children were the blank sheet on which parents and churchmen inscribed needs and desires and strategies," she writes. "They were the blue-print in which designs for the future were embodied."[10] Indeed, it is not too much to add that, in some respects, children were mirrors in which adults saw their own sexual anxieties present not merely in incipient stages but fully formed. Regulations concerning children in the Anglo-Saxon handbooks of penance suggest that even as the Church placed children in categories separate from those of adults, acts of adult sexual behavior were used to classify the children's actions. When their sex acts were analyzed, children were given but little leeway.

This preliminary inquiry into the regulation of children's sexual conduct in the Anglo-Saxon penitentials draws less on the work of Ariès than on Michel Foucault's observations about children in *The History of Sexuality* and *The Use of Pleasure*. Foucault suggests that children's sexuality signifies chiefly as a barometer of personal and institutional attitudes about the sexuality of adults. According to Foucault, the barriers between children and sex were low in the medieval and early modern periods; in the eighteenth and nineteenth centuries, when adults became more concerned with managing their own sexual conduct, the sexual conduct of children was regulated more carefully too. The "classical" period, Foucault maintained, brought to an end "a longstanding 'freedom' of language between children and adults, or pupils and teachers"; simultaneously, "the boisterous laughter that had accompanied the precocious sexuality of children for so long—and in all social classes, it seems—was gradually stifled."[11] This freedom and laughter were not replaced by silence but rather by a "regime of discourses" that made "the sex of the schoolboy"—Foucault does not mean biological sex but sex acts—"a public problem."[12] Prior to the eighteenth century, Foucault believed, the triumvirate of "canonical law, the Christian pastoral, and civil law" focused chiefly on matrimonial relations; "the rest"—other forms of sexual activity—"remained a good deal more confused." In this latter category Foucault includes sodomy and "the indifference regarding the sexuality of children." This "indifference" of earlier periods is contrasted with the later surveillance of the child's body, "in his cradle, his bed, or his room by an entire watch-crew of parents, nurses, servants, educators, and doctors," who collectively constituted "'a local center' of power-knowledge."[13]

Although the elaborate interconnected web of discourses that Foucault musters around the cradle in the eighteenth century and later is not to be found in the Middle Ages, it is difficult to support his assertion of "indifference" to the sexual behavior of children in this period. Anglo-Saxon and Anglo-Latin penitentials manifest quite the opposite, especially concerning the behavior of boys (also Foucault's chief concern in the later period). Foucault misjudges "indifference" to children in medieval Europe, but his analysis of boys' place in the sexual codes of ancient Greece established one point especially relevant to the study of the male child's sexual behavior in the Anglo-Saxon period: the child's sexual conduct was regulated with reference to the adult male he would become.

In *The Use of Pleasure*, Foucault analyzed the practice expected of Greek adults of certain classes according to which men took boys as lovers. This practice was not a license to promiscuity or an example of what we think of as "homosexuality."[14] These unions were structured very differently from heterosexual unions, especially marriage, as Foucault shows by comparing accepted attitudes among Greek adult males towards sex with their wives and sex with boys.[15] The woman's range of activity and her status were completely within the power of her husband. His faithfulness to her did not reward her fidelity, which was taken for granted, but honored "the way in which she conduct[ed] the household and herself in the household."[16] Her governance of the household was validated by his governance of her. When the man pursued the boy, however, the man's position was not supported by this firmly established economic arrangement.

With respect to the boy, the man was much more vulnerable, for the boy, unlike the woman, was not contained by a social system that kept him always subordinate. Indeed, subordination and sexual submissiveness were characteristics he would outgrow as he matured and took male lovers of his own alongside his wife. It was because the boy would become a man that he was not allowed to be degraded by consenting to a homosexual union. Sexual relations were isomorphic to social standing, with the socially dominant person taking the sexually dominant position. Sexual acts were forced on slaves or those who had lost their citizenship and had no hope of regaining social status; they were not forced on the boy. His conduct had to preserve his honor; his future social position depended entirely on it. The adult lover's risk of rejection and loss of face testifies to the boy's independence and pending maturity.[17] The system described by Foucault stresses ethics and self-mastery rather than pleasure. Already master of his wife and hence of his household and estate, the man was required to master his desire and avoid being dominated. The boy's self-mastery required that he yield to others only in ways that protected his future status. There was no question of the boy's sexual pleasure: his pleasure was to please others.[18]

ANGLO-SAXON TEXTS

Medieval authorities were no more indifferent to the sexual development of boys than were the authorities of ancient Greece. The Anglo-Saxon penitentials, and the earlier Irish and Latin documents from which they were derived, offer unusually direct evidence of sexual acts involving children and emphasize the homosexual acts of boys. The corpus consists of four handbooks of penance written c. 950–1050, each found in at least two and in as many as four manuscripts: they are the *Scriftboc,* the *Canons of Theodore*, the *Old English Penitential,* and the *Old English Handbook*.[19] I regard the *Scriftboc* as the oldest of these documents, probably not earlier than the mid-tenth century; the *Canons of Theodore*, if not contemporary with the *Scriftboc,* closely resembles it in regard to sources. Both texts draw most of their canons from the Latin *Penitential* of Theodore, compiled from Theodore's judgments and widely circulated in the early eighth century and after; neither uses introductory apparatus (similar to the *ordo confessionis*) found in later documents.[20] The *Old English Penitential* translates three books from the ninth-century *Penitential* of Halitgar of Cambrai and borrows from the *Scriftboc.* All of the canons of the *Old English Handbook* are taken from the *Old English Penitential.*[21]

Pierre J. Payer has cautioned that it is misleading to speak of "the penitentials" as a group and that standardization across the field of penitentials in a given period is difficult to determine because the documents use varying scales that complicate comparisons.[22] This caution is less necessary when dealing with the Anglo-Saxon documents. Although they preserve some important differences of form, they draw most of the canons analyzed below either from Theodore's *Penitential* (which was known in several versions) or from Halitgar's *Penitential;* they also borrow from each other. This impressive conformity among the Anglo-Saxon documents suggests that we can make significant and coherent comparisons among them. Because the documents are found in the same manuscripts, we must assume that they were used contemporaneously. Seen in terms of their sources, however, it seems clear that the texts represent a pattern of development, with the *Scriftboc* being the oldest and the *Old English Handbook* the youngest of the handbooks.[23] Canons dealing with children are usually marked by vocabulary: "cild," "bearn," "sunu," "dohtor," "cniht," and "mæden"correspond to Latin "infans," " puer," " puella," " parvulus," and "adulescens." The four handbooks contain a total of 66 references to these terms; an average of 12 percent of the canons of each text refer to children, a figure that dips to 8.5 percent for the *Old English Penitential* and rises to 16 percent for the *Old English Handbook*.[24]

Rob Meens has recently shown that the Latin vocabulary divides references to children into two categories, regulations concerning "infantes," children up to seven years of age who are mentioned only in the context of others' confessions, not their own, and "pueri," from seven to twenty, who confessed themselves. Other terms, not all of them found in the Old English texts to be discussed here, include "infantes monasterii," fourteen years of age according to the *Penitential* of Theodore, "pueri monasterii,"up to twenty-five, and the "parvulus," twenty years of age.[25] I subdivide each of Meens's categories. In the first, regarding the "infantes," I differentiate between canons that mention children only as the consequence of sexual intercourse and those that concern the death of children (with or without baptism). Neither the first nor the second category concerns the actions of children themselves. The sins in the first category are adult sexual acts that are given greater penances if children are born as a result; those in the second category are the spiritual responsibilities of those adults who raise children. Within Meens's category of "pueri" I also differentiate two groups, one dealing with actions outside the sex-gender system—that is to say, with non-sexual acts, whether voluntary or involuntary—and the other with sexual acts that localized children explicitly within that system. There are implications for children in other sections of the penitentials—arguably anything that deals with a parent deals with a child—but in the following discussion I have narrowed the evidence to specific references to children.

The first category, in which children are mentioned only because they are the result of unlawful sexual intercourse, contains only seven examples, or approximately 10 percent of the total of 66 canons related to children. Only the *Scriftboc* and the *Canons of Theodore* alter penances for sexual acts that result in conception; all but one of the references is found in the *Scriftboc*. For example, a deacon or a monk who had intercourse with a laywoman did a greater penance if she had a child; a man who had sex with another man's wife did penance for one year, but three if she had a child.[26]

The second category, which concerns the care of "infantes," contains 30 examples, nearly half of the total of 66. Most of these canons concern the death of children; such canons are found in each of the four documents between three and five times.[27] Other issues include care of a stepchild, cleansing the mother after birth, the effects of baptism on the child, and leaving the child to go on a pilgrimage. These regulations protect the "cild" ("infantes") from death by accident or murder, from death without benefit of baptism, or from abortion (to which there are six references),[28] but they seem designed to keep adults from concealing unlawful intercourse or from postponing baptism. In his analysis of infanticide, Meens cites the striking example of the continental text known as the *Paenitentiale Oxoniense II*, thought to be an eighth-century work composed by Willibrord.[29] This text assigns penances to those who deliberately suffocate children before baptism or kill a child born to a woman following the army ("in hostem"). Meens believes that this regulation pertains to "an established Frisian custom of killing children at birth"; the penitential appears to have been written "for the period right after conversion," when certain native rituals had to be accommodated.[30] The penance assigned by this penitential for the death of the child is forty days. By comparison, the *Scriftboc,* drawing on the *Penitential* of Theodore (early eighth century), assigns a penance of fifteen years to a woman who kills her child, modifying this to seven years if the woman is needy; a penance of three years is assigned to parents whose child dies unbaptized and of either ten or seven years if they kill the infant before baptism.[31]

The third category involves children in Meens's older group, "pueri" or "puella" and their acts outside the sex-gender system; there are eight examples, just 12 percent of the total. One act in this group that very likely involved the child in sexual activities, the custom of selling a child into slavery or servitude, is mentioned three times (twice in the *Canons of Theodore*, once in the *Scriftboc*). But this act itself is neither sexual nor clearly dependent on the sex-gender system.[32] A boy could be sold into slavery without his consent up to age six and after that only with his consent (a nicety perhaps); at 14 the boy could become a slave voluntarily.[33] Other acts include those aimed at curing children of fevers or concerning magical acts and children (there are three), children who eat filth, and theft by a child (one each).[34]

The fourth category, which includes all acts that engage the sex-gender system, contains 26 examples, 40 percent of the total number of canons dealing with children. These acts are divided into two categories each containing thirteen canons: non-sexual acts and sexual acts in which children participated voluntarily or involuntarily. The non-sexual canons include three that specify the age at which boys and girls achieved independence of their parents with regard to marriage or to joining the religious life; according to the *Scriftboc,* boys gained independence at age 15 and girls at 14.[35] Three concern "raptus," the act of seizing a girl before her marriage,[36] possibly but not necessarily a sexual act.[37] Five canons concern the marriage of children. Two forbid the marriage of a boy promised to the monastic life;[38] two canons concern the betrothal of a young girl; one permits father and son to marry mother and daughter.[39]

Thirteen canons concern acts of sexual intercourse, of which six are heterosexual. A boy's masturbation is mentioned once.[40] Two canons concern incest between a boy and his mother or a father and his daughter,[41] and because they focus on parents, they are related to the second category above, concerning adult responsibilities for children. The remaining three canons pertain to the marriage of young people. The rape of a maiden—distinct from "raptus"—is mentioned once.[42] Heterosexual intercourse between young people (i.e., under 20 years of age) is mentioned twice. The word for the man in the Latin source, "adulescens" ("geong man" in Old English), is not used elsewhere in Latin sources for the materials I discuss here; the stipulation of special conditions if both he and the girl ("puella") are under 20 indicates that the "adulescens" is not necessarily a child.[43] If both the "adulescens" and the "puella" are under 20 years of age, they are to fast for the three 40-day periods for one year. But their behavior could apparently have drastic results. A canon in the *Scriftboc* modifies their penance if they are sold into servitude as a result of this act, a calamitous consequence, reducing penance to 40 days and to only 20 days if they began but did not complete the act.[44] References to heterosexual acts between boys and girls are also very scarce in the earlier Irish penitentials. The *Penitential* of Cummean refers to "a boy coming from the world recently who intends to commit fornication with some girl" (20 days for thinking it, 100 for polluting himself—presumably masturbating—and one year for doing it).[45]

The boys, apparently, were not pursuing the girls; or if they were, the authors of the penitentials were not particularly concerned about their behavior. On the other hand, there was considerable concern that boys would pursue boys and be pursued by men. Seven of the thirteen sexual canons concern homosexual acts involving boys. Every one of the Anglo-Saxon penitentials includes canons concerning boys' homosexual acts; some also specify older men or older boys as the boys' partners. These acts were first described in Irish penitentials. The *Penitential* of Cummean contains a chapter "on the sinful playing of boys," which included theft and talking at improper times as well as kissing, masturbating, imitating acts of fornication, bestiality, femoral intercourse, fellatio, anal intercourse, and heterosexual intercourse.[46] Since none of the Anglo-Saxon penitentials is a monastic document, it is significant that the canons concerning young boys, although reduced in number, are retained. The penitentials are conservative documents. Even the length of penances is rarely changed from text to text, and it is rare to find sins mentioned in one text that are not mentioned in earlier texts. Given the conservative nature of the collections, it seems especially significant that the *Handbook*, the least monastic and shortest of the vernacular penitentials, retains the penances for boys.[47]

The seven examples of homosexual acts involving boys are numbered below as examples 1 through 7. Because the first canon quoted also appears in the *Canons of Theodore*, it serves as example 1 and example 2; in the *Scriftboc* it is found in a chapter on the "unlawful deeds of young men"[48] (a heading that corresponds to that in Cummean penitential):

Examples 1 and 2.

> Cnihtas gyf hi heom betweonan hæmed fremman, swinge hi man.[49]
> If boys fornicate between themselves, they are to be beaten.

The *Old English Penitential* contains one provision for boys who have sex; because it is repeated without change in the *Old English Handbook,* it serves here as example 3 and example 4.

Examples 3 and 4.

> Se man þe hine wið nytenu besmiteð, oððe wæpnedman wið oðerne mid ungesceadelicum þinge: gif he bið XX wintra eald man, þæt he understandan mæg þæt he þa sceamlican þing & þa manfullan begæð, geswice & andette & fæste XV (winter); & gif se man his gemæccan hæbbe & heo beo XL wintra & swylce ing begæð, geswice & fæste þa hwile þe his lif beo & ne gedyrstlæce þæt he drihtnes lichaman

underfo ær his endedæge. Geonge men & andgitlease man sceal þearle swingan þe swylce ðing begæð.[50]

The man who soils himself with an animal or the male who (fornicates) with another, in an irrational way, if he is twenty years old, so that he can understand that shameful and evil thing, let him desist and confess and fast fifteen years; and if he has a mate (wife), and he is forty years old and does such a thing, desist and fast for the rest of his life, and not be allowed to receive God's body before the end of his life. Young and ignorant men are to be severely beaten if they do such a thing.

The chapter is entitled "Concerning those men who have illicit fornication, that is with animals, or soil themselves with young ones, or a man who has sex with another" (Be þam men þe ungedafenlice hæmð, þæt is wið nytenum, oððe hine mid geonglingum besmiteð, oððe wæpnedman wið oðerne). The contents of the heading, found only in the *Old English Penitential*, do not correspond to the canon itself. The heading concerns men who fornicate unlawfully, either with animals or with young men or with other men. But the canon omits the reference to sexual intercourse "mid geonglingum," with young ones; instead "geonge men" are mentioned only when performing sexual intercourse together. The corresponding Latin source does not single out young men, specifying only "[cum] pecoribus quot cum masculis" and provides a penance for boys under 20 years of age ("quotquot ante vicesimum annum") who presumably have sex together; it does not provide for sex between men and boys either.[51] Presumably both sins mentioned, homosexual intercourse and bestiality, are relevant to the "young and ignorant" ones; the penance of beating is the same as that in the *Scriftboc*.

The *Scriftboc* also includes a canon that provides a penance for a small boy forced to have sex with an older boy, requiring the boy to do penance for either seven or twenty days, the latter number if he consented to the act:

Example 5.

Lytel cniht gif he byð fram maran ofðrycced in hæmede fæste VII niht; gif he him geðafige, fæste xx nihta.[52]

If a small boy is forced by a larger one into intercourse, seven nights; if he consents to it, he is to fast twenty nights.

This canon appears to originate with the *Penitential* of Cummean: "Puer paruulus oppressus a maiore annum aetatis habens decimum, ebdomadam dierum ieiunet; si consentit, xx diebus."[53] "Maran" in the Old English can be assumed to include either an older boy or a man; Cummean's text specifies "a majore puero," and the *Penitential* of Bede simply says "a maiore."[54]

The fullest discussion of the sex acts of boys is found in the *Canons of Theodore*. Two provisions for boys follow those that assign penance for adult males who commit sodomy:

Example 6.

> Gyf bædling mid bædlinge hæme .x. winter fæste. Se ðe þis werlice man deð .iiii. gear. fæste. Gyf hit cniht sy. æt ærestan .ii. gear. gif he hit æft do .iiii. gear fæste.[55]
>
> If a bædling has intercourse with a bædling, he is to fast 10 years. If he does this unaware (heedlessly) he is to fast for four years. If it is a child, two years the first time; if he does it again, he is to fast four years.

I take the third sentence ("Gyf hit cniht sy...") to mean that the "bædling" has sex with a child rather than with another adult male. "[H]it" is ambiguous, but seems to refer to the "bædling"'s partner. It is unlikely that the canon applies to intercourse between boys, already covered in this text (Example 1). The text also provides for interfemoral intercourse between a boy and a layman, and between a boy and a man in orders:

Example 7.

> Gyf he betuh ðeoh do an gear oððe .iii. feowertigo. Gyf hit cnyht sy .xx. daga fæste. oððe hine man swynge. Gyf he hit mid gehadedum men do .iii. feowertigo. oððe eal gear fæste.[56]
>
> If [an adult male] commits interfemoral intercourse [he is to fast] one year or the three forty-day fasting periods. If he is a boy, he is to fast for twenty days or he is beaten. If the boy [does it, i.e., has interfemoral intercourse] with a man in orders, [he is to fast] for the three forty-day periods or one year.

It is possible that the canon means to change both parties from adult to child, so that "gyf hit cnyht sy" could mean "if they are boys," although the language does not support this ("hine" is masculine accusative singular, not plural). Compared to the adult male, the boy received a mild penance for interfemoral intercourse; the child fasted for twenty days or endured a beating, while the man fasted for a year, or the three fasting periods. However, when a child had sex with an adult man (in orders, this time), the child's penance is the same as that for the adult who committed interfemoral intercourse.

Significantly, no penance is specified for the man involved in this act. Here, as with the boy forced into sex by an older boy (example 5), it is the younger one who does the penance. The example from the *Scriftboc* punishes the younger boy who is forced into intercourse—or abused, Latin "oppressus"—not the older boy or man who abused him. It would seem logical that these provisions sought to protect boys from the sexual advances of older boys or men, but it is plain that by assessing the penance to the younger boy, the canons hold them responsible for the sin and appear to be protecting older boys and men from the young ones. In part such a penance must have been intended to purify the boy and remove the pollution of sexual intercourse from him.[57] The demand that the boy do penance for an act he did not initiate or even participate in willingly also suggests that he is seen as a temptation to older men, and that even though he is young, he must be held accountable for his effects on them, albeit with a very light penance of seven or 20 days. One does not find penances for the older men and boys who forced younger boys into sexual relations.

Of the seven canons concerning the homosexual acts of boys, four concern boys having sex with other boys (examples 1–2 and 3–4). Three concern sex between boys and older boys or men (5, 6, and 7). However, example 3 carries a heading that provides for sex between men and boys; example 6 could be read as indicating sex between boys; example 7 could be read as indicating either sex between boys or between a boy and a man in orders. Taking these variables into consideration, it seems fair to say that at least four and probably five of these canons deal with sex between boys, and that at least three and possibly four of them deal with sex between boys and men or older boys. Further analysis of Latin sources will help to refine the categories used to differentiate a canon prohibiting sex between boys from one prohibiting sex between a younger boy and an older one. It is clear, even from this initial inquiry, that transgenerational sexual intercourse was nearly as prominent a concern among Anglo-Saxon church officials as sexual acts within generations. It is also clear that, regarding children at least, homosexual activity was as great a concern as heterosexual activity. In the penitentials as a whole, however, homosexual acts are rarely mentioned, accounting for from 2 percent to 7 percent of the canons.[58]

SOME CONCLUSIONS

It is useful to compare penances for children's sexual offenses with those for acts of adults. According to the *Scriftboc* and the *Canons of Theodore,* a man did four years penance for sodomy the first time and fifteen years if it was habitual. According to the *Old English Penitential* and the *Old English Handbook* the penance was fifteen years or a lifetime. Boys guilty of sodomy received a penance of two years for the first offense, four for the second. For interfemoral intercourse, a man did penance for one year or three 40-day fasts but a boy for only 20 days, or he was whipped. Boys who fornicated with each other were also beaten, and that was all. It appears that there was some leeway granted to boys who committed sodomy only once or who had interfemoral intercourse with each other.

The regulations specific to children's sex acts seem to regard them as part of the larger discursive world of adult sexual conduct. Indeed, a number of the regulations discussed above are concerned with the behavior of adults with whom children came into contact, not with children themselves. The sexual acts of boys conform especially closely to those of adults males; the boy's "sinful playing" includes sodomy, masturbation, interfemoral intercourse, and other acts men were held responsible for. Some canons, especially those concerning boys who are forced into sex, seem to protect children but can also be understood as seeking to shape their behavior to the demands that this system would later make on them.

The case of the young boy forced into sex by an older male is especially troubling. What does it mean that he rather than the person who forced him was assigned a penance? The canon suggests that children were not considered to be innocent even when they were. The regulation does not suggest that young boys were driven by sexual desires and that they actively pursued sexual interactions; the canon makes clear that the older boy or man initiated the act and that the younger one was forced into it. Presumably by punishing the boy for a wrong that he neither initiated nor consented to, the authorities sought to impress on the child the seriousness of sexual behavior. We should note that in examples 3 and 4 above the canon concerns "men who fornicate illicitly," not the young men ("geonglingum") with whom they had sex; both examples are directed at laymen, not clerics or monks. It is also important to compare the provision concerning the small boy forced into sex by another male with other sexual acts that are clearly not monastic in context. These include heterosexual transgenerational sex acts. When a mother initiated acts of fornication with her son, she received the penance; when a father had sex with his daughter, he received the penance.[59] Clearly heterosexual abuse of a boy or girl was of more concern than homosexual abuse. One also has to consider that the parent was held to a higher standard than the adult male—originally, and probably most frequently, a monastic—who exploited a child. The canon makes it clear that older boys took advantage of the younger ones; the educative function of the penance was not assumed to be effective.

The boy involved in the homosexual affair in ancient Greece, Foucault stresses, was expected to become a man of consequence; hence society protected his rights against those of his adult male lover. Because boys educated in monasteries were to grow up to be monks, abbots, and even bishops and kings, their sexual acts were closely watched. The penances for most children's sexual offenses were relatively light, if only for first offenses, as if the Church expected that the boys would be boys for a while. But after the first time, the sex acts of children were regarded more severely. Speaking of the Greek boys, Foucault wrote that the "asceticism" created by all the conditions that the Greeks set on man-boy love was not an interdiction. This asceticism was not a means of disqualifying the love of boys, he wrote; "on the contrary, it was a means of stylizing it and hence, by giving it shape and form, valorizing it."[60] The medieval Church did not seek to stylize or valorize the love of boys in the monastery, but by giving form and shape to the sexual activity that took place there, the Church did seek to begin to form the possibility of renouncing all sexuality that some monastic boys would have to accept. Thus it is true that the monastic boy was the father of the monk.

I will propose two conclusions based on what the penitentials tell us. First, the behavior of boys, especially in the monastery, was supervised from an early age; children were not excluded from discussions of sex and obviously must have discussed sexual acts among themselves and with adults. It did not require the eighteenth century for such supervision and discourse to come into being.

Second, the penances for childhood sexual acts reveal concern not only for children but for the adults with whom they interacted. When boys and men had sex (examples 5 and 7), the penitentials assess penances for the boys, not the men, suggesting that boys were seen not as victims of adult sexual advances but rather as causes of them. By making it worse to have interfemoral intercourse with a man in orders than with another boy, the Church emphasized both the sacredness of the older man's status and his vulnerability to seduction by the young; by providing a penance for a young boy who was sexually exploited, the Church emphasized that all his sexual deeds, even those he did not initiate, were culpable. The vulnerability of adult males to temptation by boys and young men was combined with an attempt to instill in the young a fear of all sexual acts. Whether they lived inside or outside the monastery, boys had to acquire habits of sexual purity, abstinence, and self-control, the ideals of adult sexual conduct.

Asking where the boys are can yield a simplistic answer: they are in the monastery, in the care of Church authorities who want to reproduce themselves by managing the boys' sexual development along ascetic, highly disciplined lines. Other sources, saint's lives and Latin colloquies in particular, tell us more about how boys were raised in monasteries than the penitentials can reveal. In a striking passage in a Latin colloquy, for example, the speaker calls his "wife" to kiss him; his companion calls to a "young girl." In another, "Dominus" (an older brother) asks "Fraterculus" (a boy) to accompany him to the lavatory; "Fraterculus" refuses but then receives permission from the master to do so in order to carry a lamp.[61] Colloquies, we know from the famous Old English example of the form,[62] required boys to play roles. These enigmatic and provocative episodes suggest that knowing where the boys are does not necessarily mean that we know what they were up to.

Finally, we must also ask who the boys are. Even young boys were already thought of as "men," not only because they were biologically sexed but because they were thought to be capable of the full range of male homosexual acts and were expected to act like men. Because their sex acts were usually assessed in ways equivalent to those of adult men, the process of the boys' sexual maturation was seen less as learning new behavior than as realizing an innate capacity for that behavior. One would be inclined to say that the boys were already—biologically—male and had only to become—learn to act like—men. What the penitentials suggest, however, is that they were already constructed as men. The purpose of monitoring their sexual conduct was to ensure that they also became "male." Even then the process is not simple, for some of the most striking regulations examined above show that certain men, although hardly boy-like, did not outgrow their desire to like and be like boys.

NOTES

1. Since "sexuality" as a distinct part of identity separate from other social functions is a modern concept, it is more precise, if more cumbersome, to refer only to the sexual acts of children. Some of the evidence discussed here appears in my essay, "Between the Lines: Queer Theory, the History of Homosexuality, and Anglo-Saxon Penitentials," *Journal of Medieval and Early Modern Studies* 26 (1996): 255–96. This essay, drawn from a work-in-progress to be called *Straightforward: Sodom, Sodomy and Same-Sex Relations in Early Medieval England*, was generously supported by Loyola University Chicago and the John Simon Guggenheim Memorial Foundation. For recent commentary on sexual attitudes in the Anglo-Saxon period, see Hugh Magennis, "'No Sex Please, We're Anglo-Saxons'? Attitudes to Sexuality in Old English Prose and Poetry," *Leeds Studies in English* 26 (1995): 1–27, and Anthony Davies, "Sexual Behaviour in Later Anglo-Saxon England," *This Noble Craft*, Erik Kooper, ed., Proceedings of the 10th Research Symposium of the Dutch and Belgian University Teachers of Old and Middle English and Historical Linguistics for 1989, *Costerus 80* (Atlanta: Rodopi, 1991), pp. 83–106.

2. See Vern L. Bullough, "The Sin against Nature and Homosexuality," in Bullough and James Brundage, eds., *Sexual Practices and the Medieval Church* (Buffalo: Prometheus Books, 1982), pp. 55–71, at p. 62. There are references to the sexualization of boys in several essays in Kent Gerard and Gert Hekma, eds., *The Pursuit of Sodomy: Male Homosexuality in Renaissance and Enlightenment Europe* (New York: Harrington Park Press, 1989); see index, pp. 533–34. J. A. Burrow analyzes the trope of the "puer senex" among the "ideals of transcendence" in *The Ages of Man: A Study in Medieval Writing and Thought* (Oxford: Clarendon, 1986), pp. 95–134; he points out that the hagiographers rarely sang "the praises of infant innocence" but preferred instead to associate virtue with age (see pp. 106–7).

3. Carol J. Clover, "Regardless of Sex: Men, Women, and Power in Early Northern Europe," *Speculum* 67 (1993): 363–87, reprinted in *Studying Medieval Women: Sex, Gender, Feminism*, Nancy F. Partner, ed. (Cambridge, MA: Medieval Academy of America, 1993), pp. 61–85, at p. 77.

4. Allen J. Frantzen, *The Literature of Penance in Anglo-Saxon England* (New Brunswick: Rutgers University Press, 1983), pp. 1–18, and see the new preface to the translation by Michel Lejeune, *La littérature de la pénitence dans Angleterre Anglo-Saxonne* (Fribourg: Éditions Universitaires, 1991), pp. ix–xxx. It is difficult to see why the penitentials should be disregarded, as they are in John Boswell's *Christianity, Social Tolerance, and Homosexuality: Gay People in Western Europe from the Beginning of the Christian Era to the Fourteenth Century* (Chicago: University of Chicago Press, 1980). See Pierre J. Payer, *Sex and the Penitentials: The Development of a Sexual Code 550–1150* (Toronto: University of Toronto Press, 1984), pp. 135–39, on Boswell's arguments, and David F. Greenberg, *The Construction of Homosexuality* (Chicago: University of Chicago Press, 1988), pp. 16–17 on Boswell's methodology and pp. 263–64 on Boswell's use of the penitentials. Still important to the discussion of penitentials is Derrick Sherwin Bailey, *Homosexuality and the Western Christian Tradition* (London: Longmans, Green & Co., 1955; rept. New York: Archon, 1975), pp. 100–10.

5. Compare Matthew 18: 3–4: "Unless you be converted and become as little children, you shall not enter into the kingdom of heaven. Whosoever therefore shall humble himself as this little child, he is the greater in the kingdom of heaven." Quoted, with commentary, by Burrow, *The Ages of Man*, pp. 105–6.

6. John Milton, *Paradise Regained*, Book 4, ll. 220–21. Quoted from *John Milton: Complete Poems and Major Prose*, Merritt Y. Hughes, ed. (New York: Odyssey, 1957), p. 520. William Wordsworth, "My Heart Leaps Up," quoted from *The Norton Anthology of English Literature*, M. H. Abrahms et al., vol. 2, ed. (New York: Norton, 1974), p. 174.

7. See the following texts in F. W. H. Wasserschleben, ed., *Die Bussordnungen der abendländischen Kirche* (Halle: C. Graeger, 1851; rpr. Graz: Akademische Druck-U. Verlagsanstalt, 1958): prologue to the *Penitential* of Bede, p. 221 ("juvenis, adulescens, senex, pueri"); prologue to Pseudo-Bede, p. 250 ("infans, puer, juvenis, adulescens aetate, senex"); prologue to Egbert's *Penitential*, p. 232 (same as Pseudo-Bede). The first and third of these texts are more readily available in A. W. Haddan and W. Stubbs, eds., *Councils and Ecclesiastical Documents Relating to Great Britain and Ireland*, 3 vols. (Oxford: Clarendon, 1871; rpr. 1964), 3: 327 and 417. Bede is not the author of this text, as most scholars have long agreed; when I refer to a penitential of Bede in this essay I am referring to specific, edited texts as cited in the notes.

8. Robert Spindler, *Das altenglische Bussbuch (sog. Confessionale Pseudo-Egberti)* (Leipzig: Verlag von Bernhard Tauchnitz, 1934), I.b., "Be þæs mæssepreostes gesceadwisnysse," p. 172; I have renamed this text *Scriftboc* and refer to it as such, giving references to Spindler's edition. The same text is edited by Josef Raith, ed., *Die altenglische Version des Halitgar'schen Bussbuches (sog. Poenitentiali Pseudo-Ecgberti)*, Bibliothek der Angelsächsischen Prosa, 13 (Hamburg: H. Grand, 1933; rpr. with new introduction, Darmstadt, 1964), pp. xlii–xliii.

9. Philippe Ariès, *L'enfant et la vie familiale sous l'ancien régime* (Paris, 1960); R. Baldick, trans., *Centuries of Childhood* (Hammondsworth: Penguin 1973).

10. See Janet L. Nelson, "Parents, Children, and the Church in the Earlier Middle Ages," in Diana Wood, ed., "The Church and Childhood," *Studies in Church History* 31 (Oxford, 1994), pp. 81–114. For a summary of scholarship on medieval childhood, see James A. Schultz, *The Knowledge of Childhood in the German Middle Ages 1100–1350* (Philadelphia: University of Pennsylvania Press, 1995), pp. 2–13. For a summary of scholarship on medieval childhood subsequent to Ariès' work, see Nelson, "Parents, Children, and the Church," p. 82, note 3. As Nelson notes, most of these sources say little about childhood before the eleventh century. For a discussion of earlier evidence, see Rob Meens, "Children and Confession in the Early Middle Ages," pp. 53–65. For contemporary theoretical perspectives, see Daniel T. Kline, "Textuality and Subjectivity: Theorizing the Figure of the Child in Middle English Literature," in *Children and the Family in the Middle Ages*, ed. Nicole Clifton, *Essays in Medieval Studies* 12 (1996), 23–38 at pp. 28–30 (available online: http://www.luc.edu/publications/medieval or Gopher.luc.edu[Loyola University: Information and Resources /Publications and Proceedings]).

11. Michel Foucault, *The History of Sexuality*, vol. 1, Robert Hurley, trans. (New York: Vintage, 1980), p. 27.

12. Foucault, *The History of Sexuality*, p. 28.

13. Foucault, *The History of Sexuality*, p. 98. For further comments on the pedagogization of sex, see pp. 104, 116–17.

14. Michel Foucault, *The Use of Pleasure*, Robert Hurley, trans. (New York: Vintage, 1986), pp. 187–88.

15. Foucault's section on "Economics" concerns marriage, the household, and the man's relation with his wife (*The Use of Pleasure*, pp. 141–84); the section on "Erotics" concerns the man's relation with the boy (pp. 187–225).

16. Foucault, *The Use of Pleasure*, p. 165.

17. Foucault, *The Use of Pleasure*, pp. 215–17.

18. Foucault, *The Use of Pleasure*, pp. 223–24.

19. In addition to the texts by Spindler and Raith listed above, note 8, see Roger Fowler, ed., "A Late Old English Handbook for the Use of a

Confessor," *Anglia* 83 (1965): 1–34. Franz Joseph Mone, ed., *Quellen und Forschungen zur Geschichte der teutschen Literatur und Sprache* (Aachen and Leipzig: J. A. Mayer, 1830), pp. 514–28. This text is edited in two forms by Benjamin Thorpe, *Ancient Laws and Institutes of England*, 2 vols. (London: G. E. Eyre and A. Spottiswoode, 1840), vol. 2, pp. 228–31 and pp.232–39. He joined an extract found only in Cambridge, Corpus Christi College, 190, Part B, pp. 416–18, Exeter (provenance taken from N. R. Ker, *Catalogue of Manuscripts Containing Anglo-Saxon* [Oxford: Clarendon, 1957], no. 45B) to canons selected from two other manuscripts (not indicating omissions). They are Brussels, Bibliothéque royale, 8558–63, ff. 146v–53v, southeastern (printed by Mone; Ker, *Catalogue*, no. 10), and Oxford, Bodleian Library, Laud Misc. 482, fol. 21r–27v, Worcester (Ker, *Catalogue*, no. 343). The Brussels and Oxford versions of the text are similar; the Cambridge version contains only a few of the canons found in them and some that are not. Thorpe prints all this material (2: 228–39) as part of the fourth book of the Pseudo-Egbert text edited by Raith.

20. On the use of prefatory matter in the vernacular penitentials, see Frantzen, *The Literature of Penance*, pp. 135–36 and 139–40.

21. For the sources of the *Scriftboc*, see Spindler, *Bussbuch*, pp. 21–91. On the relation of the *Scriftboc* to the *Old English Penitential*, see Raith, *Die altenglische Version*, p. xxiii, and on the dependence of the *Old English Handbook* on the *Old English Penitential*, see Fowler, "A Late Old English Handbook," pp. 8–9, and Raith, *Die altenglische Version*, pp. 75–80.

22. "Unless a method can be devised for standardizing the scales of different penitentials, there are no grounds for comparing offences in different penitentials," Payer writes. See *Sex and the Penitentials*, p. 131.

23. Some indications of the development of the vernacular handbook from rudimentary to more complex forms are outlined in Frantzen, *The Literature of Penance*, pp. 133–41.

24. The *Scriftboc* contains 42 percent of these 66 references (28), the *Canons of Theodore* 26 percent (17), the *Old English Penitential* 21 percent (14), and the *Old English Handbook* 11 percent of the total (seven canons). These statistics are derived from an electronic edition of all the vernacular penitentials now in preparation but can be confirmed in the printed editions cited above, notes 10 and 14. There will be some variation, since what constitutes one canon as opposed to one canon in two parts is debatable (some canons are complex, and editors divide and enumerate them differently). The results are not statistically significant (that is, I have not calculated frequency ratios or attempted other forms of statistical analysis; for an example of such analysis, see James Brundage, "Sex and Canon Law: A Statistical Analysis of Samples of Canon and Civil Law," in Bullough and Brundage, *Sexual Practices*, pp. 89–101).

25. Meens, "Children and Confession," pp. 53–55.

26. These examples are taken from Spindler, *Bussbuch*. For the first, see III, "De episcopis vel presbyteris seu diaconis," 2.a–2.b., p. 176; for the second, see I, "De laycis quomodo peniteant," 6.a–6.b, p. 177.

27. I give only samples from each text here. For the *Scriftboc,* see Spindler, *Bussbuch,* X, "De infantibus non baptizatis," 10.a.–10.c., p. 179. For the *Old English Penitential,* see Raith, *Die altenglische Version,* p. xxiii, II.1.d, p. 16. For the *Old English Handbook* see Fowler, "Handbook," ll. 144–45, p. 21. For the *Canons of Theodore* see Mone, *Quellen,* c. 116, p. 519.

28. See Spindler, *Bussbuch,* XVI, "Item de generationibus quomodo iunguntur," 19.k, p. 184; Raith, *Die altenglische Version,* II.2, p. 16 and IV.17, p. 55; for the *Old English Handbook,* see Fowler, "Handbook," p. 21, lines 148–51, and, for the *Canons of Theodore,* Mone, *Quellen,* c. 114, pp. 518–19, and c. 188, p. 525.

29. Edited by Ludger Körntgen, *Studien zu den Quellen der frühmittelalterlichen Bussbücher,* Quellen und Forschungen zum Recht im Mittelalter 7 (Sigmaringen: J. Thorbecke, 1993), pp. 90–205. See the review by D.A. Bullough, *Journal of Ecclesiastical History* 46 (1994): 317–20.

30. Meens, "Children and Confession," pp. 56–60; see p. 57, note 17.

31. See Spindler, *Bussbuch,* XVII, "De homicidiis vel incestis mulieribus," 19.l, p. 184, for the penance of fifteen years, and X, "De infantibus non baptizatis," 10.a, p. 179, for penances of three, ten, and seven years. The *Old English Penitential* also prescribes a penance of three years for the death of an infant; see Raith, *Die altenglische Version,* II.1.d, p. 16. There are several other examples.

32. See Ruth Mazo Karras, "Desire, Descendants, and Dominance: Slavery, the Exchange of Women, and Masculine Power," in *The Work of Work: Servitude, Slavery, and Labor in the Middle Ages,* Allen J. Frantzen and Douglas Moffat, ed. (Glasgow: Cruithne Press, 1994), pp. 16–29.

33. See Spindler, *Bussbuch,* XV, "De etate pueri vel puelle quomodo sibi dominentur," 18.c., p. 183, and Mone, *Quellen,* c. 214, p. 527.

34. The *Scriftboc* forbids a woman to place her daughter on a roof to cure her fever; see Spindler, *Bussbuch,* XVIII, "De sacrificiis que demonis immolantur," 19z, p. 185, and, in the *Canons of Theodore,* Mone, *Quellen,* c. 206, p. 526. The *Old English Penitential* also contains a general prohibition against the use of witchcraft on children; see Raith, *Die altenglische Version,* IV.16, p. 55. See also Spindler, *Bussbuch,* XXV, "De cybo sanctificato et de his qui inmunda gustant," 28.d, p. 191, which concerns a child who eats worms or bodily waste, and VI, "De iuvenis," 7.b, concerning theft, p. 177.

35. See Spindler, *Bussbuch,* XV, "De etate pueri vel puelle quomodo sibi dominentur," 18.a–18.b, p. 183. The Old English, translating the *Penitential* of Theodore, grants a fourteen-year-old girl control of her body, saying that a boy is in his father's power until fifteen, at which point he can join a monastery; that a girl of sixteen or seventeen is in her parents'

power and that she can be given in marriage after that point with her own consent. See Theodore, *Penitential*, II.12.35–36, in Haddan and Stubbs, *Councils*, 3: 201–202.

36. This act is included only in the *Old English Penitential* and *Old English Handbook*. See Raith, *Die altenglische Version*, II.15, p. 24, and IV.9, pp. 51–52, and Fowler, "Handbook," p. 23, ll. 207–11 (same as *Old English Penitential* II.15).

37. See James Brundage, "Rape and Seduction in Medieval Canon Law," in Bullough and Brundage, *Sexual Practices*, 141–48. The topic is discussed extensively in Brundage, *Law, Sex, and Christian Society*, passim.

38. See Spindler, *Bussbuch*, IV, "De monachis, sanctimonialibus et sacerdotibus," 5, p. 176, and Mone, *Quellen*, c. 111, p. 518.

39. See Spindler, *Bussbuch*, XIII, "De coniunctione et aliorum causis," 16.a., p. 181, which permits father and son to marry mother and daughter, and XIV, "De lavacro mariti vel aliorum causis," 17.c.–17.d., p. 183, regarding the marriage of the "fæmnan," translating Latin "puella."

40. Spindler, *Bussbuch*, VI, "De iuvenis," 7.c; the penance is 20 days of fasting.

41. See Spindler, *Bussbuch*, V, "De laycis quomodo peniteant," 6.d., p. 177, which concerns a father who has intercourse with his daughter; and the *Canons of Theodore*, Mone, *Quellen*, c. 148, p. 521, concerning a mother who initiates acts of fornication with her little son.

42. Raith, *Die altenglische Version*, II.13, p. 23.

43. The Old English uses "geongan men" again; see Spindler, *Bussbuch*, IV, "De monachis, sanctimonialibus et sacerdotibus," 5, p. 176, but this translates Latin "puer" from the *Penitential* of Theodore, Book 2.6.11, "Puero non licet jam nubere, prelato ante monachi voto" (Haddan and Stubbs, *Councils*, 3: 195).

44. Spindler, *Bussbuch*, XXVIII, "De apibus," 39.f, p. 194 "And gif hi ðonne for ðysum gylte genyrwode wurþað, betan XL daga, and gyf heo hit þonne beginnan & ne gefremmon, beton XX daga." This section of the *Scriftboc* is a mixture of regulations regarding use of food (e.g., honey from bees who have killed someone); the canon is obscure and highly unusual. The Latin source is the *Penitential* of Bede, III.3–4: "Si propter peccatum hoc servitio humano addicti sunt, XL dies. Si nitens tantum et non coinquinatus, XX dies peniteat." See Haddan and Stubbs, *Councils*, 3: 327. The implications of this canon too are unclear.

45. Ludwig Bieler, ed., *The Irish Penitentials*, Scriptores Latini Hiberniae 5 (Dublin: Dublin Institute for Advanced Studies, 1963), *Penitential* of Cummean, X, "Ponamus nunc de ludis puerilibus priorum statuta patrum nostrorum," canon 17, p. 128.

46. Bieler, ed., *Irish Penitentials*, pp. 126–28, chapter X, canons 2 and 3 (kissing with or without pollution), canon 4 (initiating acts of fornication), canon 5 (bestiality), canon 6 (mutual masturbation), canon

8 (interfemoral intercourse), canon 9 (abuse of a small boy by a larger one), canon 15 (sodomy, fornication in terga), canon 16 (fellatio). On the monastic context of early Irish penitentials, which were written by abbots, including Finnian and Columbanus, see Bieler's comments, pp. 3–7, and Frantzen, *Literature of Penance*, pp. 25–40.

47. Thus it is significant that the *Handbook* includes a canon about boys; this text winnows its canons to a relatively small number, only 44, compared to over 200 for the *Scriftboc* and over 160 for the *Penitential*.

48. Spindler, *Bussbuch*, VI, "Be unrihtum dædum geongra manna," p. 177, a heading found in one manuscript; another says simply "De iuvenis."

49. Spindler, *Bussbuch*, VIII, "De maritis vel pueris, cum impie agant in pecora," 9e, pp. 178–79. Mone, *Quellen*, c. 144, p. 521.

50. The text of the heading and the canon are both quoted from Raith, *Die altenglische Version*, II.6, pp. 18–19. For the text in the *Handbook*, see Fowler, "Handbook," p. 22 (lines 164–70).

51. See Raith, *Die altenglische Version*, p. 18: "De his qui fornicantur irrationabiliter, id est qui miscentur pecoribus aut cum masculis polluuntur."

52. Spindler, *Bussbuch*, VI, "De iuvenis," 7a, p. 177. Note in the apparatus that Spindler's penance of seven years is not supported by readings from any of the three manuscripts for this canon; for the first penance, all three specify five days, not seven; for the second, one manuscript provides a penance of 15 days rather than 20. The translations here and elsewhere are mine.

53. In Bieler, *Irish Penitentials*, see the *Penitential* of Cummean, 10.4 (simulating intercourse, p. 128), and 10.9 (for the older boy who forces the younger one into sex, p. 128). Davies comments on this passage, "Sexual Behaviour," p. 95. See also Bailey, *Homosexuality*, pp. 107–8.

54. For Cummean's text, see note 50; see the *Penitential* of Bede 3.32: "Parvulus a majore puero oppressus, septimanam, si consentit, dies XX." See Haddan and Stubbs, *Councils*, 3: 329. See also Bailey, *Homosexuality*, p. 103. Bailey claims that another canon in Bede's *Penitential* refers to sodomy involving boys, but both this canon and the one before it refer to interfemoral intercourse rather than anal sex (Bede, *Penitential*, 3.21 and 3.22; see Haddan and Stubbs, *Councils*, 3:328).

55. Mone, *Quellen*, c. 139, p. 521. The source is the *Penitential* of Theodore, Book I.2.7, ed. Haddan and Stubbs, *Councils*, 3: 178.

56. Quoted from Mone, *Quellen*, p. 525, canons 183–85. In Theodore's *Penitential*, this penance is assigned for masturbation: "Qui se ipsum coinquinat XL. dies peniteat: si puer sit, XL. dies aut vapuletur. Si cum ordine, III. XLmas., vel annum, si frequentaverit." See Haddan and Stubbs, *Councils*, 3:184, Book I.8.11. The Old English text omits the first clause and joins this canon with the preceding one ("Si in femoribus, I.

annum vel III. XLmas"; ibid., Book I.8.10). However, the Latin source specifies a sex act (mutual masturbation) between a boy and a man in orders; as the Old English stands (in both manuscripts) the act in question is not masturbation but interfemoral intercourse, first between a boy and an layman and then between a boy and a man in orders. The Old English translator assumed that "cum ordine" means "with *a man* in orders"; the Latin clearly means to differentiate between a boy's masturbation and that of a man with orders.

57. Meens discusses this example briefly, "Children and Confession," p. 63.

58. Homosexual acts account for less than 2 percent of the canons in the *Scriftboc* and the *Old English Penitential*, for 7 percent of the canons in the *Old English Handbook*, and for less than 5 percent of those in the *Canons of Theodore*. I report these and some other statistics in "Between the Lines," pp. 268–69.

59. See note 41 above.

60. Foucault, *The Use of Pleasure*, p. 245. See also pp. 250–51.

61. George Norman Garmonsway, "The Development of the Colloquy," in Peter Clemoes, ed., *The Anglo-Saxons: Studies in Some Aspects of their History and Culture, Presented to Bruce Dickins* (London: Bowes & Bowes, 1959), pp, 248–61. See the summaries, pp. 255–57, especially p. 256, paragraph 10. I thank Martin Foys for his comments on this material.

62. George N. Garmonsway, ed., *Æfric's Colloquy* (London: Methuen, 1939). For an analysis of the dynamics of this text, see John Ruffing, "The Labor Structure of the Colloquy," in *The Work of Work*, Frantzen and Moffat, ed., pp. 55–70.

IRONIC INTERTEXTUALITY AND THE READER'S RESISTANCE TO HEROIC MASCULINITY IN THE *Waltharius*

David Townsend

This essay examines the way readers of an early medieval epic used irony as a powerful and flexible, though ambiguous, strategy to undercut the text's ostensible investment in the heroic masculinity of Germanic legend.

If masculinities are culturally constituted (as a rich critical literature of the last decade has contended, and as the essays in this volume have set out to illustrate with respect to the cultures of medieval Europe, in particular); if such masculinities are ideologically constructed (so that the contingency of their formation is rendered invisible, and they are allowed to stand in the discursive communities that perpetuate them as a naturalized "given"); and if ideology, in turn, despite its pervasiveness, is by its very nature full of implicit fractures (which its "faultline narratives" attempt to elide), then resistances to the dominant fictions of masculinity are very likely indeed to be precipitated not only outside the canonical texts of normative masculinity but also within the very fabric of their narratives.[1]

The profoundly materialistic and honor-obsessed masculinity of the Germanic heroic age is perhaps a particularly tough nut to unveil in this regard. The palpable presence of deadly enemies, the protection of one's own in the face of direct threat, the need to intimate continually that reprisal for violations of one's person, kin, or possessions will be swift and merciless; fair words courteously spoken, aid given and received, the virtues of loyalty, cemented with the obligations imposed by hospitality, sustenance, and praise—responses to such motivations present themselves, in the surviving texts, as largely unmediated and automatic, though not as inevitable, since lapses into cowardice are always possible. The brutality of the stimuli to which the Germanic warrior responds obscures effectively the faultline between social circumstance and identity. The relentlessness of the characters and narrators of these texts is mirrored in the more or less straightforward modern scholarly acceptance of heroic roles, not only among the nationalist German philologists of the nineteenth and early twentieth centuries, but also among critics more interested in examining amalgamations of native Germanic ethos with Christian belief and thought.[2] The *Germania* of Tacitus routinely figures as the warrant that something as systematic and consistent as an indigenous "heroic code" prevailed from well before the first century of the Christian era until the eleventh in England and until even later in Iceland.[3]

If *Beowulf* and the scholarship surrounding it provide one of the most obvious illustrations of such tendencies,[4] much the same could be said for the short Latin epic known as the *Waltharius*. The poem survives in eleven full and partial manuscripts dating from the eleventh through the fifteenth centuries.[5] The identity of its author and the date of its composition have engendered lively and ongoing debate. Jakob Grimm first proposed that it was the work of Ekkehard I, a monk of St. Gall, who composed it in the early 900s, and his hypothesis held without objection until well into the twentieth century. Independent witnesses attest that Ekkehard did indeed in his early years write in some form a poem on "Waltharius manu fortis," intended as a teaching text and later revised by Ekkehard IV, also a monk of St. Gall. More recently, scholars have suggested as author one Gerald, who names himself in a prologue that appears with the poem in some manuscripts. Several Carolingians have been proposed as alternatives.[6] Whoever its author, and whatever its exact date, the poem enjoyed some popularity: writers such as Sigebert of Gembloux in the eleventh century knew and drew on the work, and it held the status of a school text.[7] But its original audience was almost certainly monastic: the first line of the poem addresses the narratees as a homosocial community of *fratres*. The *Waltharius* is the tale of an exemplary hero, for the edification or entertainment, or both, of a monastic brotherhood, or so it is generally received. In the pages that follow, I want to suggest that the paradigms of masculinity it presents are not so unproblematic nor so unsusceptible of resistance on the text's own terms as they are often assumed to be.

Perhaps I should offer a plot summary at the outset. Attila the Hun makes enforced treaties with Frankland, Aquitania, and Burgundy, taking as hostage a royal child from each kingdom. The hostages grow up as favored retainers at the Pannonian court. Hagen the Frank escapes. Later Walther of Aquitaine and Hildegund of Burgundy do likewise. Coming to the Rhine, their approach is made known to Gunther, nebbish king of the Nibelung Franks, whom the escaped Hagen now serves. Against Hagen's urgent protests, Gunther and his retinue of twelve knights pursue Walther in hopes of retrieving the treasure he carries. Walther takes refuge in the defiles of the Vosges, in a gorge where only one man can attack him at a time. The next 500-odd lines of the poem—a good third of its total length—looks more or less like the Rhineland Chainsaw Massacre, with Hagen sitting on a nearby hilltop repeatedly saying "I told you so." Finally, Hagen comes to Gunther's assistance after all—some of the dead meat was Hagen's nephew—and they ambush Walther the next day when he comes out of his stronghold. In the ensuing combat, Gunther loses a leg up to the knee, Hagen an eye and some teeth, and Walther his right hand. By this time they're all tired, so they sit down together and joke lamely about one another's missing body parts—the eye is still twitching on the sward—while Hildegund dresses their wounds and serves drinks.

My quip about chainsaw massacres is not entirely decorative. Carol Clover, a Scandinavianist who also really cares about chainsaws, has brilliantly traced the irony and gender subversion of the cheap slasher films of the seventies and eighties.[8] If you've ever had the nerve and bad taste to sit through *Texas Chainsaw Massacre II*, you may agree with Clover, as I do, that it *is* a funny movie. Halfway through her ordeals in the subterranean lair of a demented family of out-of-work meatpackers, the heroine comes upon a friend one of the ghouls has already attacked and partially flayed. Miraculously, he's still alive. As he attempts to untie her, he repeatedly stumbles and convulses. Finally, giving up, he confesses in his thick C&W twang, "I'm fallin' apart on ya, honey." Meanwhile, the self-declared hero of the film is elsewhere in the labyrinth, hacking meaninglessly at the walls with a chainsaw so big he can hardly keep it up in the air, while occasionally asking the Lord for strength to do His work.

According to the conventions of the genre, the heroine—the "Final Girl" in Carol Clover's parlance—eventually rescues herself, wielding the dusty chainsaw of the ghoul family's mummified grandmother.

My point in indulging in the preceding digression is that the humor of the *Waltharius* is as strange as the humor of *Texas Chainsaw Massacre II*, nor is it entirely unrelated. Conventions of normative masculine heroism are flouted in both. By the time Walther takes on his sixth opponent—"sextus erat Patavrid," the text announces laconically (line 846)—this reader, at least, is rolling in the aisles. And Hildegund is something of a Final Girl according to the conventions of the slasher: passive and masochistic spectator of carnage, she nevertheless survives it all to the end, thanks at least in part to her own doing.[9] But Hildegund is far less visible than the Final Girl. In this, she is something like the more peripheral love-interest character of the action film. In fact, we hardly see her, much less hear from her, at all. She begs Walther to slit her throat before she falls into hands other than his (lines 545–7). She screams when weapons land too close to her feet and then looks up to see whether her hero still lives (lines 893–4). But the reader who doesn't find herself, or himself, in Walther and his exploits, nor even in the Christian deployment that brackets the Germanic heroics, may well be left asking, "Where's Hildegund?"[10] Her peculiar status at the edge of the poem allows the reader a model for an experience of the text that both engages and diverges from its explicit frame of reference.

For the medieval woman reader of this text—for the literate nun who could also appreciate the achievements of Hrotswitha, for example—Hildegund would have provided the one possibility of a direct gender identification in this poem addressed to the *fratres*, unless we entertain the possibility that Attila's shrewd but unappealing queen Ospirin might function as a mirror for the female reader's subjectivity. But what if we admit the possibility of a cross-gender identification with Hildegund by some among the *fratres* themselves, as they read the poem either for pleasure, or as the teaching text it became? While we certainly can imagine the medieval woman reader of the *Waltharius*, it is probably fair to say that the poem's early readerships were predominantly male. But to leap from that observation to the assumption that the *fratres* would have seen the action of the showdown in the Vosges simply through the eyes of Walther, or more perversely, through those of his opponents, elides significant alternative configurations. With respect to such considerations, I would appeal again to an analogy with Clover's work on the slasher, whose audiences are also predominantly male and young.

These low-budget horror films, argues Clover, substantially complicate the gendered semiotics of the cinematic gaze. To be sure, the typical slasher audience cheers the first appearance of the killer, and the sadistic identification is often enforced by the camera itself, which photographs the action intermittently but unmistakably from the psychopath's point of view. But the shaky hand-held camera that effects this identification also adumbrates the bathetic deficiency of the killer's personality. That deficiency becomes increasingly evident as the films progress, and it is eventually confirmed as the camera's point of view shifts from the eye of the killer to that of a detached observer, and/or of the Final Girl herself. Audience reaction generally bears this out, as sympathy shifts to the heroine's successful struggles. The investment of the young men who regularly watch these films and who are thoroughly versed in their rigid conventions seems to lie, in significant measure, in seeing themselves as embodied in the Final Girl. This theatre of gender plays out archaic and fluid categories of sex difference. The phallus as social signifier is readily transferable, as portable and as subject to appropriation as the chainsaw wielded first by a killer who is seen increasingly as grotesque and contemptible, and finally by an androgynous young woman who saves her own life by destroying him. Such cross-gender identifications, moreover, are even more striking, and even less fully accounted for by straightforward assertions of the sadistically phallic gaze of cinema, in the rape revenge film, a genre Clover takes up in a subsequent chapter of her study.

To suggest that slashers and their audiences trade in these cross-gender identifications, and thereby in the transumption of sexual difference into rituals of fluidly performative gender, is hardly to rehabilitate the films in feminist terms. Indeed, the genre seems not so much to create a space for the articulation of female agency—despite some specious suggestions to the contrary—as to deploy its female characters in order to play out characteristically male anxieties about the nature of sexual difference. But Clover's observations do suggest that the fascination of the films she scrutinizes lies at least as much in anxiety over what is problematic and divided in modern male identities as with what is unified and straightforwardly phallic in their agency. In drawing the analogy between the slashers and the *Waltharius*, I run a risk of reducing the one sympathetic female presence in the poem to a cipher of male experience. What I instead want to suggest, however, is that the significance of Hildegund's presence for the *fratres* develops not so much by an eventual assimilation to male experience, as by her continued, though unstated, opposition to a normative paradigm. That opposition potentially connects readers who stand in multiple relations of difference from the heroic masculinity so conspicuously present at the poem's center. The disaffected male reader among the *fratres* is thus drawn into a relation, not so much of metaphorical identification with Hildegund has of metonymical contiguity with her perspective on the poem's events. Such a reader stands, like Hildegund, at the edge of Walther's exploits, at once materially engaged and interpretatively separated from the events in which Walther is embroiled more directly.

Irony offers a principal means to achieve this simultaneous connection to and detachment from the discursive regimes of the text. The text itself explicitly links Hildegund's most active intervention in the flow of the narrative with the consideration of irony, in a passage that raises far more questions than it lays to rest.

Near the poem's beginning, long before the combatants have collapsed and await Hildegund's ministrations, Walther announces his intentions to his fellow hostage: having just returned from a military victory, he encounters Hildegund alone, alludes to their childhood betrothal by their parents, and then asks, apparently rhetorically, why such matters have remained unstated between them.

> Provocat et tali caram sermone puellam:
> 'Exilium pariter patimur iam tempore tanto,
> Non ignorantes, quid nostri forte parentes
> Inter se nostra de re fecere futura.
> Quamne diu tacito premimus haec ipsa palato?'
> Virgo per hyroniam meditans hoc dicere sponsum
> Paulum conticuit, sed postea talia reddit:
> 'Quid lingua simulas, quod ab imo pectore damnas,
> Oreque persuades, toto quod corde refutas,
> Sit veluti talem pudor ingens ducere nuptam?'
> Vir sapiens contra respondit et intulit ista:

'Absit quod memoras! dextrorsum porrige sensum!
Noris me nihilum simulata mente locutum
Nec quicquam nebulae vel falsi interfore crede.
Nullus adest nobis exceptis namque duobus:
Si nossem temet mihi promptam impendere mentem
Atque fidem votis servare per omnia cautis,
Pandere cuncta tibi cordis mysteria vellem.'[11]

He called the dear girl with words of this sort:
'Together we have long suffered our exile,
nor are we unaware what our parents, as chance would have it,
decided amongst themselves about our future.
How long shall we suppress these matters with silent tongue?'
The young woman, thinking that her betrothed said this by way of irony,
was silent for a little while, but then responded thus:
'Why do you feign with speech what you abhor deep in your breast, and urge with your lips what you reject with all your heart,
as though it were a huge disgrace to wed such a bride?'
The wise man answered to the contrary, speaking these words:
'God forbid what you suggest! Direct your understanding rightly!
Know that I have spoken nothing with feigning intent:
do not believe that anything false or murky is involved.
No one is here except us two:
if I knew that you were ready to give me a compliant mind,
and to keep faith with careful vows in all things,
I would reveal to you all the mysteries of my heart.'

Hildegund's initial response might well perplex the reader. She bursts out angrily, "Why feign in speech what you condemn deep in your breast?" They've been betrothed since childhood, after all. The passage has puzzled scholars. If Walther and Hildegund have been so long engaged, why does Hildegund apparently think that Walther cares nothing for her? Some have suggested that two versions of the story have been awkwardly conflated here: in one, the hostages meet for the first time and fall in love at Attila's court; the second, later version, presupposes the childhood betrothal. Relatively recently, Haijo Westra suggested that, whether two versions are here conflated or not, the text as we have it handles the episode with understated psychological depth of characterization.[12] But an approach through *Quellenforschung*, or for that matter through analysis of character and its representation, sidesteps a strikingly self-reflexive interpretative cue. The narrator has told us, introducing Hildegund's retort, that she thought Walther was speaking *per hyroniam*. What does this mean?

It is clear that whatever irony is here, it instigates a hermeneutic move by which Hildegund momentarily confronts and resists Walther's construction of events. And the interpretative agency that we are told Hildegund exercizes for a few seconds is not merely described; it also functions as a sort of "reading interlude," to borrow Gerald Prince's term, which shapes our own response to the events at hand, until Walther hastily shuts it down again.[13] The passage's close texture oscillates back and forth between these two poles, the representational and the interpretative, of the narratorial aside. We are almost certainly intended to take "Virgo per hyroniam meditans hoc dicere sponsum" as a description of how Hildegund the character sees Walther at this point: given the flexible word order of Latin verse, the line obviously means that "the young woman thought that her betrothed said this by way of irony." But the reader can also wrench the modifying phrase *per hyroniam* away from the infinitive of the indirect discourse construction, and attach it instead to the participle: "the young woman, thinking through irony that her spouse was saying this...." In any case, Hildegund then falls briefly silent, going somewhere beyond the discursive structure Walther has built. The resisting reader is free to follow her into the space into which she momentarily passes. Irony, then, is here a given; but what it *is* remains an open question, since the text instantiates it without defining it. Irony at once not only characterizes Hildegund's temporary disposition nor yet only cues the reader as to how Walther's words could be interpreted (though, Walther soon protests, should not be); it also constitutes an interpretative problem in its own right. The reader who seizes on Hildegund's resistance as the cue for his own progress through the text wins a space from which to mount his own distanced reading. He may intuitively grasp that irony is his best hope, but he has yet himself to think through irony. And irony, to reapply Michel Foucault's phrase, is an "utterly confused category."[14] The resistant among the *fratres*—and, learned reader, it is only honest to admit to you that I cloak myself as well in the habit of those putatively disaffected monks dead now for nearly a millennium—had best sift his ironies carefully.

Perhaps the most obvious way of dealing with irony is to cite its classical and early medieval definitions as a trope by which one thing is said and its opposite meant.[15] The easy way out of the narrator's comment—and the most effective way to contain the moment of Hildegund's resistance—is to translate "thinking he spoke by way of irony" as "thinking he meant the opposite." So the phrase *per hyroniam* would become a pedantic alternative to simply saying that Hildegund took Walther precisely the wrong way and that, as her subsequent behavior might suggest, after further reassurances she recognized that she was a fool ever to have doubted him. Linda Hutcheon has recently addressed this more or less standard binary and antiphrastic model of ironic statement, this "*either/or* model of inversion" and has pointed out that much of what is in fact taken as ironic admits of no readily palpable negation.[16] Certainly, her observations on the inadequacy of the standard semantic definition apply to Hildegund's outburst. What precisely has Walther said that Hildegund can read as meaning the opposite of what it seems to mean? He is hardly denying that they know of their childhood betrothal. Nor can he be implicitly denying that they have indeed experienced a long exile. And his final rhetorical question, "Why do we keep silent?" admits of no direct negation whatsoever. However irony functions here, it does not operate by simple antiphrastic cancellation.

Hutcheon draws on a range of alternative models to propose a more flexible and inclusive account of a mode of discourse which she sees as both politically engaged and politically ambiguous. Irony, she suggests, is relational, inclusive, and differential (58). By this she means, first, that the rubbing up of the said against the unsaid which constitutes irony (the concrete and colloquial image is one of her more vivid creations) necessarily presupposes literary, discursive, and social contexts that allow this to happen in the mind of the interpreter: in so far as intention functions in the operation of irony, it is an intention that happens *between* ironist and interpreter, not authorial intention pure and simple. Second, she means that irony can function only when *both* or *all* meanings of an utterance are held in the mind of the interpreter simultaneously[17] and third, that the difference of these meanings held in simultaneous suspension with one another is non-binary and so defies collapse into the "real" signification of the utterance.

If we set out to explore the possibilities of Hildegund's resistance to Walther's own discursive trajectory, guided by Hutcheon's notably rich and flexible analysis, what kinds of context come into play at the moment when she "meditates through irony"? First of all, by the time we get to the scene in question, we already know that, when the occasion for it arises, Walther is duplicitous as all hell. He has just eluded Attila's proposal to marry him off to a Hunnish princess by protesting that marriage and service to his lord don't mix (lines 146–167). To prove his loyalty, he has slaughtered a rebellious nation (lines 179–214). He then comes home to speak surreptitiously with Hildegund of long exile and the silence around their shared knowledge of an early betrothal. Perhaps Hildegund thinks Walther is not to be trusted because she believes his recent protestations to Attila that he'll never marry. Or perhaps that performance has simply undermined her faith in his ability to speak the truth to her, any more than he has dealt squarely with Attila. Or perhaps she picks up the idea from some non-verbal cue of his demeanor which, according to Walther and the narrator, she misinterprets. The frames that mark irony are various and fraught with the possibility of miscarriage, as Hutcheon emphasizes in a later chapter (141–75). The intratextual circumstances of Walther's utterance may indeed be the marks on which Hildegund relies. But if the circumstantial markers by which Hildegund perceives Walther's opening speech as ironic are circumscribed within the textual representation of character, it is important to stress that other sorts of markers may come into play as well. Attention to these other markers help us to avoid the pitfall of assuming that Hildegund-as-character is a real person to whom one might impute motives and understanding in some straightforward or unproblematic way—an assumption which obscures the possibility that Hildegund as a subject in her own right might stand not within the text's frame but outside it as a reader. After all, the narrator is telling us that Hildegund misinterprets Walther. But by that very comment, like it or not, he admits that she interprets the events around her, that she is, in effect, a reader of the text that unfolds before her. If we shift, then, from a focus on the opposition between Walther's utterance and its meaning *per hyroniam* to a tension between Hildegund as character and Hildegund as a way of reading what confronts her, maybe we can find the space where her subjectivity resides. Hildegund's status as a reader who transgresses the textual frame is linked to a third mark of ironic intention/reception, to wit, the recognition of intertexts.

In addition to the cues that Hildegund-as-character may take up in order to think through irony, Hildegund-as-reader perhaps responds on another level at which said and unsaid meanings rub up against one another. Perhaps Hildegund-as-reader, and along with her the disaffected *fratres*, deploy the intertextual valence of the *Aeneid* to open a space in which the text, while drawing a substantial share of its comic force from its echoes of Vergil, simultaneously destabilizes the patriarchal trajectories upon which its parodic imitation relies.

The prominence of tags from the *Aeneid* in the *Waltharius* is no news. Karl Strecker's MGH edition provides an *apparatus fontium* which includes not only the major word-for-word transpositions but a whole range of more general associations with Vergil's language and narrative patterns.[18] Dennis Kratz has pointed out that some of these references associate Walther not with Aeneas but with Turnus.[19] He has also suggested the importance of Prudentius' *Psychomachia* and other Christian texts.[20] Peter Dronke analyses the carefully clustered allusions to the abandoned Dido's distraction in the description of Attila's sorrow at the escape of his favorite.[21] But neither mapping of the text's ironic allusions is what I need to find Hildegund and so myself as a reader wary of both Ingeld *and* Christ. Dronke's observations in particular witness to just how unhelpful to my search some takes on irony, and indeed on ironic textual reference, can be: he points out that in likening Attila to Dido the world conqueror "waxes womanish" and so becomes ridiculous.[22] No space for Hildegund here.

But the unspoken presence of the *Aeneid* behind the *Waltharius* might suggest instead the rubbing up of said meanings against unsaid in ways more likely to engender and enable Hildegund's skepticism about Walther's discursive project—and with it also to engender the reader's skepticism about the discursive project of the poem that bears Walther's name. In a work that has already repeatedly evoked Vergil's epic, an encounter between lovers that involves talk of exile points to Book Four, and to Dido, more or less automatically.[23] More specifically, just after Walther has met Hildegund in the king's chamber, we read "post amplexus atque oscula dulcia dixit"—that he speaks to her after embraces and sweet kisses, in a line lifted substantially from *Aeneid* 1.687, where it is used of Cupid, disguised as Ascanius, driving the shafts of love into the heart of Dido. I propose that Hildegund as character not only mistrusts Walther's veracity, but that as a reader of him and of the narrative that bears his name, she has every right to be suspicious of a hero who tells her she's his one and only but who immediately adds that it's time to split. It's a little too close for comfort to Dido and Aeneas, after all, in its travestied resonance against the resolve of Vergil's hero to depart Carthage. Walther, unlike Aeneas, chooses departure out of personal desire, not out of imposed duty; he intends to return to his origins, not to found of necessity a new society; and he intends to take Hildegund with him. Hildegund's response suggests the resistance of an interpreter to the narrative expectations cued by the Vergilian paradigm. Just where *does* she fit into all this, once she's sorted out the tissue of distorted motifs from Vergil to which Walther's plan alludes? It's surprising that Walther's response calms her fears: significant chunks of the first sentence out of his mouth are borrowed directly from *Aeneid* 4.109 ("quod memoras") and 105 ("sensit enim simulata mente locutam"), phrases taken from the scene in which Juno and Venus reach an uneasy and insincere agreement that they should patch up their differences and marry Aeneas off to Dido.

The work of at least two theorists of irony upon whom Hutcheon herself draws are applicable here. If Hildegund-as-reader knows her Vergil well enough to recognize a slippery Trojan when she sees one, she seems to know something of a theory of irony as echoic mention of a previously articulated utterance. According to such a model, as laid out by Sperber and Wilson, the irony of one text always assumes the preexistence of another. The ironic utterance makes mention of that preexistent text without redeploying its intended meaning.[24] At the same time, insofar as Hildegund is in the know about the generic conventions of Vergilian epic, she recognizes that Walther's proposed behavior is a profound negation of epic expectation that boy meets girl and then drops her off at the funeral pyre. She thus also seems to have read her Wolfgang Iser, who locates the irony of a text in its negations and deliberate thwartings—"blanks," Iser calls them—of the expectations one brings to a text on the basis of one's knowledge of other texts in the same genre.[25]

And indeed, much of Walther's behavior both before and after the showdown in the Vosges is profoundly unheroic. His suggestion to Attila that he should not marry because a wife would compromise the single-mindedness of his devotion to his lord is a kind of over-the-top parody of homosocial organization, one of those surpluses of social desire between men which run the risk of crossing the line into the illicit.[26] After Hildegund and Walther lay their plans to escape, Walther dons extensive and extensively described armor, in a vignette that evokes the formal arming scenes of classical epic (lines 326–40). Walther, however, is preparing not to do battle but to escape by night. His armor serves in the first instance chiefly to so encumber him that Hildegund must carry the more practical paraphernalia necessary for their sustenance en route. There is subsequently something touchingly bucolic, and hardly normatively macho, about his and Hildegund's progress through the countryside on their way west (lines 419–27). And the hangover of the Huns the morning after their escape (lines 358–401) is scarcely the stuff of vengeful wrath on an epic scale.

Hildegund's status as a reader is thus bound up with the fact that she reads more than the text of Walther immediately before her. She simultaneously reads another text, without which her interpretation of the primary text would be impossible. She construes the meaning of Walther's text, in fact, as being inseparable from its relation to another text outside itself. Still, if Hildegund is a reader, the narrator wants to reassure us (just as Walther wants to reassure her) that she's a bad one, that her interpretation is a misinterpretation, that for all her canny recognition of the Vergilian red flags, she's got it wrong. Walther's references to Vergil, and the *Waltharius*'s references to Vergil, don't mean what she imagines them to mean. Hildegund-as-character gives in to such a pronouncement rather readily—ten lines later, she is at Walther's feet saying "I want what you want, lord. I'll do everything you say." (lines 257–9) Walther and his text are thus drawing a line around the significance of one text for another. Ironic reference is all well and good, if it means what its speaker intends it to mean. Anything else it might mean is irrelevant, a red herring that can only drag one further and further afield from the properly bounded intention of an authoritative voice.

I am not entirely convinced, however, that Hildegund-as-reader ceases to resist. If ironic reference to other texts could really be controlled by pinning it securely to authorial intent, there would be nothing untoward about the allusions in the *Waltharius* to the *Aeneid*. Subtexts aren't all that threatening to common sense notions of literary signification. Allusions and lines of influence are the stuff of mainstream literary history, and they leave us admiring how deftly the *Waltharius* poet has forged his links with the great literary tradition. But there is another and far more radical possibility, namely, that lines of textual influence do not go all in one direction along a linear path. There is the possibility that once the allusions to Vergil are loose on the page—once Walther has told Hildegund to stop thinking ironically, to stop it this minute—they're fair game for a vast constellation of possible readings, as the text passes through a range of discursive communities which constitute the horizons of its reception history. The coordinates of those readings in all their polymorphous perversity are determined not only by the controlling mind of the *Waltharius* poet drawing on the controlling mind of Vergil. Such readings also depend on a vast array of further discursive vectors traversing the mind of the reader.

The paths of those vectors are not infinite, but neither are they subject to a law of linear descent from one text to its rightful successor. They are rather a web, a network of multiple potentials. I wonder whether this reading of the text as sited in a web that spreads beyond it on all sides doesn't have something to do with Hildegund's sense of the ironic applicability of *Aeneid* 4 to the events unfolding before her. Some cognoscenti of theory, including Julia Kristeva herself, who first coined the term, have objected that "intertextuality" has been misconstrued and trivialized.[27] But I think it remains a serviceable way to denote what's at stake here—namely, the difference between ironic reference as a trace of authorial intention and ironic echo as the initiation of a path of interpretation that can't be held to a single direct line. Put another way, Hildegund-as-reader can continue to resist after Walther informs her that she's got it wrong. She can do this insofar as Vergil is subsumed into the intertext of the *Waltharius* rather than simply established as its subtext.

All this makes for a somewhat postmodernist heroine in a Carolingian or Ottonian poem. But fashionable terminology aside, is the possibility that a medieval reader could have resisted the ideology of the text all that farfetched? Was disaffection from the dominant discourses of monasticism so uncommon within the monasteries themselves that a literate monk or nun might not find in Hildegund-as-character's single act of resistance the chutzpah to unleash Hildegund as a principle of resistant, ironical reading? Carolingian and Ottonian monasteries were hardly communities of homogeneous assent, nor were their inmates there by anything like the individuality of choice that marks the entry into religion today.[28] And anyone who's spent time in a twentieth-century religious community knows the range and subtlety with which individual personality expresses itself. The notion that the early medieval *fratres* to whom the *Waltharius* is addressed would have read the poem with unanimous understanding isn't any more historically rigorous, it seems to me, than the delineation of readerly resistance I propose. Totalizing projections of unanimity have as much to do with seeing *Lilies of the Field* or, God forbid, *The Sound of Music* at an impressionable age as with historicist scruples. We ignore the social diversity of the paths by which people in the ninth through eleventh centuries and beyond entered the Latinate communities of the Church if we imagine that their readings of the text cannot have incorporated all the conflicting social vectors that crossed the space of the text as they received it.

So what happens to Hildegund the resisting reader after her one outburst, and with her to a disaffected monk of St. Gall who's had enough of Cassian's obsessions with the menace of "nocturnal illusion,"[29] but who equally resents the secular family he left behind, or who abandoned *him* as a child oblate? Or to an uppity nun from Gandersheim who finally decides that martyrdom's not enough? Does Hildegund-as-reader subsequently vanish so completely from the frame of the text that we're left only with Hildegund-as-character, keeping watch for Huns and Franks while an exhausted Walther sleeps (1172–84), and begging Walther to kill her before she falls into enemy hands?

Well, maybe. But all three of the warriors who survive till the end fall down exhausted. That scene clearly relies on the codes of dark humor that mark a lot of the surviving Germanic literature. One might compare Beowulf telling Hrothgar that the Danish king won't need to bury him after Grendel has his snack, or the impaled Thorgrim in *Njal's Saga* observing that while his opponent Gunnar may or may not be hiding inside his house, his halberd certainly is at home.[30] Or the heroine's sidekick in *Texas Chainsaw Massacre II* apologizing that he's falling apart. For some, the final scene also recalls, as Dennis Kratz suggests, the words of Jesus to cut off hand or eye or foot rather than perish in sin, as well as the dictum of Exodus, "an eye for an eye and a tooth for a tooth."[31] But neither does the Christian subtext exhaust the ironic potential. In the last catalogue of spare body parts, the narrator tells the reader that "illic...palma iacebat Waltharii"—that there lay Walther's palm (line 1402). Surely *palma* suggests not only the hero's severed hand, but the palm of victory, lying now in the dust along with a leg, the odd tooth, a twitching eye, and a set of lips. Yet *palmae* lying in the dust can undermine more than Germanic heroism. Classical heroes, and along with them Prudentian martyrs, receive *palmae* as well by a metaphoric extension that coopts Christian discourse as much as Christian discourse coopts the language and imagery of heroism. At the end, we're not left with the proper ending to a Germanic lay. According to those expectations, everybody should be dead, save maybe for Hildegund, who should at least be ravaged or inconsolably bereaved. But we're not left with pure and simple Christian reconciliation either. We're left with macho jokes about Walther embracing Hildegund with his left hand, and Hagen looking sideways at guests with his one remaining eye, and with a final approving aside that Walther later married Hildegund and ruled auspiciously for thirty years. The last real action of the poem is Hildegund ministering to three incapacitated louts. She's the only one left standing and intact. As interpreting subject, she may well still hold her own opinions about what's gone on in the defiles of the Vosges.

Hildegund thus remains both a character in the narrative and, potentially, the representative of a principle of critical reading that has infiltrated the generic expectations of the text from within its own space in order to resist and subvert them. Perhaps we may even see her hermeneutic as ultimately victorious: in the final combat of Walther, Hagen, and Gunther, unlike Aeneas's savage victory over Turnus, there is no clear winner. All lie down, exhausted and mutilated, under a tree. But unlike Lavinia, the bride-prize who has disappeared at the end of Vergil's epic, Hildegund then serves the drinks. In thus remaining on the scene, she offers the possibility of a reading resistant to the norms of dominant patriarchal narrative patterns, a reading anchored within the realm of intertextual association, as well as extending out into a stereotypically feminized realm of extratextual "Reality." Her final performance as peaceweaving cupbearer may fulfil the expectations of the men around her, but it may evoke simultaneously the ironized mimesis of Irigaray.[32] At the same time, the last state of Walther, Gunther, and Hagen suggests that the price of phallic potency is amputation—that those who live by the phallus are figuratively castrated by the phallus, and that within the signifying economy of patriarchy's dominant fiction, as Kaja Silverman has contended, *all* subjectivity is castrated;[33] or put differently, that the price of the phallus is the rest of the body or at least significant portions of it. The trope of irony is here the nexus at which intertextuality and the gendered subjectivity of the resisting reader come together.

NOTES

I am grateful to my colleagues in the Work in Progress in English circle (WIPE) at the University of Toronto for trenchant and helpful criticism of an earlier version of this essay and to Professor Margaret Sinex for her work on irony in the *De nugis curialium* of Walter Map.

1. My approach to ideology is influenced in particular by Kaja Silverman, *Male Subjectivity at the Margins* (New York: Routledge, 1992), pp. 15–51 and by Alan Sinfield, *Cultural Politics—Queer Reading* (Philadelphia: University of Pennsylvania Press, 1994), pp. 21–39.

2. Stanley B. Greenfield and Daniel G. Calder, *A New Critical History of Old English Literature* (New York: New York University Press, 1986), the second edition of Greenfield's long-influential introductory account of 1965, perpetuates in its basic organization into chapters the notion that the most fundamental dynamic of Old English literary production was the amalgamation of imported Christian values with a native heroic tradition.

3. Ibid., p. 134, p. 150. Katherine O'Brien O'Keefe is more circumspect about Tacitus' descriptive value: "Heroic Values and Christian Ethics," in *The Cambridge Companion to Old English Literature*, Malcolm Godden and Michael Lapidge, eds. (Cambridge: Cambridge University Press, 1991), pp. 112–13.

4. Contrapuntal voices in *Beowulf* scholarship have begun to interrogate the "givenness" of heroic values: see, for example, Clare A. Lees, "Men and *Beowulf*," in *Medieval Masculinities: Regarding Men in the Middle Ages*, ed. Clare A. Lees, with Thelma Fenster and Jo Ann McNamara (Minneapolis: University of Minnesota Press, 1994), pp. 129–48; Gillian Overing, *Language, Sign, and Gender in Beowulf* (Carbondale: Southern Illinois University Press, 1990); James W. Earl, "*Beowulf* and the Origins of Civilization," in *Speaking Two Languages: Traditional Disciplines and Contemporary Theory in Medieval Studies*, Allen J. Frantzen, ed. (Albany:

State University of New York Press, 1991), pp. 65–89; and David Rosen, *The Changing Fictions of Masculinity* (Urbana: University of Illinois Press, 1993), ch. 1.

5. Karl Strecker, ed., *Monumenta Germaniae Historica, Poetae Latini Aevi Carolini*, vol. 6 (Weimar: Böhlau, 1951), pp. 1–83. Strecker gives an account of the manuscripts at the outset of his introduction.

6. For a useful summary of the state of the question, see Armando Bisanti, "Un decennio di studi sul *Waltharius*," *Schede medievali* 11 (1986): 345–63.

7. Robert G. Babcock, "Sigebert of Gembloux and the 'Waltharius'," *Mittellateinisches Jahrbuch* 21 (1986): 101–5; Günter Glauche, *Schullektüre im Mittelalter. Entstehung und Wandlungen des Lektürekanons bis 1200 nach den Quellen dargestellt* (Munich: Arbeo–Gesellschaft, 1970), pp. 94–9.

8. Carol Clover, *Men, Women, and Chainsaws: Gender in the Modern Horror Film* (Princeton: Princeton University Press, 1992).

9. Clover, *Men, Women, and Chainsaws*, pp. 35–41.

10. Ursula Ernst, "Walther—ein christlicher Held?" *Mittellateinisches Jahrbuch* 21 (1986): 79–83 offers one recent consideration of the poem's engagement with Christian values; Maria Luhrs, "Hiltgunt," *Mittellateinisches Jahrbuch* 21 (1986): 84–87 considers the presentation of Hildegund but along lines very different from those I pursue below.

11. Lines 230–47, as edited by Strecker. My translation follows.

12. Haijo Jan Westra, "A Reinterpretation of 'Waltharius' 215–59," *Mittellateinisches Jahrbuch* 15 (1980): 53 and n. 1.

13. Gerald Prince, "Notes on the Text as Reader," in *The Reader in the Text: Essays on Audience and Interpretation*, Susan R. Suleiman and Inge Crosman, eds. (Princeton: Princeton University Press, 1980): pp. 225–40.

14. Michel Foucault, *The History of Sexuality: An Introduction*, Robert Hurley, trans. (New York: Vintage Books, 1990), p. 101.

15. Dilwyn Knox, *Ironia: Medieval and Renaissance Ideas on Irony* (Leiden: Brill, 1989), pp. 7–37.

16. Linda Hutcheon, *Irony's Edge: The Theory and Politics of Irony* (Routledge: London and New York, 1994), pp. 57–88 and esp. pp. 61–4.

17. One of Hutcheon's favorite metaphors takes up the ambiguous drawing of what may be the head of a rabbit, or of a duck, employed by Wittgenstein and then by E.H. Gombrich. In *Art and Illusion*, Gombrich contends that we can see only one or the other at a time. Irony, counters Hutcheon, is that mode of interpretive consciousness by which we can have our bunnies and make them quack, too: "I would suggest that, when it comes to the ducks and rabbits of ironic meaning, our minds almost can [perceive both simultaneously]....But—and here the visual analogy needs adapting—it is not the two 'poles' themselves that are important; it is the idea of a kind of rapid perceptual or hermeneutic *movement between* them

that makes this image a possibly suggestive and productive one for thinking about irony." (60)

18. See also Luigi Alfonsi, "Considerazioni sul vergilianismo del 'Waltharius'," in *Studi philologici, letterari e storici in memoria de Guido Favati*, Giorgio Varanini and Palmiro Pinagli, eds., vol. 1 (Padua: Antenore, 1977), pp. 3–14.

19. Dennis M. Kratz, *Mocking Epic: Waltharius, Alexandreis, and the Problem of Christian Heroism* (Madrid: Studia Humanitatis, 1980), pp. 24–26 and pp. 52–53.

20. Kratz, *Mocking Epic*, p. 18, pp. 51–6, *et passim*.

21. Peter Dronke, "Functions of Classical Borrowing in Medieval Latin Verse," in R. R. Bolgar, ed., *Classical Influences on European Culture, A.D. 500–900*, (Cambridge: Cambridge University Press, 1971), pp. 159–164.

22. Dronke, 161: "...A moment later [Attila's] restlessness...is expressed in almost the same words as are used of Dido in the *Aeneid*. The incongruity is deliberate—the world conqueror, frustrated, waxes womanish."

23. On Dido in medieval literature, see especially Marilynn Desmond, *Reading Dido: Gender, Textuality, and the Medieval Aeneid* (Minneapolis: University of Minnesota Press, 1994) and also Christopher Baswell, *Virgil in Medieval England: Figuring the Aeneid from the Twelfth Century to Chaucer* (Cambridge: Cambridge University Press, 1995).

24. Dan Sperber and Dierdre Wilson, "Irony and the Use-Mention Distinction," in *Radical Pragmatics*, Peter Cole, ed. (New York: Academic Press, 1981).

25. Wolfgang Iser, *The Act of Reading: A Theory of Aesthetic Response* (Baltimore: Johns Hopkins University Press, 1978), pp. 180–231.

26. For an analogous example of ideological contradictions implicit in normatively homosocial bonds, see Alan Bray, "Homosexuality and the Signs of Male Friendship in Elizabethan England," in *Queering the Renaissance*, Jonathan Goldberg, ed. (Durham: Duke University Press, 1994), pp. 40–61, as well as Eve Sedgewick's foundational delineation of homosociality in *Between Men: English Literature and Male Homosocial Desire* (New York: Columbia University Press, 1985), pp. 1–20.

27. Barbara Godard, "Intertextuality," in *Encyclopedia of Contemporary Literary Theory*, Irena A. Makaryk, ed. (Toronto: University of Toronto Press, 1993), pp. 568–71.

28. Heinrich Fichtenau's representation of Ottonian society, *Living in the Tenth Century: Mentalities and Social Orders*, Patrick J. Geary, trans. (Chicago: University of Chicago Press, 1991) readily facilitates an awareness of social conflict within monastic communities and without.

29. On monastic anxieties over nocturnal emissions, see Jan Ziolkowski, *Talking Animals: Medieval Latin Beast Poetry, 750–1150* (Philadelphia: University of Pennsylvania Press, 1993), pp. 79–105.

30. *Beowulf*, lines 445–51; *Njal's Saga*, ch. 77.

31. Kratz, *Mocking Epic*, p. 50.

32. Luce Irigaray, *This Sex Which Is Not One*, Catherine Porter with Carolyn Burke,trans. (Ithaca: Cornell University Press, 1985), pp. 148–52; Toril Moi, *Sexual/Textual Politics* (London: Methuen, 1985), pp. 131–43.

33. Silverman, *Male Subjectivity*, pp. 42–8.

ABELARD AND (RE)WRITING THE MALE BODY: CASTRATION, IDENTITY, AND REMASCULINIZATION

Martin Irvine

Abelard's writings disclose that he was engaged in a project of remasculinization in response to his public identity as a feminized eunuch. This essay places his project in a historical context.

Abelard's narrative of identity anxieties in his *Letter of Consolation to a Friend*,[1] incorrectly called by its modern editorial title, the *Historia calamitatum* (c. 1132), is well known, but the significance of Abelard's representations of self and the body and his strategies for remasculinization have not yet become a focus of modern scholarship.[2] What Abelard tries to repress in this work and subsequent letters—his denied but abiding desire, his inexpressible pain, and his abject humiliation as a social castrate—continues to be repressed in most modern studies of Abelard and Heloise. In this essay I want to unfold some of the repressions and evasions in the Abelard story, both then and now, by focusing on Abelard's project of remasculating himself with new imagined objects of wholeness that flow from his pen, from his books and the power of discourse in the homosocial world of the teacher, philosopher, and monk.[3]

Recent theory has brought into focus the complicated connections among the sexed human body, the discourses and ideologies that "make sex," and the social construction of gender identities.[4] The twelfth and thirteenth centuries appear to be an era of heightened anxiety about the body and its sexuality. Discourse about the body, the marks or signs of sexual and gender identity, the soul/body dichotomy, and the correspondences between the material or physical condition of the body and the mind and soul proliferated. As recent studies like John Baldwin's *The Language of Sex* make clear, the twelfth and thirteenth centuries seem to bear out Foucault's claim that each era produces the means simultaneously to represent, manage, and control sexuality in the discourses that circulate around bodies.[5] Abelard's strategies for positioning himself as a masculine subject in a world where castrates were feminized and marked by an irrecoverable lack were thus enacted in a world of already conflicted and conflicting social categories.

Abelard's narratives of emasculation and strategies for remasculinization are part of a large field of discourse and genres that situate representations of bodily mutilation and castration in a network of social values and anxieties, and the cultural meaning of the events narrated in Abelard's letters must be sought in the larger social system of values and identities within which they were produced. Before turning to Abelard's self-representation and strategies for remasculinization, I'd like to point out a few examples of castration narratives that can serve as compass points on the larger map of twelfth-century discourse.

Narratives of emasculating mutilation abound in accounts of the crusades, local wars, and revenge in the twelfth and thirteenth centuries. For example, Guibert of Nogent relates castration anxiety nightmares in his autobiographical memoirs (*De vita sua*), and tells war stories with graphic descriptions of genital mutilation, such as the account of Thomas of Coucy, who often hung his enemies up by their testicles and penises until the organs were ripped from their bodies (3.11). Guibert also relates the story of a young man who, on a pilgrimage to repent from a non-marital sexual union, was commanded by the devil to cut off his offending sexual organ and then use the same knife to slit his throat (3.19).[6]

There are similar revenge narratives where men are castrated by other men offended by discovered sexual intercourse, usually consensual, with a kinswoman. Castration was a recognized punishment for adultery in some regions, though the courts sought to control the application of the penalty. Canon law also prescribed castration for a Christian European found guilty of adultery with a Saracen woman.[7]

Other castration stories indicate that genital mutilation was often used against clerics and monks for sexual crimes. Aelred of Rievaulx (abbot, 1147-67) preserves a bizarre story of an oblate nun at the monastery of Watton in Yorkshire.[8] The nun disliked the cloistered life, began a sexual relationship with a young lay-brother who served at the monastery, and became pregnant. When her affair and pregnancy became known to the sisters, the young man was at first caught by the nuns and beaten but then managed to flee, and his lover was cruelly mistreated by her sisters and chained in her cell. The young man was later apprehended—by other brothers cross-dressing as nuns!—and brought back to Watton. The guilty nun, in the presence of her sisters, was then forced to castrate her lover with her own hands. One of the bystanders snatched up the bloody testicles and thrust them into the young man's mouth. The nun was then compelled to return to her cell and was chained again.[9] The motivation of the sisters and lay-brothers who assisted them is clearly revenge for violated chastity, and in this respect the story is parallel with Abelard's own narrative. Also parallel is the irrelevance of the woman's consent or agency in a sexual union: for the community, it is a case of violated chastity performed by the man. The cruelty of the punishments was not unusual for the time; there are other accounts of judicial castration, sometimes combined with blinding, from the same period.[10]

Other castration narratives from this era recapitulate the story of Origen, the early patristic philosopher who castrated himself to become a eunuch for the kingdom of heaven's sake. (Abelard, though, thought Origen had overinterpreted the scriptures in this regard.[11]) For example, Hugh of Lincoln (d. 1200), from the knightly class in Burgundy, a Carthusian monk and bishop of Lincoln soon canonized after his death, was relieved of his intense sexual desire by a miraculous castration: one night a saint came down from heaven and castrated him, giving him only calm from that moment on.[12]

The French fabliaux, of course, contain many stories of violence to sexual organs and satirical representations of both male and female genitals.[13] The fabliau *Prestre crucifié*, for example, dramatizes social anxieties about middle-class adultery with clergy in the portrayal of a priest castrated by a sculptor of crucifixes who surprises his wife in bed with the priest. When the sculptor returns home, suspecting what his wife was up to, the priest jumps out of bed and decides to hide by mounting a newly carved cross and playing the body of Christ. Considering the body on the cross, the sculptor decides that the prick and balls are not right so he cuts them off, leaving the mutilated priest to flee into the street.[14]

And finally, Jean de Meun's continuation of the *Romance of the Rose* both extends twelfth-century discourse on sexuality and charts the popular reception of Abelard in thirteenth-century Paris. Jean, who translated the letters of Abelard and Heloise around 1280, reveals a fascination with castration and dismemberment in his continuation of the *Roman* (c. 1275), and in the course of the narrative he inserts various exempla dealing with the castration of Saturn, Origen, and Abelard.[15] In a famous section of the *Roman* on Friend's advice to the Lover against marriage—which, incidentally, indicates Jean's knowledge of Abelard's first letter at this time—Jean summarizes Abelard's and Heloise's life and cites Heloise's arguments against marriage. He mentions that "Pierre's testicles were removed, in his bed, at night; on this account he endured great suffering and torment."[16] Genius's speech on fertility and procreation, an extension of the speech of Nature, is formed of a series of phallic tropes—penis as stylus, hammer, and plow—for the male agency in generation. The speech concludes with diatribe against castration:

> Anyone who castrates (*escoille*) a worthy man does him very great shame and injury....It is a great sin to castrate a man. Anyone who castrates a man robs him not just of his testicles (*la coille*), nor of his sweetheart whom he holds very dear and whose fair face he will never see, nor of his wife, for these are the least; he robs him especially of the boldness in human ways that should exist in valiant men. For we are certain that castrated men (*escoillié*) are perverse and malicious cowards because they have the ways of women. Certainly no eunuch (*escoilliez*) has any bravery whatever in him, unless perhaps in some vice, to do something very malicious. All women are very bold at doing deeds of great devilishness, and eunuchs (*escoilliez*) resemble them in this respect. In particular, the castrator (*escoillierres*), even though he may not be a murderer or a thief nor have committed any mortal sin, at least has sinned to the extent of doing Nature a great wrong in stealing the power of engendering.[17]

The complex of ideas and associations here—maleness and masculinity symbolized and authenticated in the testes (not the penis), the eunuch as physically and morally deficient, the eunuch as an object of misogynist scorn—certainly would have been current in Abelard's Paris a century earlier.

These are only a few examples of numerous accounts and representations of physical emasculation, both fictional and historical, in the twelfth and thirteenth centuries, and these texts provide an important context for reading Abelard's own *vita* of masculine redefinition. In light of other castration stories, Abelard's narrative immediately stands out in its attempt to play down the significance of the physical violence and the irrecoverable loss of maleness, repressing the full psychic and social trauma in the construction of a moral and spiritual drama.

We have more than Abelard's self-dramatization for recovering the social valence of his castration and the context for his project of remasculinization. In around 1120, Roscelin of Compiegne, Abelard's former teacher and the main proponent of nominalism, wrote an attack against Abelard in response to Abelard's criticism of Roscelin's teachings.[18] Roscelin's open letter against Abelard was written soon after Abelard's relationship with Heloise, his castration, and his entry into monastic life had become widely known.[19] Roscelin begins with some verbal revenge on what he takes to be Abelard's insults: Abelard should fear divine justice for his attack on Roscelin and his church, "lest your tongue, with which you now sting, be taken away just like your tail, which you used to prick with promiscuously."[20] In the main part of the letter, Roscelin defends his theological doctrines against Abelard's criticisms, but he concludes with a sarcastic commentary on Abelard's life and identity. He opens his conclusion with a speciously sympathetic description of Abelard's condition, a description that foreshadows Abelard's own narrative: "your misery is already widely known, and though the tongue be silent about it, the fact itself proclaims it."[21] Roscelin then recites the events leading to Abelard's castration, rebuking him for teaching his student to fornicate, an act that makes him guilty of several crimes at once—traitor to his host, fornicator, and violator of a virgin. But God took revenge, Roscelin continues, by removing the part that he sinned with.[22]

Using terms from dialectic and grammar, the disciplines Abelard was famous for, Roscelin concludes his letter with a spiteful attack on Abelard's identity. Abelard has no identity in Roscelin's view: he is neither monk nor cleric or layman, and he has no name, not even Petrus, since a masculine proper name loses its signification once its referent changes gender:

> Si igitur neque clericus neque laicus neque monachus es, quo nomine te censeam, reperire non valeo. Sed forte Petrum te appellari posse ex consuetudine mentieris. Certus sum autem, quod masculini generis

nomen, si a suo genere deciderit, rem solitam significare recusabit.[23] Solent enim nomina propriam significationem amittere, cum eorum significata contigerit a sua perfectione recedere. Neque enim ablato tecto vel pariete domus, sed imperfecta domus vocabitur. Sublata igitur parte quae hominem facit non Petrus, sed imperfectus Petrus appellandus es. Ad huius etiam imperfect hominis ignominiae cumulum pertinet, quod in sigillo, quo foetidas illas litteras sigillavit, imaginem duo capita habentem, unum viri, alterum mulieris, ipse formavit. Unde quis dubitet, quanto adhuc in eam ardeat amore, qui tali eam capitum coniunctione non erubuit honorare? Plura quidem in tuam contumeliam vera ac manifesta dictare decreveram, sed quia contra hominem imperfectum ago, opus quod coeperam imperfectum relinquo.[24]

If, then, you are not a cleric, nor a layman, nor a monk, I'm unable to find a name by which I can consider you. But, to be sure, you are lying that you can be called 'Peter' from conventional usage. I'm certain that a noun (*nomen*) of masculine gender, if it falls away from its own gender, will refuse to signify its usual thing (*rem*). For proper nouns usually lose their signification when the things signified fall back from their own completion. A house is not called a house but an incomplete house when its walls and roof are removed. Therefore since the part that makes a man has been removed, you are to be called not 'Peter' but 'incomplete Peter.' It suits this heap of incomplete human disgrace that in the seal by which he seals his stinking letters he himself forms an image having two heads, one a man and the other a woman. This being the case, who can doubt how much he still burns with love for her, the one who does not blush to honor her in such a conjunction of heads? I have decided to say many true and obvious things against your attack, but since I am writing against an incomplete man, I will leave the work that I began incomplete.

According to this argument, Abelard cannot even be represented in language, since his own name is meaningless, a masculine proper noun without a referent. For Roscelin, Abelard's sexual deficiency is symbolized in the ambiguity of his seal: a Janus head with a male and female face. Man becoming woman, woman and man as, or in, *coniunctio*, or an ambiguous, dual-sexed identity?

There is another letter addressed to Abelard from this period which provides additional evidence for understanding the public identity he had to overcome. Fulco (Fulk), Prior of Deuil, in his parody of a consolation epistle addressed to Abelard around 1118, turns the public response to Abelard's castration into mock-heroic satire with close affinities to fabliau.[25] After accusing Abelard of whoring his money away, he describes in malicious detail how useful the mutilation of certain body parts has been to Abelard (*invenires quantum tibi afferat utilitatis particularum ista mutilatio)* since he is now relieved from disturbing passions and the heat of lust and sexual pleasure (*ardor libidinis et luxuriae*). Fulco then mockingly enumerates the benefits of castration for Abelard. Lacking the physical signs and body parts to perform manhood, he will be relieved of the burden of the social performance of masculinity. Husbands won't fear that he'll violate their wives and he'll be able to pass through a crowd of married women with utmost decorum. A band of virgins in the flower of youth can revive the libido of old men, Fulco taunts, but they will no have no effect on Abelard. Furthermore, he'll never have to fear the temptations of homosexual society, the need to masturbate after erotic dreams, or the pleasures of bodily contact with a wife. Abelard will be able to imitate the exemplary self-castrator, Origen, and other saints and martyrs who rejoiced to be without genitals (*gaudent genitalibus caruisse*): "blessed are they who have castrated themselves for the sake of the kingdom of heaven."[26]

As if this were not "consolation" enough, Fulco goes on to frame a scene of mock lamentations by all who learned of Abelard's castration. Bishops, canons, clerics, and citizens all lamented his wound and the outpouring of his blood that did violence to his city.[27] Fulco continues:

> Quid singularum feminarum referam planctum, quae sic, hoc audito, lacrymis, more femineo, ora rigarunt, propter te militem suum, quem amiserant, ac si singulae virum suum aut amicum sorte belli reperissent exstinctum?[28]

> How shall I relate the lament of each and every woman, whose faces were wet with tears upon hearing this news, because of you, their knight/soldier whom they had lost, as if each one of them had discovered their husband or lover had been killed in battle?

Fulco concludes the letter with a sarcastic hope that Abelard will persevere in his holy life, so that Christ will restore whatever Abelard has lost in his future body of the blessed.[29]

Fulco's sarcastic letter throws open a window onto a wide field of sexual categories: in this somatic logic, Abelard's lack is a sign of emasculated desire, both hetero- and homosexual. It is important to note how easily Fulco slips in the possibility of homoerotic experience, "the secret retreats of the sodomites" (*sodomitarum secretos recessus*), in the catalogue of pleasures denied the eunuch.[30] The implication is that Abelard must now avoid homosexual society (*consortia*) too, since he can only occupy the feminized position of the one penetrated. For Fulco it is not simply the fact of castration that unmans Abelard: the lack of genitals is a sign of a deeper lack, a deficiency or erasure of *virtus*, which alone allows the true performance of masculinity. And it was this that Abelard sought to perform through his books, a claim to this inner *virtus*, a fantasized phallus-substitute, a re-identification with symbolic power.

Contemporary castration narratives and the letters of his enemies reveal that Abelard's social identity was thus marked by the stigma of the feminized eunuch. This identity continues in the writings of Abelard's enemies right up to the time of his betrayal and condemnation at the Council of Sens (1140). During the later 1130s, Bernard of Clairvaux, Abelard's nemesis, wrote a series of scathing letters to bishops, cardinals, and the pope denouncing Abelard and his teachings.[31] Bernard's strong animus against Abelard is difficult to understand at our historical remove from the political and personal conditions of the 1120s and 1130s, but the *ad hominum* remarks in Bernard's letters provide one kind of clue. In one letter we read Bernard's fears of scholastic philosophers in general epitomized in the emasculated Abelard: he is a monk without a rule and an abbot without a community; he spends his time discussing problems with children and holding conferences with women; he is always surrounded by his students and followed by a crowd; he is like a hissing dragon, spreading poison through pen and ink; his character is known from his writings.[32] The collocation of terms here is telling: emasculated and feminized, Abelard is associated with children and women. But though politically powerless, Abelard is a force to be reckoned with in his writings. Bernard was outraged to have to contend with this upstart half-man who was known by his writings, which were even being read in the papal curia, and by his large student following. Bernard's authority and political influence prevailed, allowing him to orchestrate Abelard's condemnation at the Council of Sens, a defeat which Abelard never lived to overcome.

About twelve years after Roscelin's and Fulco's letters, at the end of his disastrous stint as abbot of the monastery of St. Gildas de Rhuys in Britanny, Abelard turned to a narrative of his own life in the form of a letter of consolation to an unnamed friend, now known as the *Historia calamitatum* (c. 1132). This letter, the first of the collected letters of Abelard and Heloise and the first major statement from Abelard since his condemnation at the Council of Soissons in

1121, is arguably the first work in a project of remasculinization that Abelard undertook in the 1130s. The letter of consolation to a friend is a rhetorical performance of the highest order, woven from several discourses and genres,[33] and a performance that discloses deep gender anxieties and the intense but repressed desire to be reunited to the social body that had rejected him.

Many commentators have noted that Abelard represents himself at the opening of the letter as a knight of dialectic, exchanging the soldier's life for the "weapons of dialectical argument" (*dialectarum rationum armaturam*). But Abelard shifts his rhetorical posture and subject position several times in the narrative, moving from representation of self as the controlling agent of conquest (in the schools and with Heloise) to one brought low by pride and lusts of the flesh (glory in his own position as *magister scholarum* and his love of Heloise), to one repeatedly emasculated, victimized, and feminized by enemies who worked to remove his masculine identity as *magister* and *philosophus*.

Abelard thus constructs the narrative as a sequence of gendered episodes, moving from his siege of Paris as the leading soldier of dialectic to his two primary emasculations and feminization at the hands of his enemies—his physical castration and his trial at the Council of Soissons—to the hope of another identity as father of the Paraclete community, which Abelard founded and later installed Heloise as abbess. The letter paradoxically draws much of its power from Abelard's gender switching, and here rhetoric and gender combine forces: Abelard deploys the conventions of the ethical appeal in rhetoric—the technique of seizing the benevolence and sympathy of the audience by constructing an appropriate image of character (*ethos*)—with the conventions of gender, representing himself occupying, quite "unnaturally," the feminine position before the authority of other men.

Abelard's self-representation is at first a story of incremental conquests, leading to his portrayal as the chief philosopher of Paris. The episode of his love affair with Heloise is at first treated as another easy conquest. A pivotal point in the letter is marked by the shift in narrative form at the point of the story of his "fall" in Paris. Abelard chooses a common narrative frame, that of the deserved fall through pride and lust. But inside this frame Abelard inserts two other master narratives or genre types—the fall of man through a woman and the *vita* of the persecuted martyr—narrative genres that conflict with the main narrative frame.[34] In fact, Abelard deploys these narrative forms to create his own myth of origins, the starting point of his ongoing persecution and victimization. After the love affair is discovered by Fulbert, a canon of Notre Dame and Heloise's uncle, the subsequent narrative becomes a story of feminized victimization, much like the classic female martyr-saints, even though the story is framed as a deserved fall through pride and lust. Although abject from his sense that he had betrayed his host, Fulbert, Abelard portrays himself as both castrated and raped by Fulbert's lackeys, a victim of patriarchal control.

Let's attend closely to the rhetoric of Abelard's account of his two emasculations. The first act was performed by Fulbert and his kinsmen and relatives (*consanguinei seu affines*):

> Unde vehementer indignati et adversum me coniurati, nocte quadam quiescentem me atque dormientem in secreta hospicii mei camera, quodam mihi serviente per pecuniam corrupto, crudelissima et pudentissima ultione punierunt, et quam summa ammiratione mundus excepit, eis videlicet corporis mei partibus amputatis quibus id quod plangebant commiseram. Quibus mox in fugam conversis, duo qui comprehendi potuerunt oculis et genitalibus privati sunt, quorum alter ille fuit supradictus serviens qui, cum in obsequio meo mecum maneret, cupiditate ad proditionem ductus est.[35]

> They plotted against me with fierce indignation, and on a certain night while I was at rest and sleeping in a private room in my lodgings, they bribed one of my servants with money, and then took the cruelest and most shameful revenge, which the whole world heard about with the greatest wonder; they cut off those parts of my body by which I committed what they complained about. They then took to flight, but two who could be caught were deprived of their eyes and genitals, one of them the servant just mentioned, who was led by greed to become a traitor while he stayed with me in my service.

Here the language of revenge for violated chastity combines with the language of rape: Abelard was invaded and assaulted in an inner, private place (*in secreta hospicii mei camera*) while he was helplessly asleep. The castration is thus presented as a violation of an overpowered victim, not as just punishment for Abelard's own act of perceived violation.

Castration was often used as a punishment for crimes against the orderly traffic in women, where specific configurations of patriarchal culture are maintained by men controlling other men's access to women by strict adherence to class and rank. Fulbert would have assumed the rights of ownership over Heloise's body, and thus the castration of Abelard would have been an act of power over Abelard for violating the traffic laws. Abelard's narrative is thus closely parallel to the story of the Nun of Watton: Heloise's consent or agency is irrelevant to the perceived violation avenged by her relatives. But there is an interesting turn here. The castrators or violators themselves are both blinded and castrated, a type of humiliation found in war and judicial uses of castration, and the servant is singled out for being a traitor, the very crime Abelard feels guilty of in his betrayal of Fulbert.

Abelard's commentary on this event is also revealing in his attempt to displace the trauma onto a narrative of moral and spiritual development. He relates that he had more pain from witnessing the outpowering of grief and sympathy from his students and feeling shame and humiliation than from the physical harm to his body.[36] While inserting this episode into the larger frame of a deserved fall, Abelard lets other realizations slip through. He calls the injury *hec singularis infamia*, this extraordinary or unique disgrace, which would make him a monstrous spectacle to everyone.[37] He then recalls the cruel letter of the biblical law against eunuchs, who are forbidden to enter a church as if unclean.[38]

The narrative of his second emasculation, his condemnation and book burning at the Council of Soissons in 1121, is even more revealing for Abelard's sense of masculinity. This scene is the narrative epicenter of the letter, a scene where Abelard extends the elision of castration and rape for powerful rhetorical effects. Abelard's political enemies staged a deceptive hearing on his book, *On the Unity and Trinity of God*, which turned into an illegal trial on his beliefs. It's clear that this council had only one purpose—stripping Abelard of his authority and reputation, a social and political emasculation. At the end of the lengthy narrative of the conflicts and events at this council—the story takes up two large sections in the letter—Abelard concludes with a rhetorical crescendo in which he not only employs the language of rape and castration, but chooses a female exemplum to identify with.[39] First, he was forced to perform what he describes as a self-emasculation: "without any questioning or discussion they compelled me to throw my book into the fire with my own hands (*propria manu*)."[40] Abelard's libidinal investment in his book clearly marks it as an extension of his own body as well as his inner masculine *virtus*. Then Abelard deploys the counter-discourse of the feminine, which uses the victimization to unmask an injustice parading as self-evident authority. At the moment in the narrative when Abelard could have chosen any exemplum, Samson perhaps, he represents himself as identifying with Susanna, an exemplum of an innocent woman facing male accusers. Abelard constructs a drama where Geoffrey, Bishop of Chartres, his defender at the council, cites Susanna as an exemplum for the current trial:

> audacter ille restit, et quasi Danielis verba commemorans, ait: 'Sic fatui, filii Israel non judicantes, neque quod verum est cognoscentes, condempnastis filium Israel.... divina hodie misericordia innocentem patenter, sicut olim Susannam a falsis accusatoribus, liberante.'[41]

> He boldly stood his ground, and recalling the words of Daniel, said, '"Are you such fools, sons of Israel, to condemn a daughter of Israel, not examining nor learning what the truth is?"...Today, with the help of divine mercy, set free one who is clearly innocent, just as Susanna was freed from her false accusers.'

Abelard clearly identifies with Susanna as an innocent victim of the false accusations of men. It is remarkable that in the central of scene of his social emasculation he represents himself as a feminized victim.

Having been feminized before the Council, Abelard further relates that the authorities reduced him to the level of a child, requiring him to recite the Athanasian Creed to prove his orthodoxy. For additional humiliation, they even supplied him with a text of the creed, in case he had forgotten it—a creed every child knows by heart. He recited the creed through tears and sobs and was then sent back to the monastery where he had been staying. The humiliation experienced through this thorough emasculation was total: Abelard states that the pain suffered at the trial was inexpressible and far worse than his physical castration. The silencing and book-burning is finally described more like a rape than a castration:

> et longe amplius fame quam corporis detrimentum plangebam, cum ad illam ex aliqua culpa devenerim, ad hanc me tam patentem violentiam sincera intentio amorque fidei nostre induxissent, que me ad scribendum compulerant.

> I wept much more for the harm done to my reputation (*fame*) than to my body (since I had come to that through some guilt); this open violence had

> come upon me only because of the purity of my intentions and love of our faith which had compelled me to write.[42]

This event is both the central episode in the narrative and the turning point in the letter for self-representation. Although Abelard appropriates the subject position of the feminine elsewhere in the letter, after the narrative of his humiliation at the Council of Soissons he shifts to an identification with a different masculine image, Origen and Jerome, who became, in medieval cultural symbolization, paternal and almost asexual authorities who directed communities of women and retained phallic power while denying the sexual use of the penis (through self-castration and chastity). Abelard quotes or uses exempla from Jerome nine times after his account of his emasculation at Soissons, a clear indication of his shift in identity.[43]

The remainder of the letter is a narrative of the assaults of Abelard's enemies, his wanderings, and his attempt to find peace through the sisters of the Paraclete. He states that he finds Heloise and her sisters to be a haven of peace and their weakness, as a community of women, a strength.[44] Abelard's ego-ideal at the close of the letter is that of father, the paternal provider of a community of daughters, Heloise's convent of the Paraclete.[45]

But Abelard's letter was only the beginning of an eight-year campaign (c. 1132-1140) to reinvent himself and demonstrate his inner masculinity. It is important to note that nearly all of Abelard's major works were written after his castration and during the 1130s, the decade of Abelard's remasculinization project.[46] The project is announced in the first letter to an unnamed friend, and continues with his commentaries, the *Theologia christiana*, the *Dialogus*, the *Ethics* (known also as *Scito te ipsum*, or *Know Yourself*), and his famous guide to disputation questions, *Sic et non*. I'd like to conclude by advancing a hypothesis that Abelard, stung by the satire and personal attacks of enemies like Fulco and Roscelin and resisting the social position constructed for him, sought to defend himself by an apology for the masculine intellect in his *Dialogue of a Philosopher with a Jew and a Christian*.[47] The *Dialogue* can be read as part of Abelard's second siege on Paris and it marks a complete revoking of the victimized feminine position that he used for rhetorical ends in his first letter. In this work Abelard represents himself as an arbiter of all philosophical and religious arguments, a supreme Christian *philosophus*, embodying a wholeness that transcends the body. Like the other works of this period, it is a demonstration, a performance, of masculine *ingenium* or force of intellect.

The *Dialogue* was probably written between 1136-1139, a time of great literary activity for Abelard and a moment of renewed intellectual influence before his final political emasculation by Bernard of Clairvaux at the infamous Council of Sens (1140). During these years, Abelard had returned to teaching in Paris and was also writing to Heloise, collaborating on the building of the Paraclete community, and reinventing his identity as an authoritative teacher. Written shortly after his *Theologia Christiana* and shortly before his *Ethics*, the *Dialogue* can be read as part of an intellectual and moral defense addressed to the academic community centered at Paris.[48]

The dialogue is framed by an attempt to reconcile natural law and Christian ethics, and the greater part of the work is devoted to a synthesis of classical and Christian approaches to the human virtues.[49] But the first part of the dialogue is a discussion of the Jewish law and the meaning of circumcision. Since so much of the Philosopher's dialogue with the Jew is concerned with circumcision, we can read here an anxiety about genital privation and emasculation refracted onto a debate about law, the sign of circumcision, and the hierarchy of mind and soul over body.

Abelard represents the Jew defending the Law based on its difficulty: "Who would not abhor or fear to receive the very sacrament of our circumcision on account of both the shame and the pain? What part of the human body is as tender as the one on which the Law inflicts its wound and also on small infants themselves?"[50] Answering the Philosopher's attack on the irrationality of circumcision, the Jew defends circumcision as a *signum*, God's indelible mark on the body of his people: the sign of circumcision is so abhorrent to the gentiles that if Jews tried to win over their women, none of the women would give their consent, believing that the truncating of this member is the height of foulness.[51] Circumcision is a *signum*, a mark or sign inscribed on the body; once done it cannot be undone (*aboleri iam non potest*). Jews are sanctified to the Lord through the member and instrument of generation, and removing the front part of this member symbolizes an internal cutting off from the beliefs and practices of the Chaldeans.[52] Abelard here stresses the inner, spiritual, and mental state, which he argues is more important than the wholeness of the body.

Abelard then represents the Jew explaining circumcision in a series of body tropes: male believers are like a vineyard (Is. 5.2), and their genitalia are shoots of the vines that need pruning to prevent the yield of wild grapes. Circumcision is also God's punishment in the male genitals equivalent to female pain in childbirth. Whereas women suffer in the same member where they have the pleasure of sex, men suffer *in genitali membro*, in the same part that produced children who will die. (It is interesting that in this context Abelard assigns both sexual pleasure and pain in childbirth to women, but simply the agency of generation to men without a reference to pleasure or lust.) The Jew continues his defense with an account of the rewards promised to the people marked by circumcision, which the Philosopher counters and refutes by proving that the Jew's religion is all outward laws and not properly focused on the state of the soul and salvation.

In the second part of the dialogue, the Philosopher defends a philosophical *voluptas*, not the enjoyment of carnal enticements but a certain inner peace of the soul (*quadam interiorem animae tranquillitatem*).[53] Since the Philosopher functions as Abelard's persona, this affirmation of inner peace as the goal of philosophy can be read as nothing less than Abelard's attempt to transcend external and bodily deprivations. Inner peace of the soul comes from control of the flesh (*domandae carnis exercitium*)[54] and the removal of suffering (*ab omni passione immunis*).[55] Concerning bodily suffering itself, the Philosopher asserts that suffering in itself produces no further virtue: "for it would not be proper that anything that pertains to bodily peace or affliction should increase or diminish our happiness if virtue keeps the mind in the same intention."[56] The Philosopher is thus Abelard's other ego-ideal, an imagined wholeness, self-absorbed in philosophical *voluptas*. The Philosopher represents the transcendence of the male body through masculine *ingenium*; he is the triumph of gender over sex.

Abelard's dialogue can thus be read as an explicit statement of his ongoing project of remasculinization. The attacks by the likes of Roscelin and Fulco are rendered impotent in the face of Abelard's superior intellect and force of argument. For Abelard, the male body is only a shell for the masculine intellect, and the wholeness of one's mind and soul transcend the physical state of the body. Abelard spent nearly two decades fashioning new images of wholeness, new substitutes for the social body he was never invited to rejoin. But throughout his career, Abelard clearly advanced a performative model of masculinity: a man is he who acts like a man, using superior intellect, the power of dialectic, and written discourse as the ultimate tools of masculine power and self-definition.

NOTES

1. The name of Abelard's letter to a friend, used twice by Heloise in her first letter to Abelard, is *ad amicum pro consolatione epistola.* References to this letter and to Heloise's first letter are from the edition by Jacques Monfrin, *Historia calamitatum* (Paris: Vrin, 1962). I will also supply page references to the widely used Penguin translation by Betty Radice, *The Letters of Abelard and Heloise* (London and New York: Penguin, 1974). For Heloise's references to what we call the *Historia calamitatum,* see Monfrin, pp. 111 and 114. Abelard and Heloise encode their letters with the genre conventions of twelfth-century culture. For background, see my article, "Heloise and the Gendering of the Literate Subject," in Rita Copeland, ed., *Criticism and Dissent in the Middle Ages* (Cambridge: Cambridge University Press, 1996): 87–114.

2. But see R. Howard Bloch, *Etymologies and Genealogies: A Literary Anthropology of the French Middle Ages* (Chicago: University of Chicago Press, 1983), Chap. 4, "Poetry, Philosophy, and Desire," 128–58.

3. In my reading of Abelard's works, I am especially indebted to the following studies: Peter Dronke, *Abelard and Heloise in Medieval Testimonies* (Glasgow: University of Glasgow Press, 1976); D. E. Luscombe, *The School of Peter Abelard* (Cambridge: Cambridge University Press, 1969); *Peter Abelard's Ethics*(Oxford: Oxford University Press, 1971), and "From Paris to the Paraclete: The Correspondence of Abelard and Heloise," *Proceedings of the British Academy* 74 (1988): 247–83; Barbara Newman, "Authority, Authenticity, and the Repression of Heloise," *Journal of Medieval and Renaissance Studies* 22/2 (1992): 121–57; René Louis and Jean Jolivet, eds., *Pierre Abélard—Pierre le Vénérable: Les Courants philosophiques, littéraires et artistiques en Occident au milieu du XIIe siècle*, Colloques internationaux du Centre National de la Recherches Scientifiques, 1975 (Paris: CNRS, 1975); and Rudolf Thomas, ed., *Petrus Abaelardus, Trierer theologische Studien*, Bd. 38 (Trier: Paulinus, 1980).

4. My thinking on the historically dynamic approach to gender and subjectivity has been informed by several recent articulations of theory and historical research, of which I consider the following to be exemplary: Judith Butler, *Gender Trouble: Feminism and the Subversion of Identity* (New York: Routledge, 1990) and *Bodies that Matter: On the Discursive Limits of*

'Sex' (New York: Routledge, 1993); Joan Scott, "Gender: A Useful Category of Historical Analysis," in *Gender and the Politics of History* (New York: Columbia University Press, 1988); Michel Foucault, *The History of Sexuality: An Introduction* (New York: Pantheon, 1978); Thomas Laqueur, *Making Sex: The Body and Gender from the Greeks to Freud* (Cambridge, Mass.: Harvard University Press, 1990); Domna C. Stanton, ed., *Discourses of Sexuality: From Aristotle to AIDS* (Ann Arbor: U of Michigan P, 1992). A full bibliography on gender and sexuality can be found in Jonathan Dollimore, *Sexual Dissidence: Augustine to Wilde, Freud to Foucault* (Oxford: Clarendon Press, 1991). On the implications of gender and sexuality theory for medieval studies research, see Nancy Partner, ed., *Studying Medieval Women* (Cambridge, Mass.: Medieval Academy of America, 1993) and Partner's essay in this collection, "No Sex, No Gender," pp. 117–41, and the papers presented at the Cultural Frictions Conference at Georgetown University, October 1995, available through the Labyrinth Website on the Internet (http://www.georgetown.edu/labyrinth/conf/cs95/).

5. See John W. Baldwin, *The Language of Sex: Five Voices from Northern France around 1200* (Chicago: University of Chicago Press, 1994) and Michel Foucault, *History of Sexuality*. See also Sarah Kay, "Women's Body of Knowledge: Epistemology and Misogyny in the *Romance of the Rose*," in Sarah Kay and Miri Rubin, eds., *Framing Medieval Bodies* (Manchester and New York: Manchester University Press, 1994), 211–35.

6. On Guibert, see George Duby, *The Knight, The Lady, and The Priest*, Barbara Bray, trans. (New York: Pantheon, 1983): 139–159, and John F. Benton, ed., *Self and Society in Medieval France: The Memoirs of Abbot Guibert of Nogent* (New York: Harper and Row, 1970).

7. See the references in James A. Brundage, *Law, Sex, and Christian Society in Medieval Europe* (Chicago: Chicago University Press, 1987), General Index, s.v. "castration."

8. The text, *De sanctimoniali de Wattun*, is printed with Aelred's other works in *PL* 195: 789–96. For an historical analysis, see Giles Constable, "Aelred of Rievaulx and the Nun of Watton," in Derek Baker, ed., *Medieval Women* (Oxford: Blackwell, 1978), 205–26.

9. *Datur ei in manibus instrumentum, ac propriis manibus virum abscidere invita compellitur. Tunc una de astantibus, arreptis quibus ille fuerat relevatus, sicut etant foeda sanguine in ora peccatricis projecit. PL* 195: 793–94. It's clear from the story that a castration of the testicles alone was performed. It should be noted that this episode of violated chastity and revenge through castration is framed within a miracle story: shortly after returning to her cell and chained by her sisters, the nun not only had her chains miraculously loosed from her arms, but the child she was carrying was no longer there.

10. See Constable, "Aelred of Rievaulx," 214–218.

11. See Monfrin, ed., *Historia calamitatum*, p. 102; Radice, p. 99.

12. See Christiane Klapisch-Zuber, ed. *A History of Women in the West, II. Silences of the Middle Ages* (Cambridge, Mass.: Harvard University Press, 1992), 204, 225.

13. On castration in the French fabliau, see R. Howard Bloch, *The Scandal of the Fabliau* (Chicago: University of Chicago Press, 1986), 59–100.

14. A major compilation of fabliaux containing this text has been conveniently edited with an English translation by Raymond Eichmann and John Duval, *The French Fabliau B.N. MS. 837*, 2 vols. (New York: Garland, 1985); vol. 2, 62–67.

15. See David Hult, "Language and Dismemberment: Abelard, Origen, and the *Romance of the Rose*," in Kevin Brownlee and Sylvia Huot, eds., *Rethinking the Romance of the Rose: Text, Image Reception* (Philadelphia: University of Pennsylvania Press, 1992): 101–130.

16. *Roman*, ll. 8766–68. Cited from the edition of Félix Lecoy, *Le Roman de la Rose*, Les Classiques Francais de Moyen Âge, 3 vols. (Paris: Champion, 1965–70). English translation is from Charles Dahlberg, *The Romance of the Rose* (Princeton: Princeton University Press, 1971): 329–30.

17. *Roman*, ll. 20007–20044. Trans. Dahlberg, 329–330.

18. Printed in *PL* 178: 357–372. For a modern critical edition of Roscelin's letter, see J. Reiners, *Der Nominalismus in der Frühscholastik* (Beiträge zur Geschichte der Philosophie und der Theologie des Mittelalters, 8) (Münster, 1910), 63–80. Quotations are from Reiners' edition with references to corresponding columns in *PL*.

19. Roscelin's letter assumes that Abelard is still a new monk at the abbey of St. Denis. Abelard entered the monastery in 1119. See Reiners, 79; *PL* 178: 370.

20. Sed valde tibi divina metuenda est iustitia, ne, sicut cauda, quae prius, dum poteras, indifferenter pungebas, merito tuae immunditiae tibi ablata est, ita et lingua, qua modo pungis, auferatur. Reiners, 64. *PL* 178: 359.

21. Miseria siquidem tua iam manifesta est, et quamvis eam lingua taceant, tamen eam res ipsa clamat. Reiners, 78; *PL* 178: 369.

22. Sed eam fornicari docuisti, in uno facto multorum criminum, proditionis scilicet et fornicationis, reus et virginei pudoris violator spurcissimus. Sed *deus ultionum dominus, deus ultionum libere agit* [Luke 16.22, 24], qui ea qua tantum parte peccaveras te privavit. Reiners, 78; *PL* 178: 369.

23. The following incomplete sentence, omitted from the edition of the letter in *PL* 178, is found in Reiners' edition: "Amodo enim neutri generis abiectionem, sicut et suum significatum, penet…, et cum hominem integrum consueverit, dimidum forsitan significare recusabit." Reiners finds damage to the text or faulty transmission (Reiners, 80, note 13).

24. Reiners, 80; *PL* 178: 371–372.

25. Fulco's letter, which was included in some later manuscripts of the collected letters of Abelard and Heloise, is printed as Epistola XVI in *PL* 178: 371–76. Migne refused to print the explicit conclusion of this letter, for which see D. Van den Eynde, "Détails biographiques sur Pierre Abélard," *Antonianum* 38 (1963): 217–20. On the satire in the letter, see Peter Dronke, *Abelard and Heloise in Medieval Testimonies* (Glasgow: University of Glasgow Press, 1976), 26–27. Many readers have mistaken this letter for a genuine consolation. Perhaps it was intended as a travesty or parody of Abelard's own first letter of consolation to a friend.

26. *PL* 178: 373–74.

27. Plangit ergo hoc tuum vulnus et damnum venerabilis episcopi benignitas, qui, quantum licuit, vacare iustitiae studuit. Plangit liberalium canonicorum ac nobilium clericorum multitudo. Plangunt cives, civitatis hoc dedecus reputantes, et dolentes suam urbem tui sanguinis effusione violari. (*PL* 178: 374).

28. *PL* 178: 374.

29. *PL* 178: 367.

30. Dripping with irony: "Sodomitarum secretos recessus, quos detestatur super omnes turpissimos divinae iustitiae veritas, et eorum turpia et maligna consortia, quae quidem semper odisti, de caetero to sine intermissione vitare verum est." *PL* 178: 373.

31. See Bernard's letters, nos. 187–189, 192, *PL* 182: 349–359.

32. See Letter 192, *PL* 182: 358.

33.See Mark Amsler, "Genre and Code in Abelard's *Historia calamitatum*," *Assays* 1 (1981): 35–50.

34. See Monfrin, ed., *Historia calamitatum*, pp. 71–75; Radice, pp. 65–70.

35. Monfrin, ed., *Historia calamitatum*, p.79, 581–87; Radice, p. 75.

36. Monfrin, ed., *Historia calamitatum*, p. 80; Radice, p. 75.

37. Monfrin, ed., *Historia calamitatum*, p. 80; Radice, p. 76.

38. Abelard cites Lev. 22.24 and Deut. 23.1; see Monfrin, ed., *Historia calamitatum*, p. 80; Radice, p. 76.

39. Monfrin, ed., *Historia calamitatum*, pp. 82–90; Radice, pp. 78–86. Radice did not retain the section headings that appear in most of the manuscripts of the letter, but they are in Monfrin's edition. I believe these headings were used in the scriptorium of Heloise's convent, which preserved the letters.

40. Monfrin, ed., *Historia calamitatum*, pp. 87–88; Radice, p. 83.

41. Monfrin, ed., *Historia calamitatum*, p. 88; Radice, p. 83. Abelard portrays Geoffrey of Chartes citing Daniel 13.48–49, part of the apocryphal addition to Daniel containing the story of Susanna.

42. Monfrin, ed., *Historia calamitatum*, p. 89, 923–27; Radice, pp. 84–85.

43. Abelard cites the following works or exempla: Jerome's *Contra Jovinianum* 8–9 (Monfrin, ed., *Historia calamitatum*, pp. 92–93; Radice, p.

89); *Epist.* 125.7 (Monfrin, ed., *Historia calamitatum*, pp. 93–94; Radice, pp. 89–90); *Liber heb. Quaest. in Genesim* (Monfrin, ed., *Historia calamitatum*, p. 94; Radice, p. 90); comparison to Jerome being driven East by the jealousy of the Romans (Monfrin, ed., *Historia calamitatum*, p. 98; Radice, p. 94); *Epist.* 45 (2 quotations) (Monfrin, ed., *Historia calamitatum*, pp. 101–102; Radice, pp. 98); *Vita S. Malchi* (Monfrin, ed., *Historia calamitatum*, p. 104; Radice, p. 101); *Epist.* 52, 45, and 14 (Monfrin, ed., *Historia calamitatum*, p. 108; Radice, p. 105).

44. Monfrin, ed., *Historia calamitatum*, p. 105; Radice, p. 102.

45. On Heloise's relationship with Abelard through the Paraclete community, see my "Heloise and the Gendering of the Literate Subject," in Rita Copeland, ed., *Criticism and Dissent in the Middle Ages* (Cambridge: Cambridge University Press, 1996): 87–114.

46. See Damien van den Eynde, "Chronologie des écrits d'Abélard à Heloïse," *Antonianum* 37 (1962): 337–49, and D. E. Luscombe, *The School of Peter Abelard* (Cambridge: Cambridge University Press, 1969).

47. Rudolf Thomas, ed., *Petrus Abelardus, Dialogus inter Philosophum, Iudaeum et Christianum.* Stuttgart-Bad Cannstatt: F. Frommann, 1970. An inferior edition can also be found in *PL* 178: 1609–1684. For a translation, see Pierre J. Payer, *Peter Abelard, A Dialogue of a Philosopher with a Jew and a Christian* (Toronto: Pontifical Institute of Medieval Studies, 1979).

48. Earlier scholars tried to associate the dialogue with Peter Abelard's final years when he was given refuge at Cluny by Peter the Venerable. See Rudolf Thomas, "Die Persönlichkeit Peter Abelards im 'Dialogus inter Philosophum, Iudaeum et Christianum' und in den Epistulae des Petrus Venerabilis," in René Louis and Jean Jolivet, eds., *Pierre Abélard—Pierre le Vénérable: Les Courants philosophiques, littéraires et artistiques en Occident au milieu du XIIe siècle* (Paris: CNRS, 1975): 255–69, and the studies cited there. For the historical context of the dialogue, see David E. Luscombe, *Peter Abelard's Ethics* (Oxford: Clarendon Press, 1971): xxvi–xxvii.

49. See Luscombe, *Peter Abelard's Ethics*, xxiv–xxx.

50. Quis non ipsum circumcisionis nostrae sacramentum, cum ex erubescentia tum ex poena, suscipere non abhorreat aut trepidet? Quae tam tenera humani corporis portio, quam illa, cui hanc plagam in ipsis quoque infantulis lex infligit? *PL* 178: 1618D.

51. *PL* 178: 1623D.

52. et a praecedente sua Chaldeorum in fidelium origine, ita moribus se amputent, sicut primam illius membri partem a se removerunt. *PL* 178: 1624.

53. *PL* 178: 1642A; cf. 1644C–D.

54. *PL* 178: 1642.

55. *PL* 178: 1643.

56. Absit enim ut quaecunque ad corporalem vel quietem vel afflictionem pertinent beatitudinem nostram vel augeant vel minuant, si in eodem proposito vitus mentem custodiat. *PL* 178: 1643.

ORIGENARY FANTASIES: ABELARD'S CASTRATION AND CONFESSION[1]

Bonnie Wheeler

This essay argues that Abelard essentializes his own masculinity as an intellectual, not a physical, capacity or prowess, and thus his castration serves to enhance and fulfill his strategies of claiming authoritative status as magisterial philosopher. Heloise colludes with him in this project.

> Virga haec est patris, non gladius persecutoris.
> *This is a father's rod, not a persecutor's sword.*
> *Letter 4*, Abelard to Heloise

> Sublata igitur parte quae hominem facit non Petrus, sed imperfectus Petrus appellandus es.
> *Since therefore the part which makes a man has been taken away, you should be called not 'Peter' but 'defective Peter.'*
> Roscelin of Compiègne

Rhetoric is the battleground and dialectic the weapon for the 'voices' of Abelard and Heloise,[2] who in the cycle of their letters inscribe sequences of multiple and competitive positions from the rich treasurehouse of theological and classical sources they share, continually appropriate, and re-script.[3] In this shifting debate about their proper roles in relation to each other,[4] there is a singular inflexible assumption about personhood: the castrated Abelard is immutably masculine.

Abelard and Heloise's discourse, as studies of Abelard's *Historia calamitatum* and the preserved Abelard-Heloise correspondence have taught us, is a sequence of taut and powerful rhetorical performances as scandalous as it is revelatory.[5] Multiple narrative structures overlap the facts of the couple's stories. They adumbrate the potentialities and impasses of the early twelfth century in the Paris region, a time marked by strides toward and resistance to institutionalization and standardization in the intellectual, political, economic, and social *milieux*. Just as Bernard of Clairvaux's tracts insist upon paradoxical entanglements, so, too, the Abelard-Heloise correspondence is constructed of contraries and engages the imbrications of, for example, public with private, innovation with profound conservatism, confession with repression.

Their discourse, I argue, manufactures and memorializes Abelard's masculinity. Abelard and Heloise collude to mythologize his masculinity, to sunder his gender from his sex and his sexuality. In resistance to and independent of his castration, Abelard asserts a fixed masculinity that inspires unending feminine desire and the relentless envy of other men. This fixed representation of Abelard's masculinity stands in opposition to the rifts their correspondence exposes in their malleable understandings of female sex and gender roles.[6] It stands in equal opposition to the record of sexual taunts hurled at Abelard in the aftermath of his castration. The voices of Abelard and Heloise project an Abelard so irreducibly male that even castration does not imperil his gender. They assert a masculinity in which mind substitutes for body, in which *intellectual* domination (even violence) extends *physical* domination. Though I have elsewhere argued that Abelard and Heloise pursued a strategy of re-masculinization after his castration,[7] further consideration of the Abelardian *corpus* and the Abelard-Heloise correspondence leads me to conclude that Abelardian discourse is rooted in and celebrates an essentialized, immutable Abelardian masculinity. Gender is privileged above sex, even eradicates sexual identity, so that Abelardian masculinity is frozen in a rhetoric of being, not becoming.

THE FATHER'S ROD

Abelard's *Historia calamitatum* is a tantalizing document, purportedly a twelfth-century autobiography guised as a private letter of consolation.[8] Among the wide-ranging rhetorical modes subsumed in Abelard's letter are those of confession, both as formal Augustinian structure and as spiritual discipline. In part, Abelard deploys his life narrative to assert the distinctiveness of his philosophical and theological arguments, voicing and craftily summarizing even those arguments contained in texts that had officially been banned and burned.[9] He manages to claim, retain, stamp, and propel into the future even those ideas he was required to consign to the flames. The *Historia calamitatum* is a skilled, dense, complex, and aggressive confession of a life and of a life's work designed to engage the sympathies of the reader—and not just the reader's sympathy. Foucault reminds us how tricky confessions are, since readers of confessions become complicit with their writers: to confess requires to some degree absolution from the reader who is the recipient of the writer's secrets. Confession is "the effect of a power that constrains us,"[10] a ritual that always "unfolds within a power relationship," and the listener is "a partner who is not simply the interlocutor but the authority who requires the confession, prescribes and appreciates it, and intervenes in order to judge, punish, forgive, console, and reconcile."[11] It is not surprising that Abelard claims to be consoling the un-named friend to whom he addresses his autobiographical letter. His strategy is psychically coercive; it diminishes the experience of the Other as it enhances the importance of the speaker : "ut in comparatione mearum tuas aut nullas aut modicas temptationes recognoscas et tolerabilius feras." [when you compare your trials to mine you may consider them of little or no account and be stronger to endure them.][12]

What does Abelard confess, for what does he show remorse, seek forgiveness, or provide consolation?

> Cum igitur totus in superbia atque luxuria laborarem, utriusque morbi remedium divina mihi gratia licet nolenti contulit. Ac primo luxurie, deinde superbie; luxurie quidem his me privando quibus hanc exercebam; superbie vero que mihi ex litterarum maxime scientia nascebatur, juxta illud Apostoli 'Scientia inflat', illius libri quo maxime gloriabar combustione me humiliando.

> And while I was laboring under my pride and lechery, God's grace provided a cure for each, though I willed it not, first for my lechery by depriving me of the organs by which I practised it, then for my pride which my scholarship especially nursed in me in accordance with the saying of St. Paul: *Knowledge puffs up*. This was accomplished by humiliating me through the burning of the book which was my special glory.[13]

Here he prefaces the story of his lechery with a seemingly parallel admission of his intellectual pride. Physically and psychically—through his books and his body—Abelard was punished, but his confession *qua* remorse is limited to his regret for his physical lusts. His castration absorbs his capacity for remorse. His narrative is cast in terms of intention and result, in terms of cause and effect, and in terms of confession and forgiveness. Abelard insists upon the deliberate, calculated quality of his seduction of Heloise. Although he definitively withdrew from physical combat, the traditional site of masculine subjectivity, his most visible trophy for his verbal performance and confirmation of his masculine identity is nevertheless stereotypical: it is the possession of a woman. He is hounded by his desire to subjugate and contain the Other. Lust for knowledge is temporarily displaced by lust for women, and each reveals in turn his drive for the power and subjugation that are crucial foundations of patriarchal subjectivity and display. Abelard later uses the metonym of his sexual member and its lust as full, objective embodiment of his various concupiscences. He *willed* his sins of the flesh. Those sins found perfect penitential compensation in the mutilation of his body, the excision of his sex. Ironically he suffers wounds as real as any warrior, any devotee of Mars. Abelard tells his always horrified readers that:

> Unde vehementer indignati et adversum me coniurati, nocte quadam quiescentem me atque dormientem in secreta hospicii mei camera, quodam mihi serviente per pecuniam corrupto, crudelissima et pudentissima ultione punierunt, et quam summa ammiratione mundus excepit, eis videlicet corporis mei partibus amputatis quibus id quod plangebant commiseram. Quibus mox in fugam conversis, duo qui comprehendi potuerunt oculis et genitalibus privati sunt, quorum alter ille fuit supradictus serviens qui, cum in obsequio meo mecum maneret, cupiditate ad proditionem ductus est.

> They became strongly incensed against me and formed a conspiracy. One night when I was sound asleep in an inner room of my lodgings, by bribing my attendant they wrought vengeance upon me in a *most* cruel and *most* shameful manner and one which the world with great astonishment abhorred, namely, they cut off *the parts of my body* by which I had committed the deed which they deplored. They immediately fled but *the two who could be* caught had their eyes put out and were castrated; one of them was my servant already mentioned who while in my service was brought by greed to betray me.[14]

In this heightened passage, full of superlatives, Abelard represents himself as a victim of those who act in a "most cruel and most shameful manner," and as victim he solicits sympathy from his audience. He interrupts the narrative flow to pair and bracket the crime committed against him with the subsequent punishment of the perpetrators: their crime inexorably leads to their punishment. This exact completion of this causal chain seems an ironically and excessively neat (as well as emphatically Old-Law) closure for the philosopher who is a foundational proponent of intentional ethics. He moves swiftly from the horror of his bodily victimization to the problem of his humiliation. The move from somatics to sentiment (or, rather, refusal to be sentimental) typifies Abelard's strategy of rhetorical displacement:

> Maxime vero clerici ac precipue scolares nostri intolerabilibus me lamentis et ejulatibus cruciabant, ut multo amplius ex eorum compassione quam ex vulneris lederer passione, et plus erubescentiam quam plagam sentirem, et pudore magis quam dolore affligerer.
>
> The clerics and especially my students by their excessive lamentation and wailing pained me so that I endured more from their expressions of sympathy than from the suffering caused by the mutilation.[15]

The castration narrative is cloistered within the humiliation narrative, which maintains Abelard's primary focus on his reputation and his renown. His castration is represented as precise retributive justice. His crime led to his punishment:

> Occurrebat animo quanta modo gloria pollebam, quam facili et turpi casu hec humiliata, immo penitus esset extincta, quam justo Dei judicio in illa corporis mei portione plecterer in qua deliqueram; quam justa proditione is quem antea prodideram vicem mihi retulisset; quanta laude mei emuli tam manifestam equitatem efferent...
>
> I fell into thinking how great had been my renown and in how easy and base a way this had been brought low and utterly destroyed; how by a just judgment of God I had been afflicted in that part of my body by which I had sinned; how just was the betrayal by which he whom I had first betrayed paid me back; how my rivals would extol such a fair retribution...[16]

Here Abelard limits his admission of transgression to sexual concupiscence and its effects.[17] Though he confesses his own crime and argues that restitution was achieved when his body was mutilated, he nevertheless encapsulates his sin in a moral and intellectual cocoon. His concupiscence narrative—the story of his desire for a woman—had a beginning, middle, and end. When he is castrated, desire itself dies. His lust for Heloise is ended. Castration as restitution provides a major trope of reversal, in which Abelard recuperates himself fully by being severed from his penis. This lack—the core of all desire, in Lacan's terms—makes the castrated Abelard whole. Appropriate restitution is achieved at the expense of bodily integrity. Abelard then proceeds as if the matters both of his restitution and his confession are fully resolved by his castration, even if they are complicated by the degree of his public shame: "In tam misera me contritione positum, confusio, fateor, pudoris potius quam devotio conversionis ad monastichorum latibula claustrorum compulit." [Filled as I was with such remorse, it was, I confess, confusion springing from shame rather than devotion the result of conversion, which drove me to the refuge of monastic cloister.][18]

Abelard's castration narrative is notoriously evasive. He claims that castration was appropriate as his punishment, yet he finds it acceptable for his castrators to be punished. If justice required that the servants who castrated him be punished, why was it not necessary that Fulbert, who propelled the castration plot, be punished equally? Eliding and avoiding these matters allows Abelard to cast his castration as an appropriate and complete act of Old-Law vengeance. Yet confession in Abelard's time—and from his own pen—had come to focus not on external acts but on the importance of internal sorrow.[19] "Sin is remitted," said Pope Alexander III, "by contrition of the heart."[20] Remission required not simply correction, but full and sincere confession that required inner contrition. Abelard is unflinchingly aware of the tendency toward emotional/rhetorical insincerity and of the danger of confusing "correction" with repentance. Abelard's own hymn on penance and the Magdalene written for the Paraclete community is instructive here:

> Paenitentum severa correptio
> Et eorum longa satisfactio
> Crebris carnem edomant ieiuniis
> Asperisque cruciant ciliciis
> Et eiectos ab ecclesia
> Confundit erubescentia.
>
> In hac nihil actum est hoc ordine
> Mitiorem sensit Deum homine,
> Rex et iudex idem legem temperat
> Nec attendit, qui cor vere iudicat,
> Tam temporis longitudinem
> Quam doloris magnitudinem.

Penitents' severe correction when they pay long satisfaction tames the flesh, with their frequent fasts and with their hair-shirts' cruel rasps. Those expelled from the church will know what it is shame to undergo. But the saint did not suffer thus, finding God gentler far than us, for the Judge uses equity, nor does God who all hearts can see, value more a long-lasting sentence than a true sorrowful repentance. [21]

Abelard states that "remorse...confusion [and] shame...drove me to the refuge of monastic cloister." Naming remorse, he claims remorse. By claiming remorse, he claims to fulfill the final requirement for forgiveness, since he thus adds requisite contrition to the "full and sincere confession" constituted by the text of the *Historia* itself, and to the restitution—the literal, bodily mutilation of the sexual member. His sin of lust is thus by these terms fully penanced. At the same time, the castration narrative engulfs his admitted, more deeply serious sin, the problem of his professional and intellectual pride. There is no Augustininan personal humility woven into the humiliation narrative.

In equating physical retribution with moral restitution, Abelard invokes a profoundly external system of confessional discipline. The loss of the 'rod' or 'sword' of his manhood is God's direct vengeance as much as Fulbert's. It is, as Abelard says, the good and proper punishment required by the Father: "Virga haec est patris, non gladius persecutoris." [This is a father's rod, not a persecutor's sword.][22]

Abelard's willingness to speak his guilt and announce his penance is tricky. There is a rapacious aggressor hiding in this figure of Abelard *qua* recuperated sinner. His confession is as much a boast of his sustained power as an admission of his physical lack. From the inception of the *Historia calamitatum*, Abelard majestically and deviously recasts his readers' understanding of masculinity as a particular kind of intellectual performance rather than as a sexual or physical capacity. His definitions of the masculine are unconventional, located not in terms of sexual organs or sexual potency nor in terms of warrior prowess, but rather in terms of intellectual swordplay. The form of competition that he finds integral to his brand of masculine identity is dialectic and disputation. Abelard arms himself with knowledge of dialectics in order to prevail in intellectual competition; he deploys the language of warfare, demonstrating the link between conflict and masculine identity. As long as the masculine subject is in open conflict with others, declaring war on opposing factions, his identity is complete. Masculinity itself is established from the beginning of the *Historia calamitatum* as intellectual rather than physical prowess:

> Ego vero quanto amplius et facilius in studio litterarum profeci tanto ardentius eis inhesi, et in tanto earum amore illectus sum ut militaris glorie pompam cum hereditate et prerogativa primogenitorum meorum fratribus derelinquens, Martis curie penitus abdicarem ut Minerve gremio educarer; et quoniam dialecticarum rationum armaturam omnibus philosophie documentis pretuli, his armis alia commutavi et tropheis bellorum conflictus pretuli disputationum.
>
> The further I went in my studies and the more easily I made progress, the more I became attached to them and came to possess such a love of them that, giving up in favor of my brothers the pomp of military glory along with my right of inheritance and the other prerogatives of primogeniture, I renounced the *court* of Mars to be brought up *in the lap* of Minerva. Since I preferred the armor of logic to all the teaching of philosophy, I exchanged all other arms for it and chose the contests of disputation above the trophies of warfare.[23]

Abelard, like Andreas Capellanus, defines language as the zone of gender contest and warfare. Disputatious speech is the site of masculine performance, the ground zero of masculine subjectivity. With words as weapons, Abelard garners trophies appropriate to his status as the most successful combatant until the trophy is Heloise herself. He brags that: "Tanti quippe tunc nominis eram et juventutis et forme gratia preminebam, ut quamcunque feminarum nostro dignarer amore nullam vererer repulsam." [I then enjoyed such renown and was so outstanding for my youthful charm that I feared no repulse by any woman whom I should deign to favor with my love.][24] Abelard's confidence in his easy success with Heloise shows that it is not the process of seduction that is important for his display of masculine superiority but rather the challenge of a new object of conquest, a new geography of knowledge, this time amatory. Heloise's protective uncle Fulbert occupies the third slot in this typical triangulation of desire—and had the insulted Fulbert later achieved his goal of un-manning Abelard, the organ that might more effectively have been excised was Abelard's tongue.

Abelard is very precise about the intellectual quality and requirement of his desire: Heloise is the perfect empty vessel whose brilliance justifies the efforts of the masculine subject. In godlike fashion, Abelard *is*, and he brings Heloise into being by desiring her. Abelard is also the object, a master who yearns to be yearned for; Heloise is the subject, the pupil, malleable, full of yearning and desire. Both Heloise and Abelard speak of Heloise's desire to bend to the task of understanding her teacher's mind as well as body, of directing her will entirely toward Abelard. Unlike Heloise's, Abelard's desire is neither immanent nor self-transforming.

Abelard does not grant subjectivity to the conquered Heloise. Abelard's possession of Heloise is an "honor" to her though a dishonorable slight to Fulbert. Heloise is cast in the role of pupil by both masters—her uncle and her lover—and the masculine subject is cast as instructor. But to one teacher, one pupil: like Abelard, Fulbert's masculine identity is confirmed by the ownership/ instruction of the feminine subject and is threatened by its loss.

When the lovers are caught by Fulbert, nothing could be more conventionally misogynistic than Abelard's self-defense. The gap between his traditionally anti-feminist statement and his account of his seduction of Heloise is bridged not by logic but by emotive display. He ritually invokes the primary and entire history of masculine vulnerability to the voracious, demanding female:

> nec ulli mirabile id videri asserens, quicumque vim amoris expertus fuisset, et qui quanta ruina summos quoque viros ab ipso statim humani generis exordio mulieres dejecerint memoria retineret.

> I told him that whoever had felt the force of love or recalled to what a crash women from the beginning have brought even the greatest men would not be surprised at my fall.[25]

This appeal to powerlessness—his "crash," his "fall"—masks the fact that Abelard's masculine prowess remains fixed not in Heloise's control of him but in his control of her. It is best seen in her acts of submission—first to his insistence that they marry:

> Hec et similia persuadens seu dissuadens, cum meam deflectere non posset stultitiam nec me sustineret offendere, suspirans vehementer et lacrimans perorationem suam tali fine terminavit : 'Unum, inquid, ad ultimum restat ut in perditione duorum, minor non succedat dolor quam precessit amor.' Nec in hoc ei, sicut universus agnovit mundus, prophecie defuit spiritus.

> When she could not divert me from my mad scheme by such arguments of exhortation and discussion and could not bear to offend me, she sighed deeply and in tears ended her final appeal as follows: 'If we do this, one fate finally awaits us: we shall both be ruined and sorrow will thereby pierce our hearts equal in intensity to the love with which they are now aflame.' And, as all the world knows, she was possessed of the spirit of prophecy in this statement.[26]

She submitted to all his terms—to marriage, to Abelard's subsequent requirement that she return to the community of Argenteuil, and (most infamously) to his post-castration demand that she accept full monastic vows. Her performance of perfect obedience in the spheres of private and public action secures, confirms, and protects Abelard's positive masculine identity.

After his castration, Abelard locates his "torture" (but not sin, not guilt) in the burning of his books and the loss of his good name. In an interesting rhetorical slippage, Abelard equates wholeness of his body with great riches and subordinates both to his concern for his fame. "[I] am tortured more by the loss of my reputation than I was from the mutilation of my body, for as it is written: *Better is a good name than great riches.*"[27] His intellectual work, always contested, was more frequently repudiated after the castration. Though he all but erases from mention the fruit of his loins, his son Astrolabe, Abelard emphasizes the power and persistence of his paternal mastership over his intellectual and spiritual progeny, when he tells the story of how Geoffrey, bishop of Chartres, before Abelard's treatise on the Trinity was condemned at Soissons, urged the council to consider Abelard's supporters and followers; he measures Abelard's fecundity as a "vine that extends its branches from sea to sea."[28] Abelard records Geoffrey warning the council:

> But if you are disposed to act canonically against him, have his doctrine and writings brought before us and let him have an opportunity freely to answer when questioned so that, if convicted or if he confesses, he may be utterly silenced. At least such action would be in accordance with the statement of Nicodemus who, wanting to free the Lord Himself, said: *Does our law judge a man unless it first give him a hearing and know what he does?*[29]

In Geoffrey's appeal, Abelard's teaching—the fecund impact of his intellectual and personal prowess—stands as a metonymic index of his identity, a formulation with which Abelard has been complicit from the inception of the *Historia calamitatum*. Abelard's masculine power reaches new heights in his conflicts with Alberic and Lotulf, as he is cast in the role of Jesus before the Pharisee-dominated Sanhedrin through the agency of the bishop of Chartres' rhetoric and his own narrative stance. After his castration Abelard asserts the force of his masculine subjectivity through the legions of his pupils, who responded to Abelard's persuasive authority. As Constant Mews argues, "[n]owhere in the *Historia calamitatum* does Abaelard define himself as a *scriptor* or an *auctor*; his self-image in both scholastic and monastic *milieux* is that of *magister*, master or man of authority."[30]

Abelard's popularity and unconventional views align him with Christ on trial in the role of masculine victim. Both were 'master' or 'teacher' to their followers; both were viewed as threats to the established order. Christ has Mary Magdalene; Abelard has Heloise. Abelard's subtle complicity with this analogy constructs his identity still more sharply along traditional masculine lines. As with Jesus' trial, Abelard's own trial revolves around the crucial concern of all masculine subjects involved—namely, the affirmation/conviction should be as public as possible and thereby should root the masculine construction of identity in its appropriate sphere. This competition for authority is confirmed in the public sphere, establishing a virtually unassailable masculine identity: Abelard is either a martyr or a sage. In either case his masculinity is continually projected into the public sphere. This history of consolation and humiliation is thus a history of authority and identity. The freely narrated calamities forge an identity of perseverance that reconfigures the slights to Abelard until they become the marks of a masculine reputation founded on mastery, creation, and unbreakable endurance.

Abelard's bodily manhood was no longer intact, but his psychic manhood, his perception of his own essentialized gender status, was never in danger. What his enemies identified as his intellectual swaggering never diminished as a result of his castration. Abelard erases the impact of the castration on his masculinity by embracing it, for he not only recognizes and accepts, but *celebrates* his bodily sin and its just punishment. Furthermore, he never entertains the notion that he is in any way culpable in his public, professional roles as a cleric or an intellectual. Proper pride in his self-avowed masculine enterprise was thus always merited. In his view and this respect, his enemies are not only wrong, but stupid—and usually maliciously jealous. In all these contexts, Abelard cloaks his defense in the guise of the victim and not of the penitent: this victimization narrative inscribes a wide range of parallel roles from the classical and biblical traditions, coming finally to match Abelard with Jerome and even Christ as victims falsely accused even with respect to women. Abelard's post-castration reputation suffers because of his continued relation to Heloise, when he "ministers to the needs of the women" of the Paraclete. He exclaims with some bitterness: "If they had lived in the time of Christ Himself and His members whether prophets, apostles, or other holy Fathers, what a charge my enemies would have brought against them when they saw them, though bodily intact, engaging with women in such close association!"[31] What little respite and solace Abelard finds from the unjust persecution by his enemies is with the Paraclete community: "And that they might revere me the more, I decided to be with them personally and to watch over them, thereby the better to meet their needs....And this would be as beneficial to me as it was necessary to them in their need."[32] Heloise grants what the masculine Abelardian subject demands:

> Hujus quippe loci tu post Deum solus es fundator, solus hujus oratorii constructor, solus hujus congregationis ediffìcator. Nichil hic super alienum edificasti fundamentum. Totum quod hic est, tua creatio est.
>
> For you after God are the sole founder of this place, the sole builder of this oratory, the sole creator of this community. You have built nothing here on another man's foundation. Everything here is your own creation.[33]

If the masculine subject creates his own universe, in Heloise's view Abelard enjoys the advantages and conditions of creation, singularity, and the ability to resist all outside attempts to usurp his power. He creates his own gendered universe, and its existence is dependent upon his flawless rhetorical performance.

In the *Historia calamitatum*, then, Abelard compresses his castration narrative within a larger discourse, that of the wronged intellectual genius, and he pre-emptively identifies manliness with intellectual prowess. He thus represses the importance of the loss of physical manliness that he confesses. In this larger life story, Abelard's prowess and creativity—the fertility of his imaginative strengths—make him male. The *Historia calamitatum* demonstrates Abelard's mastery in commodifying and mediating the experiences it relates while it asserts Abelard's identity as the truly authoritative masculine subject. In the retrospective of the *Historia calamitatum*, Abelard is founder, builder, creator, contender, and the one real man. Abelard triumphs through his castration, not in spite of it. His castration signifies his potency: Abelard, castrated, *is* the phallus. The Father's Rod has excised Abelard's rod, and gender stands free of sex.

HELOISE AND THE NAME-OF-THE-FATHER

Heloise is constructed in her letters as an unflinching suppliant who performs in every register her yearning to provoke Abelard's response. In this respect she is the intellectual embodiment of patriarchal wish fulfillment. Her letters aggressively publicize both her sustained desire for Abelard and the consistency of her strategy of submission to him. This strategy shields Abelard, assuaging his need for patriarchal superiority while asserting his overwhelming, permanent status as the object of desire. This strategy furthermore cloaks Heloise's deft, carefully couched counterpoint of moral correction to her husband-teacher and it renders almost invisible her subtle intertextonics, her system of rebuttal-by-counterquotation. If this prismatic discourse is, as most recent scholars suggest, "a contest between Heloise and Abelard, played out via shifting roles assumed by each in turn, in a pattern in which one chooses a role, which is negotiated by the other and then reprised,"[34] it is also an unacknowledged collusion to mask the castration and preserve Abelard's confident sense of masculinity. In those instances in which Heloise resists the ways Abelard had represented her in the *Historia calamitatum*, she inevitably does so to etch her even greater subordination and deeper abandonment to him. The voice of Heloise embodies Abelard's ethics of intention: she herself is a living exemplar of unswerving passionate love. She refuses all desire except desire for Abelard, even when he insists she must uproot that desire and replace it with love of God. As Juanita Feros Ruys argues, Heloise writes

> for herself roles of inferiority to Abelard, such as handmaid, spiritual daughter, and wife, and projects upon Abelard the respective classifications of superiority: master (*Domino*), spiritual father, and husband.... [Abelard] develops a competing strategy which displaces the terms of superiority (master, father, husband) onto God. He writes for himself alternative roles of equality, such as monastic brother and fellow abbot, and inferiority, such as servant of God.... Throughout the remainder of their correspondence, Heloise and Abelard dispute the roles of inferiority, equality, and superiority, and the doctrines of obligation attaching to these.[35]

Heloise's posture of adoring suppliant enhances the castrated Abelard's sense of masculine status and prowess. Abelard's correspondence with Heloise restores patriarchal calm after the shaken, shrill ending of the *Historia calamitatum*. Heloise sustains the construct of a fully masculine Abelard; her agenda is to buttress the system of Abelard's conquests and to maintain their passion in a passionate textuality: she puts him on a pedestal in order to keep him around. In these public letters, when Abelard recalls their shameless lovemaking, he is reaching out to a larger audience to perpetuate the memory of his potency. Heloise crafts a posture of humility to illumine her weakness and consequent need of Abelard since he had already identified feminine weakness with *his* benefit. Her first letter is full of the transactional language of debt, credit, and obligation, all of which recalls the marriage debt Abelard no longer pays.[36] Using imagery both biblical and sexual, Heloise portrays herself with her nuns as a plantation in need of "watering" and "careful and regular cultivation."[37] The paranoid Abelard of the *Historia calamitatum*'s closure is projected and cultivated in full, confident masculine display by Heloise's adulation, her continuous pouring of praise, her sustained statements of passionate submission. But defiance is found equally in that submission:

> God knows I never sought anything in you except yourself: I wanted simply you, nothing of yours. I looked for no marriage bond, no marriage portion, and it was not my own pleasures and wishes I sought to gratify, as you well know, but yours.... God is my witness that if Augustus, Emperor of the whole world, thought fit to honour me with marriage and conferred all the earth on me to possess for ever, it would be dearer and more honorable to me to be called not his Empress[*imperatrix*] but your whore[*meretrix*].[38]

Heloise's rhyming pun (*imperatrix/meretrix*) transvalues roles, and she represents herself equally proud and abject in her desire for Abelard. She was willing to remain passive, accepting Abelard's absence and silence about their relations, until he 'released' the *Historia calamitatum*. By that act he made the private public (if indeed there was any 'private' aspect of this relationship). In Heloise's public response she uses the feminine community of the Paraclete as a metaphor for her own state: "Sana, obsecro, ipsa que fecisti, qui alii fecerunt curare satagis...quicquid fieret tibi soli posset ascribi." ["Heal the wounds you have yourself inflicted," she says, knowing that the 'credit' will not be hers, but "yours alone."] [39] Heloise grants Abelard the power of creation and authorship and then pleads for the maintenance of that creation in both the nunnery and their marriage. Heloise deploys and extends the rhetorical devices and biblical and classical quotations used by Abelard in order to enhance Abelard's value and to highlight her public presentation of that value. At the same time, she insists on the body, its specific gravity and local importance: she is simultaneously wife importuning husband, pupil importuning mentor, nun importuning monastic founder. She invokes a wide range of masculine roles and names each Abelard.[40] Every attempt that Abelard makes at rejoinder is complicit in this enterprise, for the system that has bracketed and denied his philosophic and theological authority—that has required *his* submission—is the same patriarchal system that asserts the necessity of Heloise's claims of inferiority and subordination. "Do not think me strong," she pleads, "lest I fall before you can sustain me."[41]

As she frequently reiterates, Heloise's intention in this matter is pure and so resolute as to seem absolute—like Griselda in Chaucer's *Clerk's Tale.* Griselda creates her own subjectivity in the radical marriage vow she offers Walter; she binds herself not only to obey him but to find and follow his will:

> Lord, undigne and unworthy
> Am I to thilke honour that ye me beede,
> But as ye wole youreself, right so wol I.
> And heere I swere that nevere willyngly,
> In werk ne thoght, I nyl yow disobeye,
> For to be deed, though me were looth to deye.[42]

One can say here of the self-constructing, self-authorizing, patient (if not monstrous) Griselda what Southern says of Heloise: she "was not moved by lust, but by a fixation of her will toward Abelard. It was this that made her voluntarily submit to his will, to his commands, to his lusts, to anything he cared to put on her."[43]

Several of Abelard's contemporaries ridiculed Abelard as a eunuch, but Heloise's voice crafts a public denial of that third-sex category through the investment of her desire by naming him the Father. She thus renders impotent the contempt expressed by such contemporaries as Fulk of Deuil about Abelard's castration. Fulk's taunts are easily folded into the Abelardian narrative of sex/gender displacement, in which penis is replaced by tongue: "Abelard used to be promiscuous with his tail, but now that he has rightly lost it he has taken to pricking with his tongue instead."[44] Roscelin of Compiègne continues Fulk's scorn in similar terms, warning Abelard "Divine Justice should be greatly feared by you, lest—just as your tail, with which formerly (while you could) you pricked promiscuously was removed as your immorality deserved—now your tongue, with which you are now pricking away, be taken away as well."[45] But Roscelin changes the thrust of his abuse and threatens Abelard's masculine identity profoundly—so profoundly, I think, that it explains more satisfactorily than any theological dispute why Abelard erases the name of his formidable former teacher entirely from the *Historia calamitatum.* Roscelin here speaks not like the radical nominalist he usually was (for whom *nomina* were merely *flatus vocis*) but like a classical grammarian according substantive significance to a properly constituted noun. He abandons his own usual theory to play Abelard's own grammatical/conceptual game but insists on the reified grammatical identity of gender/penis/name:

> Si igitur neque clericus neque laicus neque monachus es, quo nomine te censeam, reperire non valeo. Sed forte Petrum te appellari posse ex consuetudine mentieris. Certus sum autem, quod masculini generis nomen, si a suo genere deciderit, rem solitam significare recusabit....Solent enim nomina propriam significationem amittere, cum eorum significata contigerit a sua perfectione recedere. Neque enim ablato tecto vel pariete domus, sed imperfecta domus vocabitur. Sublata igitur parte quae hominem facit non Petrus, sed imperfectus Petrus appellandus es.

> If therefore you are neither a cleric nor a layman nor a monk, I am unable to discover what name I should apply to you. Perhaps you lie when you say you can be called Peter, as before; I am quite certain that a name of the masculine gender will refuse to signify its accustomed object if that object is lacking in its gender....For names normally lose their proper meaning should the things they signify happen to lose their wholeness. For when a house loses its roof or a wall, it will be called not 'house' but 'defective house.' Since therefore the part which makes a man has been taken away, you should be called not 'Peter' but 'defective Peter.'[46]

As grammarian cruelly at play, Roscelin here essays a play on terms. By calling Abelard "Petrus imperfectus," Roscelin not only signals his defect (as rendered in this translation), he also implies his termination, his obsolescence. Like any verb in the imperfect tense, reserved for action or being now absolutely finished (however repetitively habitual it may once have been), Abelard is now a "former Peter"—a state worse than mere imperfection. This Peter-who-lacks can no longer be a 'rock.' Even Roscelin's malicious attack is voided by the vehemence of Heloise's patriarchal namings of Peter Abelard.

Although both Abelard and Heloise sporadically resist the gender boundaries that were beginning to harden in their time and place, Abelard is inflexibly patriarchal in his understanding of feminine weakness and masculine strength. Monastic communities, for example, should conform to the "natural order,"[47] and women in that context should always look to a man for leadership. The facts of the historical Heloise's life as abbess seem to stand at considerable odds with such direction, but in her correspondence she is stunningly submissive: "Omnes mihi denique voluptates interdixi ut tue parerem voluntati; nichil mihi reservavi, nisi sic tuam nunc precipue fieri." [I have finally denied myself every pleasure in obedience to your will, kept nothing for myself except to prove that now, even more, I am yours.][48] Heloise reaffirms what Abelard wished to achieve in his *Historia calamitatum*. She is insistently his alone, never God's. Proving herself his, Heloise proves the value he is denied by his hierarchical superiors. Proving herself his, Heloise reinforces patriarchal understandings of Abelard's essentialized masculinity.

Heloise's seeming submission seduces Abelard into continued dialogue: the gestures and the rhetoric of proving herself his engrave the glamour and prowess of Abelardian masculinity for all readers. As seen in her flexible and complex assessment of feminine roles, Heloise understood gender as act and performance. She nevertheless colludes with Abelard to maintain his masculinity as a fixed meta-category. Barbara Newman argues that the correspondence of Abelard and Heloise is a "victory for the poetics of castration over the discourse of desire."[49] I disagree. The poetics of castration *is* the discourse of their desire.

Though Abelard reinforces his victim status with parallels (noted above) to Christ and Jerome, he finds another ancient and powerful parallel in Origen, the self-castrate who Abelard frequently asserts is the greatest Christian philosopher. Abelard glories in his own luck: imprudent Origen was censured for his self-mutilation while Abelard is innocent of the crime of castration that liberates him for his philosophic life work.[50] Through the figure of Origen, Abelard connects castration with his own genius and moral integrity;

castration images his asceticism and *auctoritas*. Abelard's "Origenary" fantasy is that he not only matches but surpasses this "prince of Christian philosophers." Abelard is the male all others must become but cannot until they rise to his understanding of the Father's Rod as creation, affliction, and re-creation. Abelard erases the physical un-manning of his castration by confessing and celebrating it; Heloise colludes. She equally erases this un-manning by denying its pertinence to his sex, his gender, or to her somatic, intellectual, or emotional desires. Abelardian masculinity is the "ever-fix'd mark" that commands her passion, her loyalty, and all her formidable intelligence. Heloise essentializes Abelardian masculinity in the name of love, in the Name-of-the-Father.

NOTES

1. This paper began in conversations with the late John Benton about the authenticity of the Abelard-Heloise correspondence and the perplexing quality of Heloise's sustained submissiveness. John Benton's views of these matters, with which I often disagreed, are often caricatured: it was precisely Benton's feminist sensibilities that led him to speculate about the authenticity of the correspondence. I have benefitted greatly from the advice and careful reading given this essay in its different stages by John O. Ward, Dennis Foster, Michael Holahan, Constant Mews, John Carmi Parsons, and especially Jeremy duQ. Adams.

2. I use the distinction made by Claire Nouvet, in "La castration d'Abelard: impasse et substitution," *Poétique* 83 (1990): 259–80 between the historical figures of Abelard and Heloise and "les noms d' 'Abelard' et 'Heloise'"(259) deployed in the "body" of their letters.

3. In the most frequently remarked instance, before taking monastic vows, Heloise quotes Cornelia from Lucan's *Pharsalia*:

> 'O noble husband,
> Too great for me to wed, was it my fate
> to bend that lofty head? what prompted me
> To marry you and bring about your fall?
> Now claim your due, and see me gladly pay....'

In a crucial passage in *The Book of Memory: A Study of Memory in Medieval Culture* (Cambridge: Cambridge University Press, 19[illegible]0), Mary Carruthers amplifies R.W. Southern's argument, arguing that here "Heloise is not expressing herself, but neither is she simply expressing Lucan. She is 'expressing her character,' a function of *memoria*."(p. 182) Further, "So instead of the word 'self,' or even 'individual,' we might better speak of a 'subject-who-remembers,' and in remembering also feels and thinks and judges. In other words, we should think of the apprehending and commenting individual subject ('self') also in rhetorical terms. Her subjectivity is located in Heloise's memory, including her florilegium of texts, one of which she 'invents,' (in the ancient sense) for this occasion, thereby investing it, the occasion, and her own action with 'common' ethical value, and giving her audience 'something to think about.'"(p. 182)

4. On role-playing, see Juanita Feros Ruys, "Role-Playing in the Letters of Heloise and Abelard," *Parergon* ns 11.1 (June 1993): 53–78. Butler is particularly useful on the overlapping ideologies of gender discourse.

5. See especially Barbara Newman, "Authority, Authenticity, and the Repression of Heloise," *The Journal of Medieval and Renaissance Studies* 22 (1992): 121–58; Linda Kauffman, *Discourse of Desire: Gender, Genre, and Epistolary Fictions* (Ithaca: Cornell University Press, 1986); Mary Carruthers, *The Book of Memory*; and Juanita Feros Ruys, "Role-Playing." My thinking about gender performance is informed particularly by Judith Butler in *Gender Trouble: Feminism and the Subversion of Identity* (New York: Routledge, 1990) and in *Bodies That Matter: On the Discursive Limits of 'Sex'* (New York: Routledge, 1993). An elegant and brilliant article by Catherine Brown, "*Muliebriter*: Doing Gender in the Letters of Heloise," pp. 15–51 in *Gender and Text in the Later Middle Ages*, Jane Chance, ed. (Gainesville: University Press of Florida, 1996) came to my attention after this essay was completed. Brown's argument elaborates the point that "[i]n the correspondence, these two well-matched lover-disputants will struggle to gender, then to occupy, the paired roles (master/servant; teacher/student) here sequentially and simultaneously emptied and filled in the shuttling movement of desire."(30)

6. Femininities float more problematically, more inconsistently and are the subject of dialogue and dispute between Abelard and Heloise.

7. Most recently as "Strategies of Submission and Seduction in Heloise's (re)Masculinization of Abelard," presented to the International Medieval Congress, University of Leeds (July 1995), and "Objects of Intention: Confessional Strategies in Abelard's *Historia*," a paper presented in debate with Martin Irvine to the International Congress of Medieval Studies, Kalamazoo (May 1996).

8. David Luscombe, "From Paris to the Paraclete: The Correspondence of Abelard and Heloise," *Proceedings of the British Academy* 74 (1988): 247–83, usefully discusses the manuscript tradition: "In two MSS the letter is introduced by the words: 'Abaelardi ad amicum consolatoria' (Monfrin, p. 60). The title 'Historia Calamitatum' appears in one MS (Rheims 872) and there only as a secondary title..."(251, fn. 37). See also Mark Amsler, "Genre and Code in Abelard's *Historia calamitatum*," *Assays* 1 (1981): 35–50. The authenticity dispute, irrelevant to my argument, remains

unresolved and persistently troublesome because of the late date of the earliest manuscript.

9. Even contemporary scholars may still be swayed by Abelard's authoritative discourse and grant him a disproportionately foundational role in, for example, the development of nominalism. As a corrective, see Constant J. Mews, "Philosophy and Theology 1100–1150: The Search for Harmony, " in *Le XIIe siècle. Mutations et renouveau en France dans la première moitié du XIIe siècle*, Françoise Gasparri, ed. (Paris: Le Léopard d'Or, 1994), pp. 159–203, and the exemplary "Peter Abelard,"*Authors of the Middle Ages*, vol. 2.5, Patrick J. Geary, ed. (Aldershot, Hants.: Variorum, 1995), pp. 30–31.

10. Michel Foucault, *History of Sexuality*, vol. 1, Robert Hurley, trans. (New York: Vintage Books, 1980), p. 60.

11. Foucault, pp. 61–62.

12. Abelard, *Historia calamitatum,* Jacques Monfrin, ed. (Paris: Vrin, 1962), p. 63, 5–7; English translation from *The Story of Abelard's Adversities*, J.T. Muckle, trans. (Toronto: Pontifical Institute of Mediaeval Studies, 1964), p. 11. All references to the *Historia calamitatum* and to Heloise's first letter are from Monfrin's edition (hereafter "Monfrin"); unless otherwise noted, English translations of the *Historia calamitatum* are from Muckle (hereafter "Muckle").

13. Monfrin, pp. 70–71, 262–69; Muckle, p. 25. Is this *inflat* a self-deflating play of words? Abelard's inflated intellect had experienced *superbia*; the tumescence of another part of him had led from *concupiscentia* to *luxuria* to castration. Deflation is not, after all, as drastic as excision or extinction.

14. Text Monfrin, p. 79, 581–91 ; Muckle, p. 38; italic modifications mine.

15. Monfrin, p. 80, 596–600; Muckle, p. 38–39.

16. Monfrin, p. 80, 600–606; Muckle, p. 39. Here, where Abelard's gloria is *extincta* as well as *humiliata* (cf. n. 13, above), the adverb *penitus* is a provocative if not outrageous pun.

17. Earlier (see n. 13) he acknowledges his own sinful pride but he never admits that he was intellectually wrong or mistaken, that the book which was his "special glory" deserved to be burned for its errors, or that his professional/vocational actions and attitudes were inappropriately prideful.

18. Monfrin, p. 80–81, 623–625; Muckle, p. 40.

19. See Colin Morris, *The Discovery of the Individual 1050–1200* (New York: Harper and Row, 1972), esp. ch. 4.

20. Morris, p. 73.

21. *Analecta Hymnica* 48, p. 221, translation by Morris, p. 72. See also Migne PL 187, cols. 1773–4; *Analecta Hymnica* 48, p. 144. As Morris notes,

"What Abelard wanted...was neither external acts nor emotional gush, but true inner sorrow for sin." (p. 73)

22. J.T. Muckle, "The Personal Letters between Abelard and Heloise," *Mediaeval Studies* 15 (1953):47–94, from *Letter 4*, Abelard to Heloise, 92. English translation from Betty Radice, *The Letters of Abelard and Heloise* (London and New York: Penguin, 1974), p. 153. With the exception of Heloise's first letter (quoted from Monfrin), all subsequent references to the texts of the personal letters are from Muckle; in most cases, space limited me to the use of English translations, which unless otherwise noted are from Radice.

23. Monfrin, pp. 63–64, 19–28; Muckle, p. 12; italicized modifications to Muckle indicate my translations. Note that the (public) male Mars is replaced by (private) female Minerva.

24. Monfrin, p. 71, 291–94; Muckle, p. 27.

25. Monfrin, p. 75, 414–418; Muckle, p. 37.

26. Monfrin, pp. 78–79, 551–558; Muckle, p. 71. Note the elision from private to public: Heloise's intimate statement to Abelard, Abelard's invocation of "all the world."

27. Monfrin, p. 102, 1389–1391; Muckle, p. 47.

28. The metaphor of the fecund vine (Psalm 89.12) is again applied to Abelard in the letter sent to Innocent II by the Council of Sens in 1141: see Muckle, p. 47, n. 63. Abelard's essential masculinity must have seemed persuasive if ecclesiastical authorities of his day ordained him priest after his castration in spite of proscriptions (of which he himself shows awareness) against eunuch-priests. I have been unable to discover the circumstances of Abelard's ordination. In private correspondence, Constant Mews agrees that "he must have been ordained by the time he became an abbot, of St. Gildas."

29. Monfrin, p. 86, 809–815; Muckle, p. 47.

30. Constant J. Mews, "Orality, Literacy, and Authority in the Twelfth-Century Schools," *Exemplaria* 2.2 (1990), 479.

31. Monfrin, p. 103, 1400–1404; Muckle, pp. 71–72.

32. Monfrin, p. 105, 1477–81; 1488–89; Muckle, p. 75.

33. Monfrin, p. 112–113, 73–80; Radice, p. 111.

34. Feros Ruys, 54.

35. Feros Ruys, 56, 59, 78.

36. As quoted above, note 33.

37. Monfrin, p.113, 92–95; Radice, p. 111.

38. Monfrin, p. 114, 144–161; Radice, p.114.

39. Monfrin, p. 112, 68–69; pp. 113, 86–87; Radice, p. 111.

40. In all her approaches to Abelard, Heloise keeps the passionate engagement entirely limited to their status as partners; she never invokes herself as "mother" to his "father" or even mentions their son Astrolabe.

41. Muckle, *Letters*, p. 181: "Noli valitudinem putare ne prius corruam quam sustentes." English translation, Radice, p. 134.

42. "The Clerk's Tale," ll. 359–64 in *The Riverside Chaucer*, 3rd ed., Larry D. Benson, gen. ed. (Boston: Houghton Mifflin, 1987).

43. R.W. Southern, *Medieval Humanism and Other Studies* (Oxford: Blackwell, 1970), p. 94.

44. Epistola XVI in *PL* 178:371–6. See also Luscombe, 259, and Peter Dronke, *Abelard and Heloise in Medieval Testimonies* (Glasgow: University of Glasgow Press, 1976), pp. 26–27.

45. "Sed valde tibi divina metuenda est iustitia, ne, sicut cauda, qua prius, dum poteras, indifferenter pungebas, merito tuae immunditiae tibi ablata est, ita et lingua, qua modo pungis, auferatur," from the text of Roscelin's letter, ed. J. Reiners, *Der Nominalismus in der Frühscholastik* (Münster: Beiträge zur Geschichte der Philosophie und der Theologie des Mittelalters 8, 1910), pp. 63–80, p. 64.

46. The full statement is compelling:

Si igitur neque clericus neque laicus neque monachus es, quo nomine te censeam, reperire non valeo. Sed forte Petrum te appellari posse ex consuetudine mentieris. Certus sum autem, quod masculini generis nomen, si a suo genere deciderit, rem solitam significare recusabit. Amodo enim neutri generis abiectionem, sicut et suum significatum, penet..., et cum hominem integrum consueverit, dimidum forsitan significare recusabit. Solent enim nomina propriam significationem amittere, cum eorum significata contigerit a sua perfectione recedere. Neque enim ablato tecto vel pariete domus, sed imperfecta domus vocabitur. Sublata igitur parte quae hominem facit non Petrus, sed imperfectus Petrus appellandus es. Ad huius etiam imperfecti hominis ignominiae cumulum pertinet, quod in sigillo, quo foetidas illas litteras sigillavit, imaginem duo capita habentem, unum viri, alterum mulieris, ipse formavit. Unde quis dubitet, quanto adhuc in eam ardeat amore, qui tali eam capitum coniunctione non erubuit honorare? Plura quidem in tuam contumeliam vera ac manifesta dictare decreveram, sed quia contra hominem imperfectum ago, opus quod coeperam imperfectum relinquo.

Reiners, p. 80; translation mine. The punning field suggested by the noun *Peter* persists in colloquial modern English. On Roscelin, see Constant Mews' new study (still unavailable to me when this article went to press), "The Trinitarian Doctrine of Roscelin of Compiègne and Its Influence: Twelfth-century Nominalism and Theology Re-considered" in *Mélanges offerts à Jean Jolivet*, A., Elamrani-Jamal, Alain Galonnier, Alain de Libera, eds. (Paris: Vrin, 1996), pp. 347–364.

47. Radice, p. 101.

48. Monfrin, p. 117, 260–262; Radice, p. 117.

49. Newman, 74.

50. Monfrin, p. 102; Muckle, p. 71.

ABELARD'S BLISSFUL CASTRATION

Yves Ferroul

This essay asserts that misunderstandings about the facts of Abelard's sexual mutilation have clouded analysis of his rejection of marriage, his claustration, and his views of male sexuality and masculinity.

Ou est la tres sage Hellois,
Pour qui chastré fut et puis moyne,
Pierre Esbaillart a Saint Denis?
Pour son amour ot ceste essoyne.

Where is the wise and learned Heloise,
On whose account once Peter Abelard
Was castrated, then monk at Saint-Denis?
Because of love he knew pain.

François Villon
Ballade des dames du temps jadis

In this essay I view the story of Abelard as a rarity: a medieval example of how a man experienced and expressed his understanding of his gender through sexuality, marriage, and sexual mutilation. In addition, I propose that the reception of this story from Abelard's time to our own has tended to misrepresent the nature both of Abelard's castration and of his claustration.

To defuse the scandal of his affair with Heloise and her pregnancy, Abelard insisted upon marrying her but did so secretly. Heloise's uncle Fulbert attended the ceremony. When Fulbert divulged this secret to others, Heloise, who then lived in his house, denied the fact of the marriage. The infuriated uncle then mistreated his niece so terribly that Abelard removed his wife to the convent of Argenteuil, where she was "disguised" in a nun's habit. Since Fulbert and his family thought Abelard was trying to reject his marital relation to Heloise, Fulbert decided to punish the seducer by mutilating him. Abelard presented the circumstances leading to his castration later in his *Historia calamitatum*.[1] He concluded: "Overwhelmed with such woes, shame (*confusio pudoris*), I must confess—rather than a true vocation—pushed me into the shade of a cloister."[2] Abelard thus established a causal connection: his castration caused him to forego his marital relationship with Heloise in order to become a monk.

Commentators—chroniclers, theologians, historians, encyclopedists, and even poets like Villon, quoted above—have persistently regarded this connection as self-evidently natural. One of Abelard's contemporaries, Otto of Freising, gave an account of the philosopher's adventures in his *Gesta Friderici imperatoria*: "Ill-treated in a well-known circumstance, Abelard became a monk in the monastery of Saint-Denis."[3] Gabriel Peignot observed in his *Dictionnaire biographique* in 1813 that "they mutilated him in an inhumane way. This unfortunate husband concealed his shame and sorrow in the Abbey of Saint-Denis, where he entered into religion."[4] "There was no alternative," concludes Charles de Rémusat in his drama *Abelard*.[5] Joseph McCabe, in *Peter Abelard,* was certain that Abelard only indirectly connects his conversion to his mutilation because of modesty:

> It is a pious theory of the autobiographer himself that this mutilation led indirectly to his 'conversion.' There is undoubtedly much truth in this notion of an indirect influence being cast on his mind of life. Yet we of a later age, holding a truer view of the unity of human nature and of the place that sex influence occupies in its life, can see that the 'conversion' was largely a direct physical process.[6]

Charlotte Charrier, in her thesis on Heloise, was equally clear: "If we approve of Abelard's decision to embrace a monastic life—and was it not the only acceptable decision? Wasn't he bound to do so?"[7] Etienne Gilson shared her opinion, the received and common opinion: "The reason he entered into religion is quite clear. Nothing allows anyone to suppose he would have become a monk had he not been covered with shame by his ordeal."[8] Gilson goes so far as to assert that Abelard immediately and totally accepted this expiation as a divine command. He therefore also connects castration to monastic life.Recent interpretations of this episode are similar. According to Régine Pernoud,

> It is therefore Abelard himself who imagined and imposed this solution. He may have thought there was no other way out: Heloise was his wife before God and Man, but he could no longer be her

> husband after the flesh. The bond that subsisted could be dissolved in no other way than by their joint entry to the monastery.[9]

In her *Regard sur les Françaises,* Michèle Sarde validates Abelard's behavior:

> Love cannot ignore the sanctions of marriage with impunity; or otherwise it would be doomed to impotence. Nevertheless, the Word is a possible substitute. Halted in full swing by castration, Abelard froze. He turned away from Heloise and fixed his eyes upon heaven.[10]

The unanimous view is that Abelard's entry into monastic life was justified, but this traditional notion assumes that the couple had to dissolve. At least one other option is ignored: Abelard could have shared his misfortune with the woman he had wedded before God. What motivated Abelard's separation from his wife? Might not the couple's marriage have been maintained?

THE FOUNDATIONS OF MARITAL LIFE

It is usually thought that once Abelard could no longer be Heloise's sexually whole husband, he inevitably sought shelter in a monastery, which affirms Abelard's right to dissolve his marriage since he had been castrated. Ecclesiastical law cites castration as one form of impotence, defined as the inability to implant semen. In the twelfth century, impotence conferred the right to nullify a marriage if it occurs after the ceremony. It was an undeniable impediment if known before.[11] However, this definition did not apply to Abelard because his marriage was consummated; after that point, impotence did not constitute legal nullity.

Procreation, as one of the goals of marriage, must be possible for a true marriage. After its consummation, a marriage becomes indissoluble: "indissolubility is attached to marriage by divine law after consummation."[12] The philosopher and his disciple-wife were fecund, and thus the couple was indissoluble. An accident after that point could not alter their union. Legally, an *impotentia coeundi,* even if it is anterior and perpetual, cannot compel the spouses to separate.[13] Why then did Abelard use nullity as a cause, since his impotence was posterior to the marriage, consummation, and the birth of a child? Castration alone cannot explain Abelard's behavior, since it did not bind him to separate from his wife. Abelard's rationale is typically explained as a desire to attain the ideal of chastity promulgated by the church, which ranked celibacy above marriage. The church venerated couples who separated to remain chaste. St. Alexis, for example, pled with his young wife on their wedding night to prefer heavenly to mortal life and to regard Jesus as her sole spouse.[14] St. Simon (d. circa 1080) similarly exhorted his new wife to retain her chastity and to take a vow of virginity, and then he sent her to a monastery and donned the habit himself.[15] But these examples are irrelevant to Abelard's situation, since the most ideally chaste of couples did not consummate their marriages.

In the twelfth century, once their children were independent and inheritance problems were resolved, many couples separated after living together for a long time in order to devote the rest of their lives to God—as did Abelard's parents. Many couples did not wait for old age, and "it is noticeable how easy it was, for those who wanted to lead a monastic life, to annul their marriages, to divorce, or to separate."[16] Monastic life was privileged; recruitment to its ranks was eased. Yet the desire for devoted monastic reclusiveness was not the exclusive reason for such couples' separation. The possibility of an ecclesiastical career constituted another important incentive. Leclercq cites the example of the twelfth-century knight Ansoud de Maule, who asked his wife's permission to become a monk: "The decision after marriage to become a monk or a nun was often grounds for separation, provided it was by mutual consent."[17] Leclercq argues that Abelard and Heloise's behavior was thus not atypical:

> The favours bestowed on them by the wealthy, who helped them in founding and sustaining the Paraclete, as well as the spiritual support granted by St. Bernard, Peter the Venerable, and Innocent II: all this proves they had not been misunderstood nor banished.[18]

One should not conclude quickly that Abelard and Heloise followed this pattern. First, their move to monastic life did not occur by "mutual assent." Abelard says that "abnegating her own will, Heloise had already, as I ordered her, taken the veil and her vows,"[19] while Heloise recounts that "your order made me undergo the rigors of monastic life." Next, no decision to be chaste requires a determination to enter a monastery. By 1200, *The Life of St. Cunegunda* (d. 1040) reports that she devoted her virginity to the king of heaven with her chaste husband's assent. Before dying, the latter told his parents-in-law: "I give her back to you just as you entrusted me with her. You gave me a virgin, and a virgin I return to you."[20] So, too, the story of the Count of Hainaut, who respected his bride's wish to remain a virgin and, "despite all other women, she became his sole passionate love."[21] Though Abelard chose monastic life for himself, why did he choose it also for Heloise? Mutual consent to separate does not require that both spouses must enter religious life. Gabriel Le Bras refers to the *Decretals* of Gregory IX that queries separations "unless one of the spouses enters religious life."[22] Abelard could have permitted his wife to remain a laywoman, without asking her to enter a convent.

Despite the virulent anti-matrimonialism of Jerome's *Adversus Jovinianum*, intensified by Gregory the Great, the church professed that it regarded marriage as one way to attain sainthood. Abelard frequently cites biblical quotations to voice his awareness that marriage is no impediment to salvation.[23] Heloise is equally sure that the quest for salvation is not shackled by marriage. God has not destined only monks for beatitude: "Et quomodo honorabiles sunt nuptiae, quae nobis tantum impediunt ?" (And how can marriage be regarded as honorable if it is seen as mere shackles?)[24] Heloise is furthermore sure of the strength of her relationship with Abelard: "You know what bond binds us and obliges you, and that the nuptial sacrament unites you to me all the more tightly as my love has always been overt and boundless."[25] The couple could have lived together and benefitted from "all these marital tokens of affection" that Heloise misses. In light of Heloise's desire, Abelard's insistence upon her claustration cannot be justified, since their conjugal status was not affected by castration after consummation. Hugh of Saint Victor writes that the union of two bodies legitimates and sanctifies marriage and that the union of souls provides "the sign and symbol of the great mystery of the union of Christ and Church."[26]

His opponent Roscelin, who knew that Abelard chose the monastery "in an overwhelming plight of misery and shame," found the decision dishonorable. But—though embarrassed by his abuse of power—Charlotte Charrier is not alone in attempting to exonerate Abelard. Since Heloise was young, beautiful, and passionate, she argues, could Abelard have left her prey to temptation? Heloise "should be regarded as a lover rather than a mother," who "surrendered as an expiatory victim and relished the bitter joy of sacrifice." This reasoning is convoluted if not bizarre: how can one assert that Heloise loved Abelard so absolutely that she would always have remained faithful to him but simultaneously argue that she had to be locked in a convent to protect herself from adultery? Or that she was a loving and passionate mother but that she could not be allowed to rejoin her son? Or that she was forced to enter a convent but that she aspired to play the part of a victim? What can be said of Charrier's representation of an aging Abelard who is fed up with his wife's smothering love, embittered by imposed mediocrity, an unfaithful, deplorable husband and father. This portrait stands in contrast to typical twelfth-century examples of marital love and mutual tenderness. My analysis suggests instead that Abelard was spurred by a complex of motives combining need to exact revenge on Fulbert with possessive jealousy and frantic selfishness.[27]

THE FANTASMS OF SEXUAL RELATIONSHIP

What exactly was Abelard's situation? Commentators from his day until ours assert that they "know what sort of mutilation was inflicted on him."[28] Abelard himself says "...eis videlicet corporis mei partibus amputatis quibus id quod plangebant commiseram"[29] so that "the means to achieve fleshly depravity has been taken from me."[30] In Letter Five, he tries to convince Heloise that this mutilation was beneficial: "I have been deprived of the part of my body that was the centre of voluptuous desires, the prime cause of the lusts of the flesh," so that "I can no longer be contaminated by the flesh."[31]

The radical end of Abelard's sexuality is underscored by his contemporaries. According to the prior Fulk of Deuil, Abelard is fortunate: his meditation will no longer be impeded by movements of the flesh. He will be able to meet with indifference beautiful women (who usually excite even the most insensitive old men), and husbands will no longer fear him.[32] Roscelin gloats over the humiliation of the arrogant philosopher: "What name can one apply to you? I am not clever enough to answer....For since you have lost the characteristic of a man, you can no longer be called Peter but incomplete Peter."[33] At the end of the seventeenth century, Pierre Bayle expresses the Enlightenment view. He states that "to take their revenge, the girl's parents struck the root of the evil and tore it off, so that the offender could not relapse" though Heloise had not renounced "the possession of which her husband had been deprived."[34] So even "though the record does not say that she would have risked her life to save her husband's sex and that her shouts could have protected this precious jewel from the murderer's hand, she must have said so." The revenge of Fulbert's men becomes: "they took him unaware as he was asleep and cut off his *membrum virile*."

This representation of the castration still persists. Gonzague Truc presumes that "the aggressors left this throbbing flesh and fled," and that Abelard "cheered the mutilation removing the root of the sin he would never commit again."[35] According to Etienne Gilson, Heloise's sole concern was her husband's happiness, because "though she has been deprived of carnal delights, she still loved Abelard." Her reproaches are naive, since "after Abelard's mutilation, their respective situations were not comparable, for Heloise's sensitivity could still benefit from solace unavailable to Abelard." Gilson admires the Abelard who becomes a passionate defender of monastic continence, and who "totally forgot how easy had been his pride in a perfection that cost him so little."[36] Michèle Sarde is just as categorical: "His desire vanished with his membrum....Facing his frustrated lover, Abelard has no longer a body of his own....once this organ, the source of sexual desire, was severed."[37] These dramatic views collectively assume that Abelard's testicles and penis had been severed and that he had thus been deprived of the means whereby he could satisfy carnal desire.

A complete mutilation has brutish and permanent physiological and psychological consequences. The amputation of an arm or a leg does not *ipso facto* wipe it out from our corporeal consciousness: our mind retains the phantom presence of limbs. It is surely even more difficult to erase from memory an organ that visibly identifies one's male sexuality.

Abelard was castrated and turned into a eunuch: "factus eunuchus."[38] But what is castration? Castration is simply excision of the testicles: it has nothing to do with cutting off the penis.[39] Abelard is precise about his mutilation and suffering. His castrators were "oculis et genitalibus privati." According to all authorities, the genitals or genitalia are the testicles alone. Du Cange translates the Latin *genitalia* as "testiculi, scrotum."[40] To accomplish this mutilation, appropriate for adulterers, the scrotum is tied up at the upper part of the testicles and then cut off. In his continuation of the *Roman de la Rose*, Jean de Meun is explicit:

> Fu la coille a Pierre tolue
> A Paris en son lit de nuis. (v. 8800-8801)
>
> (His balls were taken from Peter
> At Paris in his bed at night.)

As he recovered, Abelard remembered some biblical extracts relevant to his case, that is, to eunuchs: "tanta sit apud Deum eunuchorum abhominatio, ut homines amputatis vel attristis testiculis eunichizati intrare ecclesiam...prohibeantur"[41] (God has so great an abhorrence of eunuchs that men made eunuchs by the amputation or attrition of testicles are forbidden to enter a church.) Jean de Meun translates "eunuchi" by "escoillez" in this passage and later in the poem, when Abelard recalls his visits to Heloise.[42]

I think we should permit Abelard to keep his penis! He should also retain his sensuality, since a eunuch's sexuality is granted even in the Bible.[43] Origen himself admits that "he had made a mistake describing the inconveniences and uselessness of a remedy that disturbs the body without appeasing the soul."[44] St. Jean Chrysostome says that castration "far from assuaging the lusts of the flesh, exacerbates them." According to St. Epiphanius, after castration, "more violent and no less immoderate passions" are triggered by lust.[45] These statements relate not only to desire but also to sexual capacity.

One must distinguish the castration of a child from the castration of an adult through unequivocal scientific language without the learned use of Latin as an evasive filter: "cum me puduerit de obscoenis gallice dicere, satius visum est latino sermone uti."[46] (Since I found it too shocking to use the French language in discussing such obscene matters, it seemed healthier to use Latin.) It is a medical certainty that before the age of puberty, missing testicles—the source of male hormones—make sexual maturity impossible. Therefore, physical appearance, voice (the famous voice of Italian *castrati*), and genital life remain infantile. But with post-pubertal castration, erections are possible as is ejaculation of a fluid normally associated with semen (formed by the spermatozoa), produced by the prostate and its related glands. Though the process of this sexual activity is controversial—some attribute a role of substitution in the production of male hormones to the adrenal glands; others argue that the nervous system acquires sufficient autonomy once it has fully developed and functions thanks to testicular hormonal action prior to excision[47]—there is no doubt about the product: "eunuchs whose testicles have been cut off but who kept their penis could still have erections, making them very attractive because of the unthreatening lack of consequence to such intercourse."[48] Juvenal describes such intimacy ironically:

> Some women are thrilled by puny eunuchs and their non-prickling kisses: they don't have to dread their beards, nor prepare abortions. Voluptuousness is complete, for the men are delivered to doctors only when they were blooming, when their organ-hairs had grown and the organs themselves were mature....As for children in the hands of slave-traders, they suffer from a true and pitiful impotence.[49]

Roman women who took eunuchs as lovers were the butt of Martial's jests: "Why is your dear Caelia served by eunuchs only? It is just because she wants to be serviced without having children."[50]

Studying the process of the ritual ablation of the testicles, Aline Rousselle concludes that:

> The ancients must have distinguished fecundation, connected to the *vasum deferens* and the testicles, from sexual activity capable of independent ejaculation....In the third century A.D., men knowingly and scientifically extinguished their fecundity (but not their desire or sexual activity) through a ritual ablation of the testicles....Reproductive male power was sacrificed on a voluntary basis only, which implies sexual maturity and mental conviction: the true *Galli* thus cut off their testicles with the clear consciousness of adults retaining their sexual potency.[51]

In the fourth century, Basil of Ancyra advises virgins to avoid consorting with eunuchs:

> Those who achieve virility at an age when the penis is fit for copulation are said to be brutish in their sexual desires, not from ardor but in order to besmirch women without incurring any risk.[52]

The Pseudo-Basile:

> mainly reproached these maimed men...because they maintained sensual passion and its source (i.e., lust) along with incontinence of will and spirit. It was more dramatic since they were less fit for it physiologically, increasingly becoming slaves of voluptuousness as they indulged in it with impunity and disgrace.[53]

Although Pierre Bayle was convinced that sexual relationships for Abelard and Heloise were impossible, he notices that "Father Theophile Raynaud...had read about many examples of lurid intercourse between women and mutilated men."[54]

Amputation of the penis (emasculation) is a more recent tradition. Realizing that the eunuchs who directed the harem were not really reliable, for instance, sultans began to require full amputation that included the penis. According to Dr. Zambaco Pacha, however, its practice does not date farther back than the fifteenth century:

> Knowing that the full or partial spadon (a eunuch whose penis was totally or partially retained) had not his virility, Amurat III, the conqueror of the Persians, is said to have been the first sultan to have employed complete eunuchs and to demand a full amputation.[55]

The amputation of the penis is a delicate operation. Though the vessels of the testicles are thin, and the subsequent hemorrhage is easily stopped, the arteries of the penis from which blood floods out are more difficult to control. Dr. Ionel Rapaport recounts two amputation incidents, one of them fatal: "Attis snatched a fragment of a vase and withdrew under the pine-tree to deprive himself of the marks of his sex....His blood drained away as his life withered." In another incident, however, "a young man who decided to become a *Gallus* stripped off his clothes, made his way to the assembly, shouted and seized a knife. With this, he castrated himself suddenly before running across the town holding what he had just cut off." The account of a castration in the Russian sect of the Skoptzy in the nineteenth century bears out the claim that the latter operation was done with relative facility:

> Two adepts hold and carry the neophyte while the operating surgeon drops on one knee. He makes him bend his knees and part his legs. The root of the scrotum is bandaged quickly and tightly with a simple small string....It is then severed with a razor....The maimed person usually faints and hemostasis occurs naturally, even if the ligature is not perfect....If necessary, the cruentous surface is cauterized with ferric-chloride and alum. The dressing is held by a bandage. The main drugs used to stop bleeding are ice and tar. From four to six weeks, dressings are applied with an unguent with unknown ingredients.[56]

The amputation of the penis causes physical difficulties since the penis is also used for urination. Dr. Zambaco eloquently accounts the mutilation of children destined to serve in harems as eunuchs:

> After tying their victims down to tables with straps on the arms, legs, and chests, they would bind both the penis and the scrotum and cut them off with a sharp instrument. To keep the spermatic cords from retracting into the abdomen, causing an intro-abdominal hemorrhage that was almost always deadly, these holy monks (Egyptian Coptic monks in the nineteenth century) used to apply a ligature to the cord. They would then pour boiling tar on the wound or cauterize it with a hot iron. After being mutilated, the poor little boys were buried waist-deep in the sand. A rod was inserted into the urethra to prevent its obstruction; they were left in this position for several days. Those who survived were taken out and tended with tow that had been dipped in an aromatic oil. The wound would heal only after two or three months. The pain at every urination was terrible. I was told all these details by eunuchs who sobbed as they remembered how they had suffered forty or fifty years before.... The mortality of complete eunuchs is very high...nine out of ten would die...most eunuchs inserted a silver tube so as to urinate standing without wetting their clothes. Many suffered of chronic cystitis or from recurring inflammations.[57]

The ablation of Abelard's testicles, called castration, has nothing in common with these examples of penile amputation, called emasculation.[58] Thus Abelard could have sustained a physically affective if not a fully sexual relationship with Heloise. He strangely alludes to the perception of sexual capacity as the cause of one of his misfortunes:

> I therefore visited them more often (i.e., the nuns) to support them as well as I could. This bred a lot of gossip: sincere charity from my part was shamefully interpreted by my wicked enemies who said that I was still under the influence of the fleshly lust, since I could not bear the absence of my former lover in any way.[59]

Pierre Bayle comments that "backbiting against this poor man was fierce although he was known to have been deprived of what could have contented his wife. They kept saying that he was still attached to his former mistress by a trace of sensual voluptuousness." Bayle distrusts Heloise *a priori*: "Heloise loved Abelard so passionately, even though he had been castrated, that his chastity was at risk with her."[60]

Given the intensity of Heloise's desire, as revealed by Letter Four—as well as the emerging notion in the church that conjugal sexual relationship should be maintained at the request of one's spouse—it is legitimate to ask whether Abelard should have been expected to stay with his wife. By the following century, this expectation was granted explicit theological acceptance. The *Dictionnaire de Théologie Catholique* restates thirteenth-century opinion, asserting that a "man becoming a eunuch after a legal marriage is entitled, according to some authors, to have a conjugal sexual relationship" (art. "Mutilation," 2579).

THE FANTASMS OF INTELLECTUAL LIFE AND SEMEN

Abelard's mutilation affected his behavior in different ways. Consequently, his decision to enter religious life is not as self-evident as has been presupposed. Nevertheless, his choice was freely made and was culturally valorized. Like his contemporaries, Abelard thought religious life embodied the path of perfection; he himself wanted to attempt the most heroic road. Full of this conviction, he tried to persuade Heloise of the advantages of this life.

Abelard was confident of his intellectual acumen, and he was well versed in the scientific thought of his day. He may have been persuaded by contemporary scientific authority that his intelligence was directly related to the retention or the emission of semen:

> According to Pythagoras, the semen is 'the foam of our purest blood.' Plato regards it as 'the mellow discharge of the spine marrow,' and Alcmeon as 'the purest and the most delicate part of our brain.' Democritus thinks the semen is a 'substance of our whole body.' Epicure names it 'elixir, extract or epitome of our soul and body.' Galen also thinks that 'this fluid is produced by the whole body and drains into the testicles by its specific veins and nerves. If one loses his semen, he also loses his vitality. No wonder excessive coitus is enervating, since the body is then deprived of its purest substance.'[61] If the semen is produced by the brain, it is already white. In fact, the veins linking the brain to the testicles carry the blood already bleached, to feed the brain, reads the *Anatomia Ricardi Anglici.* The *Liber al-Mansuri* (of Rhazes) also expresses this opinion: vessels branching out in the testicles coil into a series of loops coated by a white glandulous flesh that bleaches the blood it contains. From there, this white blood is then carried to the testicles where it is dramatically processed and turned into perfect semen.... Following Avicenna, Albert the Great's teaching reckoned and established an equivalence between blood and semen—the weakening of the system following the discharge of semen, the fruit of the fourth digestion,amounts to a loss of a quantity of blood that is forty times the quantity of semen.[62]

According to Isidore of Seville, the semen always emerges from bone marrow.[63] The convolutions of the seminiferous vessels are compared to an alembic. Henri de Mondeville, Philip the Fair's surgeon, sums up the prevailing common opinion: "The excess of the good nutritive blood of all the organs is carried to the testicles. After being processed, digested through the testicles and the spermatic vessels, it constitutes semen."[64] According to Vesalius, semen will always be produced in this way. He tries to prove that it is neither in the accessory glands (since castration makes people sterile) nor in the testicles that semen is produced (since the ligature of the seminal veins and arteries also leads to sterility). As a consequence, the vessels carry semen from another source.[65] Obviously, this other source is the cerebrum. Arnold of Villanova reflects the prevailing opinion in Abelard's time:

> per calorem humor eliquatur, qui est in cerebro, per venas attrahitur eliquatus, per eas quae sunt post aures ducitur ad testiculos...deducitur semen a cerebro per venas quae post aures sunt descendentes, et per eas in spinalem medullam, et a medulla in renes, et a renibus ad didimos.... Antiqui dixerunt testiculos esse principalia membra...quod a testiculis praestatur virtus toti corpori.[66]
>
> (a certain humor in the brain is liquefied by heat; once liquefied it is conducted through the veins behind the ears to the testicles...semen is conducted downwards from the brain by the veins which are behind the ears, and from them to the spinal medulla, and from the medulla to the loins, and from the loins into the testicles....The Ancients affirmed that the testicles were the most important organs...because they supply the *virtus* [manliness, manly force] of the whole body.)

From this perspective, the "virtus" released by the testicles to inform the whole body is the seed that patterns *behavior* and therefore determines masculinity as gender. Aline Rousselle states that the castrate oscillates between two meanings of his mutilation: "his regained childhood that makes him a perfect victim of Saturn, and the adulthood whose 'pneuma' can be exclusively psychic, since the waste of the semen disappeared."

Sects that proliferated in the Greco-Roman world early in the Christian era practiced castration to spiritualize the total being. For Cybele's worshippers, the *Galli*, "the essential was giving up procreation through semen, conservation of the vital force, and its transformation into a psychic force. The mother of God mutilated Attis, though he was her lover, because the superior and eternal beings want to make masculine virtue come up to heaven." Medical science proved that:

> the amputation of the *vas deferens* did not allow the purest blood to be released into the penis for fertilization and the seat of the vital force was not located in the genitals. The vital force is transmitted by the latter by fertilizing a woman and begetting a child....But this force can be sustained and become a psychic force for the superior man.... One can locate the elements of understanding and apprehension of the positive aspect of emasculation in the physiology of the vital force and in physical pneumatology.[67]

Such was the understanding of Abelard and his contemporaries. The philosopher himself voices his awareness that at the peak of his sexual activity, his intellectual life had declined almost to non-existence; he was unable to devote his considerable energies to thinking; his teaching so bored and exhausted him that he became neglectful and repetitive. Castration then suddenly plugged this huge waste of psychic energy. He regarded it as an evident intervention of God, a sign of God to his creature to make him collect his wits and devote all his "virtus" to his intellectual life.

In this context, disbanding his marital life held minor significance. What really mattered to Abelard was the new opportunity to elevate himself:

> Deprived of this part of my body which was the seat of voluptuous desires, the primal cause of the lusts of the flesh, I was able to advance in many other ways....Pulled out of the filth into which I jumped as into muck, I was physically and spiritually circumcised. I became more fit for church services since carnal contagion could no longer reach me and spoil me....I was purified rather than mutilated by divine grace....Didn't it expel vice to preserve my spiritual innocence?[68]

Like a well-pruned tree, he will bear good fruit. Freed from the burden of the flesh, his spiritual needs will no longer be limited. He sees castration as the root of his real fecundity:

> Remember how God took care of us: He seemed to have destined us to some grand work and to have been outraged to see that the treasures of semen he had entrusted us with were not applied to the honor of his name.[69]

God entrusted him with the treasures of science because He had intended him for some grand achievement. That is why Abelard was more upset when his enemies tried to wound him in his intellectual fatherhood by burning his books than when his physical fatherhood was affected:

> I compared the torture I had to undergo formerly to the ordeals I had now to go through. I thought I was the most miserable man in the world. The attack Fulbert had perpetrated seems of no importance compared to this new injustice, and I grieved more over my soiled name than over my soiled body.[70]

He is all the more desperate when he proves spiritually sterile as the abbot of a monastery of ruffians:

> I considered with sorrow the pitiful and useless life I was to lead, sterile for me and others. My life among students used to be so fertile, but I had forsaken my disciples to live with these monks, bringing no fruit to anybody.[71]

Critics have been sensitive to the passion for glory Abelard developed after his castration. Charles de Rémusat alludes to a letter he imagines Abelard wrote Heloise:

> I think that religious life only can pave the way for activity, honor, and success. I remember the prospect of ecclesiastical dignities and the spiritual glory your ambition dreamt for me in happier days. All these prospects are still mine if I am able to make them happen. This is perhaps the first time my power has ever been so great.[72]

"From this moment, Abelard's grandeur increases," remarks Etienne Gilson, who is convinced that Abelard's mutilation enabled him to benefit from the sole life fit for a son of God: spiritual life.[73] Abelard shows gratitude to this Father-God who saved his life instead of condemning him: "Corpus vulnerat, et animam sanat. Occidere debuerat, et vivificat. Immunditiam resecat, ut mundum relinquat"[74] (He wounds the body, and heals the soul. He gives life to those who deserve to be killed. He prunes the soiled man, so that he might leave the world).

Abelard's decision to enter monastic life erased the possibility that he and Heloise might provide their culture a new ideal: a union of married passionate lovers, loving parents, and admired intellectuals. Though Abelard was driven by his need to perform his maleness, his post-castration life was marked by the brilliance of his discourse. In the end, he earned accolades from, among others, Peter the Venerable, who when "informing Heloise of his death even compares him to St. Martin and St. Germanus, two models he equalled: the former by his profund humility, the latter by his extreme poverty. His soul meditated over, his mouth uttered, his behaviour heralded divine, learned and real philosophical works only."[75]

His blissful castration enabled Abelard to become what he really wanted to be: a paragon of a Christian and the greatest of philosophers, "the one that should be called the servant and the philosopher of Christ,"[76] says Peter the Venerable, "the only one that really knew what can be known," as his epitaph concluded.[77]

NOTES

This essay was translated and revised with the assistance of Bonnie Wheeler.

1. Abelard, *Historia calamitatum,* J. Monfrin, ed., Bibliotheque des textes philosophiques (Paris: Vrin, 1978), hereafter *HC*; cf. *Patrologia Latina,* J.-P. Migne, ed. (Paris: Migne, 1844), vol. 178, hereafter *PL.*

2. *HC,* pp. 80-81. Cf. *Heloise et Abelard, Lettres et vies,* Yves Ferroul, trans. (Paris: GF-Flammarion, 1996), p. 61. Hereafter *Lettres.*

3. Quoted by Charlotte Charrier, *Héloïse dans l'histoire et dans la légende* (Paris: Champion, 1933), p. 373.

4. Gabriel Peignot, "Abailard," *Dictionnaire biographique et bibliographique portatif des personnages illustres, célèbres ou fameux* (Paris: Hacquart, 1813), p. 3.

5. Charles de Rémusat, *Abélard* (Paris: Calmann Lévy, 1877), p. 329

6. Joseph McCabe, *Peter Abelard* (New York: Burt Franklin, 1901), rep. 1972, p. 120.

7. Charrier, p. 134.

8. Etienne Gilson, *Héloïse et Abélard* (Paris: Vrin, 1938), p. 87.

9. Régine Pernoud, *Héloïse et Abélard* (Paris: Albin Michel, 1970), p. 101.

10. Michèle Sarde, *Regard sur les Françaises. Xème–XXème siècle* (Paris: Stock, 1983), p. 142.

11. Jean Dauvillier, *Le mariage dans le droit classique de l'Église (1130–1314)*, vol. 1 (Paris: Sirey, 1933), ch. 9; cf. Peter Lombard, *L'impedimentum impotentiae*, quoted in Gabriel Le Bras, "Le mariage dans la théologie et le droit de l'Église du XIème au XIIIème siecle," *Cahiers de Civilisation Médiévale* 11 (1968): 195, n. 33.

12. Dauvillier, I, p. 474. The exceptions are ties of kinship, affinity, or the fact of being a clerk.

13. Dauvillier, I, p. 9.

14. Christopher Storey, *La Vie de saint Alexis,* Textes Littéraires Français, verses 61–75 (Paris: Droz-Minard, 1968).

15. Georges Duby, *Le Chevalier, la femme et le prêtre* (Paris: Hachette, 1981), p. 138.

16. Jean-Louis Flandrin, *Un temps pour embrasser, Aux origines de la morale sexuelle occidentale, VIème–XIème siècle,* L'univers Historique (Paris: Seuil, 1983), p. 127; cf. Hincmar de Reims, "Traité du divorce," *Opera Omnia* , vol. 125 (Paris: Migne, 1852), p. 619, quoted in Duby, pp. 55–56.

17. Dom Jean Leclercq, *Le Mariage vu par les moines au XIIème siècle* (Paris: Cerf, 1983), p. 36.

18. Leclercq, *Le Mariage,* pp. 152–53.

19. *Lettres,* p. 61.

20. Duby, p. 63.

21. Duby, p. 280; cf. Gregory of Tours, quoted in Pierre Bayle, "Héloïse," *Dictionnaire historique et critique* (Rotterdam: Reinier-Leers, 1967), n. Z; cf. Leclercq, *Le Mariage*, "Mariages heureux sans consommation," p. 68.

22. Le Bras, pp. 134–36.

23. For example, "a diligent wife is a crown to her husband," "whoever has come across a virtuous wife has found true good and has been bestowed a source of joy by the Lord," "one inherits one's house, one's fortune from one's parents, but only God can give you a wise wife," "blessed is a good woman's husband," "the unfaithful husband is sanctified by his faithful wife," in *Lettres,* pp. 111–12.

24. *PL* 178, 216, Letter Six; cf. Maurice de Gandillac, "Sur quelques interprétations récentes d'Abélard," *Cahiers de Civilisation Médiévale* 4 (1961): 300, n. 31. Innocent III later stipulated this item in the profession of faith required of the Waldenses: "We believe and profess that both man and woman can be saved."

25. *Lettres,* p. 99.

26. Leclercq, p. 48.

27. Charrier, pp. 134–36.

28. Gonzague Truc, *Abélard avec et sans Héloïse* (Paris: Fayard, 1956), p. 33.

29. *HC*, p. 79.

30. *Lettres*, p. 59; *HC*, p.102; *PL* 175A, 178.

31. *Lettres*, p. 143; *PL* 178, 206D and 207A.

32. *Lettres*, pp. 200–01; *PL* 178, 371–76.

33. *Lettres*, p. 196; *PL* 178, 371A: "Quo nomine te censeam, reperire non valeo (…) Sublata igitur parte, quae hominem facit, non Petrus, sad imperfectus Petrus appellandus es."

34. Bayle, "Foulques."

35. Truc, pp. 33, 49.

36. Etienne Gilson, *Héloïse et Abélard*, (Paris: Vrin, 1938), pp. 82, 83, 90.

37. Sarde, pp. 143–44.

38. *PL* 178, 53B.

39. Actually, the ablation is not the only way to castrate (disrupting the process between generative organs and vascular or nerve centres or neutralizing the testicles as generative organs by ligating, crushing, or twisting).

40. For Du Cange (*genitalia:* unde vir generat) the source is the semen and not the generative organ. In the singular "genitale" means the penis (cf. Apulée, Met., 10, 22). In the plural "genitalia" means testicles. Cf. Colummelle, 7, 11, 2: "cutes quae intervenit duobus membris genitalibus" (the septum between the testicles). Furetière, "genitoires": "the testicles or male generative sex-glands"; *testicules.* "c'est ce qu'on appelle proprement génitoires"; *eunuques:* "ceux a qui on a retranché les testicules." Cf. also Littré. The chastisement undergone by Abelard's aggressors is not unusual in the twelfth century: Pierre Bayle ("Foulques", n. L) quotes Suger who reported that in the reign of Louis VI a traitor was blinded and his genitals cut off (oculorum et genitalium amissione damnatus).

41. *HC*, p. 80; *PL* 178, 135 C. Abelard's biblical quotations include references to Leviticus 22:24, which refers to the testicles only (contritis, vel tonsis, vel sectis, ablatisque testiculis); Deuteronomy 23:1, which refers to the testicles and the penis (eunuchus, atritis vel amputatis testiculis, et absciso veretro) to allude to two types of eunuchs—cf. *The Jerusalem Bible*: "the man whose testicles had been crushed or whose penis had been cut off."

42. *Lettres,* p. 105. One can also underline the fact that Fulk alludes to the deprivation of the small parts of the body using a phrase with the same diminutive suffix as "testiculi"; these phrases would be inappropriate to refer to the loss of the penis: "haec corporis particula quam...perdidisti" (*PL* 372D), "particularum ista mutilatio" (*PL* 373B). cf. *Lettres,* p. 199 and 200.

43. Ecclesiastes 2:4 and 3:20.

44. *Dictionnaire de Théologie Catholique* (Paris: Letouzey, 1899) "Eunuques," col. 1250.

45. *Dict. théol. cath.*, "Mutilation," col. 2576; "Eunuques," 1518; I Corinthians 7:9.

46. Jean Astruc, *Traité des maladies des femmes,* vol. 2 (Avignon: Libraires Associés, 1763), ch. 12, p. 152.

47. Cf. Henri Bricaire and J. Dreyfus-Moreau, *Les impuissances sexuelles et leur traitement* (Paris: Flammarion, 1964), esp. p. 15, 17, 39. J. P. Sarramon et al., eds.,*Chirurgie de l'impuissance,* Encyclopédie Médico-Chirurgicale (Paris: Rein, 1978), Organes Génito-Urinaires, 18395 A 20, 3-1984. The complete amputation of the testicles and the penis prevents neither ejaculation nor orgasm. A recent French television program on the sexuality of eunuchs concentrated on contemporary Indian eunuchs (50,000 to 100,000 in number) whose external genitals had been cut off and who lived on the profits of rackets and prostitution. A twenty-year-old

man who was amputated by force when he was fourteen said he still desired women: "When I see a girl on the street, I dream of her. I can't help it and I feel as if I am ejaculating. Then I get up, wash, and change my clothes." Transsexuals often have orgasms after being amputated.

48. *Dict. théol. cath.*, "Eunuque," "Mutilation," col. 2578.

49. Juvenal, *Satires*, Pierre de Labriolle and François Villeneuve, eds., vol. 6 (Paris: Les Belles Lettres, 1931), p. 74.

50. Martial, *Epigrammes*, H.-Z. Izaac, ed., vol. 6 (Paris: Les Belles Lettres, 1930), p. 67.

51. Aline Rousselle, *Porneia. De la maîtrise du corps à la privation sensorielle, IIe–IVe siècles de l'ère chretienne*, Les Chemins de l'Histoire (Paris: Presses universitaires de France, 1983), pp. 159–62.

52. Rousselle, p. 159.

53. *Dict. théol. cath.*, "Eunuques," col. 1519.

54. Bayle, "Abélard," n. R.

55. Demetrius A. Zambaco Pacha, *Les eunuques d'aujourd'hui et ceux de jadis* (Paris: Masson, 1911), p. 91.

56. Dr. Ionel Rapaport, *Les faits de castration rituelle. Essai sur les formes pathologiques de la conscience collective* (Lille: Sautai, 1945), pp. 16, 23.

57. Zambaco Pacha, pp. 99–102. The Chinese seem to have used a less expensive method:

> the patient is laid on a bed, his abdomen and thighs are tied up. Two assistants fasten his legs. The surgeon cuts off both the scrotum and the penis. He then sets a peg into the urethra, washes the wound with peppered water, then lays sheets of paper that had been previously dipped in cold water and covers them with a bandage. It is left so for three days and the patient can neither drink nor urinate. If he cannot urinate after the bandage has been removed, he dies undergoing terrible pain. Usually it heals up after three months. Nevertheless the mortality rate is said not to exceed 4%. Death is due to hemorrhages or infection (Zambaco, p. 213).

The Skoptzy wishing to attain perfection do not approve of castration, but they practice it: "The organ is placed on a block. A knife is laid on it and it is struck with the fist. A lead or thin nail is then set in the urethra to make sure the vessel is permeable, but some Skoptzy do not take this precaution....One must stress the fact that mortal accidents are rare or kept secret" (Rapaport, p. 107).

58. Abelard's statement: "nichil pene fere sentiebam" [I hardly felt any pain] (*HC*, p 102) confirms my argument. When contemporary medicine counts the cases of impotence "it holds that there are three main types of organic impotence factors: the lesion of the rectile tissue, the perturbation of the nerve control and the alteration of the vascular system as well as some endocrine diseases." Surgical castration is not regarded as the cause of the perturbation of nerve control. Cf. Giblod L. Boccon,

"Impuissance sexuelle organique," *Encyclopédie médico-chirurgicale* (Paris: Rein, 1978), 18395 A 10. But it is true that attitude has an important part to play: surgeons have noticed that two out of three men who have gone through a bilateral castration without having the details of the operation explained to them are impotent, which is not actually the case for one in three of them. This proportion is quite different if the patient understands the operation. The loss of virility is a fantasm that assimilates castration to a voluntary homicide—which is not the case as far as other amputations are concerned (*Grande encyclopédie*, "Castration," p. 776). The contemporary phallic cult of psychoanalysts muddles everything, even when it is based on the *Porporino* by Dominique Fernandez (Paris: Grasset et Fasquelle, 1974), in which several castrates have sexual relationships (Eugenie Lemoine Luccioni, *Partage des femmes* [Paris: Points-Seuil, 1976], p. 164). We are therefore as surprised as Aline Rousselle: "In Antiquity and now, the sexual faculties of men deprived of their testicles are still ignored because we refuse to stick to realities" (p. 159, n. 54, and p. 162, n. 59). Note that American judges have asked rapists to choose either prison or castration (*Le Monde*, December 8, 1983), whereas the *Dict. théol. cath.* had already noted "castration would only arouse adult criminals' desires and entice them to relapse"("Mutilation," col. 2577).

59. *HC,* p. 101; *Lettres,* p. 82.

60. Bayle, "Abélard," n. R.

61. Pierre Darmon, *Le mythe de la procréation à l'age baroque* (Paris: Points-Seuil, 1977), p. 12.

62. Claude Thomasset, "La representation de la sexualité et de la génération dans la penséé scientifique médiévale," *Love and Marriage in theTwelfth Century,* Mediaevalia Lovaniensia 1, 8 (1981): 8.

63. Isidore of Seville, *Etymologies,* W. M. Lindsay, ed., vol. 9 (Oxford: Oxford University Press), p. 104.

64. Henri de Mondeville, *Chirurgie,* E. Nicaise, trans. (Paris: Félix Alccan, 1893), *Anatomie,* ch. 9.

65. Andree Vesali, Bruxellensis, invictissimi et V. Caroli, Imperatoris medici, *De humani corporis fabrica libri septem,* vol. 5 (Basel: Joannes Oporinus, 1555), 13, p. 452.

66. Arnaldi Villanovani, *De Coitu* (Basel: C. Waldkirch, 1585), pp. 307–08.

67. Rousselle, pp. 157–59, 164. But the excessive retention of semen is also a threat for it is then spoilt and has an effect on the cerebrum leading to melancholy. Her obvious remedy is then bloodletting. Cf. Jacques Ferrand Agenois, Docteur en la Faculté de Médecine, *De la Maladie d'amour ou mélancholie érotique, Discours curieux qui enseigne à cognoistre l'essence, les causes, les signes & les remèdes de ce mal fantastique* (Paris: Denis Moreau, 1623):

veu que la semence n'est qu'un sang blanchy par la chaleur naturelle, & un excrement de la troisième digestion qui irrite par sa quantité, ou qualité, la nature à l'expeller hors du corps: autrement il se corrompt dans ses réservoirs, & de là il jette, et darde par l'espine du dos & autres conduits occultes mille vapeurs au cerveau, qui troublent ses facultez et vertus principales: il sera fort utile de tirer hors du corps la qualité superfluë du sang, par la seignee de la veine basilique du bras droit.

68. *PL* 178, 206D and 207A: "Unde justissime et clementissime licet cum summa tui avunculi proditione ut in multis crescerem, parte illa corporis sum minutus in quam libidinis regnum erat...et ab his me spurcitiis, quibus me totum quasi luto immerseram, tam mente quam corpore circumcideret; et tanto sacris etiam altaribus idoniorem efficeret, quanto me nulla hinc amplius carnalium contagio pollutionum revocarent....Me divina gratia mundavit potius quam privavit, quid aliud egit quam ad puritatem munditiae conservandam sordida removit et vitia?"; cf. *Lettres,* p. 143.

69. *PL* 178, 208A "Vide ergo quantum sollicitus nostri fuit Dominus, quasi ad magnos aliquos nos reservaret usus, et quasi indignaretur aut doleret illa litteralis scientiae talenta quae utrique nostrum commiserat, ad sui nominis honorem non dispensari"; cf. *Lettres,* p. 145.

70. *HC,* p. 89: "Conferebam cum his que in corpore passus olim fueram quanta nunc sustinerem. et omnium hominum me estimabarn miserrimum. Parvam illa ducebam proditionem in comparatione hujus injurie, et longe amplius fame quam corporis detrimentum plangebam"; cf. *Lettres,* pp. 69–70.

71. *HC,* p. 99: "Considerabam et plangebam quam inutilem et miseram vitam ducerem et quam infructuose tam mihi quam aliis viverem, et quantum antea clericis profecissem et quod nunc, eis propter monachos dimissis, nec in ipsis nec in monachis aliquem fructum haberem"; cf. *Lettres,* p. 80.

72. Rémusat, pp. 329–30.

73. Gilson, p. 91.

74. *PL* 178, 210B; cf. *Lettres,* p. 149.

75. *PL* 178, esp. p. 19: "in tantum ut nec Germanus abjectior ipse Martinus bene discernenti pauperior appareret," "mens ejus, lingua ejus, opus ejus semper divina, semper philosophica, semper eruditoria meditabatur, docebat, fatebatur."

76. Charrier, p. 295.

77. *PL* 178, esp. p. 19: "Est satis in tumulo, Petrus hic jacet Abaelardus,/Cui soli patuit scibile quidquid erat."

EUNUCHS WHO KEEP THE SABBATH: BECOMING MALE AND THE ASCETIC IDEAL IN THIRTEENTH-CENTURY JEWISH MYSTICISM

Elliot R. Wolfson

This study examines the nexus of asceticism and eroticism in the zoharic kabbalah. Renunciation of sexual power facilitated the spiritual empowerment of the male mystics.

The link between asceticism and gender has been well established in scholarly literature. In the history of various classical religious traditions, particularly prominent in Christianity, ascetic behavior afforded women the opportunity to overcome not only the limitations of the natural body but also the social status determined by gender. The stereotypical construction of women (well attested in Late Antiquity and the Middle Ages) as sexual objects (expressed most dramatically as the personification of carnal desire in the form of the temptress) and domestic beings (identified principally through the roles of marriage, childbearing, and housekeeping) was disrupted by the adoption of an ascetic lifestyle. Celibacy served as the most effective way to attain the erasure of sexual difference epitomized in the baptismal formula adopted by Paul, "there is neither male nor female, for you are all one in Christ Jesus" (Gal. 3: 28).[1] However, in light of the prevailing gender hierarchy, which is affirmed by Paul himself (1 Cor. 11: 2–16, 14: 34–36), the renunciation of sexual and other bodily pleasures on the part of early Christian women meant that the female became more spiritual and hence more masculine. Sexual abstention could thus be seen as part of the redemptive process by means of which the spiritual order is restored and the female element obliterated. Alternatively expressed, one can speak of asceticism as the mechanism by means of which the feminine female (seductive Eve) is transformed into the masculine female (virgin Mary or the body of the Church). Analogously, in the case of male Christian ascetics, sexual abstinence, epitomized in the statement attributed to Jesus regarding those who "have made themselves eunuchs for the sake of the kingdom of heaven" (Matt. 19: 12), did not entail effeminization but a further empowering of the masculine, which was associated with the incorporeal. Spiritual progress was understood as a process of the female becoming male.[2] Ascetical sublimation, therefore, did not result in the complete effacing of gender differences in either a sociological or theological sense. On the contrary, the destabilization of the sociosexual roles of women only reinforced the dominant position of the male in the social and religious order.

The focus of this study is the impact of the ascetic ideal of sexual abstinence on the construction of masculinity in the mystical fraternity surrounding the literary composition of the *Zohar* in late-thirteenth-century Castile. Scholars have duly noted the ascetical dimension expressed in the classical rabbinic corpus and in the medieval pietistic treatises of both Iberian and Franco-German extraction as well as in the unique trend of Jewish Sufism that evolved amongst the descendants of Maimonides in Egypt in the thirteenth and fourteenth centuries.[3] By contrast, the function of asceticism in kabbalistic texts has not received the attention that it warrants. What has been written on the subject has concentrated for the most part on the ascetic dimensions of kabbalistic pietism expressed in sixteenth-century texts.[4] The specific connection of gender and asceticism, to the best of my knowledge, has not been treated by scholars of Jewish mysticism.

Much emphasis has been placed on the sacrality of sexuality in the kabbalistic tradition.[5] The scholarly consensus is expressed with passionate eloquence by Gershom Scholem:

> Chastity is indeed one of the highest moral values of Judaism.... But at no time was sexual asceticism accorded the dignity of a religious value, and the mystics make no exception. Too deeply was the first command of the Torah, Be fruitful and multiply, impressed upon their minds. The contrast to other forms of mysticism is striking enough to be worth mentioning: non-Jewish mysticism, which glorified and propagated asceticism, ended sometimes by

> transplanting eroticism into the relation of man to god. Kabbalism, on the other hand, was tempted to discover the mystery of sex within God himself. For the rest it rejected asceticism and continued to regard marriage not as a concession to the frailty of the flesh but as one of the most sacred mysteries. Every true marriage is a symbolical realization of the union of God and the Shekhinah.[6]

From other passages in his *oeuvre*, it is clear that Scholem not only recognized that there has been an ascetical dimension in the history of Judaism, but he was of the opinion that the early kabbalists in twelfth-century Provence emerged from groups of ascetic pietists (referred to variously as *perushim*, *nezirim*, and *ḥasidism*).[7] Indeed, the contemplative ideal proferred by the Provençal kabbalist, Isaac the Blind, and elaborated by his Geronese disciples, is predicated on an ascetic renunciation of the body and sensual desire.[8] In this connection, Scholem noted the historical similarities between the ascetic phenomenon in the Jewish communities of southern France and the monastic tendencies evident in both Catholic clergy and Cathar *perfecti* of the time. Yet, even here Scholem sounded a note of caution, asserting that there are "clear divergences resulting from the different attitudes of Judaism and Christianity toward celibacy."[9]

One cannot disagree with the claim that in the kabbalistic tradition, as in the case of rabbinic Judaism more generally, sexuality is not problematized in the way that it is in the history of Christianity.[10] The practice of unconditional celibacy is not idealized in Jewish texts nor is the image of the virgin placed on a spiritual pedestal. Indeed, from the more specific vantage point of the theosophic kabbalah, articulated especially (but not exclusively) in the zoharic corpus, the Christian ideal of monasticism is demonized. The embodiment of impurity, Satan, is portrayed as the castrated male who is contrasted with the virile, circumcised male Jew.[11] This symbolism underlies the zoharic portrayal of the kings of Edom (Gen. 36: 31–39), the archetypal representation of the historical force of Christianity, as emasculated males.[12] From the perspective of gender, therefore, Christianity is correlated with masculine impotence, which is equivalent to the feminine character of judgment. The overcoming of the primordial state of male sterility is related in the *Zohar* to Hadar, the last of the Edomite kings delineated in the biblical record, for he is the only one whose wife, Mehetabel, is mentioned. Symbolically, the zoharic author associates

Hadar with the divine attribute that corresponds to the phallus, *Yesod*, which is also called the "fruit of the tree of splendor," *peri 'eṣ hadar* (Lev. 23: 40) and is compared to the date-palm (based on Ps. 92:13), which comprises male and female characteristics.[13] Significantly, the rectification of the celibate condition of the previous seven Edomite kings, who represent the ecclesiastical hierarchy of Roman Catholicism, is connected to the androgynous phallus[14] of God (embodied in the circumcised penis of the Jewish male). That heterosexual desire is a component of this rectification is obvious from the fact that Hadar and Mehetabel are both mentioned. But the theosophical importance of the heterosexual pairing, which one may presume is expressed in the erotic bonding between the sexes, is derived from the fact that the locus of the androgyny is the phallic gradation, represented symbolically by Hadar. Erotic yearning for the feminine is indicative of the beginning of the redemptive process, which overcomes duality and division, but the consummation is marked by the restoration of the feminine to the masculine, which entails the transformation of the *Shekhinah* from feminine other to the sign of the covenant or the corona of the phallus.[15] Corresponding to this crossing of gender identities is a shift in the texture of the erotic experience from the heterosexual to the homoerotic, a point to which I shall return below.

Repeatedly, as scholars of Jewish mysticism have noted, the zoharic authorship and scores of other kabbalists emphasize that anthropological completeness is attained only in marriage. According to the graphic image of the *Zohar*, the single male or female is merely "half a body" (*pelag gufa'*), a technical term that denotes ontological (and not merely physiological or even psychological) imperfection.[16] Indeed, the distinctive holiness of the Jewish people (based on the biblical mandate in Lev. 19: 2) is linked to the sanctity that is attained when husband and wife are joined together in sexual intercourse, which is a form of *imitatio dei* insofar as the divine anthropos is imaged as a union of masculine and feminine.[17] Accordingly, in kabbalistic sources in general, and in the *Zohar* in particular, one finds a positive valorization of marriage as a means of religious devotion. In line with the rabbinic ethos, moreover, the kabbalists affirm the positive valence of human sexuality as the means to procreate.[18] Moreover, the kabbalists, building upon allusions found in some rabbinic comments, assigned theurgic significance to human sexuality as a means to cause the indwelling of the *Shekhinah* or to augment the divine image,[19] which is understood in the theosophic symbolism of the kabbalah as androgynous.[20] The failure to produce offspring is considered by the *Zohar* to be a major offense, indeed the transgression for which the punishment of transmigration of the soul is specifically prescribed.[21] The man who dies childless is judged as if he had castrated himself. Inasmuch as emasculation is a distinguishing feature of the demonic force, such a person cleaves to the side of the unholy and he is thus denied entrance before God.[22]

Although the idea that the complete human being comprises male and female is clearly rooted in earlier rabbinic exegesis of the scriptural account of creation, it is possible that the particular form of expression that this idea assumes in the *Zohar* serves as a polemic against the Christian affirmation of celibacy as the means to restore humanity to its pristine state. Precisely this intention is implied in one context where this doctrine is related to the zoharic claim that a priest who is not married cannot enter the Temple to offer sacrifices.[23] The *Shekhinah* does not rest on such a person and blessings cannot be transmitted through him since he is blemished. Indeed, he is not even in the category of a human being (*'adam*) insofar as the latter comprises both male and female.[24] In passing, I note the convergence of the theurgic-symbolic and erotic-ecstatic elements: The priest cannot draw down blessings that issue from the union of the masculine and feminine aspects of the divine unless he is erotically bound to the *Shekhinah*, but only one who is wed can be bound in such a way,[25] for, as it is recurringly emphasized in the zoharic corpus, the *Shekhinah* (or the blessing that emanates therefrom) only rests upon the man who is married.[26] The portrayal of the married Jewish priest functions in this context as an antidote to the Catholic priest who is required to be celibate. These passages and many others unquestionably support the contention of Scholem (and scholars who have followed his line of interpretation) that the kabbalistic tradition assigned a positive valence to sexuality as a sacrament that celebrates the union of masculine and feminine energies in the divine as well as the means by which children are engendered in this world.

From another perspective, however, Scholem's generalization must be qualified. Not only is it the case that there have been Jewish mystics of an ascetic orientation, but the sacralization of human sexuality, which lies at the heart of kabbalistic myth and ritual, is dialectically related to the ascetic impulse.[27] To express the matter in an alternative way, in the kabbalistic tradition carnal sexuality is celebrated only to the extent that it is transformed by the proper intentionality into a spiritual act. This dimension of the kabbalistic approach, as it has been pointed out recently,[28] is articulated clearly in one of the more important manuals on sexual etiquette written in the later part of the thirteenth-century, the *'Iggeret ha-Qodesh*, the "Holy Epistle." It is worthwhile examining some of the key passages from this work since the attitude expressed therein is rather typical of the position adopted by medieval kabbalists in general.

According to the anonymous author of this text, the ontic condition of humanity prior to the sin in the Garden of Eden was such that Adam and Eve were "engaged with the intelligible matters (*muskkalot*) and all of their intention was for the sake of heaven."[29] The erotic nature of the conjunction of the rational soul and the supernal light is underscored in another passage where it is emphasized that the Hebrew word *yedi'ah* can be used to connote both cognition and conjugal intimacy.[30] In the pristine state of human existence, therefore, the sexual impulse was itself of a spiritual quality for Adam and Eve were primarily concerned with intelligible realities, which in this context refers to the sefirotic emanations.[31] However, when the aboriginal couple lusted after physical pleasures (*hana'ot ha-gufaniyyot*) detached from concentration on the spiritual matters, they were lowered to the level of base sexuality, and, consequently, eros itself became problematized for the physical was separated from the intelligible. Thus, before the sin Adam and Eve felt no shamefulness with regard to their nakedness (Gen. 2: 25); the shamefulness felt after the sin and the need to cover the genitals (ibid., 3:7) results from the fact that sensual desire was severed from its metaphysical basis.[32] The dichotomization of carnal passion and spiritual eros is reflected, moreover, in the interpretation of the rabbinic tradition[33] that designates Sabbath eve as the proper time for scholars to engage in conjugal sex: The physical act of sex is appropriate for the sages on the eve of Sabbath precisely because it is a time of increased spirituality, the day "that is entirely cessation and repose," the "foundation of the world," which is "in the pattern of the world of souls."[34] The offspring produced by the union of husband and wife on that night is endowed with a rational soul, which derives ontically from the world of souls, for in the act of coitus the intention of the sage is directed to the divine attribute called the "rational soul," which is elsewhere identified in this treatise as the source of thought.[35] The operative principle here is the scientific belief of the Middle Ages, based on philosophical works of Antiquity, that the mental intention of the parents is one of the key factors that helps determine the nature of the foetus.[36] So unequivocal is the author of this text in his rejection of carnal sex without a spiritual element that in another passage he remarks that if someone marries a woman only on account of her physical beauty, their conjugal union is not for the sake of God. Moreover, since his intention during intercourse is focused exclusively on physical pleasure, the child born from their union is considered a "stranger" and "foreigner" in whom God has no portion. The parents cause the *Shekhinah* to depart from them, and they are rebellious in relation to God.[37] By contrast, the partriarchs are signaled out for their being in constant conjunction with God even when engaged in corporeal matters.[38] Thus, Jacob was said to merit the twelve tribes on account of the fact that he was never separated from the supernal light, and they are described as being "in the image of the cosmic order, bearers of the instruments of God, for their thought was not separated from the supernal conjunction even in the moment of union and intercourse."[39]

The kabbalistic ideal articulated by this author can be explained on the basis of the pronounced influence that Platonic dualism of spirit and matter had on the pietists and mystics of the different religious traditions in medieval society.[40] Beyond the evident privileging of the spiritual over the material, the Platonic ontology also imparted to mystics the correlation of eros and noesis, which allowed for the expression of the latter in terms of the former.[41] As I argue in more detail below, in zoharic theosophy there is a correspondence between contemplative experience and seminal emission; indeed, the *semen virile* is homologized to the light-seed of the brain.[42] Hence, mental activity assumes a decidedly erotic character. When viewed dialectically, however, it can be said that the intensely anthropomorphic and erotic representations of the divine, which are characteristic of the theosophic forms of kabbalah that evolved in the high Middle Ages, are predicated on the devaluation of the physical body and the senses. In kabbalistic theosophy, the symbolic retrieval of the body to characterize incorporeal realities is based on the abnegation of the human body. The kabbalist experiences God in erotic terms, but such an experience is dependent on the subjugation of physical eros: the spiritualization of the erotic leads to the eroticization of the spiritual.[43] The erotic characterization of the noetic thus serves seemingly antithetical goals: the mental concentration required of the man in the act of coitus transforms the generative force of physical desire into the creative energy of contemplation, but the latter is experienced in a distinctively sensual manner.[44] The erotic nature of mystical ecstasy is based on an ascetic denial of the body, which facilitated the spiritual marriage of the kabbalist and the divine. In that sense, it is appropriate to posit an ideal of celibacy developed by the zoharic circle, albeit one that is far more limited than Christian monasticism. Indeed, for these kabbalists, the very process of becoming male was predicated to some degree on the ascetic transformation of eros and the upward channeling of the phallic energy from the genitals to the mind.

The key passage in the *Zohar* wherein the ascetic ideal is expressed is an extraordinarily bold reading of the following biblical text: "For thus said the Lord: As far as the eunuchs who keep my Sabbaths, who have chosen what I desire and they hold fast to My covenant, I will give them, in My house and within My walls, a monument and a name better than sons and daughters, I will give them an everlasting name that shall not perish" (Isa. 56: 4–5):

> Who are the eunuchs? These are the comrades engaged in Torah. They castrate themselves the six days of the week and study Torah, and on the night of Sabbath they prepare themselves for intercourse, for they know the supernal secret concerning the time when the Matrona unites with the King. The comrades who know this secret direct their hearts to the Faith of their Master and they are blessed with the fruit of their loins on that night....They are truly called eunuchs because they wait for the Sabbath, to discover the desire of their Master, as it is written, 'who have chosen what I desire.' What is [the meaning of] 'what I desire'? It is intercourse with the Matrona. 'And they hold fast to My covenant,' it is all one. 'My covenant,' without qualification. Praiseworthy is the portion of the one who is sanctified in this holiness and who knows this mystery.[45]

The scriptural reference to the eunuchs who keep the Sabbath is applied allegorically to the members of the kabbalistic fraternity. In the course of the six weekdays the kabbalists abstain from sexual intercourse, but on the eve of Sabbath they engage in marital sex because they know the secret of the holy union of the feminine and masculine aspects of God consummated precisely at that time.[46] The zoharic passage is based on the rabbinic recommendation (mentioned above) that Torah scholars ideally should fulfill their conjugal obligations only on Friday evening.[47] Going beyond the talmudic injunction, however, the kabbalistic idea is linked to the assumption that the abstinence of those occupied in the study of Torah reflects the ontological condition of the divine potencies. During the days of the week the *Shekhinah* is entrapped in the demonic shells (symbolic of exile), and she is thus compared to a gate that is closed so that the unholy male will not be afforded the opportunity to have intercourse with the holy female. By contrast, on Sabbath the *Shekhinah* is liberated and the gate is opened to allow the holy male to have intercourse with the holy female (symbolic of redemption).[48] On Friday evening, therefore, it is the task of the comrades to direct their intention to the *Shekhinah*, referred to by the technical term "Faith of their Master," when they are having intercourse with their wives, for by so doing they will draw down the blessing of the divine in their procreative act and thereby merit to have righteous children.[49] The intention of the kabbalist in the act of coitus facilitates the union above between the King and the Matrona, a theurgic deed referred to in the scriptural expression, "they hold fast to My covenant," i.e., by means of his sexual activity the kabbalist fortifies the phallic aspect of God.[50]

The mystics are called eunuchs, therefore, for their sexual abstinence during the week is a metaphorical castration. Paradoxically, the kabbalists can engage in carnal sex only at the time of heightened spirituality in the world, the eve of Sabbath. The zoharic imagery underscores a deep ambivalence about celibacy as a religious ideal for the mystical elite, on the one hand, and the marital obligation to procreate, on the other.[51] A careful examination of the relevant passages, however, has led me to the conclusion that the ascetic dimension is not pitted against the erotic; on the contrary, as I have already remarked, asceticism and eroticism in the *Zohar* (and other kabbalistic sources) are dialectically interrelated: the impulse to chastity is itself a sexual impulse.[52] The symbolic castration of the kabbalist does not imply sexual impotence, which would be equivalent to effeminization, but the transformation of the phallic energy from carnal intercourse with one's earthly wife to spiritual intercourse with the *Shekhinah*. The imaginal contemplation of the divine ensues from the erotic attachment of the mystic to God.[53]

The erotic and ultimately phallic nature of the image of the eunuch can only be gathered from a careful scrutiny of the passages that describe in more detail the activities of the comrades in the weekdays when others are engaged in marital intercourse. According to the *Zohar*, the propitious time for the conjugal act is midnight,[54] which is the hour when God is said to visit the souls of the righteous in the Garden of Eden in order to take delight in them.[55] In almost every instance, the delight that is attributed to God is related to the study of Torah on part of the kabbalists.[56] Hence, at the very moment that most Jewish males engage in marital sex, the mystical elite renounce physical sexuality in favor of a spiritualized relationship with God that is consummated through midrashic activity of an intensely erotic nature. One passage in particular underscores the nexus of different motifs:

> The sexual intercourse of [the Jewish] male is restricted to designated times so that he may direct his will to be conjoined to the Holy One, blessed be he. Thus they have taught: At midnight the Holy One, blessed be he, enters the Garden of Eden to take delight with the righteous, and the Community of Israel praises the Holy One, blessed be he, and this is the acceptable time to be conjoined to them. The comrades who are engaged in [study of] Torah join the Community of Israel in praising the holy King as they are occupied with the Torah. For the rest of the [Jewish] males this is the acceptable time to be sanctified in the sanctity of the Holy One, blessed be he, and to direct their intention to be conjoined to him. With respect to the comrades who are engaged in [study of] Torah, the time for their sexual intercourse is the time that another intercourse takes place, and this is on the eve of Sabbath.[57]

The mystics rise at midnight to study Torah at precisely the time that other Jewish males should ideally engage in sexual intercourse. The hermeneutical activity of the kabbalist is viewed as distinct from yet isomorphic to the conjugal sex of the layman: Just as the latter is conjoined to God through the proper intention in sexual intercourse, so the former attains the state of conjunction by means of textual exegesis. The phenomenological structure of the two experiences is identical: by uniting with the female (in the case of the ordinary male his wife and in the case of the mystic the *Shekhinah*) the male gains access to the masculine potency of the divine. Thus, in another passage the zoharic author states that at midnight the scholars "rise to study Torah, to be united to the *Shekhinah* in order to praise the holy King."[58] The act of self-castration suggested by the use of the metaphor of the eunuch in no way implies emasculinization of the male mystic.

On the contrary, according to the *Zohar*, the kabbalist who abstains from carnal sex is united with the feminine *Shekhinah*. The masculine virility of the kabbalist is left intact, indeed augmented, albeit translated from the physical to the spiritual. The renunciation of sexual power results in the empowerment of the mystic.[59] As the zoharic author puts the matter: "With respect to the sages who separate from their wives all the days of the week in order to be involved in [the study of] Torah, the supernal union (*ziwwuga' 'ila'ah*) is conjoined to them and it is not separated from them so that male and female will be found. When the Sabbath arrives, the sages must bring joy to their homes[60] on account of the glory of the supernal union, and they must direct their hearts to the will of their master."[61] The perspective of the *Zohar* was well understood by the sixteenth-century kabbalist, Elijah de Vidas, who thus commented: "The time of the intercourse of the rest of the people during the week, which is at midnight, is the time that the scholar is sanctified through intercourse with the Community of Israel, to rise to study Torah. Thus, he is sanctified through the holy, spiritual intercourse (*ziwwug ruḥani we-qadosh*), just as the rest of the people are sanctified through the physical intercourse (*ziwwug gashmi*)."[62] One can speak of the kabbalist's spiritual marriage to the *Shekhinah*, a matrimonial bond predicated on the separation from one's physical wife.[63] To be sure, only the kabbalist who is married can attain a state of conjunction with the *Shekhinah*, but to achieve that experience it is necessary to abstain from conjugal intercourse.[64] As a number of scholars have noted, the model of the abstinent mystic was Moses who, according to older rabbinic sources, separated from his wife after having received the Torah. The aggadic tradition is the basis for the zoharic idea that the union of Moses and the *Shekhinah* is consequent upon his adopting a life of celibacy.[65] The primary means by which the kabbalist emulates Moses and is united with the *Shekhinah* is study of Torah, a spiritually erotic experience that presupposes the negation of physical eros.

Hence, the image of the eunuch, by which the kabbalist is portrayed, is paradoxically transformed into a symbol of masculine fecundity. Indeed, for the Castilian kabbalists who participated in the zoharic circle, becoming male in the full sense was predicated on the ascetic sublimation of the erotic. As I have already indicated, the form that this forbearance took may be referred to as the upward displacement of the phallic energy from the genitals to the brain. Contemplative study of Torah, which for the zoharic author involved visually meditating on the shape of God embodied in the script of Torah, is predicated on the homology of the psychomental and the erogenic.[66] To a degree, this homology is derived from the zoharic understanding of the divine anatomy. Of particular relevance is the entity that is named by the zoharic authorship *boṣina' de-qardinuta'*, the "hardened spark," which is the aspect of the divine that gives shape to the luminous forms of being, a process that is often related more specifically to the act of writing or engraving. In other studies, I have argued that this spark functions like an upper phallus in the mind of God.[67] Moreover, the zoharic author depicted the very seed whence the sefirotic emanations come to be as made up of the letters of the Hebrew alphabet. The linguistic evolution of God's becoming, therefore, is a process of spermatogenesis.[68]

It goes without saying that the author of the *Zohar* understood the operation of the human mind in terms that correspond to the divine mind. Thus, the hermeneutical activity of the kabbalist, which is linked to the phallic imagination, is comparable in structure and function to the creative effort of God. The prooftext that serves in the *Zohar* to anchor both divine illumination and mystical enlightenment is Dan. 12:3, "And the enlightened will shine like the splendor of the sky."[69] The radiant ecstasy that arises from textual engagement involves the erotic union of the kabbalist and the *Shekhinah*, an experience that takes the place of conjugal sex with one's earthly wife.[70] From that vantage point, eroticism and aceticism are to be seen in a dialectical, not oppositional, relationship. Becoming male for the mystical elite entails metaphorical self-castration. The true male is he who willfully adopts the posture of the eunuch, for only the castrated mystic can realize the ultimate act of masculine virility by becoming one with the divine feminine. The most potent form of eroticism is actualized through the retention rather than the discharge of the seminal fluid from the genitals and its restoration to the supernal source in the cavity of the head.

With respect to this interdependence of asceticism and eroticism, there is an interesting parallelism between the *Zohar* and Tantrism, although there is no explicit instruction in the former (or in kabbalistic literature in general) to immobilize the emission of semen in the act of coitus as part of a spiritual exercise of mental concentration like we find in the latter.[71] Nevertheless, the proscribed behavior of the kabbalist to refrain from sexual intercourse at the precise moment that he contemplates the divine in his imagination suggests that in the *Zohar* there is a comparable phenomenon to the tantric practice of awakening and driving the *kuṇḍalinī* (the feminine vital energy in the form of a coiled snake at the base of the spine) by drawing up the semen (*biṇḍu*) from the genitals through the spinal cord to the spiritual center of the brain.[72] That is, only after having mastered physical eros can the kabbalist creatively interpret Scripture and contemplate the symbolically anthropomorphic image of the divine form. Exposition of esoteric doctrines, both in oral and written discourse, is itself a reified type of sexual copulation.[73] The splendor of mystical insight is the light-seed in the head that corresponds to the *semen virile* of the genitals. The aim of the kabbalist, therefore, is not only to cause the seminal energy to flow from the brain to the phallus whence it overflows to the feminine receptacle wherein the holy union is realized. The moment of mystical assimilation into the Godhead is attained by a reverse flow of the seminal energy from the phallus to the brain. What sets the upward trajectory into motion is the withholding of the ejaculation of seed on the part of the kabbalist. The ultimate theurgic role of the kabbalists who rise to study at midnight is to draw down the influx of divine energy from the upper recesses of the Godhead upon the masculine attribute of *Tiferet* and from there to the feminine *Malkhut*.[74] I would argue, nonetheless, that the downward motion of the seminal light in the divine anthropos is occasioned by the upward motion of the *semen virile* in the body and mind of the kabbalist.

From yet another perspective there is a striking similarity between the kabbalistic and tantric positions. It has been argued that the conjunction of masculine and feminine is fundamentally different in the two traditions: The kabbalist affirms carnal sex as a means to foster procreation below and to mimic the mystical coupling of the male *Tif'eret* and the female *Shekhinah* above; by contrast, the yogin seeks to overcome gender polarity by reintegrating the feminine power of *śakti* and the masculine power of *śiva* in the uppermost *cakra* (center) of the subtle body called *sahasrāra* (thousand-petaled lotus) or *brahmarandhra* (located on the crown of the skull) so that the primary state of nonduality is attained in the reconfiguration of the androgyne.[75] In this state masculine and feminine are logically distinguishable without signifying duality or division; in the oneness of the Absolute the polarity of gender is transcended but not negated. Although it is certainly true, as I have previously noted, that in the theosophic kabbalah great emphasis is placed on the sacrality of heterosexual union, a close reading of the sources indicates that the spiritual ideal for the kabbalist likewise entails the overcoming of the duality of gender, which is achieved by reintegrating the feminine in the masculine.[76]

Ontological fission within the Godhead, reflected in the historical condition of Israel's exile, results in the bifurcation of the male androgyne into the masculine and feminine hypostases, which, in turn, yields the desire of the masculine to overcome duality and separation, a desire that is manifest in images of heterosexual fantasy. The lust of the male for the female is interpreted in the *Zohar* (and related kabbalistic literature) as the attempt of the male to restore the part of himself that has been severed.[77] In the state of redemption, the otherness of the feminine is transcended and the primordial male androgyne is reconfigured. In the overcoming of duality, however, gender is not abolished in the face of a neutered unity. On the contrary, the union of the sexes results in the feminine being transformed into an aspect of the masculine. More specifically, the kabbalists embrace the idea that the male and female are united through the phallus: the organ itself corresponds to the male and the corona to the female. With respect to this structure, we again find an interesting phenomenological parallel to the symbol of the androgynous linga in tantric doctrine. Consider, for example, the following description of the unity achieved through the union of the sexes according to the method of *kulayāga*: "Since the stem of the median channel is also visualized as inseparably linked to the sex organs—as it indeed is in the esoteric experience—there results a symbolic identification of the male and female united through the phallus with the sexually polarized triangular lotuses strung on and united through the median channel. It is no doubt here, in the reciprocal 'sexualization' of the median channel and the 'spiritualization' of the coital exchange, that the mythical identity of the *axis mundi* with the *liṅga* has its true rationale."[78] Bracketing the obvious differences between Tantrism and zoharic kabbalah, the conceptual similarities are indeed conspicuous: The union of the sexes in both traditions results in the integration of the feminine in the phallus. Returning to the zoharic texts, the phallicization of the feminine implies that heterosexual eros (desire for the other as self) gives way to homoeroticism (love of self as other). In the symbolic worldview of the *Zohar*, therefore, the same-sex union is possible to the degree that physical sexuality has been abandoned for the sake of a spiritualized erotics. To put the matter somewhat differently: Homoeroticism is the carnality of celibate renunciation. A prolepsis of the eschatological transmutation of erotic energy from the bisexual to the monosexual is found in the fraternity of mystics whose study of Torah takes the place of sexual mating with their female partners.[79]

What are the implications of this dynamic for the question of the masculine identity of the medieval kabbalist? In previous scholarly discussions on the nature of eros in the *Zohar*, attention has been paid almost exclusively to the heterosexual nature of the relationship of the male mystic and the feminine *Shekhinah*. The erotic bonding of the male mystic and the divine feminine, however, must be seen as only the first stage in an integrative process that culminates with a restitution of the feminine to the phallus. To avoid potential misunderstanding, let me emphasize that I do not deny the obvious fact that eros in the theosophic symbolism of the *Zohar* entails the heterosexual yearning of the male for the female. The task before the scholar, however, is to evaluate how gender types are constructed in the particular cultural context of the medieval kabbalists. The mystery of faith, as the zoharic author reminds the reader time and again, consists of the unification of male and female. But what is the nature of masculinity and femininity in light of the kabbalistic understanding of coitus? As I have already noted, the goal of sexual intercourse is to restore the feminine to the masculine. The most startling image used to convey this restoration is the symbol of the penal corona, which is identified with the feminine.

To highlight the hermeneutical value of this approach, let me review a topic that a number of scholars have previously analyzed: According to the *Zohar*, the righteous man stands between two females, his earthly wife and the *Shekhinah*.[80] In that respect, the mystic emulates the pattern of the divine gradations for the masculine *Tif'eret* is situated between *Binah* and *Malkhut*, the upper and lower *Shekhinah*. But just as *Tif'eret* is between two females, so the lower *Shekhinah* occupies a position between two righteous males, *Yesod* and the mystic sage.[81] The primary function of the righteous man below is to stimulate the *Shekhinah* so that she arouses the desire of the masculine above. From this vantage point, the eroticism is to be viewed in purely heterosexual terms. However, this arousal is also expressed in the homoerotically charged image of the righteous below, causing the divine phallus to become erect. Two zoharic passages are particularly noteworthy:

> Come and see the secret of the matter: When the righteous man is in the world, the *Shekhinah* does not depart from him, and her desire is for him. Consequently, the desire of love for her from above is like the desire of a male for a female when he is jealous of her.[82]

> Rachel gave birth to two righteous men, and this was appropriate for the *Shemiṭṭah*[83] always sits between two righteous men, as it is written, 'The righteous men shall inherit the land' (Ps. 37: 29), the righteous above and the righteous below. From the righteous above the supernal waters flow and from the righteous below the feminine emits fluid in relation to the masculine in complete desire.[84]

The critical point here, which has been ignored by scholars, is the shifting gender valences implied by this chain of desire: the erotic conjunction of the mystic with the *Shekhinah* transforms the latter from a passive female to an active male and the former from an active male to a passive female. To arouse the supernal male, the female must assume a role that is characteristically masculine; what facilitates the assumption of this role is the insemination of the female by the male mystic. In the language of one zoharic passage, which is a homiletical reflection on "And your people, all of them righteous, shall possess the land for all time" (Isa. 60: 21): "There is none to possess that land except for the one that is called righteous, for the Matrona is conjoined to him in order to be sweetened, and the righteous man verily possesses the Matrona."[85] The mystical meaning of the prophetic claim that the righteous shall inherit the land is that only the righteous male can be mystically conjoined to the *Shekhinah*. The effect that this conjunction has on the *Shekhinah* is (in the technical zoharic terminology[86]) that it sweetens her, i.e., the union with the righteous male ameliorates feminine judgment by masculine mercy. The ultimate goal of the mystic's interpretative efforts is the union of the masculine and feminine aspects of the divine, but this union results in the restoration of the latter to the former.

The mystery of the gender transformation is related in another zoharic passage to the verse, "Isaac then brought her into the tent of his mother Sarah, and he took Rebekah as his wife" (Gen. 24: 67):

> The secret of the matter: The supernal mother [*Binah*] is found with the male [*Tif'eret*] only when the home [*Malkhut*] is in order, and the male and female are united. Then the supernal mother showers blessings upon them. In a similar way, the lower mother [*Malkhut*] is found with the male only when the home is in order, and the male comes to the female and they are joined as one. Then the lower mother showers blessings upon them. Thus the male in his home is crowned by two females in the manner of the world above.[87]

The complexity of gender symbolism reflected in the above citation (as well as numerous other passages) renders it far too simplistic to say that the dominant orientation in the zoharic composition is that the mystic is masculine in relation to the feminine *Shekhinah*.[88] The erotic union of the male mystic and the feminine *Shekhinah* results in the mutual transformation of the two: the masculine below is feminized and the feminine above is masculinized. In the language of the *Zohar*, the man is crowned by two females, one above and one below; the upper feminine assumes a masculine role and showers blessings upon him, whereas the lower feminine receives sustenance from him.

A fascinating account of this gender transformation is found in the extended passage in the *Zohar* that presents the technique of gazing at a candle in order "to know the wisdom of the holy unity."[89] The zoharic author recommends that one should contemplate the flame that rises from the coal or upon a candle that is burning. It is the second image that engages the imagination of the zoharic author, but the importance of the first image, which can be traced to *Sefer*

Yeṣirah, is that it underscores the point that a flame only rises when it is united with gross matter. In accord with the standard medieval hierarchy, the flame is the spiritual element that is sustained by the material. It is also evident that this can be transmuted into gender terms: the flame is the masculine and the coal the feminine. Even if this correlation is not stated explicitly, it is consistent with the symbolism adopted by the *Zohar* and with the larger intellectual world of the Middle Ages.

But the example of the candle offers a somewhat more complex symbolism. There are three flames: the "concealed flame," the "white flame," and the "blue-black flame." This particular text is an example of a ubiquitous phenomenon in the *Zohar* to refer to the sefirotic potencies in terms derived from the world of sense experience. Hence, the implicit meaning of this passage is the unification of the *sefirot*. Most of the discussion concerns the white flame and the blue-black flame; the concealed flame refers to one of the highest *sefirot*, most likely *Binah*. The radiant white flame rises above in a direct line and the blue-black flame serves as the throne of glory for the white flame. The white flame is thus described as resting upon the blue-black flame and uniting with it so that everything is one. The symbolic intent of this imagery is given by the *Zohar* itself through the voice of Simeon ben Yoḥai: the blue-black flame is the final *he'* of the Tetragrammaton, i.e., the feminine *Shekhinah*, which is united with the white flame or the *yod-he'-waw* of the name, i.e., the masculine *Tif'eret*. The unification of the two flames, therefore, represents the perfection of the name. But the blue-black flame is the final *he'* of the Tetragrammaton only when the righteous men of the community of Israel are conjoined to the *Shekhinah* from below so that she is united with the masculine potency from above. When Israel is not conjoined to the *Shekhinah*, she is in the form of a *dalet*, which clearly symbolizes her state of impoverishment or weakness (related to the word *dal*). Significantly, the verse that the zoharic author quotes to make this point is "If there be a damsel that is a virgin," *ki yihyeh na'arah betulah* (Deut. 22: 23). According to the masoretic orthography, the word *na'arah* is written *na'ar*, i.e., without the final *he'*. In response to the query why this is so, the zoharic author writes: "Because she is not united with the masculine, and wherever male and female do not exist, the *he'* does not exist. It departs from there and she is left *dalet*. When she is united with the radiant white flame, she is called *he'*, for then everything is united as one." When the *Shekhinah* is united with Israel from below, she is united with the male above, and this unification transforms her semiotic status from *dalet* to *he'*.

Underlying this linguistic symbolism is an ontological presumption: the *Shekhinah* is transformed from the impoverished feminine (the virgin written as *na'ar*) to the enriched feminine, the virgin that has united with and transformed into the male (symbolically represented as the *na'arah)*. The esoteric exegesis proferred here overtly contradicts the literal sense of Scripture. The damsel, *na'arah*, is not only not a virgin but the female that has been metamorphosized into a male as a result of sexual intercourse. Concomitantly, the body politic of Israel is transformed from masculine to feminine as the righteous males are assimilated into the *Shekhinah* in the image of the material wax that feeds the flame. The term *na'arah*, therefore, symbolically denotes both Israel below (the feminized male) and the *Shekhinah* above (the masculinized female).

In line with this gender metamorphosis, we should expect a shift from the heterosexual to the homoerotic. As I have already indicated, the position of the *Zohar* is that the mystic becomes fully male only when he abstains from heterosexual intercourse, an abstinence that facilitates the reintegration of the feminine into the masculine. The masculinization of the feminine effects a change in the texture of the erotic experience: Heterosexual desire is fulfilled in the homoerotic bonding of the mystic to the male body of God,[90] which is constituted by the members of the kabbalistic fraternity. The homoerotic nature of the ascetic lifestyle is conveyed most vividly in the *Zohar* by means of the mythical image (to which I referred above) of God taking delight with the souls of the righteous in the Garden of Eden at midnight. One may presume that the souls referred to in these contexts are those of the departed who dwell in the Garden of Eden. Yet, from a number of these passages it may be concluded that the reference is also to the righteous souls of the living who rise at midnight to study Torah. Let us consider as representative the following text:

> R. Isaac said: It is written, 'A river issues from Eden to water the garden' (Gen. 2: 10). This is the pillar upon which the world stands, and it waters the garden and the garden is irrigated by it. By means

> of it she produces fruits and all the fruits disseminate in the world, and they are the pillar of the world, the pillar of Torah. Who are they? The souls of the righteous for they are the fruit of the actions of the Holy One, blessed be he. Thus every night the souls of the righteous ascend and at midnight the Holy One, blessed be he, comes to the Garden of Eden to take delight in them. In which ones? R. Yose said: In all of them, those whose dwelling is in that world and those who reside in their dwelling in this world. At midnight the Holy One, blessed be he, takes delight in all of them.[91]

The homoerotic implication of this passage cannot be ignored: God delights in the souls of the righteous, which includes both the dead who have a permanent residence in the Garden of Eden and the living who are visiting there temporarily. In the first instance, it would appear that the word *'ishta'sha'* (or, in the infinitive, *le'ishta'she'a*) signifies a form of delight related to the exercise of the mind, which would be appropriate in light of the fact that the righteous souls are involved in the study of Torah when God comes to visit them. Thus, the image of God's taking delight with the righteous is certainly meant to convey the idea of intellectual joy. On the other hand, the erotic connotation of this term is also quite evident.[92] Indeed, the two significations are not ultimately separable given the homology of the noetic and the erotic to which I have already referred. There is another important dimension to this relationship that is made clear in the continuation of the aforecited passage: "When the souls of the righteous depart from this world and ascend above, they are all garbed in the supernal light, in the glorious image, and the Holy One, blessed be he, delights in them and desires them, for they are the fruit of his actions. Thus they are called 'Israel,' for they have holy souls, and they are the sons of the Holy One, blessed be he, as it is said, 'You are sons of the Lord your God' (Deut. 14: 1), sons in truth, the fruit of his actions."[93] The righteous souls in whom God delights are the fruits of his own labor and indeed his own sons who are in his image. Taking delight in the righteous mystics who study Torah is tantamount to God taking delight in himself. The erotic bond between God and the righteous, therefore, is not incestuous, but narcissistic: God's love of the righteous is an expression of self-love.[94] God delights in his own image reflected in the faces of the mystics even as the mystics delight in their own image reflected in the face of God. From this perspective, moreover, it can be said that the homoeroticism is an aspect of divine autoeroticism.[95]

One might argue that even if I am correct to assert that from the human perspective heterosexual eros is fulfilled in the homoerotic union of the male mystic and God, surely from the divine perspective the homoeroticism only serves as a catalyst to bring about the heterosexual union of the male and female attributes within the sefirotic pleroma. Thus, according to one zoharic passage, when God enters the Garden of Eden to take delight with the righteous, the *Shekhinah* brings forth the words of innovative Torah study that were stored away, and God is said to contemplate these words in joy. As a result of this contemplation, God is crowned in the supernal crowns and is united with the *Shekhinah*.[96] In this case, it would seem, the homoerotic relation of God and the righteous facilitates the heterosexual mating of God and the *Shekhinah*. Upon closer examination, however, it should become apparent that the feminine *Shekhinah* is made up essentially of the members of the kabbalistic fraternity and she is thus constructed as masculine. This is the esoteric significance of the repeated claim that God's heterosexual relationship to the *Shekhinah* is actualized through his homoerotic bonding with the kabbalists. For example, at the conclusion of an intricate discourse on the verse, "How good and how pleasant it is that brothers dwell together" (Ps. 133: 1), the author of the *Zohar* remarks that the word *gam* in the expression *gam yaḥad*, "together," signifies the inclusion of the *Shekhinah* with the mystical brothers in whom God takes joy for their words of study are pleasing to him.[97]

The degree to which the *Shekhinah* is composed ontically of the male mystics is underscored in a second passage, which is an exegetical reflection on the verse, "O my dove, in the cranny of the rocks, hidden by the cliff, let me see your face, let me hear your voice; for your voice is sweet and your face is comely" (Song of Songs 2: 14): the *Shekhinah* (referred to by the technical name "Community of Israel" and symbolized by the scriptural image of the "dove") is described as being constantly with the scholars who have no rest in the world (thus they are "in the cranny of the rocks") and who are "modest" and "pious" (signified by the expression "hidden by the cliff"). God desires the *Shekhinah* on account of the sages who have adopted an ascetic lifestyle (implied by the designations "modest," *ṣenu'in*, and the "pious who fear the Holy One, blessed be he," *ḥasidin daḥale qudsha' verikh hu'*), a passion that is linked to the words, "let me see your face, let me hear your voice." The voice of the feminine *Shekhinah* turns out to be the voice of the male mystics engaged in nocturnal study of Torah. That the face of the *Shekhinah* likewise is related to the male mystics[98] implied in continuation of the passage: "It has been taught: The images of those engaged in [the study of] Torah at night are engraved above before the Holy One, blessed be he, and the Holy One, blessed be he, takes delight in them all day and he gazes upon them. That voice [of Torah] rises and breaks through all the heavens until it ascends before the Holy One, blessed be he."[99] The voice and the face of the *Shekhinah*, which God desires to encounter, refer respectively to the voices and the iconic representations of the kabbalists involved in exegesis of Torah according to the theosophic secrets. Heterosexual language is used, therefore, to describe the homoerotic relationship between God and the kabbalist, but this is to be expected since the weaker party will be valorized as female. By this same logic, it is possible for God's erotic union with the righteous male to be portrayed by quintessentially heterosexual images such as that of the king and the queen.

Indeed, we find a remarkable articulation of this phenomenon in a passage from the thirteenth-century Castilian kabbalist and probable member of the zoharic circle, Joseph Gikatilla.[100] The comment of Gikatilla occurs in the context of his delineating the different phases of divine disclosure in the world in terms of the Tetragrammaton and the various cognomens.[101] When God appears before the nations of the world, he does so "in the image of a king who stands before his ministers and all his servants, garbed in the attire of royalty or the attire of warfare." Gikatilla concludes, therefore, that God in his essence is not really seen by the nations for he is concealed in the garb of the cognomens when he is revealed to them. By contrast, when God stands before the Jewish people, "he stands with them like a king with the members of his household and he removes something of his clothing as is the way of the king to remove some of his clothing when he stands with the members of his household." Gikatilla links this phase to the verse, "Three times a year—on the feast of unleavened bread, on the feast of weeks, and on the feast of booths—all your males shall appear before the

Lord your God in the place that he will choose" (Deut. 16: 16), and to the talmudic principle underlying the ruling that one who is blind in one eye is exempt from the commandment to be seen in the Temple during the three festivals, "just as one comes to see so one comes to be seen" (Babylonian Talmud, Ḥagigah 2a). The biblical commandment and the rabbinic dictum as understood by Gikatilla involve the obligation to see God, a seeing that is connected more specifically to the disclosure of God in his true essence, the Tetragrammaton. The disclosure is a form of divestiture, a removal of the garments, which are the cognomens that conceal the essential name. But even when God appears before Israel there must be a measure of concealment since there are some who are not worthy to apprehend the truth of the Tetragrammaton. Only when God is alone with the righteous (*ṣaddiqim*) and pious (*ḥasidim*) of Israel is the disclosure complete. Here it is worth citing Gikatilla's language verbatim:

> When God, blessed be he, unites with the righteous and pious, the patriarchs of the world and the mighty ones, he removes from himself all cognomens and the Tetragrammaton alone is exalted.[102] Thus, the Tetragrammaton alone stands with Israel like a king who has removed all his garments and unites with his wife. This is the secret, 'Turn back, O rebellious children, for I have united with you' (Jer. 3: 22), and it says, 'I will espouse you forever' (Hosea 2: 21). 'I will espouse you'—like a king who removes his garments and unites with his wife, so too the Tetragrammaton removes all cognomens and garments, and unites with Israel, with their pious (*ḥasidim*), ascetics (*perushim*), and the pure ones (*ṭehorim*). This is the secret, 'I had taken off my robes, was I to don it again?' (Song of Songs 5: 3).

The unique relation that God has to the spiritual elite of Israel is depicted metaphorically as the erotic relationship of the king and the queen.[103] Gikatilla articulates in a lucid manner an orientation found in the *Zohar* as well: the homoerotic bond between God and the mystic is expressed in heterosexual images.[104] From this we may deduce, moreover, that relationships depicted in strictly heterosexual terms can be understood homoerotically. The overtly feminine characterizations of the divine in kabbalistic texts do not in and of themselves instruct us about the valence imputed to the female gender by the medieval mystics. It is possible, as I have argued, that the feminine images must be seen as part of an androcentric, indeed phallocentric, perspective whereby the female is part of the masculine. The attitude toward gender had a profound impact on the nature of the mystic's experience with God. The preponderance of heterosexual imagery in the tradition and the positive affirmation of carnal sexuality as a means for procreation cannot be denied. On the other hand, being male for the thirteenth-century Castilian kabbalist meant restricting conjugal intercourse to the eve of Sabbath and adopting an ascetic lifestyle during the week. Ironically enough, the self-inflicted castration augmented rather than weakened the mystic's masculine virility. The vow of abstinence enabled the kabbalist to participate in a nocturnal ritual of Torah study that led to both mystical communion with the *Shekhinah* and an erotic relationship with the masculine aspect of the divine. Celibacy provided the members of the mystical fraternity an opportunity to transpose the heterosexual into the homoerotic. However, by expressing the homoerotic in heterosexual terms, the medieval kabbalist was able to appropriate standard Jewish sexual norms even as they were radically transfigured by him.

NOTES

1. See E. A. Clark, *Ascetic Piety and Women's Faith: Essays on Late Ancient Christianity* (Lewiston, 1986), pp. 175–208; G. Clark, "Women and Asceticism in Late Antiquity: The Refusal of Status and Gender," in *Asceticism*, V. L. Wimbush and R. Valantasis, eds. (New York, 1995), pp. 33–48; D. Boyarin, *A Radical Jew: Paul and the Politics of Identity* (Berkeley, 1994), pp. 180–200. On women ascetics and mystics in the Christian Middle Ages, see C. W. Bynum, *Holy Feast and Holy Fast: The Religious Significance of Food to Medieval Women* (Berkeley, 1987), pp. 82–87, 103–104; idem, *Fragmentation and Redemption: Essays on Gender and the Human Body in Medieval Religion* (New York, 1991), pp. 53–78, 131–134; E. A. Petroff, *Body and Soul: Essays on Medieval Women and Mysticism* (New York, 1994), pp. 205–206.

2. For a list of scholarly investigations of this motif in early Christian and Gnostic sources, see E. R. Wolfson, "Woman—The Feminine as Other in Theosophic Kabbalah: Some Philosophical Observations on the Divine Androgyne," in *The Other in Jewish Thought and History: Constructions of Jewish Culture and Identity*, L. J. Silberstein and R. L. Cohn, eds. (New York, 1994), pp. 192–193, n. 6.

3. On asceticism in the rabbinic materials, see E. E. Urbach, "Askesis and Suffering in Talmudic and Midrashic Sources," in *Yitzhak F. Baer Jubilee Volume*, ed. S. W. Baron (Jerusalem, 1960), pp. 48–68 (in Hebrew);

S. Fraade, "Ascetical Aspects of Ancient Judaism," in *Jewish Spirituality From the Bible to the Middle Ages*, A. Green, ed. (New York, 1986), pp. 253–288; D. Biale, *Eros and the Jews: From Biblical Israel to Contemporary America* (New York, 1992), pp. 34–36; M. L. Satlow, "Shame and Sex in Late Antique Judaism," in *Asceticism*, pp. 535–543. For the ascetic dimension of the medieval philosophical tradition, see G. Vajda, *La Théologie Ascétique de Bahya ibn Paquda* (Paris, 1947); A. Lazeroff, "Bahya's Asceticism Against Its Rabbinic and Islamic Background," *Journal of Jewish Studies* 21 (1973): 11–38; Y. Silman, *Philosopher and Prophet: Judah Halevi, the Kuzari, and the Evolution of His Thought*, Lenn J. Schramm, trans. (Albany, 1995), pp. 97–98, 233. On ascetism and medieval Ashkenazi pietism, see G. Scholem, *Major Trends in Jewish Mysticism* (New York, 1954), pp. 92–97. On the Sufi–like pietism cultivated by the descendants of Maimonides, see S. Rosenblatt, *The High Ways to Perfection of Abraham Maimonides*, I (New York, 1927), pp. 48–53, 66, 82–85; P. Fenton, *The Treatise of the Pool: Al-Maqāla al-Ḥawḍiyya by 'Obadyāh ben Abraham ben Moses Maimonides* (London, 1981), pp. 1–24. A useful discussion of the various shades of asceticism in the rabbinic traditions of the classical and medieval periods is found in M. Z. Sokol, "Attitudes Toward Pleasure in Jewish Thought: A Typological Proposal," in *Reverence, Righteousness, and Rahamanut: Essays in Memory of Rabbi Dr. Leo Jung*, J. J. Schachter, ed. (Northvale, 1992), pp. 293–314. I am grateful to the author for drawing my attention to his study and for helping me clarify some of my own opinions regarding the ascetic dimension of the kabbalistic tradition, especially as expressed in the zoharic corpus.

4. See G. Scholem, *Kabbalah* (Jerusalem, 1974), p. 245 (on the role of asceticism in the Sabbatian movement, see pp. 251 and 261); R. J. Zwi Werblowsky, *Joseph Karo: Lawyer and Mystic* (Philadelphia, 1977), pp. 38–83, 113–118, 133–139, 149–152, 161–165; M. Pachter, "The Concept of Devekut in the Homiletical Ethical Writings of 16th Century Safed," in *Studies in Medieval Jewish History and Literature*, II, I. Twersky, ed. (Cambridge, Mass., 1984), pp. 200–210; L. Fine, "Purifying the Body in the Name of the Soul: The Problem of the Body in Sixteenth-Century Kabbalah," in *People of the Body: Jews and Judaism from an Embodied Perspective*, H. Eilberg-Shwartz, ed. (Albany, 1992), pp. 117–142; Biale, *Eros and the Jews*, pp. 113–118.

5. See S. Rubin, *Heidenthum und Kabbala: Die kabbalistische Mystik, ihrem Ursprung wie ihrem Wesen nach, gründlich aufgehellt und populär dargestellt* (Vienna, 1893); M. D. G. Langer, *Die Erotik der Kabbala* (Prague, 1923); A. E. Waite, *The Holy Kabbalah: A Study of the Secret Tradition in Israel* (London, 1913), pp. 377–405; Scholem, *Major Trends*, pp. 225–229; idem, *On the Mystical Shape of the Godhead: Basic Concepts of the Kabbalah*, J. Neugroschel, trans., and J. Chipman, ed. (New York, 1991), pp. 183–196; I. Tishby, *The Wisdom of the Zohar*, D. Goldstein, trans. (Oxford, 1989),

pp. 300–302, 992–993, 1355–1379; C. Mopsik, *Lettre sur la sainteté: Le secret de la relation entre l'homme et la femme dans la cabale* (Paris, 1986), pp. 45–219; idem, "Union and Unity in the Kabbala," in *Between Jerusalem and Benares: Comparative Studies in Judaism and Hinduism*, H. Goodman, ed. (Albany, 1994), pp. 223–242; M. Idel, "Sexual Metaphors and Praxis in the Kabbalah," in *The Jewish Family: Metaphor and Memory*, D. Kraemer, ed. (New York, 1989), pp. 197–224; Y. Liebes, *Studies in the Zohar*, A. Schwartz, S. Nakache, and P. Peli, trans. (Albany, 1993), pp. 67–71; idem, "Zohar and Eros," *Alpayyim* 9 (1994): 67–115, esp. 99–103 (in Hebrew).

6. *Major Trends*, p. 235. According to Scholem, the use of erotic imagery to describe the structure of the Godhead is a substitute for the passionate relation of the mystic to God (see op. cit., p. 227). The textual evidence, however, overwhelmingly indicates that the theosophic kabbalists, and particularly the zoharic circle, cultivated ecstatic experiences of the divine of an erotic nature. For a critique of Scholem, see Tishby, *Wisdom of the Zohar*, pp. 991–993. On the correlation of mystical union (*devequt*) and the theurgical task of rectifying the divine (*tiqqun*), see Liebes, *Studies in the Zohar*, pp. 52–55. On the erotic ecstasy of the zoharic circle, see idem, "Zohar and Eros," pp. 70–80, 87–98, 104–112.

7. See G. Scholem, *Origins of the Kabbalah*, A. Arkush, trans. and R. J. Zwi Werblowsky, ed. (Princeton, 1987), pp. 229–233; idem, *Kabbalah*, p. 44.

8. *Origins*, p. 307.

9. Ibid., p. 230.

10. Cf. Matt. 19: 3–12; 1 Cor. 7: 1–9, 25–38. See A. Rouselle, *Porneia: On Desire and the Body in Antiquity*, F. Pheasant, trans. (Cambridge, Mass., 1988), pp. 129–193; E. Pagels, *Adam, Eve, and the Serpent* (New York, 1988), pp. 78–97; Boyarin, *A Radical Jew*, pp. 158–179; P. J. Payer, *The Bridling of Desire: Views of Sex in the Later Middle Ages* (Toronto, 1993), pp. 42–60, 132–178.

11. *Zohar* 2: 103a, 108b–109a.

12. *Zohar* 1: 108b, 177a–b; 2: 108b, 111a; 3: 128a, 135a, 142a, 292a; Tishby, *Wisdom of the Zohar*, pp. 276–277, 289–290; Liebes, *Studies in the Zohar*, pp. 65–68, 149, 190, n. 201; Wolfson, "Woman—The Feminine as Other in Theosophic Kabbalah," pp. 168–169, 189–190. I have expanded on the role of gender in the zoharic polemic against Christianity in "Re/membering the Covenant: Memory, Forgetfulness, and the Construction of History in the Zohar" to appear in the *festschrift* in honor of Yosef Hayim Yerushalmi.

13. *Zohar* 3: 292a; cf. 1: 223b. According to a passage in the *'Idra' Rabba'* (3: 142a), Hadar is identified as the attribute of *Ḥesed*, but in that context the rectification of the Edomite kings is depicted as the sweetening of the feminine judgment by the forces of mercy revealed in the "mouth of the penis" (*puma' de-'amah*). For the elaboration of the zoharic

symbolism in the sixteenth-century Lurianic kabbalah, see E. R. Wolfson, *Circle in the Square: Studies in the Use of Gender in Kabbalistic Symbolism* (Albany, 1995), pp. 116–119.

14. I have discussed the symbol of the androgynous phallus in a number of studies. See *Through a Speculum That Shines: Vision and Imagination in Medieval Jewish Mysticism* (Princeton, 1994), pp. 275, n. 14, 315–317, 342, 344, 357–359, 371, n. 155; "Woman—The Feminine as Other," p. 187; *Circle in the Square*, pp. 85–92; *Along the Path: Studies in Kabbalistic Myth, Symbolism, and Hermeneutics* (Albany, 1995), pp. 84–88, 175, n. 329, 186, n. 376, 222, n. 172.

15. See my brief remarks in *Through a Speculum That Shines*, pp. 274–275, n. 14, and the more elaborate discussions in "Woman—The Feminine as Other;" *Circle in the Square*, pp. 85–92; and "Re/membering the Covenant."

16. *Zohar* 3: 7b, 109b (*Ra'aya' Mehemna'*), 296a; Tishby, *Wisdom of the Zohar*, p. 1355; Y. Liebes, *Sections of the Zohar Lexicon* (Jerusalem, 1976), pp. 277–278, n. 459 (in Hebrew); Wolfson, *Circle in the Square*, pp. 94–95.

17. *Zohar* 3: 81a-b.

18. See Biale, *Eros and the Jews*, pp. 33–59; D. Boyarin, *Carnal Israel: Reading Sex in Talmudic Culture* (Berkeley, 1993), pp. 53–57, 71–75, 142.

19. See C. Mopsik, "The Body of Engenderment in the Hebrew Bible, the Rabbinic Tradition and the Kabbalah," in *Fragments for a History of the Human Body*, M. Feher with R. Naddaff and N. Tazi, ed. (New York, 1989), pp. 56–57; Idel, "Sexual Metaphors and Praxis," pp. 202–203; Liebes, *Studies in the Zohar*, pp. 71 and 190, n. 199.

20. Tishby, *Wisdom of the Zohar*, pp. 298–300.

21. Scholem, *On the Mystical Shape*, p. 209; Tishby, *Wisdom of the Zohar*, p. 1362; Liebes, *Studies in the Zohar*, p. 71; Wolfson, *Circle in the Square*, p. 93.

22. *Zohar* 2: 108b, 112a.

23. Cf. *Zohar* 1: 239b; 3: 90b, 145b.

24. *Zohar* 3: 5b; cf. 1:55b; 2: 55a; 3: 7a.

25. *Zohar* 3: 37b.

26. *Zohar* 1: 49a–50a, 55b, 122a, 165a, 182a, 228b, 233a–b; 3: 5b, 109b (*Ra'aya' Mehemna'*), 145b, 148a, 296a; *Zohar Ḥadash*, ed. R. Margaliot (Jerusalem, 1978), 50c, 65b. For an earlier rabbinic precedent, cf. Babylonian Talmud, Soṭah 17a.

27. The dialectic of which I speak in the kabbalistic literature is related to the medieval scholastic notion of the intellectual love of God, expressed succinctly in the writings of Maimonides (see below, n. 30). For discussion of this phenomenon in medieval Christian sources, see J. Leclercq, *The Love of Learning and the Desire for God: A Study of Monastic*

Culture, C. Misrahi, trans. (New York, 1961), pp. 212–217. The importance of this dialectic for understanding the erotic characterization of cleaving to God in thirteenth-century kabbalistic sources has been noted by S. Shokek, *Jewish Ethics and Jewish Mysticism in Sefer ha-Yashar* (Lewiston, 1991), pp. 219–224.

28. Biale, *Eros and the Jews*, pp. 105–113; Sokol, "Attitudes Toward Pleasure," pp. 305–306. Regarding this text, see also M. Harris, "Marriage as Metaphysics: A Study of the *Iggereth ha-Kodesh*," *Hebrew Union College Annual* 33 (1962): 197–226; K. Guberman, "The Language of Love in Spanish Kabbalah: An Examination of the *'Iggeret ha-Kodesh*," in *Approaches to Judaism in Medieval Times*, D. R. Blumenthal, ed. (Chico, 1984), pp. 53–95; Idel, "Sexual Metaphors and Praxis," pp. 205–206. A similar tension between the use of erotic language and the ideal of sexual abstention in Christian mysticism has been noted by B. McGinn, "The Language of Love in Christian and Jewish Mysticism," in *Mysticism and Language*, S. T. Katz, ed. (New York, 1992), p. 209.

29. *Kitve Ramban*, C. Chavel, ed., 2 vols. (Jerusalem, 1962), 2: 323.

30. *Kitve Ramban*, 2: 334. It is likely that the erotic characterization of the intellectual conjunction of the soul and the divine intelligibles reflects Maimonides's notion of *'ishq*, the intellectual love of God, which is identified as the contemplative ideal of prayer, the true worship of the heart. See *Guide of the Perplexed* III.51; *Mishneh Torah*, Teshuvah 10:6. For recent discussions of this aspect of Maimonides' thought, see M. Fishbane, *The Kiss of God: Spiritual and Mystical Death in Judaism* (Seattle, 1994), pp. 24–30; Ehud Benor, *Worship of the Heart: A Study in Maimonides's Philosophy of Religion* (Albany, 1995), pp. 52–53; Peter E. Gordon, "The Erotics of Negative Theology: Maimonides on Apprehension," *Jewish Studies Quarterly* 2 (1995): 1–38.

31. According to the author of *'Iggeret ha-Qodesh*, the ideal Adam was not a disembodied spirituality but a spiritualized body. Regarding these two anthropological approaches in thirteenth-century kabbalah, see B. Safran, "Rabbi Azriel and Naḥmanides: Two Views of the Fall of Man," in *Rabbi Moses Naḥmanides (Ramban): Explorations in His Religious and Literary Virtuosity*, I. Twersky, ed. (Cambridge, MA, 1983), pp. 75–106. See also S. Pines, "Naḥmanides on Adam in the Garden of Eden in the Context of Other Interpretations of Genesis, Chapters 2 and 3," in *Exile and Diaspora: Studies in the History of the Jewish People Presented to Professor Haim Beinart on the Occasion of His Seventieth Birthday*, A. Mirsky, A. Grossman, and Y. Kaplan, eds. (Jerusalem, 1988), pp. 159–164 (in Hebrew).

32. *Kitve Ramban*, 2: 323–324.

33. Palestinian Talmud, Ketuvot 5:8 (ed. Venice, 30b); Babylonian Talmud, Ketuvot 62b; Bava Qama 82a; Maimonides, *Mishneh Torah*, De'ot 5: 4; Shabbat 30: 14; 'Ishut 14: 1; Jacob ben Asher, *'Arba'ah Turim*, 'Oraḥ

Ḥayyim, 240; 'Even ha-'Ezer, 25, 76; Joseph Karo, *Shulḥan 'Arukh*, 'Oraḥ Ḥayyim, 240: 1; 'Even ha-'Ezer, 76: 2.

34. *Kitve Ramban*, 2: 327. Isaac ben Samuel of Acre, a contemporary of the author of *'Iggeret ha-Qodesh*, put the matter as follows in his *Sefer Me'irat 'Einayim* (ed. A. Goldreich [Jerusalem, 1981], p. 20): On Friday evening the enlightened mystics can "sense" through their "intellectual eyes" the "increase of the joy of the heart and the power of reproduction."

35. *Kitve Ramban*, 2: 333.

36. Ibid., 2: 331. For discussion of this philosophical view, see the evidence adduced by Mopsik, *Lettre sur la sainteté*, pp. 300–302, n. 133.

37. *Kitve Ramban*, 2: 332.

38. This, too, seems to reflect the influence of Maimonides' characterization of the patriarchs in *Guide* III.51 as being in constant intellectual conjunction with God. The ideal set forth by the author of *'Iggeret ha-Qodesh* also bears a similarity to Naḥmanides' characterization of *devequt* in his commentary to Deut. 11: 22. The resemblance between Maimonides and Naḥmanides was already noted by G. Scholem, *The Messianic Idea in Judaism and Other Essays on Jewish Spirituality* (New York, 1971), pp. 204–205.

39. *Kitve Ramban*, 2: 333–334; cf. 336–337.

40. In some zoharic passages, the ascetic life is necessitated by the association of the body and the demonic force. See *Zohar* 1: 180b; Tishby, *Wisdom of the Zohar*, pp. 764–765.

41. The Platonic tradition of eros and its impact on the Christian idea of love is discussed by Anders Nygren, *Agape and Eros* (London, 1953).

42. With respect to this issue, there is a striking phenomenological resemblance of theosophic kabbalah and tantrism. Regarding the latter, see M. Eliade, *Yoga: Immortality and Freedom*, W. R. Trask, trans. (Princeton, 1969), pp. 200–273; idem, *Occultism, Witchcraft, and Cultural Fashions: Essays in Comparative Religion* (Chicago, 1976), pp. 93–119.

43. On a similar use of erotic imagery in Christian mysticism, see McGinn, "Language of Love." On the fusion of asceticism and eroticism in the case of medieval women mystics depicted as the bride or lover united with the humanity of Christ through the ecstatic ingestion of the eucharist, see Bynum, *Fragmentation and Redemption*, pp. 133–134, 184–186.

44. An excellent example of this phenomenon can be found in the passage from the sixteenth-century kabbalist, Moshe Cordovero, cited in Mopsik, "Union and Unity in the Kabbala," pp. 234–236. It must be pointed out, however, that Cordovero's elaborate description of the meditational practice linked to conjugal sex is limited to the intercourse of the scholars on the eve of Sabbath and does not apply to the general practice of most people, an impression that one gets from reading Mopsik's analysis of the text.

45. *Zohar* 2:89a; cf. 2: 204b–205a; 3: 82a. See Waite, *The Holy Kabbalah*, p. 382; Tishby, *Wisdom of the Zohar*, pp. 1232–1233, 1357; Liebes, *Studies in the Zohar*, p. 15.

46. A similar interpretation of Isa. 56:4 is found in Moses de León, *Sefer ha-Mishqal*, J. H. A. Wijnhoven, ed., Brandeis University, Ph.D. thesis, 1964, p. 142; Joseph Gikatilla, *Sha'are 'Orah*, J. Ben-Shlomo, ed. (Jerusalem, 1981), 1: 107; idem, *Sod ha-Shabbat*, printed in *Hekhal ha-Shem* (Venice, 1601), 40a; Bahya ben Asher, *Be'ur 'al ha-Torah*, ed. C. Chavel, 3 vols. (Jerusalem, 1981), 2: 521–522. It is of interest to recall in this connection the description in *Zohar Ḥadash*, 8d (*Midrash ha-Ne'elam*), of a group of ascetics (*perishe 'alma'*) who supposedly hid during the week in caves and returned on Sabbath eve to their homes. See Tishby, *Wisdom of the Zohar*, p. 1331. One may infer that with respect to the issue of sexual practice, what is attributed to these ascetics matches the lifestyle of the mystical fraternity described in other parts of the *Zohar*. Regarding those who abstain from wine, cf. *Zohar Ḥadash*, 22c (*Midrash ha-Ne'elam*). In *Zohar* 2: 187a there is a reference to a band of ascetics (*perushim*) who meet Simeon ben Yoḥai.

47. For the talmudic reference, see above, n. 33. The rabbinic passage figures prominently in the zoharic anthology. Cf. *Zohar* 1: 14a–b; 50a; 112a (*Midrash ha-Ne'elam*); 2: 63b, 89a, 136a, 204b–205a; 3: 49b, 78a, 81a, 82a, 143a; *Tiqqune Zohar*, Reuven Margaliot, ed. (Jerusalem, 1978), 16, 38b; 21, 57a, 61a; 36, 78a; 56, 90a.

48. *Zohar* 1: 75a–b; *Tiqqunei Zohar* 18, 34a; 21, 19, 38a; 21, 61a; 30, 73a–b; 36, 78a; Tishby, *Wisdom of the Zohar*, pp. 438–439, 1226–1227; E. K. Ginsburg, *The Sabbath in the Classical Kabbalah* (Albany, 1989), pp. 115–116, 292–293. The *Zohar* is not totally consistent on this point because it does describe a form of union between the masculine and feminine potencies of the divine even during the week, albeit in a less complete manner than the union on the eve of Sabbath, which is the most appropriate time for the *hieros gamos*. Moreover, the recommended time for conjugal relations is based on the assumption that at midnight God visits the Garden of Eden, which must be understood as a symbolic depiction of the erotic union of the male and female. Cf. *Zohar* 3: 81a; Tishby, *Wisdom of the Zohar*, p. 1357.

49. Tishby, *Wisdom of the Zohar*, p. 1391, n. 101.

50. The arousal of the divine phallus by means of the sexual activity of the kabbalist in relation to his earthly wife and to the *Shekhinah* is a recurrent theme in the *Zohar* and related theosophic literature. See Tishby, *Wisdom of the Zohar*, p. 301; Liebes, *Sections of the Zohar Lexicon*, pp. 378–379, n. 92; idem, "'Tsaddiq Yesod Olam'—A Sabbatian Myth," *Daat* 1 (1978): 107, n. 171 (in Hebrew); Wolfson, *Through a Speculum That Shines*, pp. 371–372, n. 155. In another kabbalistic text that preserves material from the zoharic period, *Shoshan Sodot* (Korets, 1784), 79a, the author states that the righteous person engages in conjugal sex on Friday evening, not for

the sake of his own pleasure but to assist in the conjunction of the supernal righteous one, the phallic *Yesod*, and the feminine persona of the divine, the attribute of *Malkhut*.

51. Biale, *Eros and the Jews*, p. 111.

52. My formulation is indebted to W.D. O'Flaherty's description of a Tantric Sahajiya sect of Bengal in *Asceticism and Eroticism in the Mythology of S'iva* (London and New York, 1973), p. 261.

53. On the erotic nature of the contemplative state described in zoharic literature, related especially to exegetical activity, see Wolfson, *Circle in the Square*, pp. 16–19; idem, *Through a Speculum That Shines*, pp. 326–392; and see the reference to studies of Liebes above at the end of n. 5.

54. That midnight is the appropriate time for sexual intercourse is implied in a statement attributed to the wife of R. Eliezer in the Babylonian Talmud, Nedarim 20b. This practice is codified in the standard codes of Jewish law. Cf. *Mishneh Torah*, 'Issure Bi'ah 21: 10; *'Arba'ah Ṭurim*, 'Oraḥ Ḥayyim, 240; 'Even ha-'Ezer, 25, 76; *Shulḥan 'Arukh*, 'Oraḥ Ḥayyim, 240: 7; 'Even ha-'Ezer, 25: 3. On the basis of the zoharic passages (see following note) it became a standard theme in kabbalistic literature.

55. *Zohar* 1: 72a, 82b, 92a, 136b, 231b, 243a; 2: 46a, 130b, 136a, 195b; 3:13a, 67b–68a, 260a; *Zohar Ḥadash* 13b, 18a, 47d. See E. R. Wolfson, "Forms of Visionary Ascent as Ecstatic Experience in the Zoharic Literature," in *Gershom Scholem's Major Trends in Jewish Mysticism 50 Years After: Proceedings of the Sixth International Conference on the History of Jewish Mysticism*, P. Schäfer and J. Dan, eds. (Tübingen, 1993), pp. 227–228; idem, *Through a Speculum That Shines*, p. 371, n. 154; idem, *Circle in the Square*, pp. 190, n. 175 and 228, n. 167.

56. On the ritual of midnight Torah study, see Wolfson, "Forms of Visionary Ascent." For the later development of the zoharic tradition in the sixteenth-century Lurianic kabbalah, see S. Magid, "Conjugal Union, Mourning and *Talmud Torah* in R. Isaac Luria's *Tikkun Hazot*," *Daat* 36 (1996): xvi–xlv.

57. *Zohar* 3: 49b.

58. Ibid., 3: 81a. My translation follows the version of this passage preserved in Menaḥem Recanaṭi, *Be'ur 'al ha-Torah* (Jerusalem, 1961), 11d and 90b.

59. For recent discussion of this theme, see R. Valantasis, "Constructions of Power in Asceticism," *Journal of the American Academy of Religion* 63 (1995): 775–821.

60. A euphemism for engaging in conjugal intercourse.

61. *Zohar* 1: 50a.

62. *Re'shit Ḥokhmah*, Sha'ar ha-Qedushah, ch. 7 (Brooklyn, 1965), 149b.

63. This is implied as well in the zoharic description of the union of the *Shekhinah* and the righteous man who goes on a journey and

separates from his earthly wife. See *Zohar* 1: 49b–50a; Tishby, *Wisdom of the Zohar*, p. 1357.

64. Idel, "Sexual Metaphors and Praxis," p. 206, provides an interesting example of this phenomenon from Isaac of Acre. In my opinion, however, there is no need to explain Isaac's view that spiritual union with God is achieved only after physical union with one's wife is severed as a synthesis of the positive valorization of marriage in theosophic kabbalah and the emphasis on the spiritual nature of man's relationship to God in the ecstatic kabbalah. One can find the same dialectical overcoming of carnal sex through ascetic attachment to the divine in the theosophic material. An interesting example of this phenomenon in Christian mysticism is Margery Kempe who could not be a bride of Christ while she was still a bride of her earthly husband. Jesus was not only a substitute husband, but he subverted the social function of husbandry. See S. Beckwith, *Christ's Body: Identity, Culture and Society in Late Medieval Writings* (London, 1993), pp. 84–86.

65. *Zohar* 1: 21b, 236b, 239a; 2:5b, 245a; 3: 4b, 148a, 180a, 261b; Waite, *The Holy Kabbalah*, pp. 355–356; Scholem, *Major Trends*, pp. 226–227; Tishby, *Wisdom of the Zohar*, p. 1333; Idel, "Sexual Metaphors and Praxis," p. 206; Liebes, *Studies in the Zohar*, p. 15; idem, "Zohar and Eros," p. 102.

66. For fuller discussion of this motif, see Wolfson, *Through a Speculum That Shines*, pp. 383–392.

67. "Woman—The Feminine as Other," pp. 179–182; *Circle in the Square*, pp. 60–69; Liebes, "Zohar and Eros," p. 80.

68. See *Circle in the Square*, pp. 68–69.

69. *Through a Speculum That Shines*, pp. 356–357, 389–391; Liebes, "Zohar and Eros," pp. 73–80.

70. On the erotic nature of Torah study, see M. Idel, *Kabbalah: New Perspectives* (New Haven, 1988), pp. 227–229; Wolfson, *Circle in the Square*, pp. 16–19; idem, "Beautiful Maiden Without Eyes: *Peshaṭ* and *Sod* in Zoharic Hermeneutics," in *The Midrashic Imagination: Jewish Exegesis, Thought, and History*, M. Fishbane, ed. (Albany, 1993), pp. 169–170, 185–187; Liebes, "Zohar and Eros," pp. 97–98.

71. The kabbalistic and tantric approaches to human sexuality are compared and contrasted in Mopsik, *Lettre sur la sainteté*, pp. 159–160; idem, "Union and Unity in the Kabbala," pp. 238–240; Idel, "Sexual Metaphors and Praxis," pp. 205–206; McGinn, "Language of Love," p. 221. McGinn perceptively noted that the kabbalistic affirmation of human sexuality as an *imitatio dei* bears a resemblance to the Latin Hermetic text, *Asclepius* 21, where the conjunction of male and female is portrayed as a means of imitating the fecundity of the divine androgyne.

72. Regarding this tantric practice, see Eliade, *Yoga*, pp. 245–249; O'Flaherty, *Asceticism and Eroticism*, pp. 261–277; E. Chalier-Visusalingam, "Union and Unity in Hindu Tantrism," in *Between Jerusalem and Benares*,

pp. 195–222. From the perspective of gender, there is an interesting ambivalence in the tantric philosophy. On the one hand, the *kuṇḍalinī*, which must be drawn up through the different *cakras* from the base of the spinal column to the top of the head, is identified with *śakti*, the feminine aspect of the creative force. On the other hand, it is evident that the most critical part of the yogic meditational practice, which leads to enstasis and the reintegration of the feminine and the masculine, is drawing up the semen. See Thaiyar M. Srinivasan, "Polar Principles in Yoga and Tantra," in *Sexual Archetypes, East and West*, Bina Gupta, ed. (New York, 1987), pp. 106–115, esp. 108–111. Similarly, in the *Zohar*, the vital energy is depicted as a coiled snake that is feminine in nature yet incarnate in the male's semen. I have discussed this in "Re/membering the Covenant."

73. See E. R. Wolfson, "From Sealed Book to Open Text: Time, Memory, and Narrativity in Kabbalistic Hermeneutics," in *Interpreting Judaism in a Postmodern Age*, S. Kepnes, ed. (New York, 1996), pp. 149–150; and the text of Cordovero analyzed by Mopsik, "Union and Unity in the Kabbala," pp. 240–241.

74. *Zohar* 1: 92a; 3: 13a.

75. See reference to the studies of Mopsik given in n. 71.

76. See "Woman—The Feminine as Other," pp. 185–191; *Circle in the Square*, pp. 92–98.

77. See *Circle in the Square*, pp. 80, 195–196, n. 3.

78. Chalier-Visuvalingam, "Union and Unity," p. 207. On the androgynous linga of the Hindu tradition, see W. D. O'Flaherty, *Women, Androgynes, and Other Mythical Beasts* (Chicago, 1980), pp. 317–318.

79. I have discussed the homoerotic nature of the mystical fraternity in *Through a Speculum That Shines*, pp. 357–377 and *Circle in the Square*, pp. 107–110. This phenomenon has been discussed independently by Liebes, "Zohar and Eros," pp. 104–112, although he still privileges the heterosexual as the most perfect expression of the erotic orientation.

80. Tishby, *Wisdom of the Zohar*, p. 1357; Liebes, *Studies in the Zohar*, pp. 15, 72–73; idem, "Zohar and Eros," pp. 101–103; Idel, "Sexual Metaphors and Praxis," p. 206; Wolfson, *Circle in the Square*, pp. 209, n. 64 and 217, n. 118.

81. *Zohar* 1: 153b. For a Hebrew parallel to the zoharic passage, see *The Book of the Pomegranate: Moses de León's Sefer ha-Rimmon*, E. R. Wolfson, ed. (Atlanta, 1988), pp. 138 and 142.

82. *Zohar* 1: 66b.

83. Literally, the "sabbatical year," which is one of the names of the *Shekhinah* in kabbalistic symbolism.

84. *Zohar* 1: 153b.

85. *Zohar* 1: 216a. Cf. *Sha'are 'Orah*, 1: 98–99.

86. See Scholem, *Major Trends*, pp. 165 and 388, n. 44.

87. *Zohar* 1: 50a. Cf. *Book of the Pomegranate*, p. 223.

88. See Idel, "Sexual Metaphors and Praxis," p. 206; idem, *Kabbalah: New Perspectives*, pp. 209–210. The experience of the mystics being female in relation to God who is male, which Idel associates with ecstatic kabbalah, can be found as well in the theosophic kabbalah. Consistent with other mystical traditions, both theosophic and ecstatic kabbalists portrayed the soul of the mystic as feminine in relation to the male deity. The reversal of gender roles is particularly significant in the Christian mystical tradition, based in great measure on the appropriation of Song of Songs to depict the soul's relationship to Christ: the male mystic assumes the voice of the female beloved and Jesus that of the male lover. See McGinn, "Language of Love," pp. 202–203, 207, 211–212.

89. *Zohar* 1: 50b–51b.

90. On the zoharic locution of being conjoined to the "body of the king," see Liebes, *Sections of the Zohar Lexicon*, p. 227, n. 250. In some of the relevant passages (1: 219a; 3: 294b), the primary concern is the return of the soul to the divine after the death of the body, but in other contexts (1: 216a, 223b; 2: 86a) the issue is clearly the conjunction of the righteous to the divine, especially the phallic aspect of God.

91. *Zohar* 1: 82b.

92. On the dual signification of this term, see *Circle in the Square*, pp. 69–70, 124–125, n. 6, 189–190, n. 174, 190–192, nn. 175–180. See also Liebes, "Zohar and Eros," p. 81; and Magid, "Conjugal Union," pp. xxix–xxxi.

93. *Zohar* 1: 82b.

94. A similar argument has been made by R. A. Segal, *The Poimandres as Myth: Scholarly Theory and Gnostic Meaning* (Berlin, 1986), pp. 33–34, with respect to a passage in *Poimandres* regarding God's love of his son's beauty.

95. In *Circle in the Square*, pp. 49–78, I explore the motif of divine autoeroticism in the kabbalistic tradition, principally in zoharic and Lurianic sources, as it pertains to the emanative process by means of which the Infinite comes to be in the differentiated world of the *sefirot*. The autoeroticism of which I here speak occurs on a lower ontic level, but it clearly reflects what takes place in the initial phase of divine creativity.

96. *Zohar* 1: 243a. God's erotic relationship to the words of innovative Torah study is also described in *Zohar* 1: 4b.

97. *Zohar* 3: 59b; and see extended analysis in *Through a Speculum That Shines*, pp. 370–372.

98. On the members of the fraternity constituting the face of the *Shekhinah*, cf. the zoharic sources cited and analyzed in *Through a Speculum That Shines*, pp. 368–369.

99. *Zohar* 3: 61a.

100. Gikatilla's relationship to the zoharic authorship has been well documented in scholarly literature. See Liebes, *Studies in the Zohar*, pp.

99–102, and references to other scholars cited on pp. 203, nn. 77–79 and 204, n. 87.

101. *Sha'are 'Orah*, 1: 205–206.

102. Based on Ps. 148: 13.

103. See, however, *Sha'are 'Orah*, 1:196, where Gikatilla employs the image of the king and queen to characterize the erotic relationship of the masculine and feminine aspects of the divine.

104. A similar tendency is prominent in the Christian mystical tradition wherein the relationship of Jesus and the soul of the male mystic, frequently a celibate monk or priest, is portrayed as the erotic union of the bridegroom and bride as described in the Song of Songs. See above, n. 88.

SHARING WINE, WOMEN, AND SONG: MASCULINE IDENTITY FORMATION IN THE MEDIEVAL EUROPEAN UNIVERSITIES

Ruth Mazo Karras

This essay examines the experience of student life at medieval universities which functioned to create an elite masculine identity, including aristocratic mores, male bonding, and misogynistic attitudes.

That medieval European universities were exclusively masculine is so obvious as to be hardly worthy of comment. This very obviousness has meant that scholars have not seen the need to look more closely at the complex ways in which these universities were in fact gendered institutions. Scholars have focused on the intellectual achievements of the universities, their role in the philosophical, theological, or politico-legal issues of the day and have considered the authors of those achievements as thinkers rather than as men.[1] Scholars of women's history have focused on those areas of medieval life in which women were active rather than those in which they were absent.[2] Only a few authors have considered the consequences, either for the place of women in society and culture or for the production of knowledge itself, of the exclusion of women from the universities.[3] Very little work has been done on the role of the university in the preparation of men for their social roles.

But the universities were not primarily training scholars; they were training men. Very few of those who attended medieval universities pursued higher degrees and spent their careers in study. For most students, the university was a place to acquire skills, credentials, and connections that would help them in their career, whether within the church or without. The time spent at the university acculturated them into a world of shared experience that set them off from the uneducated perhaps even more than their actual learning. That world of shared experience, of course, was exclusively masculine. The experiences of young men at this formative stage in their lives helped shape what it meant to be an elite man in the medieval world. This brief account sketches the outlines of three interrelated aspects of the universities' role in the creation of a new masculinity: the way they helped create a social class identity for students, promoted male bonding, and structured men's relations with women.

Students at medieval European universities generally came from what could be termed a social elite but not the highest social class. Although social origins varied over time and from university to university, many of the students came from the middling sort: their fathers were merchants or prosperous artisans rather than aristocrats or peasants.[4] Some students, in fact, were quite poor and had to earn their way through the university.[5] There were members of the aristocracy at the universities, but these were for the most part churchmen, at least until the fifteenth century. The universities had not yet become a finishing school for the aristocracy, as they would become in the early modern period.[6] Undergraduate students were on average somewhat younger than their modern counterparts—beginning study at age fourteen to sixteen.[7]

For most of these students, learning was not an end in itself but a means to patronage and a lucrative career. They did not pursue higher degrees unless this would further their careers. When they did become Masters of Arts and taught at the universities, it was as a temporary position and not a long-term career.[8] Many did not even stay to get a bachelor's degree; they might end up as unbeneficed clergy or in some sort of lay career, perhaps that of a manorial official.[9] Those who completed their education did not all go into the church, although many did.[10] In effect, the universities were vocational schools, a conclusion not obviated by the fact that many great works emerged from among the small group of scholars who remained in the university to pursue study for its own sake.[11]

Given these motivations for university study, it is not too surprising if students went to the university to make connections as much as to learn—and, especially given their stage in life, before they took on the responsibility of career and possibly family, to have a good time as well. And to the extent they did go to the university to learn, it was to learn a system of behavior as well as a body of knowledge.

The life style that students came to adopt may have been beyond the means of many. In effect, they were learning from their peers to live like the elites they hoped to become. The letters home from medieval students asking their families for money are often amusing to modern readers, especially those with college-age children, but they reveal that the students were spending money for many of the same reasons students do today or did between then and now: they must dress and behave appropriately so as to fit in with their peers, and the peers who were emulated were often the wealthiest. The student who assured his parents that he did not "spend his substance on royal raiment and costly furs in the pursuit of ladies' love" knew the reputation of students.[12] Statutes from various medieval universities, and colleges within them, required a particular costume and forbade the wearing of fashionable, indecent clothing, which was a clear attempt to emulate aristocratic masculinity.[13]

The wearing of fashionable clothing, of course, signifies most prominently that one can afford it. One characteristic of aristocracy was largesse, a willingness to spend on others and on oneself. The desire to display this virtue must have caused serious problems for those who were not actually in a position to do so. It was custom at many universities, for example, for new students to treat their colleagues to a feast, and this custom became so enshrined that it was a requirement, a form of hazing of the *beanus* (*bejanus, bejaunus*) or freshman. At Orléans, the authorities were very concerned because this practice was impoverishing many students who had only a little money laboriously acquired by their parents and relatives. These students were being bullied into providing a banquet for their fellows, led to the tavern "like sheep to the slaughter," and seduced into drunkenness, housebreaking, and other offenses too serious to mention.[14] Yet for the students involved it was not just a question of hazing, a rite of passage, or a free meal; it was also a matter of demonstrating that one did not hesitate to spend on one's companions and was in a position to become part of the community. The use of feasting one's colleagues as a rite of passage was not limited to the newcomer to the university; masters had to do so, for example, when they incepted (gave their first lecture), and from the very beginnings of the universities there was concern that these solemn banquets not turn into wild parties.[15]

An aristocratic life style—one that in some ways echoed ideals of heroic masculinity, albeit in a very attenuated form—also required the bearing of weapons. This was almost universally forbidden in university and college statutes which were almost universally violated.[16] The records of medieval Oxford provide a good example. Students were frequently arrested for carrying not only daggers but also shields and swords. Occasionally the offense was compounded by the weapons actually having been used.[17] Students from the middling classes would not likely have had much occasion to use swords and shields; their adoption of these weapons signified both a rejection of the clerical status which university study might imply and an attempt at social mobility.

With weapons, of course, came fighting. This one cannot attribute to an effort to emulate heroic ideals. The town-gown riots that broke out in Oxford, the battles among the different student nations at Paris, were in the nature of street brawls more than aristocratic duels. At the risk of essentializing "the masculine," I would suggest that this should be no surprise to anyone who has seen groups of male adolescents, not very strictly controlled, consume large amounts of alcohol. The St. Scholastica's Day riots in Oxford in 1355, for example, began when two students (who were beneficed clergymen) in a tavern threw wine in the bartender's face and ended several days later with the deaths of a number of townspeople and members of the university.[18] Not only undergraduates but also masters were involved.

The need to demonstrate one's masculinity through participation in brawls of this sort may seem incongruous in a population where so many were clergy, regular or secular, or were presumed to be preparing for a life in the church. Precisely that circumstance, however, may have made students so ready to defend their honor with force. Someone who by reason of his tonsure might not be expected to fight back might be seen as fair game for frauds or insults. Students, therefore, had to be ready at all times to show their willingness to stand up for themselves manfully. The emulation of an aristocratic culture may have been somewhat at odds with the ostensible clerical nature of the universities.

One reason students were able to get into such brawls was the general lack of supervision. Colleges had detailed regulations for the behavior of their members, both masters and undergraduates; most students, however, were not members of colleges, which did not become the focus of student life and education in the English universities until the very end of the Middle Ages and never did in the other universities. Students might live in lodging halls, where the head of the hall was simply a student who sublet rooms to other students, although again by the fifteenth century the universities were trying to control student residences more closely and requiring students to live under the supervision of a senior member of the university. Coupled with the lack of supervision in daily life were the privileges of scholars, ensuring that the university rather than the town had jurisdiction over them for most offenses. University students, whether or not they had taken orders (or intended to), were deemed clerics for the duration of their university study, and accordingly were given special treatment under the law. The University of Paris in 1446, trying to obtain the release of seven students imprisoned in the Chatelet, argued that "Students are young people and commit youthful folly from time to time, for which, in lighter things, the responsibility belongs to their masters."[19]

Despite the lack of university control of residential life, the universities did promote a sense of community or bonding among their members that gave them a collective social identity. Members of the university distinguished themselves from the community in which they lived through legal privileges, distinctive clothing, and (for some) the tonsure, and also through their spoken language. Latin was spoken for all university business. Not all students spoke Latin as well as might be desired when they first came to the university—especially for fifteenth-century Germany, there are manuals for students intended to teach them the sort of Latin phrases they might need to know in daily life, and there were officials whose responsibility was to make sure that students were not speaking the vernacular among themselves.[20] But Latin was still the language of everyday business as well as of classroom activity, and it served to set members of the university off from the populace, even though they might also have to learn enough of the local vernacular to deal with landlords and shop clerks. Speaking Latin gave an automatic entreé into the community of educated men, distinguishing the student from the "plowmen, swineherds, and rural dwellers."[21] Although in the later Middle Ages there were women who spoke and wrote Latin, these women did not tend to be associated particularly with universities. Latinity was a mark of elite masculinity, and the process of learning Latin also served as a bonding ritual and a marker of identity with an extrafamilial group.[22]

Students were bonded together not only through their Latinity and their shared educational experience but also through their shared life. Some students lived in colleges, but most (apart from the regular clergy) lived in residence halls more or less regulated by the universities. There they shared their leisure hours. In addition to the residence halls many students belonged to other organizations that gave them some sort of group identity: confraternities, for example, or the "nations" at some of the universities. The bond among the members of each nation at Paris, for example, led on several occasions to serious violence between nations.[23]

Within these groups—colleges or nations—or within the faculty of arts in general, new undergraduate students were sometimes hazed. They might be compelled, as I have already discussed, to buy their way into the student community, but they were also subjected to other forms of initiation. The *Manuale Scolarium*, from fifteenth-century Germany,[24] a book of dialogues apparently intended to familiarize the student with Latin phrases he would need to know at the university, includes one dialogue in which two students encounter a wild, stinking beast. It proves to be a *beanus* or freshman; they cut off its horns and shave it in order to civilize it.[25] This ritual in German universities is better attested in the sixteenth and seventeenth centuries.[26] It is also discussed in a satirical text from 1494 from Erfurt, which states that a *beanus* had to purify himself not only by the removal of his horns by also by treating his colleagues to drinks. The 1447 statutes of the University of Erfurt, indeed, prohibit the *beanus* being charged more than a third of a Rhenish florin "for the deposition of his *beanium*" unless the rector and council of the university had given permission![27] A process of ritual humiliation like this, after which the initiate is admitted to membership in the group, functions to create a sense of solidarity among the members against outsiders. Similar procedures were in place elsewhere: at the College of St. Nicholas at the University of Avignon, *bejauni* could not be addressed as "Dominus" ("Sir"), had to serve at table, and had eventually be cleansed or purged of their "freshman disgrace."[28] In Leipzig the members of the Collegium

Minus had to be prohibited from throwing things out the window at *beani* entering the college.[29]

The social interactions of the community to which the *beanus* sought entrance were well lubricated by wine (or ale). In both secular and monastic colleges the penalty for any infraction of the rules was to purchase wine for all the masters in the college.[30] For all students and masters, the tavern was a regular retreat. The English-German Nation at the University of Paris, for example, spent a good deal of its budget on wine in the tavern after its regular meetings; in addition, every time a new procurator was elected or a new master incepted he had to treat the nation to drinks or a banquet. The records of the regular meetings always give as one part of the agenda petitions and requests: at one meeting, "as to the third item on the agenda, no one had any supplications, except for one, whose supplication was, that we should go to the tavern." In 1370 the nation voted "that the nation's funds should be preserved faithfully and diligently for the use, undertakings, and progress of the nation, and by no means vainly expended in taverns or elsewhere," but this did not have much effect.[31] It is possible to plot a geography of drinking establishments on the Left Bank of the Seine from a study of the records of the nations.[32] And these were the informal meetings; there was also a more formal feast every year in honor of the patron saint, St. Edmund, which also involved copious alcohol. On one occasion, in 1398, when the nation was trying to economize, they decided to have only the liturgical celebration and no feast at all, because "it seemed more expedient to have no feast at all, than to have half a feast."[33] These shared rituals of feast-days for their respective patron saints helped cement the communal identity of the nations, but they sometimes led to fights and even riots, so that universities required them to restrict the celebrations to liturgical rather than bibulous.[34]

The tavern was also a place for students to bond together by sharing other activities: gambling, for example, was universally execrated by officials, and no doubt as universally practiced.[35] Student drinking-songs are widely known—some have survived as the *Carmina Burana*, but students who led a more serious and stable life than the Goliardic poets no doubt sang them as well. When drunk, the students were also given to playing music loudly, dancing in the streets, and breaking into the houses of the townspeople.[36]

The whole spectrum of indecent behavior to which the taverns gave occasion led some college authorities to attempt (unsuccessfully) to prohibit their students' frequenting them.[37]

The fact that future clergymen and other leaders of the next generation formed attitudes about women under the peculiar circumstances of the universities must have had a powerful effect on the perpetuation of gender roles within medieval culture. Alcohol, besides lubricating male bonding rituals, was also a factor in the students' relations with women. Taverns, of course, were notorious for the availability of prostitutes.[38] But there was also great concern that students, especially when drunk, would harass or even rape the wives and daughters of the townspeople.[39] Indeed, the fellows of Merton College, Oxford, in 1494 disciplined a master of the college for his uncontrolled tongue, including "the foul gestures and indecent conversation he had with an honest woman at the sign of the Fleur de Lys."[40] In 1251 in Paris the masters were asked to take an oath that they would not abuse the university privileges against the town's incarceration of students by attempting to obtain the release of students accused of major crimes like murder or rape.[41]

Relations with townswomen were especially a concern because students had very little opportunity to interact with women under everyday social circumstances. Colleges had strict regulations against women servants: only men were to do the laundry, for example, or if no man could be found, the woman selected had to be old.[42] Students or masters were expelled for bringing women onto the college premises, although some of the colleges, like the Fromagerie at the University of Angers, seemed more concerned with the reputation of the college than the morals of its members: no scholar was to bring into the college "any whore, nor *within it* have carnal knowledge of any woman. [emphasis added]"[43]

Prostitution was ubiquitous in university towns. Jacques de Vitry complained that in the Street of Straw, where the lectures at the University of Paris were held, prostitutes occupied the lower floors of the very buildings where students were hearing lectures on the upper. The prostitutes called anyone who refused their services a sodomite.[44] In 1358 the Street of Straw had to be closed off at night because prostitutes were doing business in the lecture halls at night.[45] The universities of Heidelberg and Vienna were concerned with bachelors spending too much money treating their friends to the baths after their examinations, so legislated that they were to invite no one but their examiners.[46] Given the reputation of bathhouses at the time, this may represent a custom of students treating their examiners to the services of a prostitute.[47]

Women other than prostitutes were not by any means absent from the university community. Students would have dealt with women in shops and taverns. They might pay their rent to a landlady. College officials had numerous occasions to come into contact with women: they dealt with tenants of college property, with vendors of victuals and other necessities, and with women donors.[48] By the end of the Middle Ages, there were even married masters at some German universities.[49] But students would not normally have come into contact with women of their own social class. A dialogue in a student manual of the fifteenth century indicates that church attendance provided an opportunity for such contact, but this would not have been the case at a larger university like Paris.[50] For most medieval students, then, women were a social other: they provided services or a sexual outlet, but they were outsiders to the social world through which the students moved.

Within this womanless environment it is not surprising that the curriculum, when it considered women at all, was misogynous in the extreme. This was to some extent deliberate: the critique of marriage, and of women who might lure a man into marriage, was important to a celibate clergy wishing to recruit new members.[51] Sometimes the goals of the clergy came into conflict with those of the students' families who did wish them to marry. One book of model letters for students to use in writing to their families has a student at Siena writing home that he did not want to leave the university to make a good marriage, "for one may always get a wife, but science once lost can never be recovered."[52] This reasoning is a far cry from treatises opposing marriage absolutely but probably reflects the reasoning students and masters would have used with each other.

Misogyny found its way into various aspects of the curriculum, for example medicine.[53] It also appeared in the student culture. For example, the *Manuale Scolarium* included dialogues in which one student tries to talk another out of his interest in young women of the town, in one case on the grounds that the woman in question is already pregnant by another man and trying to acquire a father for her child, in another that dancing with women for half an hour will make him unable to study for two weeks, in yet another that a particular woman is menstruating and therefore poisonous.[54]

For those students who did become clerics, the general attitudes and misogynous teaching, as well as the life styles they had learned at the university, could well have affected their pastoral activities. The effects would not all be negative: a man who had spent a somewhat dissolute youth might well be a better parish priest, more sympathetic to his parishioners, than one who had done nothing at the university but study. Nevertheless, the attitudes toward women that the university education and the university experience would have reinforced would hardly be conducive to sensitive pastoral care.

For those students who did not go on to be priests or for those clerics who went into administrative rather than pastoral work, the misogynous aspects of the university experience might not have the same direct effect. The university, however, had provided training not only in the lecture hall but in the residences, taverns, and streets in how a university man behaves. It had shaped the masculine identities of a privileged elite who adopted behavior patterns that would identify them as such. It gave them a bond with other men who had gone through the same experiences and shared more than a set of intellectual tools. Student conviviality was more than youthful high spirits, it was the ritualized expression of a new masculine ethos.

Medieval university students behaved the way young men in groups, from varying social classes, behaved in the Middle Ages and today: they got drunk and rowdy. What set this process at the medieval university apart from the behavior of other young men in the Middle Ages was the extent to which it was privileged and ritualized. The drinking, gambling, and womanizing were not just incidental activities on the way to an education, although university authorities, and the parents who financed the education, may have wished to see them that way. They were part of the formation of the student as a university man. The universities trained graduates by transmitting knowledge and inculcating habits of mind, but they also socialized the students and helped create their mature masculine identities.

NOTES

1. Even this aspect of the universities has important implications for the medieval construction of gender categories. Before the rise of the universities, when intellectual activity was largely situated within monasteries, both male and female monastics participated. The shift to the universities—and to the dominance of intellectual life by the mendicants rather than monastics—functioned to exclude women from the most rarefied levels of learning. The relation of this process to the affective forms of feminine piety characteristic of the late Middle Ages is an important topic which cannot be discussed here.

2. There have been some efforts to recover the missing women. See, for example, Michael H. Shank, "A Female University Student in Late Medieval Kraków," *Signs: Journal of Women in Culture and Society* 12 (1987): 373–80.

3. Vern L. Bullough, "Achievement, Professionalization, and the University," in *The Universities in the Late Middle Ages*, Jozef Ijsewijn and Jacques Paquet, eds., Mediaevalia Lovaniensia Series 1, Studia 6 (Leuven: Leuven University Press, 1978), p. 509; David F. Noble, *A World Without Women: The Christian Clerical Culture of Western Science* (New York: Knopf, 1992).

4. See William J. Courtenay, *Schools and Scholars in Fourteenth-Century England* (Princeton: Princeton University Press, 1987), pp. 13–14; Guy Fitch Lytle, "The Social Origins of Oxford Students in the Late Middle Ages: New College, c. 1380–c. 1510," in Ijsewijn and Paquet, 452; Hilde De Ridder-Symoens, "Les Origines géographiques et sociales des étudiants de la natio germanique de l'ancienne université d'Orléans (1444–1456). Aperçu général," in *ibid.*, 463; Jacques Verger, "L'histoire sociale des universités à la fin du moyen âge: Problèmes, sources, méthodes (à propos des universités du midi de la France)," in *Die Geschichte der Universitäten und ihre Erforschung*, Siegfried Hoyer and Werner Fläschendräger, eds. (Leipzig: Karl-Marx-Universität, 1984), pp. 39–40; Klaus Wriedt, "Bürgertum und Studium in Norddeutschland während des Spätmittelalters," in *Schulen und Studium im sozialen Wandel des hohen und späten Mittelalters*, Johannes Fried, ed.,Vorträge und Forschungen herausgegeben vom Konstanzer Arbeitskreis für mittelalterliche Geschichte 30 (Sigmaringen: Jan Thorbecke Verlag, 1986), p. 497.

5. Jacques Paquet, "Coût des études, pauvreté et labeur: fonctions et métiers d'étudiants au moyen âge," *History of Universities* 2 (1982), 15–52; Léo Moulin, *La Vie des étudiants au moyen âge* (Paris: Bibliothèque Albin Michel de l'histoire, 1991), pp. 59–65.

6. Nicholas Orme, *From Childhood to Chivalry: The Education of the English Kings and Aristocracy 1066–1530* (London: Methuen, 1984), pp. 66–72; Joel T. Rosenthal, "The Universities and the Medieval English Nobility," *History of Education Quarterly* 9 (1969): 418. See also Rosemary O'Day,

Education and Society, 1500–1800: The Social Foundations of Education in Early Modern Britain (New York: Longman, 1982), p. 81. Some of the late medieval universities, particularly in Germany, made a real effort to recruit the sons of the nobility, but these never composed the majority. J.M. Fletcher, "Wealth and Poverty in the Medieval German Universities," in *Europe in the Late Middle Ages*, J.R. Hale, J.R.L. Highfield, and B. Smalley, eds. (Evanston: Northwestern University Press, 1965), pp. 411–13; see also Rainer Christoph Schwinges, *Deutsche Universitätsbesucher im 14. und 15. Jahrhundert: Studien zur Sozialgeschichte des alten Reiches*, Veröffentlichungen des Instituts für europäische Geschichte Mainz, Abteilung Universalgeschichte, 123 (Stuttgart: Franz Steiner Verlag, 1986), esp. pp. 375–465.

7. The extremely young ages sometimes cited are probably due to the lack of a clear distinction between university students and those at the grammar schools controlled by the universities. John M. Fletcher, "Commentary," *History of Universities* 6 (1986–87), pp. 139–41.

8. Courtenay, pp. 25–26.

9. For numbers who achieved the baccalaureate and other degrees, see Rainier Christoph Schwinges, "Student Education, Student Life," in *A History of the University in Europe*, vol. 1, *Universities in the Middle Ages*, Hilde De Ridder-Symoens, ed. (Cambridge: Cambridge University Press, 1992), pp. 196–200.

10. Lytle, "The Careers of Oxford Students in the Later Middle Ages," in *Rebirth, Reform and Resilience: Universities in Transition 1300–1700*, James M. Kittelson and Pamela J. Transue, eds. (Columbus: Ohio State University Press, 1984), pp. 213–53; Peter Moraw, "The Careers of Graduates," in *Universities in the Middle Ages*, pp. 244–79; John W. Baldwin, "Masters at Paris from 1179 to 1215: A Social Perspective," in *Renaissance and Renewal in the Twelfth Century*, Robert L. Benson and Giles Constable, eds. (Cambridge: Harvard University Press, 1982), pp. 138–72.

11. Alan B. Cobban, "Reflections on the Role of Medieval Universities in Contemporary Society," in *Intellectual Life in the Middle Ages: Essays Presented to Margaret Gibson*, Lesley Smith and Benedicta Ward, eds. (London: Hambledon Press, 1992), pp. 227–41; Gordon Leff, *Paris and Oxford Universities in the Thirteenth and Fourteenth Centuries* (London: John Wiley & Sons Inc., 1968), p. 117; Walter Rüegg, "Themes," in *Universities in the Middle Ages*, pp. 20–21; Stephen C. Ferruolo, "'Quid dant artes nisi luctum?' Learning, Ambition, and Careers in the Medieval University," *History of Education Quarterly* 28 (1988): 1–22.

12. Quoted in Charles Homer Haskins, *Studies in Medieval Culture* (Oxford: Clarendon Press, 1929), p. 15. See pp. 7–16 for more examples, mostly model letters.

13. Schwinges, "Student Education," p. 226; Moulin, pp. 36–38; Orléans, 1365, Marcel Fournier, *Les Statuts et privilèges des universités*

françaises depuis leur fondation jusqu'en 1789 (Paris: Larose et Forcel, 1890), 1:122; Nantes, 1461–62, Fournier 3: 48; Dole, 1424, Fournier 3: 115; Cambridge, 1342, Charles Henry Cooper, *Annals of Cambridge* (Cambridge: Warwick & Co., 1842), 1: 94.

14. Fournier, 1:122 (1365), 1:125–26 (1367), 1:127 (1368). Cf. also Jan Pinborg, ed., *Universitas Studii Haffnensis Stiftelsesdokumenter og Stattuter 1479*, trans. Brian Patrick McGuire (Copenhagen: University of Copenhagen, 1979), pp. 116–117; Heinrich Denifle and Emile Chatelain, *Chartularium Universitatis Parisiensium* (Paris: Delalain, 1889–97), 2: 523–24.

15. Nancy Spatz, "Evidence of Inception Ceremonies in the Twelfth-Century Schools of Paris," *History of Universities* 13 (1994), p. 4.

16. Orléans, Fournier, 1: 22, 1:73ff, 1: 88, 1: 105; Caen, Fournier 3: 164, 3: 212; Bordeaux, Fournier 3: 330; Lisbon, A. Moreira de Sá, ed., *Chartularium Universitatis Portugalensis* (Lisbon: Instituto de alta cultura, 1966), 1: 60; Cambridge, *Documents Relating to the University and Colleges of Cambridge* (London: Longman, Brown, Green & Longmans 1852), 1: 319–20.

17. H.E. Salter, ed., *Registrum Cancellarii Oxoniensis 1434–1469*, 2 vols., Oxford Historical Society 93–94 (Oxford: Oxford Historical Society, 1932), 1: 2, 2: 3, 1: 5, 1: 6, and passim. This register also contains numerous cases of violence by members of the university against women and men of the town. See also *Oxford City Documents, Financial and Judicial, 1268–1605*, J.E. Thorold Rogers, ed., Oxford Historical Society, 18 (Oxford: Oxford Historical Society, 1891), pp. 150ff, for coroners' inquests.

18. W.A. Pantin, *Oxford Life in Oxford Archives* (Oxford: Clarendon Press, 1972), pp. 99–104; Thorold Rogers, *Oxford City Documents*, pp. 245–68. For another town-gown brawl, see Denifle and Chatelain, *Chartularium*, 3: 166.

19. Denifle and Chatelain, *Chartularium*, 4: 668.

20. E.g., Zarncke, *Die Statutenbücher der Universität Leipzig* (Leipzig: S. Hirzel, 1861), p. 426.

21. Statutes of Collège de Foix, University of Toulouse, 1427, Fournier 1: 828.

22. Walter Ong, "Latin Language Study as a Renaissance Puberty Rite," in *Rhetoric, Romance, and Technology: Studies in the Interaction of Expression and Culture* (Ithaca: Cornell University Press, 1971), pp. 115–19.

23. Pearl Kibre, *The Nations in the Mediaeval Universities* (Cambridge, Mass: Medieval Academy of America, 1948), pp. 22–23.

24. The *Manuale* as we have it comes from Heidelberg, but it is taken almost verbatim from a text written at Leipzig by Paulus Niavis (Schneevogel). Gerhard Streckenbach, "Paulus Niavis, 'Latinum ydeoma pro novellis studentibus'—ein Gesprächsbüchlein aus dem letzten Viertel des 15. Jahrhunderts," *Mittellateinisches Jahrbuch* 6 (1970): 152–91; 7 (1971), 187–251. The *Manuale Scholarium* itself is edited by Friedrich Zarncke in

Die deutschen Universitäten im Mittelalter (Leipzig: T.D. Weigel, 1857), pp. 1–48.

25. *Manuale Scholarium*, pp. 4–10.

26. Wilhelm Fabricius, *Die akademische Deposition. Beiträge zur deutschen Literatur- und Kulturgeschichte, speciell zur Sittengeschichte der Universitäten* (Frankfurt am Main: Lichtenberg, 1895), although dated in its methodology and conclusions, is the most detailed work on the subject.

27. "Non sufficiet sola depositio, sed ut bono vino (ceterum bono cerevisia) sociorum fiat refecto..." Johannes Schram, "Monopolium der Schweinezunft," Zarncke, ed., *Die deutschen Universitäten*, 111; *Acten der Erfurter Universität*, J.C. Hermann Weissenborn, ed., Geschichtsquellen der Provinz Sachsen, 8 (Halle: Otto Hendel, 1881), 1: 18. Hastings Rashdall, *The Universities of Europe in the Middle Ages*, 2nd ed., F.M. Powicke and A.B. Emden, eds. (Oxford: Clarendon Press, 1936), 3: 377–81, discusses this ritual based largely on the *Manuale*, which Fabricius, 8, cites as the only pre-Reformation source. The "deposition" referred to in the Erfurt documents may not be an identical ritual. A ritual referred to in the 1400 statutes of New College, Oxford, may be related: "this most vile and horrible game of shaving beards, which is done the night before the inception of masters in arts of our college." *Statutes of the Colleges of Oxford* (Oxford: J.H. Parker, 1853), 1: 48.

28. Fournier, 2: 439–40 (1450).

29. Zarncke, *Die Statutenbücher*, p. 238.

30. E.g., Robert Marichal, ed., *Le Livre des prieurs de Sorbonne (1431–1485)* (Paris: Aux Amateurs de livres, 1987), p. 29.

31. *Auctarium cartularii Universitatis Parisiensis, Liber procuratorum Nationum Anglicanae (Alemanniae) in Universitate Parisiensi*, Heinrich Denifle and Emile Chatelain, eds., 2nd ed. (Paris: Henri Didier, 1937), quotations at 1: 345, 1: 361, discussion at 2:vii, and examples in vols. 1–2 passim.

32. Pierre Champion, "Liste des tavernes de Paris d'après les documents du XVe siècle," *Bulletin de la société de l'histoire de Paris* 39 (1912): 259–67.

33. *Auctarium*, 1: 788.

34. In Orléans, for example, in 1365: Fournier, 1: 121.

35. E.g., on gambling and singing, Collège du Bois, Caen, 1496, Fournier 3: 259; for Erfurt, Weissenborn 1:21; "Die Statuten der Juristen-Universität zu Bologna vom J. 1317–1347, und deren Verhältnisse zu jenen Paduas, Perugias, Florenz," H. Denifle, ed., *Archiv für Litteratur-und Kirchengeschichte des Mittelalters* 3 (1887), 367. See also the ordinances on the bearing of arms cited in n. 16, many of which also deal with gambling.

36. Moulin, 96–101, gives a number of examples. For university statutes, see Ádám Ferencz Kollár, ed., *Analecta monumentorum omnis ævi Vindobonensia*, vol. 1 (Vienna: Tratner, 1761, rpt. Westmead, Hants.: Gregg International, 1970), 226; Eduard Winkelmann, *Urkundenbuch der*

Universität Heidelberg (Heidelberg: Winter, 1886): 19, 120, 157; *Documents Relating to the University and Colleges of Cambridge*, 1: 334–35; Denifle and Chatelain, *Chartularium*, 2: 484 (College of St. Bernard).

37. Johannes Kerer, *Statuta Collegii Sapientiae. The Statutes of the Collegium Sapientiae in Freiburg University. Freiburg, Breisgau, 1497*, Josef Hermann Beckmann, ed. (Lindau: Jan Thorbecke, 1957), 60.

38. See Ruth Mazo Karras, *Common Women: Prostitution and Sexuality in Medieval England* (New York: Oxford University Press, 1996), pp. 71–72.

39. E.g., in Paris, Denifle and Chatelain, *Chartularium*, 1: 481; Copenhagen, Pinborg, p. 117; Heidelberg, Winkelmann, p. 19.

40. H.E. Salter, *Registrum Annalium Collegii Mertonensis, 1483–1521*, Oxford Historical Society 76 (Oxford: Clarendon Press, 1923), p. 186. Moulin, p. 102, cites a case involving students from Bologna attacking women whom they believed to be prostitutes.

41. Pearl Kibre, *Scholarly Privileges in the Middle Ages* (Cambridge: Medieval Academy of America, 1962), p. 102. Similarly, for Orléans from 1307: Fournier, 1: 22.

42. St. Peter's College, Cambridge: *Documents Relating to the University and Colleges of Cambridge*, 2: 30; King's College, Cambridge, *ibid.*, 2: 596; Oriel College, Oxford, *Statutes of the Colleges of Oxford*, 1: 15; All Souls' College, Oxford, *ibid.*, 1: 58; Magdalen College, Oxford, *ibid.*, 2: 26. The College of the Sorbonne, however, had women as porters (janitrices): Marichal, pp. 231, 272.

43. Fournier, 1: 353 (1408); similarly, Collège de Mirepoix, Toulouse, 1423–24 (Fournier, 1: 790), Grosse Fürstencolleg, Leipzig, 1439 (Zarncke, *Statutenbücher*, 196); Kerer, *Statuta*, 28, 38; David Sanderlin, *The Medieval Statutes of the College of Autun at the University of Paris*, Texts and Studies in the History of Medieval Education, 13 (Notre Dame: Medieval Institute, 1971), 99. Other colleges, however, prohibited their members from consorting with prostitutes anywhere: e.g. Angers, Collège de Breuil, 1424, Fournier 1: 381. For examples of infractions of this type of rule, see Marichal, p. 106.

44. Jacques de Vitry, *The Historia Occidentalis of Jacques de Vitry: A Critical Edition*, John Frederick Hinnebusch, ed., Spicilegium Friburgense 17 (Fribourg: The University Press, 1972), ch. 7, p. 91.

45. Denifle and Chatelain, *Chartularium*, 3: 53.

46. Winkelmann, *Urkundenbuch*, 117 (1410); Rudolf Kink, *Geschichte der kaiserlichen Universität Wien* (Vienna: Carl Gerold & Sohn, 1854), 1: 55 (1427).

47. Other things besides consorting with prostitutes may have been going on in the bathhouses. In Paris in 1431, the clerk of one of the masters of the Sorbonne was beaten for having spent the night in the stews (baths)

with a man from outside the college, apparently another cleric. Marichal, pp. 41–42.

48. John W. Fletcher and Christopher A. Upton, "'Monastic Enclave' or 'Open Society'? A Consideration of the Role of Women in the Life of an Oxford College in the early Tudor Period," *History of Education* 16 (1987): 1–9; the point is equally valid for the Middle Ages.

49. Fletcher, "Wealth and Poverty," pp. 418–21.

50. *Manuale Scholarium*, pp. 35–36.

51. See Katharina M. Wilson and Elizabeth M. Makowski, *Wykked Wyves and the Woes of Marriage: Misogamous Literature from Juvenal to Chaucer* (Albany: SUNY Press, 1990).

52. Quoted in Charles Homer Haskins, *The Rise of the Universities* (Ithaca: Cornell University Press, 1957), p. 81.

53. Helen Rodnite Lemay, "Some Thirteenth and Fourteenth Century Lectures on Female Sexuality," *International Journal of Women's Studies* 1 (1978), 391–400.

54. *Manuale Scholarium*, pp. 40, 38, 36.

WOLF MAN[1]

Leslie Dunton-Downer

Werewolf literature efficiently sets questions of gender against those of humanness. Marie de France's Bisclavret, *examined here, asks whether maleness and humanness constitute two mutually exclusive kinds of identities.*

> Humanity recognizes no sex; virtue recognizes no sex; mind recognizes no sex; life and death, pleasure and pain, happiness and misery, recognize no sex.
>
> Rose, *The History of Woman's Suffrage*[2]

> But once again that analogizing power, which belongs to body and mind analogically and mutually and which body and mind share with each other in the art of invention, is inconsequential compared to an irreparable transcendence inscribed on the body by gender difference. Not only calculation, but even analogy cannot do away with the remainder left by this difference. This difference makes thought go on endlessly and won't allow itself to be thought.
>
> Lyotard, "Can Thought Go on Without a Body?"[3]

> Now the universal cannot exist as such, because if definition transforms it into another particularity, then non-definition dissipates it entirely. The universality of the human as horizon, for instance, can only have being if it is delimited by the not-human-enough until it vanishes into a paradox worthy of Zeno....If it is to have being, therefore, humanity must occur as a universality that appropriates the particularity of its own negation by lodging the inhuman at its heart.
>
> Devji, "The In-Human"[4]

The subject positions and pronominal systems of Western languages, whose attraction to the clarity and simplicity of the binary opposition runs deeper than any desire to accommodate the complexity of life, have essentialized maleness and femaleness.

Thinking itself necessarily occurs if not in a male or female body, then at least in a male or female-identified voice, suggests Lyotard, whose essay about whether thought can go on without a body is divided into two sub-categories entitled "He" and "She." Culture appears to prefer its genders in clearly delimited, either/or slots, in spite of biological evidence that nature is not so essentialist when it comes to sex differences.[5] As soon as we deploy the opposition male/female we participate in the tyranny of cultural and linguistic overdeterminations of identity as resolutely gendered; the assignment of sex to the human being in Western cultures can be understood, therefore, as a means to pattern identities on the unthinking ground of differentiation itself, including the linguistic ground of the sex difference.[6]

Yet humanness, as an ontological problem, is not the same as the category designating what male or female human beings are in opposition to animals.[7] When we are being human, we are bound up in the paradoxes defining the essence of language, its problematic, poetic qualities and functions; humanness in this sense attempts to go beyond the problem of identity as it is constituted in and delimited by language. The sex difference may itself analogize the essentially differentiated ground of language (so that when we turn to questions of our humanness we desire to transcend our gendered particularities as they are given in language), but is only one of many kinds of differences through which the non-identifications that qualify our humanness are played out. Consider the differences between signifier and signified; singular and plural; present and past; utterance and its lack; self and non-self; all of these, too, motivate systems in language and thinking that rely at once on identification and non-identification in order to produce meaning, itself imperfect and indirect yet characterized by a desire to transcend the inevitable gaps through which it is produced. The sex difference, insofar as it is a cultural rather than a biological problem, works not as a master difference encompassing all "subordinate" differences; rather, it is a difference among others preserved in language. The human desire to be or speak beyond differences, to occupy an ontological realm of humanness not defined by limitations of gender, number, discourse, or any other category of discrimination, is precisely what allows us to reflect on while continuing to exist within boundaries limiting the formation of identity. To put this point as succinctly as possible, it is in striving for humanness as such that we come as close as possible to understanding the paradoxical essence of our existence in language. Werewolf literature offers an excellent resource through which to examine this phenomenon precisely because it very efficiently sets questions of gender against those of humanness.

Bisclavret is a werewolf story composed in Anglo-Norman French octosyllabic couplets by Marie de France in the second half of the twelfth century.[8] It bears the double distinction of being the earliest surviving werewolf story in the Western tradition to portray the shape-changer sympathetically and of having been composed by the first known woman to have written in the vernacular in the European West. Marie de France transforms conventional representations of the werewolf (Petronius, Pliny, Herodotus, Ovid, Virgil, and Augustine provide good surviving examples, but the Celtic-Breton oral tradition to which Marie refers in the prologue to her *Lais* stands, alongside her explicit reference to this tradition in *Bisclavret* itself, is another important source) in this text to correlate the essentially paradoxical nature of humanness with poetic language. I will argue that in Marie's rendering the animal violence associated at once with traditional maleness and the werewolf figure is, along with the violence of writing itself, attributed a human and humanizing function that describes an important twelfth-century moment in the evolution of maleness.[9]

Usually the wolf-man is a malevolent figure whose unforeseeably rapacious activities and irrational destructiveness have been understood, at least since Boethius,[10] to capture the animal aspect of the human being, the capacity each of us bears to act without humanity or reason. But we may also ask whether it is at times helpful to look at the wolf-man not as a figure for the universal animal in the universal human but rather as a figure for violence in the male human. Save the remarkable exception,[11] the werewolf is male and his maleness not accidental. The story material derives from the old and, geographically speaking, broadly dispersed practice of donning wolf skins in order more effectively to undertake hunting and warring,[12] markedly male activities. If traditional werewolf material dilates most crucially on the periodic lack of humanity in men overtaken by an impulse to destroy, lust, and cannibalize,[13] Marie's treatment of the wolf-man as a victim deserving our sympathy is all the more forceful for its striking differences from this tradition.

Remarkable in the case of *Bisclavret* is the representation of werewolf violence as sign or, say, semiotic action. Unable to speak when he has shifted shape, Bisclavret is nevertheless still able to make signs; he transforms (unreadable) animal violence into *écriture*. Devouring, here a form of poetic language, reveals the werewolf's human interior, his possession of *entente* (157), *reisun* (208), and *sen* (157) or, to put it in post-Augustinian language, his existence as an *animal rationale mortale*.[14] Recall that, for Augustine, rationality, which distinguishes humans from animals, is a prerequisite for salvation.[15]

Let me refresh your memory by summarizing the action of this brief lay. In former times, we are told, many men would become werewolves, savage beasts, who would go into a rage and devour people. But you are to hear the story of Bisclavret, the Breton word for werewolf—"man" + "wolf." (It has been argued that Bisclavret derives from *bleiz*= "wolf"+ *laveret*= "rational," from the word for "speaking."[16]) Bisclavret is a baron well loved by his wife, neighbors, and king. Now Bisclavret is mysteriously absent three days of each week.[17] One day his wife decides to get to the bottom of this situation to learn that her husband is periodically transformed into a wolf. Mortified, she persuades another knight—a knight who has long pursued her affection unsuccessfully—to prevent Bisclavret from regaining his human shape by stealing the clothing he hides during his episodes in the wild. The wife, we learn, here betrays Bisclavret, who remains in his wolf form as a result of her trickery. With Bisclavret assumed gone for good, she then marries her accomplice.

A year later, the king, out hunting, encounters Bisclavret in the woods and recognizes his *entente* (157) and *sen* (157), his humbling himself (*s'humilie* [153]), and other traits suggesting humanness. At this stage, taken in by the king as a kind of pet, Bisclavret remains gentle until the day when his wife's new husband shows up at court. The wolf-creature begins to attack the man brutally, but the court intervenes to restrain him. The court then decides that the wolf's behavior must be rational since he has never been violent. Later, when Bisclavret accompanies the king on a hunt near Bisclavret's old house, the wife comes to pay her respects to the king. Bisclavret then tears her nose from her face and his action is interpreted by a wise man as having significance. The wise man recommends subjecting the wife to torture in order to extract a confession, which she provides; she is also persuaded to produce the clothes required for Bisclavret's metamorphosis from wolf to human form. Restored to his human shape, Bisclavret is preferred by the king, who lavishes gifts on him; the wife and her new husband are exiled. We learn that some of the daughters in their line are born without noses.

There are two moments of violence, when what initially appears to be animal eating or attacking is ultimately taken (through the interpretative agency of the king's court or wiseman) as the human act of signifying. The first occurs when Bisclavret sees the new husband of his wife arrive in the king's court:

> Si tost cum il vint al paleis
> E li bisclavret l'aparceut,
> De plain esleis vers lui curut:
> As denz le prist, vers lui le trait.
> Ja li eüst mut grant leid fait,
> Ne fust le reis ki l'apela
> D'une verge le manaça.
> Deus feiz le vout mordre le jur!
> Mut s'esmerveillent li plusur,
> Kar unkes tel semblant ne fist
> Vers nul hume ke il veïst.
> Ceo dient tuit par la meisun
> K'il nel fet mie sanz reisun.
> Mesfait li ad, coment que seit,
> Kar volontiers se vengereit. (196–210)

> As soon as he came to the palace
> Bisclavret saw him,
> ran toward him at full speed,
> sank his teeth into him, and started to drag him down.
> He (Bisclavret) would have done him (the knight) great damage
> if the king hadn't called him(Bisclavret) off,
> and threatened him with a stick.
> Twice that day he (Bisclavret) tried to bite the knight.
> Everyone was extremely surprised,
> since the beast had never acted that way
> toward any other man he had seen.
> All over the palace people said
> that he wouldn't act that way without a reason:
> that somehow or other the knight had mistreated Bisclavret
> and now he (Bisclavret) wanted his revenge.
> (Hanning and Ferrante, 97)

The attack is righteously motivated, Marie goes on to say, by the beast's desire to avenge himself; but, more importantly, Bisclavret's potential danger to the court (eüst mut grant leid fait [200]) is eclipsed by his increasingly legible *reisun* (208). Notice how in this instance the werewolf's violence is not only humanized but even judicially sanctioned (and witnessed by the king) as a form of revenge.

The second instance of the werewolf's violence takes place during the hunt back in the woods near his house. When his wife appears before the king, Bisclavret pounces:

> Vers li curut cum enragiez
> Oiez cum il est bien vengiez:
> Le neis li esracha del vis!
> Que li peüst il faire pis?
> De tutes parz l'unt manacié;
> Ja l'eüssent tut depescié,
> Quant uns sages hum dist al rei:
> 'Sire, fet il, entent a mei!...' (232–240)

> When Bisclavret saw her coming,
> no one could hold him back;
> he ran toward her in a rage.
> Now listen how he avenged himself!
> He tore the nose off her face.
> What worse thing could he have done to her?
> Now men closed in on him from all sides;
> they were about to tear him apart,
> when a wise man said to the king,
> "My lord, listen to me!" (Hanning and Ferrante, 98)

This time revenge is exacted: Bisclavret tears the nose from his wife's face. The text suggests this is the best possible revenge Bisclavret could execute. As with the first attack, there is a moment of troubling chaos and general violence until an interpreter (the wise man, in this case, rather than the court in general) explains how to take the action as a motivated sign rather than an outburst of animal ferocity.

The wise man is not the only one to find significance in the beast's violence. Many critics have lined up behind him to explain the rationale of the wolf's selecting his wife's nose as the object of his aggression. Freudian-Lacanian psycho-sexual readings designate the nose a female phallus (a sign of the wife's excessive lust and her effort to dominate her husband), whose removal installs a visible gap, or an absence as presence.[18] Historical approaches have discovered in the episode evidence of the contemporary practice of punishing adulteresses by cutting off their noses, so that Bisclavret's violence acts within a recognizable judicial discourse.[19] And philological observations have drawn on the acoustic proximity of *lupa* (a she-wolf or prostitute) to *lepra* (female leper), who were often co-identified during this period as lascivious marginals, or even outlaws. So the tearing off of the nose makes the wife, as figurative *lupa*, look like a *lepra* and exposes her bestial nature while, by contrast, Bisclavret's wolf shape conceals (even as it invites people to marvel at) his human nature.[20] I would add another motivation, which further supports the violent act as poetic: the Old French expression "n'avoir point du nez" means "n'être pas raisonable, n'avoir pas du bon sens."[21] By removing her nose, Bisclavret literalizes this expression, demonstrating at once that he possesses reason and sense (il a du nez) while his wife does not (elle n'a point du nez).

No one of these readings alone is exclusively meaningful; the point is that the de-nosement becomes a richly significant act precisely because it is irreducible to a specific, referential meaning. The poetic nature of the act (i.e., its ipseity, that no other act or body part would mean as much or as well as the nose) is the supreme sign of the wolf's humanness and of his possession of a self, a linguistic interiority. The problem of the missing nose returns again in the closing lines of the lay. Marie writes of Bisclavret's wife, ultimately exiled:

> Enfanz en ad asez eü
> Puis unt esté bien cuneü
> E del semblant et del visage
> Plusures des femmes del lignage,
> C'est veritez, senz nes sunt neies
> E sovent ierent esnassees. (309–314)

> She had several children
> who were widely known
> for their appearance:
> several of the women of the family
> were actually born without noses,
> and lived out their lives noseless. (Hanning and Ferrante, 99)

The sound game here, a virtual aural palindrome (*sen-nes*) can be seen to perform poetically the curse on the wife's female line. The acoustic effects offer a repetition through time (the final two verses shifting yet doggedly repeating units of sound to form an extended *annominatio*) of a poetic sign: the absence of the nose recalling with each generation an original *grant mal* in this genetic *transfère du mal.*[22] The werewolf nature of the male is also transferred to the female, now a *lepra-lupa* of sorts in her own right.[23] The *annominatio* on *nes*, then, enacts poetically the character of Bisclavret's attack and, placed as it is in the significant final lines of the narrative, emphasizes the integral role of the nose episode in the composition as a whole.

Perhaps precisely because the lay is innovative in its sympathy toward the werewolf, leaving readers eager to locate the more simple villainy of the traditional werewolf somewhere in this composition (in order to preserve, as it were, some signature function of the traditional werewolf story), there has been a strong tendency among critics of *Bisclavret* to interpret the wife as a negative figure: adulteress, betrayer of love, breaker of courtly codes of conduct, and so on. One scholar even proposes that the cunning wife who dismantles the fabric of domestic and feudal social order is ejected so that the lay terminates on a note of comic resolution.[24] Nevertheless, the wife is not treated unsympathetically herself. She acts out of understandable fear, a fear detailed several times, of her husband's other self; she is tortured at the king's court as a confession is forced from her (she has been bad, granted, but the extremity of the torture—mut grant destresce [264]—may remind us of the language of virtual martyrdom; one thinks of the torture of Fénice in Chrétien's contemporary romance *Cligés*); and she is finally exiled to produce facially deformed females. In the end, there is no clear correlation between gender and righteous behavior in this lay.[25] In fact, the whole point of the composition appears to be that human beings, whether regarded in terms of their gender or any other category, are complicated; and since the story is primarily concerned with the differences between Bisclavret and other, previous werewolves, it is not so much taken up with preserving functions of good and evil as it is with capturing the irreducibility of human beings, including males prone to recurring periods of animality, to either of these types.

The wife's lineage performs the potentially infinite transmission of a sign of violence, but violence also circulates at every level of the lay. Members of the court, whether in torturing her or preparing to attack or dismember Bisclavret himself, are first ready to use violence, rather than to turn to language, interpretation, or other, exclusively human and peaceful modes of resolution. The wife, then, may be read as a scapegoat figure whose expulsion removes an original violence (the werewolf identity of Bisclavret? certainly not her own), which will be passed down through her line rather than circulating viciously within the social and territorial economies of the king's court and land.[26]

Post-Derridean readings of Marie, such as Howard Bloch's, insist on the violence of writing itself. Bloch argues that in Marie's poetics the recorded word, just as the translated word, "always betrays, and even kills"[27] whatever it attempts to convey or capture fully. But in spite of the admittedly problematic nature of *écriture* in general and in Marie's post-oral literary poetics in particular, her lay suggests that writing is also able to accomplish something of value: it transforms violence into meanings that reflect on the problematic nature of humanness and on the necessity of living (whether socially or spiritually, publicly or internally) with the fragile distinction between violence and language, chaos and order, the animal and the human.[28] It is precisely because poetic language is inherently problematic (or *écriture* violent) and because its indeterminacies capture the conflicts that come to define social or psychical life that poetic language is the material extraordinarily well suited for a praxis of humanness.

To put this in other terms, we could say that the gender distinction between male and female is one of many distinctions emanating from the basic system of differentiation that grounds the poetic function in language and, by extension, the human function in social and psychical life. The essential feature of poetic language, succinctly articulated by Roman Jakobson, is its dual capacity at once to identify and to refuse identification: "[B]esides the direct awareness of the identity between sign and object (A is A1), there is a necessity for the direct awareness of the inadequacy of that identity (A is not A1)."[29] This paradoxical set of equations defines the connection between signifier and signified as well as the absence of connection between these two "terms," if one could call them that. Systems of meaning operate according to this (seemingly pathological) rule: identifications yield up non-identifications so that humanness, with all its "irrationality" and "imperfection," resides in the impossibility of any collapse between terms. Poetic language, which Lyotard would perhaps recognize as the *sine qua non* of the analogical, is remarkably equipped to reflect on this essential nature of difference. Philosophy—and one may observe this as explicitly in the writings of Aquinas as in Wittgenstein— perceives the impossibility of thinking through the essence of this basic paradox of our being in language. But poetic language, like humanness itself, thrives on the messes offered up by categories of differentiation. And while language remains systematically violent in the sense Bloch deploys, it is nevertheless through the very same conditions that motivate its violence that it conveys meanings, enacts culture, humanizes males and females.

These issues are all the more pressing in the context of late twelfth-century Anglo-Norman court culture, in which selfhood was to be re-codified in new discourses, texts, and practices. Following such work as that found in the volume edited by Ariès and Duby for the series *The History of Private Life*, one could no doubt fruitfully study *Bisclavret* as a text about the social oppressiveness of courtly codes and their impact on the emergence of a newly-valued space of the private, the asocial, or the self. The sympathetic werewolf found in *Bisclavret* as well as other material in this period (the anonymous *Histoire de Biclarel*, *Lai de Melion*, *Guillaume de Palerne*, and Gerald of Wales's *Topographia Hibernica*) appears particularly well equipped to perform new ontologies of maleness in such twelfth-century courtly contexts as those occupied by Marie herself.[30]

The transformation of the literary werewolf in terms of reevaluations of humanness must also be understood in the context of twelfth-century preoccupations with the Eucharistic rite and the important debates regarding the nature of the host.[31] These debates included the problems of Christ's dual nature (human and divine), the host's dual nature (as bread and body of Christ) and the difficult nature of its reception (did one masticate Christ's body cannibalistically, or was it a representation of Christ's body that one ingested?).[32] In dealing with the werewolf as a dual creature, a man who appears to be an animal, the secular *Bisclavret* invites its audience to reflect on and redefine itself in relation to sacred models of the miraculous. The lay suggests that one of the most difficult of human tasks (besides looking beyond the illusory appearances of things or people) is to be found in acknowledging the proximity of human understanding to animal violence and learning to live soundly in a world where their distinction is so precarious yet necessary. For the problem of humanness is all the more vibrantly at stake when its nature is clearly understood to reside on the fragilities of a paradox.

The miraculous quality of Bisclavret's human nature existing as it does in a beast's form derives, after all, from the same system of identity and non-identity that informs Christ's presence in the host and offers related opportunities to reflect on the human through the not-human. Furthermore, both the story material and the ritual activities take as problems the devouring of human flesh. In the case of the Eucharist, ritual eating of the body of Christ is guaranteed to accomplish a merging of identities (human/divine), temporal modes (past/present), and extreme ontological states (life/death), such that the problems surrounding identity and difference are, in the moments where oppositions motivating humanness and poeticity are collapsed, at least temporarily resolved. The werewolf before Bisclavret, with his bloodthirsty cannibalizing and devouring, could equally be said to signify a desire for total identification and mergence, not with the divine but, very unreflectively, with his prey, demonstrating a lack of (human) reason and affection. Both kinds of ingestion (Eucharistic and lycanthropic), unlike as they may be, occur beyond the scope of language and its imperative systems of differentiation.[33] Yet Bisclavret, acting at once as an animal and a human, pushes signifying activity to its limits and for a brief time (one could even think of this as a ritual time) is able to exist in a realm in which humanness is recognized as a kind of idealized, translinguistic poeticity.

But if humanness becomes most visible in figurations of the translinguistic, to what extent may humanity be obstructed by the oppositional systems, including that of gender, in which language is grounded? "Humanity recognizes no sex," Ernestine L. Rose once said.[34] Ideally, too, the experience of the self as human is necessarily ungendered; it is an experience defined by a kind of thinking or, better, being, which has managed to incorporate what Lyotard has called "[the] difference [that] makes thought go on endlessly and won't allow itself to be thought."[35] The Eucharistic ritual and Marie's *Bisclavret* are perhaps both exploring that translinguistic space of mergence in which significance survives in spite of the collapse of systems of opposition, a space in which one can be human above and beyond one's gender or any other mark of identity. In the end, though, one returns to language and the analogical: when the ritual comes to a close, one rediscovers the distinctness of one's self, the inescapable linguistic fact of gender. After all, the werewolf has, in spite of his discovering the human, produced a line of females whose bodies, deformed, are co-extensive with the poetic function yielding the on-going riddle of their noses.

"[H]umanity must occur as a universality that appropriates the particularity of its own negation by lodging the inhuman at its heart."[36] Being male...becoming human. In certain texts and practices of the twelfth century, and notably in *Bisclavret*, we may recognize an emerging desire to remain other than merely "human" in order to continue, precisely through the particularity of maleness and the violence of language, becoming as human as possible.

NOTES

1. An initial version of this paper was presented at the first International Medieval Congress, July 4–7, 1994, at Leeds University in England. I am grateful to the American Council of Learned Societies for a grant that allowed me to attend the conference and to the Harvard Society of Fellows for the fellowship that nurtured this research. I would also like to express my gratitude to Margaret Bridges, Matilda Tomaryn Bruckner, and Derek Pearsall for their responses to this essay as a work-in-progress. And I am indebted to David Haig for his explanations of biological research pertaining to maleness and for directing my attention to relevant publications in this area.

2. Ernestine L. Rose, as quoted in *The History of Woman's Suffrage*. Vol. 1., Elizabeth Cady Stanton, Susan B. Anthony, Matilda Joslyn Gage, Ida Husted Harper, eds.(n.p., 1881; rpt., Salem, NH: The Ayer Co. Publishers, Inc., 1985), p. 238.

3. Jean-François Lyotard, "Can Thought Go on Without a Body?" in *The Inhuman: Reflections on Time*, trans. Geoffrey Bennington and Rachel Bowlby (Stanford: Stanford University Press, 1991), p. 23.

4. Faisal Devji, "The In-Human," in *Violent Mediations*, ed. Sandhya Shetti (Durham, NC: Duke University Press, forthcoming).

5. Evidence suggests that the biology of human gender as necessarily either male or female is problematic. Conditions of intersexuality, whereby humans are more complexly sexed, have been documented in individuals as well as populations. One such condition, a form of male pseudo-hermaphroditism, exists in two village populations of the Dominican Republic. Individuals born with ambiguous external genitalia are raised

as females until the age of puberty, after which time external genitalia are masculinized (testes are visible); a rite of passage allows individuals to be reassimilated into the culture as males. See Julianne Imperto-McGinley, Luis Guerrero, Teofilo Gautier, Ralph E. Peterson, "Steroid 5a–Reductase Deficiency in Man: An Inherited Form of Male Pseudohermaphroditism," *Science* 186 (1974): 1213–1215, and Julianne Imperto-McGinley, Ralph E. Peterson, Teofilo Gautier, Erasmo Sturla, "Androgens and the Evolution of Male-Gender Identity Among Male Pseudohermaphrodites with 5a–Reductase Deficiency," *The New England Journal of Medicine* 300 (1979): 1233–1237.

6. On the question of assigning male or female sex to intersexual individuals in Western medical practice and biological theory, see Anne Fausto-Sterling, *The Myths of Gender: Biological Theories About Women and Men* (New York: Basic Books, 1985); eadem, "The Five Sexes: Why Male and Female Are Not Enough," *The Sciences* 44 (1993): 2026.

7. In other words, an ontological idea of the human is quite different from the usual descriptive sense that opposes the human to the animal. Consider this observation about males in Marie de France's animal fables: "Her [Marie's] males are not the 'us' of traditional fables but the 'other' of a female artist looking at her world, defined by a male hierarchy she accepts at least in the abstract. If Marie's 'otherness' makes her an outsider, denied any significant position of public power, it also gives her an especially strong voice as a satirist and fabulist, able to look at her world simultaneously from both within and without, and seeing the populace as both 'them' and 'us,' as both male and female, as both beast and (hu)man" (Harriet Spiegel, "The Male Animal in the Fables of Marie de France," in *Medieval Masculinities: Regarding Men in the Middle Ages*, ed. Clare A. Lees [Minneapolis: University of Minnesota Press, 1994], pp. 123–24). Here, opposed as it is to 'beast,' the human is an attribute of both male and female human beings; in this sense the male is by definition human.

8. All references to Marie de France's text will be given by verse number for convenience. Citations are from *Les Lais de Marie de France,* ed. Jean Rychner (Paris: Champion, 1983). All translations are from *The Lais of Marie de France,* trans. Robert Hanning and Joan Ferrante (Durham, NC: The Labyrinth Press, 1978).

9. *Bisclavret* asks what happens when the male human being is pressed to convey (precisely in spite of his wolf form) his humanness as distinct from his maleness or masculinity. And this problem invites us to think differently about the relations among the terms: male, female, and human. At the same time, I do not want to suggest that studies looking at the social significance of Bisclavret's maleness are not themselves important. Kathryn I. Holten in "Metamorphosis and Language in the Lay of Bisclavret," in *In Quest of Marie de France, a Twelfth-Century Poet*, ed. Chantal E. Maréchal (Lewiston: The Edwin Mellen Press, Ltd., 1992), in

particular, reads gender relations carefully in the story to discover evidence of "the dangerous social instability of feudalism," p. 204. In "Of Men and Beasts," *Romanic Review* 81 (1991), Matilda Tomaryn Bruckner's interpretation of the richly-layered implications of sex differences in Bisclavret also develops our understanding of the "oxymoronic character of human nature: not only the man/beast pair....but also those of woman and man, forest and court, nature and society," p. 253. I hope my approach to the problem of humanness in this text will, rather than contesting the validity of previous interpretations of maleness in it, reveal that the human, while at times opposed to the animal, also functions as a category of being irreconcilable with gender as given in language.

10. Boethius, *De Consolatione Philosophiae* 4.3

11. One example may be found in Gerald of Wales's *Topographia Hibernica* 2.19, which features not only a male but also a female werewolf.

12. Caroline Taylor Stewart, "The Origin of the Werewolf Superstition," *University of Missouri Studies* 2 (1909): 1–37.

13. These characteristics of the werewolf are virtually signature attributes in material pre-dating Marie, as she makes clear (5–12), but they also appear in accounts after the twelfth century. Consider, for instance, Gervaise of Tilbury's description of the English man who, "infantes in forma lupina devoravit" (*Otia Imperialia* 3.120). At the same time, though, in Marie's treatment of the werewolf there emerges a new figure that will evolve into the complicated wolf-men of the twentieth century, such as Lon Chaney's various cinematographic incarnations of werewolves during the 1940s and Jack Nicholson's more recent impersonation, in the film *Wolf*, of a middle-aged editor suffering from unwanted physical changes and loss of power in the workplace. The modern werewolf protagonist, evolved from the sympathetic medieval werewolf epitomized in the figure of Bisclavret, may also be better understood with regard to maleness *per se* rather than as a figure for the psychological complexity of human beings for whom the animal comes to trope a universalized "dark side." On problems of male metamorphoses in modernity, see Stern's "Feminine Artifice and the Fate of the Man in Makeup: Wilde, Mann and Proust on the Problem of Male Metamorphosis" (Ph.D. diss., Princeton University, 1991).

14. Augustine, *De Civitate Dei,* 16.8

15. See the discussion by Dennis M. Kratz, "Fictus Lupus: The Werewolf in Christian Thought," *Classical Folia* 30 (1976): 57–79 of relevant differentiations between humans and animals in Christian thought.

16. H.W Bailey. "Bisclavret in Marie de France," *Cambridge Medieval Celtic Studies* 1 (1981): 96.

17. The regularity of his transformations (three days of each week) indicates that Bisclavret is an involuntary or 'constitutional' werewolf who,

unlike the Teutonic werewolf of shamanistic powers, undergoes a metamorphosis against or in spite of his own volition. For a discussion of this typology, see Smith, "An Historical Study of the Werewolf in Literature," *PMLA* 9 (1894): 1–42.

18. Jean-Charles Huchet, "Nom de femme et écriture féminine au Moyen Age: Les Lais de Marie de France," *Poétique* 48 (1981): 407–30; Bruckner, "Of Men and Beasts"; see also François Suard, "*Bisclavret* et les contes du loup-garou: Essai d'interprétation," *Marche Romane* 30 (1980): 267–276.

19. William Sayers, "*Bisclavret* in Marie de France: A Reply," *Cambridge Medieval Celtic Studies* 4 (1982): 77–82.; Glyn S. Burgess, *The Lais of Marie de France: Text and Context* (Athens, GA: University of Georgia Press, 1987).

20. Kathryn I. Holten, "Metamorphosis and Language in the *Lay of Bisclavret*" in Burgess, *Lais*; Sayers, "*Bisclavret* in Marie de France: A Reply."

21. Frédéric Godefroy, *Dictionnaire de l'ancienne langue française et de tous ses dialectes du IXe au XVe siècle.* 10 vols. (Paris: Champion, 1880–1902) 5: 492.

22. One may think, here, of Eve and the post-lapsarian transfer of original sin from her to all humans. On the co-identification of the female (Eve) and the animal (serpent) in this paradigm and its relation to Bisclavret, see Bruckner, "Of Men and Beasts."

23. Could it be that the deforming mark Bisclavret inserts in the lineage of his former wife also functions as punishment for her having taken a new husband and procreating with him rather than with her initial and "rightful" husband?

24. Paula Clifford, *Marie de France: Lais* (London: Grant and Cutler Ltd., 1982).

25. One unfortunate tendency in much of the work on Marie is to supply meanings that motivate her writing as "feminist" or "female." Consequently, a number of readers who see women portrayed relatively favorably in much of Marie's material find themselves fretting when encountered with Bisclavret's wife, who then needs to be carefully handled so as to fit into whichever authorial ideological system the reader has attributed to Marie. The concluding paragraph of Leo Spitzer's study "Marie de France—Dichterin von Problem-Märchen," *Zeitschrift für romanische Philologie* 50 (1930): 1–67 summarizes the ill-suitedness of Marie's lays to any programmatic reading: "Marie de France gibt nicht Anekdoten, sondern symbolisch deutbare Erzählung, nicht Allegorien, sondern musikalisch umspielte, organisch sich entfaltende Symbolik, die der Leser erzeut, ohne vom Autor auf eine These hingestofsen zu sein, sie gibt träumerisch aufgelöste These, 'Problem-Märchen,' Problematisches, Vieldeutiges—Lebendiges," 66.

26. Most readers find that the wife gets her due for having betrayed her husband. An example from Joyce E. Salisbury, *The Beast Within: Animals in the Middle Ages* (New York; London: Routledge, 1994): "Before his wife becomes involved in his plight, he is an animal half the time. In this we see most clearly the beginnings of the twelfth-century acceptance of an animal side of people. The animal side consumes the human through the agency of a woman, more carnal and closer to animals than even the half-wolf man," p. 165.

27. R. Howard Bloch, *Medieval Misogyny and the Invention of Western Romantic Love* (Chicago; London: University of Chicago Press, 1991), p. 138.

28. The fragile distinction between oral and more strictly literary modes of communication also informs the poetics of humanness in this text. Marie herself addresses these specific characteristics of her writing in the General Prologue to the *Lais*. See Bruckner, "Conteur oral/ Recueil écrit: Marie de Fance et la clôture des *Lais*." *Op. Cit.* 5 (1995): 5–13.

29. Roman Jakobson, "What Is Poetry?" in *Language in Literature*, ed. Krystyna Pomorska and Stephen Rudy (Cambridge, MA; London: Belknap Press, 1987), p. 378.

30. See the discussion by Bambeck in "Das Werwolfmotiv im Bisclavret," *Zeitschrift für romanische Philologie* 89 (1973) on the cultural centrality of the court of Henry II in both Marie and Gerald of Wales, whose *Topographia Hibernica* "hatte er 1188 Heinrich II gewidmet" (146).

31. Bambeck argues that the figure of the king in Marie's story captures the problem of the *persona mixta* as developed in the study by Ernst H. Kantorowicz, *The King's Two Bodies: A Study in Mediaeval Political Theology* (Princeton: Princeton Univ. Press, 1957) and indicates the likely importance of contemporary debates surrounding the Eucharist in evaluating the central themes of *Bisclavret.* See also Salisbury and Bruckner (1994); on the question of werewolves and illusory change as it was understand by the Church, see Kratz.

32. For a helpful review of these arguments as they evolved from around the year 1000 through the twelfth century, see the study by Miri Rubin, *Corpus Christi: The Eucharist in Late Medieval Culture* (Cambridge: Cambridge University Press, 1991), esp. pp. 1–163.

33. Dunton-Downer, "Languageless Places and Poetic Language: The Boundless Desire of Cannibal Clément X," *Analecta Husserliana* 44 (1995): 13–143.

34. Stanton et al., eds. *The History of Woman's Suffrage,* vol. 1, p. 238.

35. Lyotard, p. 23.

36. Faisal Devji.

GOWTHER AMONG THE DOGS: BECOMING INHUMAN C. 1400

Jeffrey Jerome Cohen

Using the postmodern identity theories of Gilles Deleuze and Félix Guattari, Cohen maps the gendering of a monstrous male body in a late Middle English Romance. The essay demonstrates that the medieval body is always in process, always in production.

> The Church has always burned sorcerers, or reintegrated anchorites into the toned-down images of a series of saints whose only remaining relation to animals is strangely familiar, domestic.[1]

OEDIPAL CANINES

Vladimir Slepian writes of a man who decides to become a dog.[2] Dogs, he reasons, have more freedom than humans, because they do not suffer the same constraints. One limb, one organ at a time he transforms himself, mapping the affects of the canine body across a human form in the strangest kind of diagramming. Dogs are quadrupedal, and so he ties shoes to hands and feet; when his new paws prevent him from lacing the fourth shoe, he utilizes his mouth, which becomes a dog's clever snout. His metamorphosis almost succeeds, but then he comes to the tail and can find no somatic analog. For him to involve his sexual organ in this wild fit of becoming would tear him completely from the cultural meaning system that he has begun to flee; who would he be if the signs of his identity were not readable from his anatomy? In the end he chooses being a man over becoming something other, something freakish or monstrous. A "psychoanalytic drift" descends, he is flooded with childhood memories ("all the clichés about the tail, the mother...all those concrete figures and symbolic analogies," *ATP*, p. 259).

Suddenly it becomes clear

> what constraint was being escaped: Oedipus, phallocentrism, molar personhood itself. The man's anti-Oedipal desire was not strong enough, or his powers of analysis not refined enough, to pull the linchpin (Massumi 94).

The man's becoming-dog fails, mainly because he has mapped his escape across a body already too constrained: no freedom animates the household dog.[3] Canine bodies, like human bodies, receive their meaning-in-being only to the extent to which they are oedipalized, made to signify within a geometry of familial relations. Sir Gowther, a rapinous murderer born of a demon and revered as a saint, could have taught our failed cynocephalus that.

ENFANCES

It may seem strange to begin an essay on the Middle Ages with an anecdote about a man intent on becoming man's best friend. But readers of the Middle English verse romance *Sir Gowther* (c. 1400) will already recognize in the vignette a familiar story.[4] Gowther gains his adult identity as knight, hero, and saint through a similar process of transformation, mapping the potentialities of his unsocialized self across the grid of the canine bodies with whom he shares food and place. Through an equation formulated by the Church and officially sanctioned by the State, Gowther's becoming-animal curves into his being-man. This odd but wonderful little romance plots, through the wilds of identity, a monstrous route to becoming male in the Middle Ages.

Gowther's life does not begin well. His mother and father, the Duke and Duchess of Estryke (Austria), have been wedded for ten childless years. The text holds the duke as much at fault for the lack of an heir as his wife ("He chylde non geyt ne sche non bare," 50), but he blames only her:

> 'Y tro thou be sum baryn,
> Hit is gud that we twyn;
> Y do bot wast my tyme on the,
> Eireles mon owre londys bee—'
> For gretyng he con not blyn. (53–57)

> 'I believe that you're barren,
> So it would be good for us to part.

> I'm wasting my time on you.
> My lands are heirless—'
> For weeping he could not finish.

In the duke's rhetoric, culpability falls upon the maternal body, which is indeed destined to become a problematic site of origin in this romance. Yet the father's body does not fare much better. No son exists to carry into the future the family name, the "paternal metaphor" condensed in the ducal title. This impersonal title is the only signifier of identity attached to the Duke and Duchess of Estryke, who *both* remain without personal names throughout the narrative.

Aristocratic, familial history is germane to the "ancestral romances" (*Guy of Warwick, Beves of Hampton*): such stories detail the foundational moments of provincial aristocracies in order to trace the phantasmatic power of family names. "Fair Unknown" romances (Malory's "Tale of Sir Gareth," *Lybeaus Desconus*) enact the same narrative without invoking the illusory "real" of particularized history. Jacques Lacan's notion of "the Name of the Father" (*nom du père*)[5] is useful in describing the textual mechanics of both genres: these "identity romances" often trace how young men (*juvenes*) mature into their proper name through a series of adventures—and, "as it turns out," the adult identity into which they wander exactly coincides with a family name that may have been hidden from them until that point. Even when (or especially when) romance heroes do not know who their father is, their movement into adulthood is dictated nonetheless by the ghostly agency that the Name-of-the-Father embodies in its narrative determinacy: the Name is revealed at the precise moment when the hero becomes the history for which it stands.

Sir Gowther is neither ancestral nor Fair Unknown romance but plays with the conventions of both in order to create a hybrid kind of identity romance. The Name-of-the-Father, that ghost which passes like Hamlet's father to each son and whispers "Remember me," will stop appearing when the (nameless) Duke of Estryke dies, for he has no son to compel with its impossible charge to repeat. The duke despairs and breaks apart his family. His wife, however, finds a way to reconfigure the circuit of that Name, by invoking a "real" phantasm, an incubus, as well as a larger history than the local one of ancestral romance.[6] The duchess prays to "God and

Maré mylde" that, through some miracle, she will have a child, "on what maner scho ne roghth" (63). She wanders into the orchard and encounters a man resembling her husband who seeks her love. He leads her to a tree and "With hur is wyll he wroghtth" (69):

> When he had is wylle all don,
> A felturd fende he start up son,
> And stode and hur beheld.
> He seyd, 'Y have geyton a chylde on the
> That in is yothe full wylde schall bee.' (70–74)
>
> Whe he had worked his will on her,
> He leapt up, a hairy fiend,
> And stood and looked upon her.
> He said, 'I have engendered a child on you
> Who, in his youth, will be very wild.'

She runs from the garden, terrified at this supernatural revelation—terrified that her desires have been simultaneously spoken and realized.

But she is not so frightened that she cannot see an advantage in the impregnation. The duchess informs her husband that an angel has descended from bright heaven to declare that they will conceive a child that night (80–81). The tableau wickedly repeats in secular, imaginary history a foundational moment in salvation history. The duchess speaks as if she were Mary after the Annunciation, declaring the impending arrival through the agency of a Holy Spirit of a miraculous birth. The duke believes his wife, and "he pleyd hym with that ladé" all night, unaware that a "fende" has already "bownden" with her (91–92). Joseph lost his "paternal imperative" to God; the duke loses his to a demon.

The baby is born and christened Gowther—christened *in nomine patris*, just as the romance is constructed around the search for a father's Name under which to be. The evil deeds Gowther commits while still a youth cause the duke to sicken and die within a single line: no possibility of inheriting any identity-giving history from someone who has been, all along, a non-entity. Of Gowther's "biological" father we know little, other than that he was the same evil fiend who begot Merlin (95). A prologue in the British Library (MS. Royal 17.B.43) version of the story yields some additional prehistory. Foul fiends, we are told, once roamed the earth, passing themselves off as men in order to have intercourse "with ladies free" (6–7):

> A selcowgth thyng that is to here:
> A fende to nyeght wemen nere,
> And makyd hom with chyld,
> Tho kynde of men wher thei hit tane
> (For of homselfe had thei never nan). (13–17)
>
> It is a strange thing to hear:
> A fiend would lie with women,
> And engender a child on them,
> Through the mens' forms [*or* semen] they had taken
> (For of themselves they have none).

The creature described here is the incubus, a monster with a complex medieval genealogy. Incubi would temporarily reside in illusory male forms to work their sexual crimes, engendering monstrous offspring before reverting to their disembodied state. Patristic exegesis connected these airy demons to the fallen angels, tracing their history to an ambiguous passage from Genesis:

> Gigantes autem erant super terram in diebus illis. Postquam enim ingressi sunt filii Dei ad filias hominum illaeque genuerunt. Isti sunt potentes a saeculo viri famosi. (Genesis 6:4)
>
> Now giants were upon the earth in those days. For after the sons of God went in to the daughters of men, they brought forth children. These are the mighty men of old, men of renown.

According to a tradition dismissed by Augustine but influential throughout the Middle Ages, the sons of God (*filii Dei*) were angels, the daughters of men (*filiae hominum*) mortals, and the offspring of this illicit mingling of the purely spiritual and overly physical were the giants, the most wicked and pervasive race of monsters in the bible—and in romance tradition.[7] Trevisa's translation of Higden's *Polychronicon* (1387), for example, declares that it may be that "Incubus, such feendes" that lay by women "in liknesse of men" once begot giants.[8] The Pearl Poet and Andrew of Wyntoun likewise explicate the biblical narrative as an encounter between a devil or *incubi* (a "fende" or "sindry spretis") and earthly women who fall prey to their sexual lures and give birth to giants.[9] From the Annunciation we have moved back to those iniquitous days preceding the Flood.

But we also recede into a specifically English history. Late in the thirteenth century, numerous prose and verse chronicles circulated that detailed the settlement of the island by exiled Greek or Syrian princesses. These popular histories were still well known at the time *Gowther* was composed. According to these accounts, the oldest of the sisters, Albina, convinced her siblings to murder their husbands in their sleep. Their father punished his transgressive daughters by casting them adrift in a rudderless boat. Arriving after a long journey on English shores, Albina named this new world "Albion" after herself. Before long, the women yearned for the company of men and were visited by incubi or devils who impregnated them with giants, and England thus received its aboriginal population of monsters. Many years later, the Trojan warrior Brutus arrived to do battle with this evil progeny, wiping England clean for nationhood.[10]

Unlike the mother in *Robert le diable*, who vows her son to the devil at conception, the duchess in *Sir Gowther* is replaying a particularly English scene which wholly transforms the French romance upon which *Gowther* is based, giving it a "local habitation" along with a new name.[11] History repeats: the intercourse of fiend and errant daughters of men in biblical history becomes the intercourse of fiend and transgressive princesses in national history, which in turn becomes the intercourse of fiend and disconsolate wife in the local or familial space of romance.[12] But even if these successive repetitions threaten to become a funnel that trickles out smaller versions of the same story, Gowther is nonetheless something of a giant. Like the monstrous progeny of the biblical and chronicle narratives, Gowther grows at a prodigious rate: "In a twelmond more he wex / Then odur chylder in syvon or sex" (142–43). His exceptional growth is the product of the flow of violence that nourishes him as much as the breast milk with which it mingles: his father arranges for him to have the best wives of the country as his wetnurses, and Gowther "sowked hom so thei lost ther lyvys" (110). At the age of one, he has drained nine nurses of milk and life. The duchess is then forced to take over the feeding of this little monster:

> His modur fell a fowle unhappe;
> Apon a day bad hym tho pappe,
> He snaffulld to it soo,
> He rofe tho hed fro tho brest;
> Scho fell backeward and cald a prest. (124-29)

His mother suffered a foul misfortune;
Upon a day she tried to breastfeed him,
He worried at it so,
He tore the nipple from the breast;
She fell backwards and called for a priest.

The physical violence that attends every attempt at nurture demonstrates that no place exists for him within the domestic spaces represented by the parade of nurses and his mother; Gowther, from infancy, resists familialism. Nor does his behavior improve much as he grows older. By the time he is fifteen, he is wielding a "fachon," a sword with a curved blade that signifies both his uncontrolled aggression (he and the sword are never parted) and his alterity (the falchion is an Eastern weapon, suggestive of Saracens and other fiendish heathens). His father knights him, then dies of grief; his mother flees to a fortress, where she immures herself against his energetic evil.

Gowther, now a "duke of greyt renown," passes his days happily beating up churchmen, hunting, and chasing away mendicant friars. "Erly and late, lowde and styll, / He wold wyrke is fadur wyll" (172–73): like the young Jesus discovered preaching in the Temple, Gowther must be about his father's business, only he has no idea who his father is even as his actions inscribe him under that paternal Name ("fiend"). In one bout of wickedness he and his men rape a group of nuns who have issued in procession from their convent to beg mercy; he then locks the women in their church and burns them alive ("Then went his name full wyde," 189). The catalog of crime also includes spoiling virgins so that they cannot marry, violating wives and then slaying their husbands, forcing friars to leap off cliffs, hanging parsons on hooks, slaying priests, and igniting hermits and widows (190–201).

Sex and violence or sex as violence: sex is the violence directed against women; unprovoked and unsanctioned murder its equivalent toward men. Gowther's crimes are doubly anti-chivalric. If chivalry is that code which regulates the proper construction of masculinity within the domain of bourgeois and aristocratic relations (and is simultaneously a fiction and an effective cultural intervention into "real world" gender codification), then Gowther embodies everything which that code excludes. As the son of a demon and *filia hominum*, Gowther is the stereotyped giant of romance, that masculine body out of control whose abnormal size signifies rampant appetite, both somatic and social.[13] The giant embodies everything Freud labeled "pre-oedipal": his is the body unimpressed by social coding, a playground of unchannelled forces (aggression, orality, desire, and drive without boundary) that explode outward in monstrous acts. Deleuze and Guattari have argued that the Oedipal construct ("Oedipus") is the organizing principle of Western culture, the primary structuration through which desire is regulated into identity.[14] In classical psychoanalysis, submission to Oedipus means recognition of the dictative power of the father (Freud's "Oedipus complex"), or of that transcendental principle which the father ineptly embodies, beyond choice or control (Lacan's "Name-of-the-Father"). In the theatre of psychoanalysis, the Oedipal drama is a critical success when the dénouement is acceptance of one's place within an identity grid mapped across a triangle of familial relations. Oedipus is a productive prohibition whose outcome is a "global person," an "ego," an "individual."[15] The equation for Oedipus might be written as 3 + 1: the three members of the family triangle, plus a master signifier, a principle "outside the structuration" that acts as guarantor of its truth.[16] The Oedipalized body which is the equation's resultant is a predictable distribution of forces and affects across a culturally coherent identity. This body can then be exactly placed on a social grid by reference to filiation.

Oedipus works rather differently as a constitutive principle in the Middle Ages, depending on the particular culture employing its organizational power (and sometimes, of course, it does not obtain at all).[17] In romances involving *juvenes* (young men progressing toward adulthood), the moment of Oedipalization usually occurs during the fight against the giant. The young hero defeats his monstrous double in a battle whose outcome announces that the knight has learnt to channel the multiple drives that traverse the body, rendering a multiplicity of becoming (only the danger of which the giant encodes) into a unitary being, the one who bows down to the One. Oedipus in identity romance is not predicated upon rivalry with the father for the affection of the mother, with all its various displacements; it perhaps takes Freud's claustrophobic domestic interiors for that family drama to be scripted. Romance geographies are wider, the cast of characters more numerous and less quotidian, but the Name-of-the-Father becomes their cartographer all the same.

The young hero learns what expression the historical, sexual, social forces at work upon his body are to take and willingly steps into that sanctioned role: Yvain becomes master of his castle, settling down after long errantry to be both husband and lord. The romance ideal of masculinity involves a single heterosexual object choice (the requisite loving wife) coupled to an unambiguous situation within the grid of homosocial relations (ideally, as lord or king, the high position a final representational validation of the worth of the attainer). Oedipus ensures that, in the imaginary but culturally effective space of romance, young bodies particularly prone to troublemaking are brought under social ("familial") control—even if that family is the celibate family of the Holy Church.

THE NAMES OF THE FATHER

What happens, though, when the restraints of Oedipus fail to produce a sufficiently docile body? From the point of view of the power structures whose interplay composes a society or culture, that body is unstable, dangerous, monstrous. Scrutiny of such abjected, "impossible" (but nonetheless socially produced) identities yields important insight into what is assumed as the foundation of self-identity. By encoding what one must not become, the monster demonstrates what, in the gaze of its terrifying face, one is compelled to be.

Despite his wicked ways, Gowther possesses this monstrous insight. When an elderly earl accuses him of being the son of a fiend, he is horrified (210). He imprisons the man, gallops to the fortress where his mother is hiding, and demands to know the truth of his paternity. "Who was my fadur?" becomes the central question of the text, which now works with the efficiency of a riddle to resolve it. The first reply is situational: the duchess states simply that he was fathered by the duke "that dyed last" (223). Gowther is not satisfied, and asks again. This time the answer is historical, as the duchess invites her son to witness, through her narrative, the primal scene of his own biological and metaphysical formation:

> 'Son, sython Y schall tho sothe say:
> In owre orcharde apon a day,
> A fende gat the thare;
> As lyke my lorde as he myght be,

Undurneyth a cheston tre.'
Then weppyd thei bothe full sare. (226–31)

'Son, since I must tell you the truth:
In our orchard one day,
A fiend begot you;
He looked as much like my lord as might be,
Underneath a chestnut tree.'
Then they both wept, full of sorrow.

The scene of the no-longer-immaculate conception is detailed, with Gowther as its onlooker: the sexual relation, stripped of its mythology (no courtly love here, no rhetoric of the symbolic to clothe the naked Real of the act) reduces Gowther to a genital outcome. This brief but disturbing account functions similarly to the psychoanalytic drama of a *pornographic* moment.[18] The sexual act, Slavoj Zizek argues, works narratively as "an intrusion of the real undermining the consistency of [the] diegetic reality" (111). The love stories that structure identity romances are built around an approach toward the "unattainable/forbidden object" of desire, but the object itself is never supposed to be reached. The sexual act exists "only as concealed, indicated, 'faked'":

> As soon as we 'show it,' its charm is dispelled, we have 'gone too far.' Instead of the sublime Thing, we are stuck with vulgar, groaning fornication. (110)

The orchard scene which opened the romance repeats precisely in order to push the narrative "too far," to expose the vulgarity of Gowther's conception as the vulgarity of *all* conception. Despite its revelatory power, however, the moment of origin remains indecipherable (was it rape? was it desired? a rape-in-desire? how does one judge such an event? how does one represent the Real of the sexual relation?). The seamlessness of the Symbolic (the system of representation which structures culture) is momentarily tattered by an intrusion of the Real (the utterly "material," that which resists representation).[19] Gowther is faced suddenly with the elemental nonsensicality of his coming into being. Through his mother's testimony he witnesses the act in its inescapable materiality, and now he must find a way to symbolize that encounter, to incorporate it into a meaning-system not reducible to "mere" sex.

A theological reading of the passage must stress that Gowther has just been faced with the stark reality of his *human* birth into

Original Sin, the fallen state of humankind.[20] The fiend is not really any different from the duke; indeed, a fiend attends upon every sexual relation. If the "kynde of men" that the incubus steals (12) refers to man's semen rather than man's shape, then the fiend is a disembodied delivery system, the sexual act in effect but not in a particular body; the *materia* is still the Real of the father. Another way of putting it: the fiend *is* the duke, or at least the "father in reality" (the father in his corporeality, as a sexual and fallible body), as opposed to the pure and incorporeal function of paternity (as "metaphor," as *nom du père*). "Who was my fadur?" After the situational and historical responses which his mother provides, the only answer that now remains to the riddle of masculine identity is a purely transcendent one that can leave behind the soiled physicality of this originary moment. Through transcendence lies the only possibility of escape.

Gowther enjoins his mother to make confession, promises to do likewise, and then leaves for Rome. He prays to "God that Maré bare" and "God and Maré mylde": his new family will be the Holy Family, and he will gain entrance through audience with the pope, Father of the Church, who commands Gowther to "Lye down the fachon" (286). The knight refuses; the sword is too much a part of his identity, a materialization into extrapsychical space of what he inside *is*. But the next papal commandment Gowther obeys without hesitation:

> 'Wherser thou travellys be northe or soth,
> Thou eyt no meyt bot that thou revus of howndus mothe,
> Cum thy body within;
> Ne no worde speke for evyll ne gud,
> Or thou reydé tokyn have fro God
> That forgyfyn is thi syn.' (292–97)
>
> 'Wheresoever you travel, north or south,
> You must eat only what meat you snatch from dogs' mouths,
> Nothing else may come into your body.
> Speak no word, for evil or for good,
> Until you have a clear sign from God
> That your sin is forgiven.'

Gowther's body is to be completely closed from social intercourse: his food prechewed, his mouth an organ that receives and ingests rather than reacts and interacts through language. In order to become fully embedded within the Symbolic (in order, that is, to become a Name divorced from the corporeality a name might signify), Gowther's body must become a passive object, a still surface upon which will be inscribed new codes of conduct and a new organization.

In order to be a man, Gowther is going to have to become a dog.

TRANSITIONAL BODIES

In acceptance of his penance, Gowther kneels before the throne of the pope: this bowing to the Name is his first gesture of submission. In Rome he eats meat only from the mouths of dogs, wholly obedient to his vow; then he wanders from the Eternal City (the city of the transcendental principle, of Universal Truth) and arrives in "anodur far cuntre" (305). A greyhound delivers a loaf of bread for each of three days. When on the fourth the dog fails to appear, Gowther discovers the castle of a mighty emperor.[21] Trumpets resound upon the high wall; knights process into the main chamber; and Gowther follows as if he were that vanished greyhound:

> [He] gwosse prystely thoro tho pres,
> Unto tho hye bord he chesse,
> Therundur he made is seytt.
> Tho styward come with yarde in honde;
> To geyt hym thethyn fast con he fonde
> And throly hym con threyt. (328–33)

> [He] goes quickly through the crowd,
> Went right to the high table,
> And he sat underneath.
> The steward came carrying a stick;
> He tried hard to drive him out from there,
> And threatened him fiercely.

Like a dog, Gowther scurries under the table; the steward, quick to enter the drama of resemblance, threatens to beat Gowther with a stick, like a dog. Yet the penitential knight retains a strange dignity even as he maps the trajectory of his becoming through a domestic, shaggy body: the canine with which he will form an alliance, his point of departure to becoming something other than the son of a fiend, will not be any household pet, but the special favorite of the castle's master. Gowther seats himself under the high table, where the emperor recognizes that some higher calling may compel this man-dog, perhaps even a penance (343–44). He has Gowther provided with meat and bread from his own board, and watches curiously as the stranger refuses to eat; when the Emperor sees the speechless man snatch a bone from a "spanyell," he provides the hounds with extra food so that Gowther can share in the secondary feast. "Among tho howndys thus was he fed" (364), and at night he is led to a "lytyll chambur" ringed with curtains. He quickly becomes a court favorite, and they name him Hob.

The episode is similar in many ways to Marie de France's lay *Bisclavret*, whose protagonist becomes the favorite knight of the king by spending many months as his favorite hunting hound. Bisclavret is a werewolf trapped permanently in canine shape after his fearful wife steals his clothing. The king comes across the wolf-man in the forest and refrains from killing him when he makes signs of submission. He adopts the metamorphic knight as a pet, not realizing that the beast was formerly one of his men. Bisclavret endears himself to his master, sleeping with him in his chamber at night and passing the day at his feet. In quadrupedal form, he sees his wife for the treacherous woman she is, and realizes the superiority of the bond that ties him to the king over that which had joined him to his spouse. By learning to be a proper dog (that is, by submitting to his allotted place within the masculine hierarchy) Bisclavret learns to be a proper man; *bisclavret*, the Breton noun for "werewolf," becomes Bisclavret, a proper name. In Marie's narrative, an antinomy exists between male-male and male-female bonds; Bisclavret is rewarded with his "true" body only after he takes his revenge on his traitorous spouse by biting off her nose to expose her crime. The wife, not the werewolf, is the monster. Rather than lycanthropy being transmitted to successive generations, the wife's noselessness is passed along congenitally to her female children.

Gowther's body receives a "domesticating" (or, better, "familializing") imprint similar to Bisclavret's. He is trained into the functional Symbolic of the court just as a canine or infantile body is made to internalize the regulatory mechanisms that render it (through habit and repetition) coherent, legible, self-same. For both Bisclavret and Gowther, a wild, multiple, "molecular" identity is constrained through a mapping across an animal body, receiving its "molar" being only after this interstitial (transitional, transferential) form has been successfully passed through.[22] In both cases, the liminal canine body has as much to do with the anthropomorphization of dogs as the becoming-animal of humans.

Dogs are readily incorporated within human meaning systems because their bodies have been bred to be easy to imprint: we like dogs as household pets to the extent to which they act as if human, like a simultaneously exaggerated and diminutive version of ourselves. Dogs are easy to Oedipalize.[23] "Docility" is the canine affect that Bisclavret and Gowther become-dog in order to instate. Rather than fight a giant to confront Oedipus, these monstrous knights are Oedipalized more slowly, through a grammar of transformation that will fix the undisciplined and metamorphic multiplicity of their bodies into the stasis of a molar identity.

Another way of putting it: Gowther and the hound (or Bisclavret and the wolf) enter into a masochistic relation. They seem simply to be imitating the dog but in fact are engaged in a more complex process of intersubjective embodiment. To return to Deleuze and Guattari's terminology, the instinctive forces that animate the human body are being overcoded by transmitted forces. D&G provide the example of a masochist who transforms himself through a similar somatic mapping into a horse.[24] *Why a horse?*

> Horses are trained: humans impose upon the horse's instinctive forces transmitted forces that regulate the former, select, dominate, overcode them. The masochist transmits an inversion of signs: the horse transmits its transmitted forces to him, so that the masochist's innate forces will in turn be tamed (155–56).

And so with the dog: all of the forces that are transmitted through the canine body rebound to overcode the human. An interstitial monster springs temporarily into being: a dog-man, a cynocephalus, a werewolf. But once the overcoding "takes," the body passes out of its freakish hybridity to be inscribed more fully than ever into the secure space of the Human.

Gowther's becoming-dog ultimately follows a rather different trajectory from Bisclavret's—or at least a more geometrically complicated one. A trigonometry unites not only Gowther and the animals under the table but also the knight and the emperor's daughter, who is likewise mute ("was too soo dompe as hee," 372). Her body is the next mediating "partial object" which will pull him closer to a full identity. Conjoined by their mutual affect (silence),

Gowther and the princess use the canine bodies as the bridge across which they communicate, beginning a new diagram that allows Gowther to leave these docile animals for new transitions. When the princess sees that he takes his food only from dogs' mouths, she reacts with kindness: she calls two fine greyhounds to her side, washes clean their mouths with wine, places a loaf of bread in one and some meat in the other, and sends the pair to Gowther, who devours the food eagerly. The dogs become mediating rather than restrictive forms, and through the princess' intercession Gowther begins the final process of transubstantiation. For the first time, Gowther's own corporeality is inserted into the text through a vigorous exclamation: "That doghthy of body and bon" (447). No coincidence, then, that the bread, wine, and "flesch" she sends to him have their analogs in the Eucharist, where "lofe" and "wyn" become a body, the "flesch" and blood of Christ.

But first Gowther's desire must alight upon the princess as object, for without the connection of desire he cannot be pulled by a new investment of force from his place beneath the table. This process is initiated through mimesis. No sooner does Gowther first see the emperor's daughter than she is constituted as object of desire through the gaze of another: a "sawdyn" (sultan) of great might declares he shall wage war against the emperor "dey and nyghtt" until the princess is given him (376–84). The emperor refuses with the resonant phrase "Y wyll not, be Cryst wonde, / Gyffe hor to no hethon hownde!" (388–89). The declaration demarcates for us Gowther's third relational body, connected to him both by its rhetorical contiguity to the dogs he imitates ("hethon hownde!")[25] and by its fascination with the emperor's daughter (dumb, like him; object of the gaze, like him). This third body will break the closed circuit of his identity diagramming. Gowther is connected to the animal and feminine bodies by relationships of becoming and movement; this new enemy will teach him the necessities of abjection as differentiation, as entrance into stable being. The Sultan takes the place of the giant which Gowther no longer is.

A series of miraculous transformations occurs as the sign from God that Gowther is triangulating his passage well. When the sultan first attacks the emperor's lands, Gowther retreats to his chamber and prays for all the material signifiers of knighthood (weapons, armor, a horse). These are the first words he has spoken since undergoing his penance, and the utterances have the potency of a speech act ("He had no ner is preyr made, / Bot hors and armur bothe he hade," 406–07). That which he names is instantly materialized: signifier and signified are united. Gowther is close to being his name.

Nor is he any less effective on the battlefield. With his beloved falchion he bursts enemy heads (422), spills blood and brains (426), and decapitates scores of heathens. Having ensured that the emperor's men will carry the day, Gowther returns home, where his black horse and black armor vanish. He enters the hall where the emperor's men are celebrating their victory and promptly seats himself "too small raches betwene" ("between two small hunting dogs," 441). No one knows the identity of the mysterious Black Knight but the princess, and she cannot speak her knowledge.

The sultan repeats his assault the next day, and this time Gowther is dressed by God in red armaments. Again he dismembers Saracens by the dozen, but this time it is his enemy who is "blake" ("black"): Gowther is moving through an alchemical process, becoming refined, impurities removed. His slicing of the sultan's men into little bits has an analog earlier in the poem, when on the day of his wedding the duke cracked men's skulls ("mony a cron con crake," 45) during a nuptial tournament. Gowther's violence is similar ("Mony a crone con he stere," 422) but sanctioned in ways that his father's could not be. Gowther's aggression is not for celebration.

The self-effacing space of the battlefield substitutes for the performative arena of the tournament.[26] Gowther is most strongly himself when he learns the power of masochism. In self-denial is his self-assertion. The falchion that was the symbol of his unrestrained violence now becomes the visual signal of his proper control, the weapon by which those bodies antithetical to Gowther's new ethos are torn into pieces. This psychomachia upon the battlefield has its analog in miniature upon Gowther's body with real effects: he suffers. After the battle and after the customary dinner among the hounds, the battered knight retreats to his chamber to rest his wounds and meditate upon the sins that they signify.

The alembic process of Gowther's transformation is completed on the third day, when he charges into combat dressed in white. Gowther is as white as the alimental milk that he drained from his wetnurses along with their lives; only no trace of the monster now remains. The emperor thinks that multiple mysterious knights have been coming to his aid (520), and in a way he is correct: these are multiple Gowthers in that they are "Gowther under process," Gowther the fiend becoming Gowther the savior through a series of transubstantiations that culminate in this final version. Just as white is not a single color so much as the spectrum of all possible colors, Gowther as the white knight is the product of a long combinatory equation whose alchemical outcome is an elemental hero who has passed through a multiplicity of difference to become the sanctioned One. The battlefield Gowther is the continuation and culmination of all these other Gowthers, of the narrative's manifold past that is moving its multiplicity toward a unity.

GOWTHER TRIUMPHANT

When the sultan succeeds in capturing the emperor, Gowther rides to his liege's rescue. The sequence of events (623–30) is extraordinary in its toppling domino effect. Gowther strikes off the head of his enemy, overcoming and vanquishing the very thing he once was, renouncing monstrousness forever. In the exultation which this liberatory feat provokes, he is reminded all the more forcefully of his corporeality: even as he praises God for constructing his body from the raw materials of flesh and bone, even at the triumphant moment when he experiences a transcendence from the fleshliness of that frame, his body is transfixed by an enemy weapon. The somatic chain reaction culminates in the princess for the first time finding her voice, a visceral response to the visible sign of Gowther's vulnerability—and to his being fixed, metaphorically and literally, in place.

The princess' fall into the signifying chain has its price: she tumbles from the window of her tower and lies dead. When the pope arrives to pronounce her obsequies, a miracle occurs: "scho raxeld hur and rase" in order to speak "wyse" words to Gowther (652). The message she delivers is straight from God, who declares through her that the mute knight who still eats among the dogs is forgiven all his sins, that he may now speak without fear, that Gowther should eat, drink, and "make mery," and that he is numbered among the chosen of heaven (656–60). To her father she announces Gowther's true identity as the knight that fought as his polychromatic ally for three glorious days. The pope consecrates these proceedings by declaring to Gowther "Now art thou Goddus chyld" (668), no longer a "warlocke wyld" ("wild devil," 669). With the assent of these two new earthly fathers (the pope, the emperor), Gowther marries the princess and becomes heir to the land. Gowther is inscribed beneath a new family Name, a mightier one: emperor, rather than duke.

But Gowther is not yet ready to remain in place. He journeys back to Estryke and marries his mother to the old earl who precipitated his metamorphic journey. He finds something satisfying in returning the country to the normalcy of the family triad. Simple domestic bliss is not the interest of this romance; indeed, this return to the maternal only prepares for a second and final renunciation of it. He memorializes and expiates his early sins by building an abbey where monks will pray "unto the wordus end" for the nuns he victimized. Nuns to monks: as the maternal vanished, so does the feminine. The narrative now moves toward the eternal, the immutable, the transcendent, as Gowther assumes his full identity as "Goddus chyld." Full of remorse as he recalls the crimes of his youth, Gowther can escape the return of the romance's triply enfolded past (biblical, national, familial) only by finding a way to stand outside of it.

Gowther journeys "hom" to the demesnes he rules as emperor and spends his life performing good works. The princess is never mentioned again after the marriage. Nor is the existence of an heir: the body disappears as a textual concern in preparation for a final transfiguration out of all corporeality. Gowther dies, is buried in the abbey he constructed, and is worshipped as "a varré corsent parfett," a true saint (721). Pilgrims seek his shrine and are rewarded with divine metamorphoses of their disfigured bodies: the blind see; the mute speak; hunchbacks are straightened. Because "geyton with a felteryd feynd" (742) and sanctified after a long journey through a series of transitional bodies, Gowther has come to signify a transformative, corrective, normalizing principle. Gowther in triumph is Gowther abstracted, the hero who becomes an incorporeal Name under which miracles are performed: from inhuman origins to superhuman transfiguration, an inhuman end.

"Who was my fadur?" Gowther has at long last found his purely transcendent answer to the riddle of paternity. God is his father:

this simple fact guarantees his legitimacy, the truth of his identity, by allowing his body to be placed outside of the chains of filiation that would otherwise delimit him as the son of a fiend, the son of a nameless duke, the son of an all-too-human father rather than of an abstract principle that looks down upon him from heaven and smiles. The British Library manuscript of the romance rightly ends with the phrase *explicit vita sancti*, "here ends the saint's life": from identity romance through multiple transformations into an eternity of hagiography.[27]

The "transcendent principle" is the same as the "master signifier" that ensures the truth value of Oedipus; in the equation 3 + 1, it is that exterior One which allows belief in the interior structure. This disembodied principle as it works its transfigurations on Gowther is equated with the Holy Spirit: "For he is inspyryd with tho Holy Gost, / That was tho cursod knyght" (731-2). Perhaps this "inspiration" allows us to see why the mother and the princess vanish so suddenly from the text. Gowther is Oedipalized into the celibate family of the Church, where the place of the feminine body in the triangle has been usurped by a pure and mysterious spirit. The Holy Trinity of familialism is supplanted by the Holy Trinity of Father, Son, and sexless disembodied Principle. Gowther submits to this sacred trigonometry by learning to disavow the merely corporeal, aligned in the beginning and then in the end with the maternal and the feminine. His reward is to be rendered not a hero but a saint.

AS OPPOSED TO WHAT?

> We know nothing about a body until we know what it can do, in other words, what its affects are, how they can or cannot enter into composition with other affects, with the affects of another body, either to destroy the body or to be destroyed by it, either to exchange actions and passions with it or to join with it in composing a more powerful body. (*ATP*, p. 257)

We may as well reformulate Sedgwick's famous question about nationalisms and sexualities and demand "Oedipus, as opposed to what?"[28] I am not arguing that Gowther had any choice within this long process of Oedipalization; after all, even if such things as choice and intentionality do exist, he is a literary representation of a subject that does not see outside of his own generative text (a fact which perhaps makes him more human, not less). Oedipus was probably the same structural inevitability in England c. 1400 as it is in the United States c. 2000, but as this essay demonstrates, its phantasmatic workings were at once very different and equally complex. By tracing the genealogy of Oedipal configuration, and mapping its affects across the body of Gowther, this essay argues that gender is constructed and that bodies are sexed in culturally specific ways. Freud and Lacan depict the unconscious as a classical theatre whose secret dramas are played out externally by actors who keep repeating the same roles before dying and leaving them to understudies. This model is in many ways deeply Christian (especially in Lacan's formulation) and fits well with medieval ideas like the sacred Trinity because it derives in part from them.[29] But I would like to suggest that the Middle Ages are far more complicated than they are often made out to be. Before it hardens into the armor of his final identity, Gowther's plastic body illustrates well two of the most remarkable assertions of Deleuze and Guattari: that the body is a site of multiplicity, process, and becoming ("a discontinuous, nontotalized series of processes, organs, flows, energies, corporeal substances and incorporeal events, intensities, and durations")[30]; and that the unconscious is not a theatre but a factory (Gowther's body is the sight of endless production that grinds to a halt only at the imposed limit of saintliness, at the transubstantial death that is the reward for a successful embrace of transcendentals). Gowther before Oedipus can only be represented as a monster, because romance is a normalizing genre; but Gowther as monster, as a playground of somatic signification, is a site as intriguing in its multidirectionality as it is frightening in its excess.

Just as the dogs with which Gowther shared his meals and identity were interstitial (transitional, transferential) bodies for him, Gowther's own body has been interstitial for this essay, the corpus between the Middle Ages and the Post-Modern Ages where some identity exploration followed an eccentric trajectory. We could even go so far as to say that the process of engaging the romance is the process of becoming-Gowther, of mapping how Being acquires its cultural meaning only as it ceases to become; it is the process also of finding a line of flight within that performative mapping, despite the fact that some determinative *telos* strives to freeze its meaning into place. Gowther among the dogs teaches that bodies, genders, and identities have no limits other than the illusory "final," "stable" selves that culture manufactures and sanctifies and that never in the end constrain.

NOTES

My thanks to Mary Cain, John Block Friedman, Connie Kibler, Sarah Higley, Juris Lidaka, and especially Michael Uebel for assistance with this essay.

1. Gilles Deleuze and Félix Guattari, *A Thousand Plateaus: Capitalism and Schizophrenia*, tr. Brian Massumi (Minneapolis: University of Minnesota Press, 1987), p. 248. Originally published in French as *Mille plateaux, v. 2 de Capitalisme et Schizophrénie* (Paris: Les Editions de Minuit, 1980). Further references will be marked *ATP*, followed by the page numbers in Massumi's translation.

2. "Fils de chien," *Minuit* 7 (January 1974). The story is retold in *ATP*, pp. 258–9 and further explicated by Brian Massumi in *A User's Guide to Capitalism and Schizophrenia: Deviations from Deleuze and Guattari* (Cambridge, MA: Swerve Editions, MIT Press, 1992), p. 93ff.

3. What would success have been like? Massumi offers his own vision: "The man, having superposed human and canine affects, faces a choice: fall back into one or the other molar coordinate, or keep moving toward the great dissipative outside stretching uncertainly on the wild side of the welcome mat. He may either revert to his normal self or suffer a breakdown...or he may decide not to look back and set out instead on a singular path of freakish becoming leading over undreamed-of quadrupedal horizons" (p. 95). The Middle Ages suggests another possibility: a cynocephalus, an exotic body where human and canine affects play—and the body, also, of Saint Christopher, at least in many Eastern accounts (see John Block Friedman, *The Monstrous Races in Medieval Art and Thought* [Cambridge, MA: Harvard University Press, 1981], pp. 72–5; and David Gordon White, *Myths of the Dog-Man* [Chicago: University of Chicago Press, 1991], especially pp. 1–70).

4. The romance exists in two manuscripts, National Library of Scotland Advocates 19.3.1 and British Library Royal 17.B.43. The latter is generally held to be the superior version, and I have relied on it throughout in the edition of Maldwyn Mills (*Six Middle English Romances* [Rutland, Vermont: Everyman's Library / Charles E. Tuttle, 1988]). The Middle English version retells the French *Robert le diable* story but with important differences; see Laura A. Hibbard, *Mediaeval Romance in England* (New

York: Burt Franklin, 1963), pp. 49–57; Mortimer J. Donovan in J. Burke Severs (ed.), *A Manual of the Writings in Middle English 1050-1500,* vol. 1 (New Haven: The Connecticut Academy of Arts and Sciences, 1967), pp. 141–2; and Shirley Marchalonis, "Sir Gowther: The Process of a Romance," *The Chaucer Review* 6 (1971): 14-29.

5. Malcolm Bowie describes this difficult concept well: "The Name-of-the-Father is the 'paternal metaphor' that inheres in symbolization and thereby potentiates the metaphorical process as a whole; and it is an essential point of anchorage for the subject" (*Lacan* [Cambridge, MA: Harvard University Press, 1991], p. 109). The Name-of-the-Father is the illusory coherence sutured around a name that binds the symbolic into a genealogical identity-system with individuated, historical, familial subjects. Its nearest equivalent in the Middle Ages is the ancestral title (e.g., "Duke of Gloucester") in its mythy existence outside of particular bearers. On ancestral romance and the ubiquity of family crisis, see Susan Crane, *Insular Romance: Politics, Faith, and Culture in Anglo-Norman and Middle English Literature* (Berkeley: University of California Press, 1986), pp. 16–17.

6. Margaret Robson writes that the romance "could be said, from some points of view, to be [Gowther's mother's] story"; it is disturbing, then, that the maternal should so quickly become a vanishing point in the narrative. Fathers abound; by Robson's count, Gowther has five. See "Animal Magic: Moral Regeneration in Sir Gowther," *The Yearbook of English Studies* 22 (1992): 140, 146.

7. On the complex history of this biblical passage, see Nicholas Kiessling, *The Incubus in Medieval Literature: Provenance and Progeny* (n.l.: Washington State University Press, 1977); James Dean, "The World Grown Old and Genesis in Middle English Historical Writings," *Speculum* 57.3 (1982): 548-68; and Walter Stephens, *Giants in Those Days: Folklore, Ancient History, and Nationalism* (Lincoln, NE: University of Nebraska Press, 1989), pp. 76–84. On giants in romance see my essay "Decapitation and Coming of Age: Constructing Masculinity and the Monstrous," *The Arthurian Yearbook* III (New York: Garland, 1993), pp. 171–190. On medieval *incubi*, see Augustine, *De civitate Dei* 15.23 (PL 41.468); Thomas Aquinas, *Quaestiones de potentia Dei*, 6, 'De miraculis,' 8, *Opera omnia and Summa theologiae* I.51.3.6; Kiessling; and Andrea Hopkins, *The Sinful Knights: A Study of Middle English Penitential Romance* (Oxford: Clarendon Press, 1990), pp. 165–8. Hopkins' book contains the most useful discussion of Gowther and the mythology of the incubus.

8. *Polychronicon Ranulphi Higden monachi Cestrensis, together with the English translations of John Trevisa and of an unknown writer of the fifteenth century*, ed. Joseph Rawson (Nendeln, Liechtenstein: Kraus Reprints, 1964).

9. See "Cleanness" in *The Poems of the Pearl MS*, ed. Malcolm Andrew and Ronald Waldron (Berkeley: University of California Press,

1979), ll. 269-73; Andrew of Wyntoun's *Original Chronicle*, ed. F. J. Amours (Edinburgh: Scottish Text Society, 1903-14), Book I, l. 297ff. Andrew, like Trevisa and Higden, cannot decide between the orthodox, Augustinian interpretation of the story (in which the sons of God and daughters of men are all mortals) and the older, fallen angel or incubus version, so he provides both. The Pearl poet gives only the anti-Augustinian narrative. As a result of the survival of this tradition, romance giants were often described as the sons of fiends. In *Torrent of Portyngale*, for example, "There ys a gyant of gret renowne, / He dystrowythe bothe sete and towyn / And all that euyr he may; / And as the boke of Rome dothe tell, / He was get of the dewell of hell, / As his moder on slepe lay" (ed. E. Adam, EETS-ES 51 1973), ll. 921–6.

10. The Albina story was widely popular, appearing in Anglo-Norman, Latin, and Middle English versions, but has received little critical attention. See *Des Grantz geanz: An Anglo-Norman Poem*, ed. Georgine E. Brereton (Oxford: Basil Blackwell Publishing, 1937); *An Anonymous Short English Metrical Chronicle*, ed. Ewald Zettl (EETS-OS 196, 1935); *The Brut or the Chronicles of England*, ed. Friedrich W. D. Brie (EETS 131, 1906 [rpr. 1960]); and "Constructing Albion's Past: An Annotated Edition of *De Origine Gigantum*," ed. James P. Carley and Julia Crick, *Arthurian Literature* XIII (1995): pp. 41–114.

11. See Andrea Hopkins' thorough discussion in *The Sinful Knights*, p. 147.

12. This localizing movement finds its best expression in the Royal MS, which conflates Gowther and "Seynt Gotlake" [St. Guthlac], the heroic hermit who fought legions of airy spirits (fiends, demons, perhaps even incubi) and founded the abbey of Croyland. E. M. Bradstock argues that there is little continuity between the two "saints" ("The Penitential Pattern in *Sir Gowther*," *Parergon* 20 [1978], 6), but I disagree: both fight for a coherent identity versus a fiend or legions of fiends that represent a dangerous multiplicity of becomings and desires.

I label romances like *Gowther* "familial" simply because their scope tends to be limited to discovering the ways in which intersubjectivity configures personal identities, rather than (say) proving how manifest destinies dictate national histories through exceptional bodies, such as those of heroes. The familial in romance tends to exist as an "exterior," idealized fantasy space that pulls the hero through and out of the "real" horror of actual family space: for example, the knight Gregorius is the offspring of brother-sister incest who unknowingly marries his own mother but turns out well in the end (Hartmann von Aue, *Gregorius: Bilingual Edition*, ed. and tr. Sheema Zeben Buehne [New York: F. Ungar, 1966]).

13. "Decapitation," p. 178 and note 11.

14. See especially *Anti-Oedipus: Capitalism and Schizophrenia*, tr. Robert Hurley, Mark Seem, and Helen R. Lane (Minneapolis: University

of Minnesota Press, 1983 [*L'anti-Oedipe: Capitalisme et Schizophrénie* (Paris: Les Editions de Minuit, 1972]), but also *ATP*. The translator's note to *L'anti-Oedipe* explains "Oedipus" well: "The term Oedipus has many widely varying connotations. It refers, for instance, not only to the Greek myth of Oedipus and to the Oedipus complex as defined by classical psychoanalysis, but also to Oedipal mechanisms, processes, and structures" (p. 3). Or, as Massumi summarized in the earlier quotation, Oedipus stands for "phallocentrism, molar personhood itself."

15. Oedipus, argue Deleuze and Guattari, produces "a definable and differentiable ego in relation to parental images serving as co-ordinates (mother, father). There we have a triangulation that implies in its essence a constituent prohibition, and that conditions the differentiation between persons.... But a strange sort of reasoning leads one to conclude that, since it is forbidden, that very thing was desired. In reality, global persons—even the very form of persons—do not exist prior to the prohibitions that weigh on them and constitute them, any more than they exist prior to the triangulation into which they enter" (*Anti-Oedipus*, pp. 70-1).

16. "This common, transcendent, absent something will be called phallus or law, in order to designate 'the' signifier that distributes the effects of meaning throughout the chain and introduces exclusions there.... This signifier acts as the formal cause of triangulation—that is to say, makes possible both the form of the triangle and its reproduction: Oedipus has as its formula 3 + 1, the One of the transcendent phallus without which the terms considered would not take the form of a triangle" (*Anti-Oedipus*, p. 73). Even though this "transcendental signifier" appears to be exterior to the structuration it sanctifies, it is actually generated by an interior necessity.

17. How, for example, would Oedipus work in the early Germanic sex/gender system described by Carol J. Clover in "Regardless of Sex: Men, Women, and Power in Early Northern Europe" (*Speculum* 68 [1993]: 363–87)?

18. My remarks derive from Slavoj Zizek's analysis in *Looking Awry: An Introduction to Jacques Lacan through Popular Culture* (Cambridge, MA: October Books / MIT Press, 1992), pp. 107–22. Cf. the similar but more graphic moment in Chaucer's *Merchant's Tale* ("And sodeynly anon this Damyan / Gan pulled up the smok, and in he throng" (*The Riverside Chaucer*, 3rd edition, Larry Benson, gen. ed. [Boston: Houghton Mifflin Company, 1987], ll. 2352–3).

19. In Lacanian psychoanalysis, the Symbolic refers to the meaning-system which orders signification, that makes "reality" possible through representation. Bowie usefully describes the Real as "that which lies outside the symbolic process,...to be found in the mental as well as the material world: a trauma, for example, is as intractable and unsymbolizable as objects in their materiality" (p. 94).

20. Dorothy S. McCoy uses the various versions of the Robert the Devil story to gauge differences in attitude toward human sexuality and resists such a generalized, theological reading of Gowther: "For his own restless reasons, the Devil intervenes directly in the sexual act. This evil intrudes upon the Duchess from another world; it is external" ("From Celibacy to Sexuality: An Examination of Some Medieval and Early Renaissance Versions of the Story of Robert the Devil," in *Human Sexuality in the Middle Ages and Renaissance*, ed. Douglas Radcliff-Umstead [Pittsburgh: Center for Medieval and Renaissance Studies of the University of Pittsburgh, 1978], pp. 29–39). I am arguing that it is necessary to read through the monster here, rather than dismissing it as an "external," extraneous evil: the fiend embodies in inverted form the transcendent principle of Original Sin as embodiment.

21. Hopkins sees in the daily deliveries of bread by the hound an echo of the sojourn of Elijah in the wilderness, where he was fed flesh and bread by ravens (1 Kings 17: 6, Hopkins p. 154).

22. A good idea of what D&G mean by molar (and its relation to "personal" bodies) is conveyed by Steven Shapiro: "The relations of power in our society...select and organize the singularities of an anarchic, molecular sexuality, subject them to the laws of morality and the signifier, arrange them hierarchically, distribute them around a statistical norm, and finally construct heterosexuality as a majoritarian standard or as a transcendent model." (*The Cinematic Body* [Minneapolis: University of Minnesota Press, 1993], p. 71).

23. "Puppies are cute and cuddly (just 'like' a baby! Both have to be toilet trained). Soon, they learn to wait whining at the door for the return of their master (whose voice of authority they always recognize, 'like' a good wife). Love and regression in a fur coat" (Massumi, p. 97). D&G speak of dogs as Oedipal animals in *ATP*, pp. 28-9, 240, 248 (Massumi p. 179, #5).

24. See *ATP*, pp. 155-6. I treat this episode in my essay "Masoch/Lancelotism" (http://www.georgetown.edu/labyrinth/conf/cs95/papers/cohen.html).

25. Dogs were associated (via "lurid Christian propaganda") with Islam throughout the Middle Ages, and numerous manuscript illustrations of Muslims depict them as cynocephali (see Friedman, 67–9, and C. Meredith Jones, "The Conventional Saracen of the Songs of Geste," *Speculum* 17 [1942]: 201–25). Stories involving Christopher, Mercurius, and the wonderfully named cannibal Abominable detailed the conversion of such dog-headed men into proper Christians; on some level *Sir Gowther* is a reworking of these narratives. Gowther's becoming-animal is, then, also a complex way of his becoming-other, becoming-monstrous.

26. Donna Crawford contrasts the violence against the Saracens with Gowther's earlier aggression against nurses and nuns, finding in the former a rejection of the diabolical, but we may as well call this rewriting of violence

a rejection of the *paternal.* See "'Gronyng wyth grysly wounde': Injury in Five Middle English Breton Lays," in *Readings in Medieval English Romance*, ed. Carol M. Meale (Cambridge, UK: D.S.Brewer, 1994), p. 45.

27. The status of Sir Gowther itself as a kind of interstitial monster, a hybrid of romance and saint's life, has caused much critical anxiety; see especially E. M. Bradstock, "Sir Gowther: Secular Hagiography or Hagiographical Romance or Neither?" *AUMLA: Journal of the Australasian Universities Language and Literature Association* 59 (May 1983): 26–47.

28. Eve Kosofsky Sedgwick, "Nationalisms and Sexualities: As Opposed to What?" *Tendencies* (Durham: Duke University Press, 1993), 143-153.

29. On Lacan and Christianity, see (for example) Judith Butler, *Bodies That Matter: Feminism and the Subversion of Identity* (New York: Routledge, 1990), p. 56; and Franco Rella, *The Myth of the Other: Lacan, Deleuze, Foucault, Bataille*, tr. Nelson Moe (Washington, DC: Maisonneuve Press, 1994), p. 21.

30. Elizabeth Grosz, "A Thousand Tiny Sexes: Feminism and Rhizomatics," in *Gilles Deleuze and Theater of Philosophy*, ed. Constantin V. Boundas and Dorothea Olkowski (New York: Routledge, 1994), pp. 193–4. Grosz argues that Deleuze and Guattari's work is useful to feminists as a way to reconceive bodies "outside of the binary polarizations imposed on the body by the mind/body, nature/culture, subject/object, and interior/exterior oppositions. They provide an altogether different understanding of the body than those that have dominated the history of Western thought in terms of the linkage of the human body to other bodies, human and nonhuman, animate and inanimate; they link organs and biological processes to material objects and social practices while refusing to subordinate the body to a unity and homogeneity provided either by the body's subordination to consciousness or to organic organization" (p. 194).

EROTIC DISCIPLINE...OR "TEE HEE, I LIKE MY BOYS TO BE GIRLS": INVENTING WITH THE BODY IN CHAUCER'S *Miller's Tale*

Glenn Burger

This essay details ways that The Miller's Tale *resists the sadism constructing medieval hegemonic masculinity by desiring instead a "desexualized" body operating within, yet not completely controlled by, the ideological structures of desire.*

> With Sade and Masoch the function of literature is not to describe the world, since this has already been done, but to define a counterpart of the world capable of containing its violence and excesses. It has been said that an excess of stimulation is in a sense erotic. Thus eroticism is able to act as a mirror to the world by reflecting its excesses, drawing out its violence and even conferring a 'spiritual' quality on these phenomena by the very fact that it puts them at the service of the senses.[1]

Despite the very best efforts of the Host to forge an orderly and homogeneous pilgrimage body, the unexpected intervention of the Miller irrevocably alters the nature of the Canterbury game. Fabulously excessive, *The Miller's Tale* remains one of Chaucer's best-known and most popular stories, not least because of its brilliantly layered and doubled plot that parodies both the courtly love stories of *The Knight's Tale* and the biblical stories of Noah's Flood and the Annunciation. Moreover, the drunken Miller and his parodic fabliau are insistently and volubly iconoclastic in their attempts to "quite" the refined nobility and transcendent assurance of the sober Knight and his courtly epic. Set in the now of late medieval domestic life and reproducing the flavor of day-to-day life and conversation, his tale asserts a natural order and bodiliness almost asphyxiated by the Knight's excessively symbolic and institutionalized ordering of existence. However churlish, the Miller offers a breath of fresh air by providing a moment of fictional verisimilitude more directly mirroring the present of the Canterbury pilgrims.

But *The Miller's Tale*, for all its carnivalesque bawdy, ends with a vision of chastened masculinity and restored social control that in many ways reproduces the *moralitas* of *The Knight's Tale*, albeit in starker colours and bolder strokes. In the tale's climactic moment, with one thrust of the hot "kultour," Absalon finally behaves like a proper man, Nicholas's excess heat is dissipated, and John's overweening social pride—that a carpenter could know God's "pryvetee"—is brought down to earth by his ignominious fall. Directed at the female body as punishment for the shame that Absalon has undergone because of the misguided kiss, the branding actually punishes Nicholas's wayward *male* body. The *physical* violence represented in the branding thus works to "remasculinize" the potentially effeminate behavior of the men in the tale, correcting a humoral imbalance that has resulted from their loss of control of the body.[2] But more important for the tale's fabliau moral, the *symbolic* violence in the laughter that follows generalizes and institutionalizes this process of remasculinization. As a result, John's delusions of special favor above his station, Alison's lack of governance as wife, Nicholas's and Absalon's inattention to professional duty, indeed the general lack of good governance represented by the Miller's hijacking of the Canterbury game, are all "corrected," and communal order reasserted, by the tale's disciplining of the body.[3]

To the extent, then, that the laughter of *The Miller's Tale* works to restore proper masculinity, the tale "quites" *The Knight's* only so far as it translates *The Knight's* message into another discursive terrain.The generic difference of *The Miller's Tale*, rather than absolutely distinguishing it from *The Knight's Tale*, instead allows it to bring to the surface, with all the obscenity and immediacy of the fabliau medium, the erotic violence animating the Knight's encounter with the body and power in his tale. In the process, *The Miller's Tale* foregrounds the bodily signifiers and first rank of signification and understanding that *The Knight's Tale* takes for granted in its absolutist, transcendent account of the formation of masculine subjectivity. The severity of such attempts to rebalance the male body at the end of *The Miller's Tale*, and consequently to restore the hegemony of a "proper" masculinity and heteronormativity, thus reproduces *in extremis* the sadism of *The Knight's Tale* and its impositions of institutionalized masculine power and knowledge.

In describing the project of these tales as sadistic, I want to point to the larger representational questions posed by their attention to physical domination and eroticization of violence. What we find in both tales is pornology rather than pornography; that is, a literature "aimed above all at confronting language with its own limits, with what is in a sense a 'non-language' (violence that does not speak, eroticism that remains unspoken)." For as Deleuze reminds us: "[w]ith Sade and Masoch the function of literature is not to describe the world, since this has already been done, but to define a counterpart of the world capable of containing its violence and excesses." Paralleling the symbolic violence that takes place in these tales with the disciplinary regulation of Sade's fictions will, I hope, draw attention to the ways the eroticism of both tales "is able to act as a mirror to the world by reflecting its excesses, drawing out its violence and even conferring a 'spiritual' quality on these phenomena by the very fact that it puts them at the service of the senses."[4]

The Knight's Tale underscores again and again the need to discipline "the body." Emilye's desire for unproductive virginity gives way to marriage; Palamon's solipsistic devotion to love is replaced by a dutiful attention to the institutions that further the common good; Arcite's productive activity as loyal retainer to Theseus and knightly advocate for Emilye allow his heroic stellification in death. At another level the actions of Theseus (and the tale's fictionalized relationship with tale-teller and audience) inscribes the necessity for the personal to turn by reflection upon itself into the impersonal and institutional. *The Knight's Tale* thus emphasizes its own apparently inevitable enactment of a series of increasingly schematic substitutions. The chaotic desire of Palamon and Arcite is organized by the restraint of the Knight as tale-teller directing our attention to Theseus as embodiment of properly ordered masculine desire. In turn the magisterial artistry of Theseus and the tale as a whole allows desire to be directed even higher to the purified order of Egeus's Boethian mastery of individual desire.

Yet, as Bataille has pointed out, Sade's language is paradoxical because it is essentially that of a victim: "Only the victim can describe torture; the torturer necessarily uses the hypocritical language of established order and power."[5] While for some readers of the tale, both Theseus and the Knight might seem to fit the bill of "torturer," such an obfuscatory use of violence better describes the interventions of the Reeve in his tale.[6] The Knight, as victim of that very order he seeks to embody absolutely, instead maps out the kinds of systemic and systematic disciplining of the individual and social body necessary to achieve that perfect institutionalization. In Sade's fictions the spiritual and the obscene, symbolic violence and literal physical violence, are fused; in Fragment I of *The Canterbury Tales* these functions are split between *The Knight's* and *Miller's Tales*. Both, however, enact the turn to the purely demonstrative that Deleuze underscores as essential to the project of sadism:

> With Sade we witness an astonishing development of the demonstrative use of language.... The libertine may put on an act of trying to convince and persuade.... But the intention to convince is merely apparent, for nothing is in fact more alien to the sadist than the wish to convince, to persuade, in short to educate. He is interested in something quite different, namely to demonstrate that reasoning itself is a form of violence, and that he is on the side of violence, however calm and logical he may be. He is not even attempting to prove anything to anyone, but to perform a demonstration related essentially to the solitude and omnipotence of its author. The point of the exercise is to show that the demonstration is identical to violence.[7]

For in different but mutually constitutive ways, the eroticism of the first two Canterbury tales forces its participants and readers to conform to an institutionalized hegemonic view of the body—whether individual or social—as organic hierarchy. The lower regions of the body are ruled by its head just as the individual is ruled by the stars and matter by the transcendent will of God. This universal hierarchical principle in turn produces and naturalizes a series of interlinked binaries and essentialisms. In the social sphere, the noble is naturally going to rule the baser elements of society just as (and because) the head rules the baser elements of the body and as spirit takes precedence over matter. In terms of gender, the masculine is to the head and nobility as the feminine is to the lower limbs (especially the genitalia) and baseborn churls. In *The Knight's Tale* these "truths" are read back onto biological sex in an essentializing and stabilizing fashion that creates a chilling memorialization of that medieval masculinist hegemony in which, as Will Sayer has stated,

> Women passively carry a sex identity while men are actively engaged in gender. Male sex is the 'default'...in that its possession is not a matter of concern since attention is turned to the more important issue of gender realization. Women are marked, not least by the Church, with the sign of the deviant sex (non-male and variously virginal, reproductive, maternal, socially destabilizing, voracious) and this marking limits the types and degree of gender realization that are possible. Gender is then contained by the female sex and the force is centripetal. For the man, male sex, like superior physical strength, is the given, the point of departure is the elaboration of gender; movement is centrifugal.[8]

Thus, in *The Knight's Tale* "good" femininity (i.e., the [female] body seeking the guidance and control of a properly masculine will) acts as a frame that throws into relief true masculinity (generally arising out of noble and heroic [male] activity). And in *The Miller's Tale* "bad" femininity (whether the female body left untended or male bodies sliding into effeminate confusion because of improper desire) finds the rod of correction it so achingly needs in order to take on proper desire and true masculine agency.

Let us return again to the branding scene. If Absalon's original intention for the hot "kultour" had been successful, his action would have scored a violently misogynistic blow against the female body that humiliated him. The action of the tale's plot, however, substitutes Nicholas for Alison. With one stroke, as it were, the focus shifts to the male body and Absalon's cauterization of it. The branding thus reproduces that sealing off of the male body that Absalon attempted earlier when he tried to purify his lips, abandon lovemaking, and rededicate his body to the proper pursuits for which it is intended. However much Absalon's unreasoning desire for revenge may want to destroy the (female) body, the tale's plot rearranges that desire into a more constructive, disciplinary, and hierarchized relationship of reason and body. We laugh at both men because they're "getting what they deserve," and what they deserve is the necessary disciplining of the body that will restore the mind-body balance that constructs proper masculinity and the social and cosmic order that depends upon it. Implicitly, then, the tale reassures its readers that the truly masculine subject position lies outside the tale, accessible via the distantiating laughter of the community: a masculinity that will put everything in its place and conform to a pre-existent transcendent order of things. In short, it is the hegemonic masculine subject position outlined by the Knight's tale but now imagined as always already present *within* the present moment—that is, discoverable within the moment of pilgrimage dialogue as much as through the transcendence of "olde stories," and available to the wider category of "gentils" rather than limited to an aristocracy of blood.

For this reason, the apparent otherness of fabliau carnival to courtly restraint can be seen as the disguise necessary to mask its complicity in articulating for the masculine an erotics of domination and power as knowledge. And Foucault's ambivalence about Sade's apparently subversive sexuality is also applicable to the drunken Miller's "quiting" of the Knight. According to Foucault, the body as Sade sees it is still strongly organic, anchored in this hierarchy, the difference being that the hierarchy is not organized—as in old fable (such as *The Knight's Tale*)—as starting from the head but as starting from the genitalia. Thus Sade formulated an "eroticism appropriate to a disciplinary society: a regulated society, anatomical, hierarchized, with its carefully allotted times, its controlled spaces, its duties, and surveillance."[9] The Miller may restore "the body" that the Knight so often occluded. But he restores that body in order to remasculinize it and to incorporate it within the gender politics that the Knight's tale initiated.

***

> If the regulatory fictions of sex and gender are themselves multiply contested sites of meaning, then the very multiplicity of their construction holds out the possibility of a disruption of their univocal posturing.[10]

Although the "end" of the Miller's tale—its trajectory of desire as fabliau—may be erotic discipline, the activity unleashed in achieving such control also works to resist a "pure" demonstration of the sadism I have just outlined. Let us return to the branding scene once more.

As I have said, in the first instance this is the sadistic moment that "makes sense" of the tale...if we accept it as effective substitution for the earlier kiss, if we substitute proper masculinity in place of the effeminate activity of Nicholas, John, and Absalon, if we leave behind any desire for contact with the female body. In short, if we accept its "end" as teleological and absolutely necessary, we will not be lost irrevocably from the world of the Knight and its disciplined, heteronormative epistemology. The tale "works" in this way, however, only if we *can* leave behind the story. Even by the end, though, can it really only be said that Alison passively carries a sex identity or that the tale has succeeded in containing gender by the female sex in a force that is reassuringly centripetal? Could the layering of the tale, its redoubling of plot events within the tale (and by placement within *The Canterbury Tales* in relationship to *The Knight's Tale*), also work to keep us close to its parts in ways less easily normalized and hierarchized than the ending's substitutions would like?

Peter Beidler has pointed out that in all the European analogues "it is the male lover who presents *his* buttocks out the window for the kiss, while the woman stays in the shadows. Chaucer is unique among early tellers of the story in having the woman execute the trick."[11] And as countless readers of the tale have commented, Alison is the one character not explicitly forced to undergo a comic fabliau comeuppance in the climactic moments of the tale. For even as the branding successfully reaches the wayward male body, the female body that it has intentionally aimed for steps back into the safety of the tale's margins.[12] Similarly, Alison's earlier "Teehee" (I.3740)[13] underscores Absalon's unexpected relationship to the female body and the consequent disruption of knowledge/control that ensues with his misguided kiss. Absalon's return and the tale's attempt to substitute his "meaningful" encounter with Nicholas for the earlier kiss depend upon and can never leave behind that earlier encounter with Alison's bottom. Branding and kiss remain contiguous and mutually constitutive, however much the tale's ending attempts to hierarchize and substitute one for the other, just as the meaning of *The Knight's Tale* is (re)constructed by *its* forced encounters with the world of *The Miller's Tale*. Alison's "Teehee" is thus an instance of category confusion that reverberates throughout and in spite of the tale's ending—much like the "nether ey" (I.3852) that Absalon kisses and then attempts to see from the panoptic position of masculinity.

Although her "Teehee" cannot constitute "voice," in the sense that it is not ascribed meaning within the dominant culture of the tale, Alison's marginal notation of masculinity in the tale does "speak," to the extent that it marks the physicality of the feminine as that "other" without which masculine identity could not "be" *and* that place of shame and humiliation to which *The Miller's Tale* keeps returning us as readers.

Such a countermovement of signification within the tale challenges its final imposition of disciplinary order, blurs the "difference" between "hende Nicholas" (I.3199) and this "Fair yonge wyf" (I.3234), and suggests that both sex and gender are slippery and sliding signifiers, as much multiply contested sites of meaning as regulatory fictions. Indeed, what makes the tale useful to Chaucer and his audience is its attention to the politics of representation: that under the guise of generic and social difference—a churl's tale in opposition to the nobility of the Knight's—it can take into account the fluid and ambiguous status of gentility in the later Middle Ages as well as their own contradictory position as "new men" within nobility.[14] On the one hand, such an enlargement of hegemonic subjectivities takes place on the backs of "others" by writing a more mobile masculinity through the exclusion of "churls" and "women."

On the other hand, in order to achieve such representational flexibility, the reader must be aware of the advantages of activity for individual gain and the need to keep "the body" in motion. To that extent, the reader remains "with" Alison as much as or more so than with the men of the tale. And the tale explores and gives voice to the instabilities of any identity such "new men" might find for themselves, ready at any moment to slide into abjection. This kind of activity thus works to inscribe the body and the feminine as necessary, useful, even privileged, in ways that the explicitly masculinist trajectory of the tale's plot and "moral" would choose to obscure or deny.[15]

This loosing of gender is necessary in order to mobilize a fabliau masculinity that will authorize a "lower" part of society and the social body as having as much access to knowledge and power as the higher. To allow—if only as fantasy—that a churl might have access to knowledge that a knight does not have, makes possible the creation of an inscribed reader that is male and properly masculine (in the sense that he, unlike Nicholas, Absalon, or John, comes out on top and with controlling knowledge) but not limited to the static univocal subject position of *The Knight's Tale* and its presumptive nobility. This new reader is authorized to turn the leaf based on the wider-ranging, more mobile "trothefulness" of his judgment. In doing so, *The Miller's Tale* can represent change and movement within stable categories in ways *The Knight's Tale* was unable to do.[16]

In order to accomplish this degree of representational movement within hegemonic masculinity, *The Miller's Tale* must therefore bring us into contact with the feminine and the body in ways that disorganize the stable heteronormativity of *The Knight's Tale*. The latter fantasizes a static spectacular moment *sub species aeternitatis* and *The Miller's Tale* (with its various distantiation techniques) also aims for its own kind of cold theatricality. But *its* continued contact with the feminine represents a far more mobile, provisional masculine subject—embroiled with the material in disconcerting and unsuitable ways but, because of that, accessible to a far wider variety of individuals. By allowing the body its place, *The Miller's Tale* makes possible a more open understanding of who warrants access to masculine agency, yet only by foregrounding even more systematically than *The Knight's Tale* the need to regulate that masculine body. The abjection of Nicholas, Absalon, and John because of their excessive, effeminate physicality becomes the necessary fulcrum that will turn desire away from the fe(male) body toward that "proper" masculinity happening at the outer boundaries of the tale—in the laughter of John's neighbors and in the projected laughter and superiority of the inscribed audience (fictional Canterbury pilgrims and textualized reader). Proper masculinity then finds articulation as that which welcomes such violent disciplining of the body, whether imagined as the doer or receiver.[17]

Yet there is also a second, "forgotten" abjection that lingers within *this* instantiation of fabliau and marks the political work of the Canterbury game: that is, Alison as the putative recipient of Absalon's hot "kultour," and with it, the projected, but forgotten, abjection of Alison within the tale. The branding is ostensibly directed at Alison, fantasizing the impossible as possible: banish the feminine, seal up the body, and secure a transcendent masculine identity. Yet as we have seen, part of the project of *The Miller's Tale*—as a specific textual moment in the here and now—is to "open up" a hegemonic masculine identity supposedly securely anchored in transcendent notions of class and blood in order to admit "new men" like Chaucer and his immediate audience. And such a move requires fantasizing the male body as abject, open, and effeminate.

That the turn from physicality and the feminine constructed by the ending of the tale might itself be a fantasy therefore becomes a threatening byproduct of this process of abjection/remasculinization. Such a mediated recognizing and forgetting of gender instability and the riskiness of identification constitutes that excess produced by the politics of representation that marks its production of an individual identity within and outside generic and social discipline. The same male reader who "necessarily" submits to the discipline of masculinity must also choose "necessarily" to take on Alison's part in order to learn the truth of the tale. In other words, the generic sadism of fabliau—as it is experienced within the specific textual moment that is *The Miller's Tale*—constructs an alternative *masochistic* trajectory of desire: back toward a (humiliating) acknowledgment of the bodily, toward persuasion rather than instruction, contract rather than demonstration.

By way of illustration, consider the reverberant energy of Alison's tonic laugh within the tale and its difference from the disciplinary laughter of John's neighbors and the Canterbury pilgrims that ends the tale. Alison's "Teehee" focuses our attention—and Absalon's—on her "nether ey." In highlighting the misguided kiss, her laughter makes explicit a masochistic contract already initiated by Absalon's desire. That is, Absalon has chosen the humiliating position of the courtly lover, not as the way to discipline and masculinize its subject (as the sadistic pattern of *The Knight's Tale* would suggest) but instead as a pleasurable escape from masculine activity itself. Absalon, as fabliau structure demands, may later reject this masochistic contract for the pure demonstrative of proper masculinity (represented by his hot "kultour"). But can such a substitution of an instructive, pure demonstrative for the persuasions of the masochistic contract ever be completely secure within the dynamic relationship this tale constructs with its audience? Alison's reverberant presence/absence in the tale suggests otherwise. So too does the Miller's embrace of his humiliating position in oppositionality to the Knight.

The Miller's Tale reorients the Host's stabilizing plans for the Canterbury game almost before it gets started: both by the tale's presentation of Alison as female body outside masculine control and by its (re)presentation of that threatening possibility in the Canterbury frame itself by means of a drunken Miller who refuses to know his place. In this way, the tale challenges its audience to "see" via the nether eye; that is, to learn through a feminine, queer touch as much as a masculinist, dominating gaze.[18] The reader who embraces the full potential of the textual moment offered "him" by *The Miller's Tale* (whether in reading on *or* in turning the leaf) to some extent at least enters into a contractual agreement to choose the "humiliation" of the tale's category confusion and thereby choose contact with the unnameable "hole" (I.3732) that Alison's characterization offers as mediation/margin/boundary between individual desire and ideological mastery.[19] Such a reader, choosing pleasurable excess, seeks to defer the closure of disciplinary control for the present inventiveness and mobility of fiction. While the panoptic masculine gaze shapes fabliau by casting it as nobility's fantasized "other," *The Miller's Tale* as feminine/effeminate nether eye also works to bring its reader up close to the liberatory potential of fantasizing what is not known.[20]

Thus *The Miller's Tale*, even as it reproduces the turn to discipline *The Knight's Tale* so adamantly adumbrates, resists the sadism constructing medieval hegemonic masculinity. In doing so, the tale queers the heteronormative sexual politics of the *Knight's* and *Reeve's* tales by desiring instead a "desexualized" body operating within, yet not completely controlled by, the ideological structures of desire. The tale strives, as Foucault puts it, "to invent with the body, with its elements, its surfaces, its volumes, its depths, a nondisciplinary eroticism: that of the body plunged into a volatile and diffused state through chance encounters and incalculable pleasures."[21] This strategy serves an immediate political end of multiplying subject positions that confer masculine agency, opening up discursive space for new social groups, and recognizing the new uses possible for fiction as fiction. To do so, it must also necessarily disorganize sex, gender, and sexuality so that masculinity and femininity, male and female difference, heteronormative and effeminate/sodomitical as regulatory fictions become multiply contested sites of meaning in the spaces that open up between reader/frame/story and desire/knowledge/power.

NOTES

1. Gilles Deleuze, *Sacher-Masoch: An Interpretation* (London: Faber, 1971; Fr. ed. 1967), p. 33. I want to thank Carol Everest for talking me through medieval sex, and Jeffrey Cohen for introducing me to the masochistic contract in his paper "Masoch/Lancelotism" presented at Cultural Frictions Conference, Georgetown University, October 1995; available from http://www.georgetown.edu/labyrinth/conf/cs95/papers/cohen.html.

2. According to medieval medicine, the combination of Absalon's lack of virile heat and lovesickness without relief would actually make *him* the most likely candidate for cauterization. One cure for such humoral imbalance was cauterization, whether potential—performed by caustics applied to the inflicted area—or actual—performed by fire on the afflicted area. Absalon applies a version of the former to his lips and mouth after the misguided kiss, and the latter, to Nicholas's buttocks with the hot "kultour." Nicholas's problem, of course, is not a lack of virile heat—as his night of lovemaking and flatulence indicate. But a non-sexual release of this excess heat—via the branding—would restore a humoral balance more appropriate for a single clerk and perhaps make a lively female mate sexually available once more to a chastened husband. Carol Everest, in "Medicine, Aging, and Sexuality in Chaucer's 'Reeve's Prologue,' 'Merchant's Tale' and 'Miller's Tale'" (Ph.D. diss., University of Alberta, 1992), pp. 160–208, argues persuasively for cauterization and against David Williams's suggestion that Absalon's punishment of Nicholas involves anal penetration by a hot poker and consequently parodies the operation for *fistula in ano* ("Radical Therapy in the *Miller's Tale*," *Chaucer Review* 15 [1981]:227–35). See also Edward C. Schweitzer, "The Misdirected Kiss and the Lover's Malady in Chaucer's *Miller's Tale*," pp. 223–34 in *Chaucer in the Eighties*, ed. Julian N. Wasserman and Robert J. Blanch (Syracuse: Syracuse University Press, 1986); and Danielle Jacquart and Claude Thomasset, *Sexuality and Medicine in the Middle Ages* (Princeton: Princeton University Press, 1988; Fr. ed. 1985); and Joan Cadden, *Meanings of Sex Difference in the Middle Ages: Medicine, Science, and Culture* (Cambridge: Cambridge University Press, 1993), esp. pp. 167–227.

3. Various critics have noted the relationship between the generic differences between the *Knight's* and *Miller's* tales and the representation of a social contest. For examples of this approach, see Peggy Knapp, *Chaucer and the Social Contest* (New York: Routledge, 1990), pp. 15–44; Lee Patterson, *Chaucer and the Subject of History* (Madison: University of Wisconsin Press, 1991), pp. 244–79; and Paul Strohm, *Social Chaucer* (Cambridge, Mass.: Harvard University Press, 1989), esp. pp. 130-82. Strohm points out, as well, the ways in which even narrative structuring of time and space in the two tales has a social dimension. The Knight works in symbolic "church time," advancing a longstanding sacralized notion of

fixed social relationships, while the Miller works in quantifiable "merchant's time," inscribing the new contractual, communitarian relationships governing postfeudal medieval society (pp. 123–25).

4. Deleuze, p. 21.

5. Deleuze, p. 16.

6. See also Dolores Warwick Frese, "The Homoerotic Underside in Chaucer's *Miller's Tale* and *Reeve's Tale*," *Michigan Academician* 10 (1977): 148.

7. Deleuze, p. 18.

8. "Medieval Masculinities: Heroism, Sanctity, and Gender," Jeffrey Jerome Cohen and the Members of Interscripta, available from http://www.georgetown.edu/labyrinth/e-center/interscripta/mm.html.

9. "L'érotisme propre à une société disciplinaire: une société réglementaire, anatomique, hiérarchisée, avec son temps soigneusement distribué, ses espaces quadrillés, ses obéissances et ses surveillances." "Sade, sergent du sexe," interview, *Cinématographe* 16 (December 1975–January 1976): 5; trans. James Miller, *The Passion of Michel Foucault* (New York: Doubleday, 1993), p. 278.

10. Judith Butler, *Gender Trouble* (New York: Routledge, 1990), p. 32.

11. "Art and Scatology in the *Miller's Tale*," *Chaucer Review* 12 (1977): 92.

12. This might seem yet another oppressive illustration of the female and the feminine once again being marginalized and pushed into the background. And certainly in the first instance Alison's marginality would appear to signify only the fact that the (female) body has served its purpose. The marginality of *her* body thus forms an outline that brings into view the sealing off of male bodies and construction of a secure hegemonic masculine subject position outside the tale that the tale's plot is trying to effect. But this marginalization, although set up as a binary that will authorize production of masculinity, also works to keep us in touch with the tale as tale, with character as developing, unknowable in any final sense, the production of all identity as performative. For margins also tell their own story. They mark the embodied facticity of text and can register a textual excess that, although "unknown" or "forgotten" by the ideological directive as to what a text means, may yet excite its own peculiar curiosity in the reader or author. A textual reader who chooses such a wayward position might thus contract for a different engagement with story than the submissive posture of the tale's "conclusion" demands. In the case of *The Miller's Tale*, female marginality can serve as a reminder that the "ending" of the tale is itself a kind of margin. Hegemonic masculinity tries to declare that margin as "end," in a way that seals off what the tale means, bounds it as if it were the property of such masculine subjects. A reader of the margins, however, might question the stability and "trothe" of such a hierarchized version of masculinist binaries such as surface and depth, centre and margin. Of course, as V. A. Kolve reminds us, "the baring of an arse

has, in fact, its own humble area of provenance within medieval art—the borders of illuminated manuscripts" (*Chaucer and the Imagery of Narrative: The First Five Canterbury Tales* [Stanford: Stanford University Press, 1984], p. 191). For discussion of such marginalia in the context of *The Miller's Tale*, see Kolve, pp. 191–97; and for speculation about the dialogic reading such marginalia might provoke or represent, see Michael Camille, *Image on the Edge: The Margins of Medieval Art* (London: Reaktion Books, 1992), *passim.*

13. All quotations from *The Canterbury Tales* are taken from *The Riverside Chaucer*, 3rd ed., Larry D. Benson, gen. ed. (Boston: Houghton Mifflin, 1987).

14. Cf. Strohm's discussion of the contradictions and anxieties inherent in the position of late-medieval "gentles," contradictions exacerbated in the new class of gentlepersons "en service" to which Chaucer and much of his audience belong:

> As a preliminary observation, then, we may say that every knight and esquire of the late fourteenth century, including Chaucer himself, was subject to two conflicting social evaluations: each shared with the great lords of the kingdom a common assessment of gentility, even as each shared with his fellow merchants, citizens, and burgesses of the middle strata the fact of nonaristocratic status or social rank....But Chaucer's stratum of gentlepersons 'en service' eludes confident characterization. Though inserted in a social hierarchy between knights and other *gentils gentz*, they lack the traditional support of lands and rents. Though aligned by their work with the growing body of clerks, scribes, lawyers, and literate tradespeople, they are separated from that body by their gentility. (pp. 11–13)

15. Sarah Kay has recently argued in "Women's Body of Knowledge: Epistemology and Misogyny in the *Romance of the Rose*," in *Framing Medieval Bodies*, ed. Sarah Kay and Miri Rubin [Manchester: Manchester University Press, 1994], p. 210):

> changing attitudes towards the problem of knowledge between the twelfth and thirteenth centuries trouble the equations between femininity and carnality, and between masculinity and the mind or spirit, which are extensively invoked in classical and patristic writing to justify the subordination of women to men. The increasingly complex treatment of the mind-body dichotomy in this period [the twelfth and thirteenth centuries], and the growing emphasis (under the influence of new translations and adaptations of Aristotle) on the senses as a source of knowledge, lead to the body figuring in intellectual discourses other than those propounding moral or theological hierarchies, and pose the threat that the alleged physicality of the feminine implies not women's inferiority, but the possibility that they might enjoy more immediate access to knowledge than men.

See also Michael Camille ("The Image and the Self: Unwriting Late Medieval Bodies," *Framing Medieval Bodies*, pp. 62–99) for a discussion of "the ways in which a host of competing notions of the body existed in the thirteenth and fourteenth centuries that were articulated, not through texts, but through images," p. 62).

16. Cf. Strohm's argument in *Social Chaucer* that "Chaucer preeminently occupied what Eagleton calls a 'dissentient conflictual position' within his own society, a position that throws the ideological faultlines of his literary production into high relief" (p. 142). Thus, "Chaucer's generic and stylistic variation, and his multiplication of the different vocalities by which this variation is sustained, may be viewed as a mediated response to factionalism and contradiction within his own social experience.... Viewed in relation to this challenge, Chaucer's *aesthetic* enterprise of defining a literary space that permits free interaction of different forms and styles may be placed in reciprocal relation with the *social* enterprise of defining a public space hospitable to different social classes with diverse social impulses" (p. 164).

17. Cf. Deleuze's comments that "[t]he sadist enjoys being whipped as much as he enjoys whipping others.... It would therefore be difficult to say that sadism turns into masochism and vice versa; what we have in each case is a paradoxical by-product, a kind of sadism being the humorous outcome of masochism, and a kind of masochism the ironical outcome of sadism." (pp. 34–35).

18. I am indebted here to Carolyn Dinshaw's recent attempt to distinguish what she has called "the touch of the queer," a critical category that might help resist the metaphoric, substitutive, colonizing power of the gaze: "I begin with this representation of a hand on a thigh, and I speak of the tactile—'the touch of the queer'—because I want to highlight the metonymic workings and corporeal impact of queerness on its surroundings. Queerness works by contiguity and displacement, knocking signifiers loose, ungrounding bodies, making them strange; it works in this way to provoke perceptual shifts and subsequent corporeal response to those touched." ("Chaucer's Queer Touches / A Queer Touches Chaucer," *Exemplaria* 7.1 [Spring 1995]: 76).

19. For other medieval conflations of female vagina and rectum, see E. Jane Burns, *Bodytalk: When Women Speak in Old French Literature* (Philadelphia: University of Pennsylvania Press, 1993), esp. pp. 31–47.

20. Cf. the provocative discussion by Leo Bersani in "Is the Rectum a Grave?" on the value of powerlessness:

> A reflection on the fantasmatic potential of the human body—the fantasies engendered by its sexual anatomy and the specific moves it makes in taking sexual pleasure—is not the same thing as an *a priori*, ideologically motivated and prescriptive description of the essence of sexuality. Rather, I am saying that those effects of power

> which, as Foucault has argued, are inherent in the relational itself...can perhaps most easily be exacerbated, and polarized into relations of mastery and subordination, in sex, and that this potential may be grounded in the shifting experience that every human being has of his or her body's capacity, or failure, to control and to manipulate the world beyond the self.
>
> Needless to say, the ideological exploitations of this fantasmatic potential have a long and inglorious history. It is mainly a history of male power, and by now it has been richly documented by others. I want to approach this subject from a quite different angle, and to argue that a gravely dysfunctional aspect of what is, after all, the healthy pleasure we take in the operation of a coordinated and strong physical organism is the temptation to deny the perhaps equally strong appeal of powerlessness, of the loss of control. Phallocentrism is exactly that: not primarily the denial of power to women (although it has obviously also led to that, everywhere and at all times) but above all the denial of the *value* of powerlessness in both men and women. I don't mean the value of gentleness, or nonaggressiveness, or even of passivity but rather of a more radical disintegration and humiliation of the self.

(*Reclaiming Sodom*, ed. Jonathan Goldberg [New York: Routledge, 1994], p. 256; first printed *October* 43 [1987]: 197–222).

21. "Il faut inventer avec le corps, avec ses éléments, ses surfaces, ses volumes, ses épaisseurs, un érotisme non-disciplinaire: celui du corps à l'état volatil et diffus, avec ses rencontres de hasard et ses plaisirs sans calcul." ("Sade,"5; trans. Miller, p. 278).

THE PARDONER, VEILED AND UNVEILED

Robert S. Sturges

Whereas the Pardoner's vernicle signifies his participation in the phallogocentric economy, Sturges argues here that his other veil conceals a performative masculinity, perpetually under construction.

The dust jacket on my hardcover copy of David F. Greenberg's book *The Construction of Homosexuality*[1] features a drawing by Dennis Anderson of two figures, shown from the shoulders up against a vaguely modern urban background; one figure has (his? her?) its hand around the other's shoulder. The most striking aspect of the drawing is that both heads are heavily veiled in white cloths like pillowcases, whose folds, loosely clinging to their features, both reveal that there are invisible faces underneath the veils and conceal what those faces look like. Paperback reprints of this book have an entirely different cover; perhaps this mysterious drawing puzzled other readers as much as it does me. Given the book's topic, is it meant to suggest that there is an authentic face of homosexuality whose true nature is hidden by the veil of social construction, and that the relationships of gay people more than others are mediated by these social veils? Or have the veils actually enabled the depicted encounter, allowing the two figures to recognize their similarities in structure (or construction) as more important than their differences in detail? Gender itself seems to be at issue here as well: the veils prevent us from identifying the two figures as male or female, and perhaps this gender ambiguity, too, is to be seen as a component in "the construction of homosexuality."

***

The veil as a metaphor for that which both conceals and reveals, of course, has a long rhetorical history, especially in the Middle Ages, and Marjorie Garber has recently pointed out the veil's historical association with the crossing of gender (and other) boundaries as well.[2] Dennis Anderson's drawing can thus be regarded as a late example of both metaphorical uses of the veil, and this essay will examine a hitherto neglected medieval point on the same historical continuum: Chaucer's description of the Pardoner's veils in the *General Prologue* to the *Canterbury Tales*.

The Pardoner, while ostensibly male, is also a figure of fluid gender, erotic practice, and even sex: over the years, he has been identified variously as "feminoid,"[3] as a literal or metaphorical eunuch,[4] as a hermaphrodite,[5] as "homosexual"[6] or "gay,"[7] as a "normal" (i.e., "heterosexual") man,[8] etc. Only recently have literary historians begun to emphasize this fluidity in itself, rather than trying to pin the Pardoner to any single definition.[9] This is an important distinction: the Pardoner's body and behavior gesture toward a variety of incompatible identities without fully conforming to any. Chaucer's language, continuously oscillating among these various possibilities for the Pardoner, thus suggests less a stable, finished gender identity than one that is perpetually under construction.

The Pardoner's veils, like those in Anderson's drawing, can be construed as metaphors for this fluid construction of gender: veiling is crucial to the construction of the Pardoner's ambiguous masculinity. His veils, as multivalent gender signs and also, indeed, as signs in themselves of multivalent signification, provide a useful point of entry into the question of just how this gender identity is endlessly constructed and reconstructed.

In particular, the Pardoner's masculinity has heretofore been largely taken for granted: while a wide variety of explanations has been offered for his deviations from this supposed norm, the construction of his masculinity itself has received little attention, as is demonstrated by the large amount of commentary attracted by the controversial line in which the narrator of the *General Prologue* declares of the Pardoner, "I trowe he were a geldyng or a mare" (I, 691)[10]. Almost every word in this line has received special attention from scholars: "I trowe" as expressing either the narrator's belief or the uncertainty of his judgment,[11] the subjunctive "were" as reinforcing the air of doubt,[12] "a geldyng" as a reference to the Pardoner's presumed state of eunuchry,[13] "or" as implying the narrator's indecision,[14] "a mare" as suggesting homosexuality or hermaphroditism.[15] The only word in this line whose meaning has been virtually taken for granted is the masculine pronoun "he"; the present essay may be seen as an investigation into how such a problematic character as the Pardoner assumes this unexamined masculinity. The veils associated with him should prove a useful tool in exploring masculinity as a social construction, performance, or masquerade.

The first of the Pardoner's veils mentioned in the *General Prologue* might better be termed a *representation* of a veil: "A vernycle hadde he sowed upon his cappe" (I, 685). This "vernycle," or vernicle, is one of the badges worn by those who had made a pilgrimage to Rome and represents the original cloth, supposedly belonging to St. Veronica, on which, according to her legend, an image of Christ's countenance was miraculously imprinted. The vernicle was thus a representation of the face of Jesus as it appeared on this miraculous cloth; it is clearly visible in the Ellesmere manuscript's miniature portrait of the Pardoner.

Different versions of Veronica's legend describe the original of the vernicle in various ways: in the *Legenda aurea*, for instance, it is merely a piece of linen on which Veronica intended to have Jesus' portrait painted until the miracle provided her with a better image.[16] Some later adaptations of her legend suggest that the cloth was Veronica's handkerchief and that she used it to wipe Jesus' face on the road to Calvary. A persistent version of the story, however, which appears both in the early *Mors Pilati*[17] and in Chaucer's period, describes Veronica's cloth specifically as a veil;[18] the Middle English *Siege of Jerusalem*, for example, dated to the last decade of the fourteenth century,[19] is quite clear:

> & þat worliche wif, þat arst was ynempned,
> Haþ *his visage in hir veil*, Veronyk ȝo hatte,
> Peynted priuely & playn, þat no poynt wanteþ;
> For loue he left hit hir til hir lyues ende.[20]

This veil would appear to be at odds with the traditional metaphor of the veil as it occurs, for example, in medieval rhetorical theory, where it is commonly used to describe the figure of allegory, both theological and poetic. This metaphorical use of the veil originates in St. Paul's reading of the veil of Moses:

> And not as Moses put a veil upon his face, that the children of Israel might not look steadfastly on the face of that which is made void. But their senses were made dull. For, until this present day, the selfsame veil, in the reading of the Old Testament, remaineth not taken away (because in Christ it is made void). But even until this day, when Moses is read, the veil is upon their heart. But when they shall be converted to the Lord, the veil shall be taken away.[21]

Those who read the Old Testament only literally see the veil but not the truth concealed beneath it; only the Christian reading of Scripture can remove the veil of allegory and reveal the spiritual truths beyond the literal level. The veil, in other words, is a figure for a figure, deferring proper interpretation until Christian enlightenment allows direct, unmediated knowledge of the truth. St. Augustine's account of his own conversion in the *Confessions* 6.4 suggests a similar reading of the veil, when St. Ambrose reveals the hidden truth of Scripture to him: "...those things which taken according to the letter seemed to teach perverse doctrines, he spiritually laid open to us, having taken off the veil of the mystery."[22] The *Glossa ordinaria* expands the meaning of the veil to include the literal level of Scripture generally, not just of the Old Testament, in its discussion of the wedding at Cana.[23] In Chaucer's period, secular allegory, too, was described as a fictional veil concealing spiritual truth, for instance in the commentaries on classical authors by Theodulphus of Orleans, Bernard Silvestris, Boccaccio, and Petrarch:[24] "...can anyone believe [Virgil] wrote such lines without some meaning or intention hidden beneath the superficial veil of myth?"[25] All these veils are figures for concealment and mediation, for the deferral of truth pending proper interpretation.

At the same time, to the Christian interpreter, the veil does not merely conceal, but reveals the presence of a hidden truth; from this perspective, the veil actually protects spiritual mysteries from the prying eyes of the uninitiated while allowing enlightened interpreters to perceive their outlines. The veil in this reading represents a readable code for those in the know; others won't even notice the presence of such a code, much less be able to interpret it. As Robert Grosseteste suggests in his commentary on the *Celestial Hierarchy* of Pseudo-Dionysius, "somehow the sacred veils, to some, are manifestations of the thing veiled under them, but to others they are concealments."[26] This revealing function of the veil, too, is extended to secular literature by the fourteenth century, as in Boccaccio's defense of the classical poets: "If, then, sense is revealed under the veil of fiction, the composition of fiction is not idle nonsense."[27]

The vernicle, on the other hand, is a veil that seems to function in a rather different way: it neither conceals nor encodes but instead provides direct, unmediated access to the *Logos*, the bodily visage of Christ, God's word embodied. It is important to remember that the original veil of Veronica is not imagined merely as an image or representation but as a true icon;[28] indeed, *vera icon* is a medieval etymology for "Veronica," from which the term "vernicle" is derived.[29] This is a veil that does not perform the usual functions of veiling: the veil of Veronica actually carries the Truth, the miracle of God's presence, on its surface rather than covering it up. It neither defers ultimate meaning nor encourages the enlightened reader to interpret but displays truth itself for direct apprehension.

It is worth pointing out that Veronica's veil was itself veiled during the Middle Ages; it hung in the Chapel of Veronica at St. Peter's in Rome, and as Rhodes (citing Giraldus Cambrensis) points out,

> Usually the cloth remained in the Chapel under a protective covering, but...the veil proved so popular that it was frequently given public displays with its covering removed, most often on feast days or as a climax to the journey made by so many pilgrims during the mass pilgrimages of the late Middle Ages.[30]

The original vernicle here functions not as the concealing or encoding veil, but is itself the spiritual truth hidden beneath a different veil; it is the second, outer veil, the one covering the vernicle, that, by suggesting what it conceals, inflames the pilgrims' desire to behold this truth "face to face."

Individual vernicles like the one worn by the Pardoner, then, may be only representations of the original veil, but they can be traced back to this originary truth. In itself, the Pardoner's vernicle is thus only one link in a chain of signifiers, but this chain is not endless: the chain finds its endpoint, and its signification comes finally to rest, in the transcendental signified, the *Logos* in its full presence. The Pardoner, by wearing the vernicle, inserts himself into this chain, thereby implying that his own authenticity is guaranteed by its relation to the Logos.

***

In twentieth-century feminist theory, the *Logos* is associated, if not equated, with the phallus, as is suggested by the term "phallogocentrism," originally coined by Derrida[31] and quickly adopted in deconstructive feminist discourse. As Carolyn Burke suggests, Derrida's term

> implies that psychoanalytic discourse is guilty of identifying the phallus with the *Logos* as transcendent and, therefore, unexamined (and unexaminable) grounds of signification, of assigning meaning...when it puts the phallus in the central position as a kind of *Logos*, as the "signifier of all signifiers"[32]

The *Logos*, of course, is not only signifier, but also signified; in this sense, the phallus and the *Logos* are simply two versions of this same transcendental signified, now seen as the illusion or fantasy of an ultimate, prescriptive, and oppressive authority, gendered masculine. Indeed, modern psychoanalysis is seen here as theorizing signification in a manner quite comparable to that of medieval rhetoric: both ground meaning in the transcendental signified, whether *Logos* or phallus. We may find a similar connection in *The Canterbury Tales* by examining the Pardoner's second veil described in the *General Prologue*, one of the false relics he carries with him to deceive ignorant villagers: "For in his male he hadde a pilwe-beer, / Which that he seyde was Oure Lady veyl" (I, 694–95).

This veil, too, is only a representation, but of a distinctly different sort than the vernicle. Not only is this pillowcase a *false* representation of Mary's veil, but what it conceals suggests even more starkly the contrast between the body of Christ and the Pardoner's body, a contrast that has already been implied by the immediate juxtaposition of their two faces earlier in the Pardoner's *General Prologue* portrait: "Swiche glarynge eyen hadde he as an hare. / A vernycle hadde he sowed upon his cappe" (I, 684–85). The Pardoner's "glaring eyes" are here distinguished from the serene face of Christ directly above them on his cap (the Ellesmere miniature confirms that this vernicle depicts a calm, not a suffering, Jesus), and the contrast implies differences beyond those of facial expression. The reference to the hare, supposed in medieval lore to be hermaphroditic and associated with sodomy as well,[33] is one of several details in the description of the Pardoner that hint at gender ambiguity and, indeed, at an ambiguity concerning the nature of his anatomical sex. Other such references include, most famously, the narrator's comment in the *General Prologue*, "I trowe he were a geldyng or a mare" (I, 691), the line that led Curry and the other commentators cited above to the conclusion that the Pardoner is depicted as a eunuch.

If, then, the vernicle represents a unitary, phallogocentric truth that finds its ultimate authority in the body of Christ, the Pardoner appears to represent the opposite: neither clearly male nor clearly female, indeterminate in gender and erotic practice as well as in anatomical makeup, his fragmented gender identity and possibly dismembered body are without authority and hence excluded from the unambiguous truth of the vernicle. Barred by Chaucer's language from participation in the *Logos*, as a possible eunuch he can lay no clear-cut claim to the phallus, either. The importance of the second veil is that it allows the potential rhetorical construction of a masculine role from this mass of ambiguous details. As a kind of costume or drag, the veil also suggests that this masculinity is *only* a role, never achieved but only assumed.

What is it that this supposed veil covers? It is carried, significantly, in a "male," apparently the same "walet" or traveller's bag in which the Pardoner carries his pardons "biforn hym in his lappe" (I, 686).[34] "Lappe" may be glossed (as in the *Riverside Chaucer*) as a fold or pocket in the Pardoner's clothing, but given its position "biforn him" as he rides horseback and its description as "his lappe," it makes more sense to read it as "lap" in the modern sense.[35] And while "male" itself is an unambiguous noun meaning "bag" here, it may also carry overtones of the modern noun or adjective "male" (i.e. the opposite of "female"): the *OED* (s.v. "male") lists a number of occurrences contemporary with Chaucer for this sense of the term, and several critics have also pointed out the common metaphorical link drawn in the Middle Ages between the traveller's bag and the testicles.[36]

For it is, of course, the Pardoner's testicles, the organs that, etymologically, "testify" to one's masculinity, which are at issue here. While it is unclear precisely which sex organs the Pardoner may lack, his final encounter with the Host at the end of the *Pardoner's Tale* implies that the other pilgrims identify the nature of his possible lack with his "coillons"; as the Host says,

> I wolde I hadde thy coillons in myn hond
> In stide of relikes or of seintuarie.
> Lat kutte hem of, I wol thee helpe hem carie;
> They shul be shryned in an hogges toord! (VI, 952–55)

The Pardoner's furious silence here also suggests that the testicles are his specific point of vulnerability. Lacan reminds us that the phallus is not identical with the penis but "symbolizes" it:

> In Freudian doctrine, the phallus is not a phantasy, if by that we mean an imaginary effect. Nor is it as such an object...in the sense that this term tends to accentuate the reality pertaining in a relation. It is even less the organ, penis or clitoris, that it symbolizes.[37]

For the Pardoner, the symbolic function of the phallus seems to be associated with the testicles rather than the penis, precisely because they are what he (possibly) lacks, as we shall see. The various suggestions of castration, then, might seem to place the Pardoner outside the boundaries of phallogocentric discourse, preventing any identification with the divine truth represented by the vernicle. However, Lacan can also assist in our reading of the second veil as that which also allows the potential for such an identification.

As Lacan suggests in "The Signification of the Phallus," the phallus

> can play its role only when veiled, that is to say, as itself a sign of the latency with which any signifiable is struck, when it is raised (*aufgehoben*) to the function of the signifier. The phallus is the signifier of this *Aufhebung* itself, which it inaugurates (initiates) by its disappearance.[38]

It is the disappearance of the phallus that makes it a signifier: not its mere absence but its disappearance beneath a veil, that which may suggest presence without fully revealing it. Neither clear presence nor mere absence allows the phallus to "play its role," but veiling does so, the simultaneous concealment and revelation familiar from medieval rhetorical theory. In fact, the Lacanian veil can be understood as a better analogue of the medieval rhetorical figure of the veil than can the vernicle, whose immediate manifestation of the *Logos*, as we have seen, allows direct access rather than signification. The Pardoner's second veil, like the cloth covering Veronica's veil rather than the original vernicle itself, increases, or, indeed, creates, the significance of the phallus/Logos which it conceals.

Garber's discussion of the veil in terms of gender ambiguity draws on another aspect of Lacan's discussion of the veiled phallus: "the 'to seem' that replaces the 'to have' in Lacan's trajectory of desire."[39] She refers to Lacan's description of

> the intervention of a "to seem" that replaces the "to have"...which has the effect of projecting in their entirety the ideal or typical manifestations of the behaviour of each sex, including the act of copulation itself, into the comedy.[40]

Only the veiling of the phallus can have this effect; thus the "typical manifestations of the behaviour of each sex" are projected by the veiling itself. Indeed, gender (not anatomical sex but its ideal manifestation) is constructed behind the veil. Or, more precisely, gender is always *under construction* behind the veil, projected as an ideal to be approached rather than achieved.

We may observe this process in the Pardoner's case. As Dinshaw has brilliantly and painstakingly shown, the Pardoner's bulls and relics, including the supposed veil of Our Lady, are transmuted into fetishes, part-objects that both substitute for what is lacking and simultaneously signify lack itself .[41] Again like the veil of allegory, the fetish both conceals and reveals, though what it conceals and reveals is absence rather than the presence of the *Logos*, specifically the mother's lack of a phallus and hence the possibility of castration.

Related to this aspect of the fetish, and more important for our purposes, is its social function: the fetish does not satisfy desire, but rather, in Lacan's terms, reifies "the desire of the Other."[42]

> The infant's main means of obtaining satisfaction is by identifying himself with the mother's object of desire—his desire is then the desire of the Other. To please her...he must at one level *be* the phallus. He informs the mother that he can make up to her what she lacks, and he will be, as it were, the 'metonymy' of the phallus, replacing the desired phallus by himself. It is around this lure that the fetishist articulates his relation to his fetishistic objects...which are symbols of the woman's phallus insofar as it is absent, and with which he identifies. The transvestite identifies with the phallus as hidden under the mother's clothes—he identifies with a woman who has a hidden phallus.[43]

The fetish, then, represents an attempt to identify with that which is desired by the Other, the absent or hidden phallus. Because metonymy is not identity, such representations cannot achieve the status of true icon like the vernicle. This attempted identification is therefore bound to fail, and its failure requires another attempt; rather than coming to rest in the transcendental signified, these veiled representations demand endless repetition.

The Pardoner is described as attempting to incite this kind of fetishistic desire in his various audiences. The ignorant villagers to whom he sells his wares must be made to desire what he has to offer, his relics and pardons; only through their desire can his fetish-objects be identified with the phallus:

> But with these relikes, whan that he fond,
> A povre person dwellynge upon lond,
> Upon a day he gat hym moore moneye
> Than that the person gat in monthes tweye;
> And thus, with feyned flaterye and japes,
> He made the person and the peple his apes (I, 701–06).

A more detailed description of how the Pardoner uses the relics to create this desire of the Other appears in his own *Prologue* (VI, 329–88), but the point is clear: the fetishes have value insofar as they are desired by others. The supposed veil and the other false relics create that desire, which in turn grants the Pardoner not only a comfortable living but the ability to project a potent gender identity too: the authority that comes with access to the Logos. That this identity is phallic as well also seems clear from the sharpening, piercing, stretching imagery associated with his verbal authority over the audience of villagers: "He moste preche and wel affile his tonge" (I, 712); "Thanne peyne I me to strecche forth the nekke" (VI, 395); "Thanne wol I stynge hym with my tonge smerte" (VI, 413), etc.

For the Pardoner, at least, these "typical manifestations" of masculinity can be constructed only beneath the veil. The Pardoner's money and authority, the components of his phallogocentric identity, are derived from the villagers' desire; desire is constructed through the fetishized relics; the relics, including the veil itself, are fetishized in the veiling of the phallus. The Pardoner's masculinity is thus constructed in a chain of signifiers, but this chain, unlike that in which the vernicle takes its place, ends neither at the *Logos* nor at the phallus but at the veil: at "seems" rather than definitive truth.

Thus the Pardoner can never be satisfied; since he cannot achieve full, iconic identification with *Logos* or phallus, he must repeat his performance endlessly as a direct expression of anxiety about his own authenticity:

> Or elles taken pardoun as ye wende,
> Al newe and fressh at every miles ende,
> So that ye offren, alwey newe and newe,
> Nobles or pens, whiche that be goode and trewe.
> It is an honour to everich that is heer
> That ye may have a suffisant pardoneer...(VI, 927–32).

The audience is invited to manifest its desire for what the Pardoner supposedly has repeatedly, indeed continually, in the vain hope that this constant repetition can reassure him that he is indeed "suffisant." Full identification—or identity—cannot be achieved behind the veil but is always under construction.

Lacan implies that this performative construction of masculinity is not atypical: if the phallus is not an organ, whether or not the Pardoner actually has "coillons" to be found beneath the veil is, as it were, immaterial, because the veil, as we have seen, is necessary to the phallus as signifier. Indeed, unveiling always undoes the signification of the phallus:

> This is why the demon of Αιδως (*Scham*, shame) arises at the very moment when, in the ancient mysteries, the phallus is unveiled (cf. the famous painting in the Villa di Pompei).[44]

This shameful unveiling, too, and the concomitant destruction of the signifier, can be observed in the Pardoner's case, in the famous scene that concludes the *Pardoner's Tale*. Having tried, as now seems inevitable, to create in the audience of pilgrims that same desire of the Other which he usually successfully creates in his less sophisticated audiences of villagers, the Pardoner attempts to assert his authority over them by inviting the Host to kiss his supposed relics:

> Com forth, sire Hoost, and offre first anon,
> And thou shalt kisse the relikes everychon,
> Ye, for a grote! Unbokele anon thy purs (VI, 943–45).

The Host, however, refuses to grant the Pardoner any part of his own phallogocentric authority, declines to fetishize the relics, and verbally unveils the Pardoner's phallus instead:

> I wold I had thy coillons in myn hond
> In stide of relikes or of seintuarie.
> Lat kutte hem of, I wol thee helpe hem carie;
> They shal be shryned in an hogges toord! (VI, 952–55).

Critics have usually, and rightly (if somewhat contradictorily), emphasized both the threat of castration in these lines and their direct reference to the Pardoner's presumably already missing "coillons" as the sources of his subsequent anger and silence. I would like to emphasize instead the threat of exposure or unveiling: the "coillons" are to be taken from beneath Our Lady's veil, carried publicly in a procession, and enshrined (like Veronica's veil?) for public display, even if only in a hog's turd. For Lacan, after all, as we have seen, the possibility of castration is essential to the construction of the phallic signifier, and the sexual organs themselves are not to be identified with the phallus anyway. But the veil is necessary; it is exposure that destroys the signification of the phallus and its significance. That is the threat that undermines the Pardoner's masculine authority, the threat that deconstructs performative masculinity.

***

As we have seen, Lacanian psychoanalytic theory draws explicitly on the "ancient mysteries" of the veil and places itself in the same tradition as medieval rhetorical theory. Both refer to the figure of the veil as simultaneously concealing and revealing, or deferring, and in this process creating desire for, an authority gendered masculine. Both can be therefore be criticized as phallogocentric, and the best recent readings of the Pardoner acknowledge Chaucer's perhaps inevitable, but still conflicted, implication in this phallogocentric economy. Dinshaw, for instance, suggests that the Pardoner as a eunuch, necessarily outside the boundaries of such binary oppositions as male/female, points the way toward a medieval poetics of pure presence:

> ...he suggests the possibility of a poetics based not on such mediations as gender and language but, perhaps, on something unmediated. And that, for Chaucer, would be a poetics based on the incarnate Word, on the body of Christ, which is itself an embodied word; it would be a poetics founded on the body of Christ who is God, in whom there is no lack, no division, no separation, no difference.[45]

Dinshaw's vision is of a *Logos* that includes the feminine as the Pardoner's body does, a *Logos* that is not phallogocentric. Although she correctly claims throughout this chapter that the Pardoner's anatomical status remains a mystery,[46] her argument thus depends centrally on the idea of the Pardoner as a eunuch. Yet, as the process of veiling and unveiling shows, this cannot be assumed: the veil allows the Pardoner to gesture toward a masculine identity regardless of what may lie beneath it, and even the Host's verbal unveiling suggests that something may be there to be cut off—even as it reminds us that this something may also not be there. Masculinity is indeed assumed in this process, though only as a reiterated performance fraught with anxiety. Chaucer's investment in the phallogocentric economy may therefore be less gender inclusive than Dinshaw believes.

Nevertheless, regardless of this reproduction of masculine authority in Chaucer's discourse, we are also free to draw on other discourses in speculating about further possible meanings for the Pardoner's veils. In some ways, for example, that final unveiling seems comparable to the story of Salome and the stripping off of her veils as Garber analyzes it:[47] both unveilings are also associated with a symbolic castration (the beheading of John the Baptist and the Host's threat), with a silencing (of the prophetic voice and of the Pardoner), and with a kiss (Salome's kiss of the severed head, which is destined to become a relic, the Pardoner's invitation to the Host to kiss his relics, and the kiss of peace between Host and Pardoner arranged by the Knight [VI, 960–68]).[48] For Garber, reading the story of Salome through Lacan's figure of the veiled phallus, it is a story of

> the paradox of gender identification, the disruptive element that intervenes, transvestism as a space of possibility structuring and confounding culture.... The cultural Imaginary of the Salome story is the veiled phallus and the masquerade.[49]

Given the similarities in their stories, might the Pardoner, too, be seen as participating not only in the performative construction of masculinity but unconsciously in its transvestic deconstruction as well? For the Pardoner's veils both specifically represent women's garments, the veils of Veronica and of Our Lady. As Benvenuto and Kennedy point out in the passage cited above, "the transvestite identifies with the phallus as hidden under the mother's clothes—

he identifies with a woman who has a hidden phallus."[50] From this point of view, Our Lady emerges as the phallic mother, the mother whose imagined body provides a transgressive gender identification for the male child. The veiled phallus in this case is even more clearly a construction: a performance or masquerade, and the Pardoner's veils a kind of drag.

Both veils. For the vernicle, too, represents a man's face in a woman's veil, a male head cut off from its body (which may remind us that the Crucifixion, too, is a symbolic castration, and that some vernicles showed the face of a suffering Christ). That this is the face of Christ is all the more disturbing: Jesus in drag suggests that the *Logos* itself, like the phallus, is, after all, only a masquerade.[51]

NOTES

1. David F. Greenberg, *The Construction of Homosexuality* (Chicago: University of Chicago Press, 1988).

2. Marjorie Garber, *Vested Interests: Cross-Dressing and Cultural Anxiety* (1992; New York: HarperCollins, 1993), pp. 304–52.

3. Donald R. Howard, *The Idea of the Canterbury Tales* (Berkeley: University of California Press, 1976), p. 344.

4. Walter Clyde Curry, *Chaucer and the Mediaeval Sciences*, 2nd ed. (New York: Barnes and Noble, 1960), 54–70; Robert P. Miller, "Chaucer's Pardoner, the Scriptural Eunuch, and the *Pardoner's Tale*" (1955), in *Chaucer Criticism: The Canterbury Tales*, ed. Richard Schoeck and Jerome Taylor (Notre Dame: University of Notre Dame Press, 1960), pp. 221–44; Carolyn Dinshaw, *Chaucer's Sexual Poetics* (Madison: University of Wisconsin Press, 1989), pp. 156–84.

5. Beryl Rowland, "Animal Imagery and the Pardoner's Abnormality," *Neophilologus* 48 (1964): 56–60; Rowland, "Chaucer's Idea of the Pardoner," *Chaucer Review* 14 (1979): 140–54.

6. Monica McAlpine, "The Pardoner's Homosexuality and How It Matters," *PMLA* 95 (1980): 8–22.

7. Steven Kruger, "Claiming the Pardoner: Toward a Gay Reading of Chaucer's *Pardoner's Tale*," *Exemplaria* 6 (1994): 115–39.

8. C. David Benson, "Chaucer's Pardoner: His Sexuality and Modern Critics," *Mediaevalia* 8 (1982): 337–49; Richard Firth Green, "The Sexual Normality of Chaucer's Pardoner," *Mediaevalia* 8 (1982): 351–58.

9. Glenn Burger, "Kissing the Pardoner," *PMLA* 107 (1992): 1143–56.

10. References to *The Canterbury Tales* are by fragment and line numbers, according to *The Riverside Chaucer*, 3rd ed., Larry D. Benson, gen. ed. (Boston: Houghton Mifflin, 1987).

11. Benson, "Chaucer's Pardoner," 339; Dinshaw, *Chaucer's Sexual Poetics*, pp. 256–57, n. 1.

12. Ralph W. V. Elliott, *Chaucer's English* (London: André Deutsch, 1974), pp. 87–88; Ewald Standop, "Chaucers Pardoner: Das Charakterproblem und die Kritiker," in *Geschichtlichkeit und Neuanfang im sprachlichen Kunstwerk: Studien zur englischen Philologie zu Ehren von Fritz W. Schulze*, Peter Erlebach, Wolfgang G. Müller, and Klaus Reuter, eds. (Tübingen: Gunter Narr, 1981), pp. 63–64.

13. Curry, *Chaucer and the Mediaeval Sciences*, p. 59.

14. J. Swart, "Chaucer's Pardoner," *Neophilologus* 36 (1952): 45.

15. McAlpine, "The Pardoner's Homosexuality," 8–19; Rowland, "Chaucer's Idea," 143.

16. Th. Graesse, ed., *Jacobi a Voragine Legenda aurea vulgo historica lombardica dicta*, 2nd ed. (Leipzig: Arnold, 1850), p. 233.

17. See James F. Rhodes, "The Pardoner's *Vernycle* and His *Vera Icon*," *Modern Language Studies* 13 (1983): 35–36.

18. The complex history of the Veronica legend is carefully described by Rhodes, "The Pardoner's *Vernycle*," 34–37.

19. E. Kölbing and Mabel Day, eds., *The Siege of Jerusalem*, EETS o.s. 188 (1932; New York: Kraus Reprint Co., 1971), p. xxix.

20. *The Siege of Jerusalem*, ll. 161–164; emphasis added. See also ll. 231, 249, 259.

21. 2 Corinthians 3: 12–16 (Douay–Rheims).

22. St. Augustine, *Confessions*, W. H. D. Rouse, ed., William Watts, trans. 2 vols. (Cambridge, MA: Harvard University Press, 1912), 2: 279.

23. I am indebted to D.W. Robertson, Jr., *A Preface to Chaucer: Studies in Medieval Perspectives* (Princeton: Princeton University Press, 1962), p. 291, p. 294, and pp. 319–20 for all these examples of the veil as a figure for Scriptural allegory.

24. O.B. Hardison et al., eds., *Medieval Literary Criticism: Translations and Interpretations* (New York: Ungar, 1974), p. 20; Robertson, *Preface*, p.280.

25. Giovanni Boccaccio, *Boccaccio on Poetry: Being the Preface and the Fourteenth and Fifteenth Books of Boccaccio's* Genealogia Deorum Gentilium, Charles G. Osgood, trans. (1930; New York: Bobbs-Merrill, 1956), p. 53.

26. Quoted in A. J. Minnis and A. B. Scott, eds., *Medieval Literary Theory and Criticism, c. 1100–c. 1375: The Commentary Tradition*, rev. ed. (Oxford: Clarendon Press, 1991), p. 172, n. 40.

27. Boccaccio, *Boccaccio on Poetry*, p. 48.

28. The reference to Veronica's veil in *The Siege of Jerusalem*, cited above, is unusual in its description of the image of Christ's face as a painting; more typically, it is miraculously imprinted on the veil, transferred directly by contact with Christ's body. See, for instance, Veronica's narrative in

Graesse, ed., *Legenda aurea*, p. 233. Even the *Siege*, however, traces the image directly back to Christ ("for loue he left hit hir"), thus linking the vernicle once again to the originary transcendental signified.

29. Rhodes, "The Pardoner's *Vernycle*," pp. 36–37.

30. Rhodes, "The Pardoner's *Vernycle*," p. 34.

31. Jacques Derrida, *Spurs: Nietzsche's Styles / Eperons: Les Styles de Nietzsche*, Barbara Harlow, trans. (Chicago: University of Chicago Press, 1979), pp. 62–65.

32. Carolyn Burke, "Irigaray Through the Looking Glass," in *Engaging with Irigaray: Feminist Theory and Modern European Thought*, Carolyn Burke, Naomi Schor, and Margaret Whitford, eds. (New York: Columbia University Press, 1994), p. 42. Burke's entire discussion of this term's history is useful and relevant, pp. 41–43.

33. Beryl Rowland, *Blind Beasts: Chaucer's Animal World* (Kent, Ohio: Kent State University Press, 1971), p. 100; John Boswell, *Christianity, Social Tolerance, and Homosexuality: Gay People in Western Europe from the Beginning of the Christian Era to the Fourteenth Century* (Chicago: University of Chicago Press, 1980), pp. 137–8, p. 306.

34. Critical opinion is divided as to whether or not the "walet" and the "male" are in fact the same bag. The Ellesmere miniature depicts only one, suggesting that they are indeed identical, although, departing from the verbal description, it depicts the bag neither in the Pardoner's lap nor in a fold but hanging from his horse's neck.

35. Chaucer uses the term unambiguously in this modern sense later in the *Canterbury Tales*: Ugolino's children lie "in his lappe adoun" to die (VII, 2454). The text's unambiguous uses of the term in its other sense do not include the possessive pronoun but refer to "a lappe" or "the lappe" (VIII, 12; IV, 585). Another occurrence of "lappe" with the possessive pronoun (V, 635) could also be read either way, but again the modern sense seems more likely.

36. See, for example, Dinshaw, *Chaucer's Sexual Poetics*, p. 164.

37. Jacques Lacan, "The Signification of the Phallus," in his *Ecrits: A Selection*, Alan Sheridan, trans. (New York: Norton, 1977), p. 285. The slippage between "phallus" and "penis" in Lacan's own usage, however, has been noted by several critics as itself an instance of the phallogocentrism Derrida exposes in psychoanalytic discourse; see Jane Gallop, *Reading Lacan* (Ithaca, NY: Cornell University Press, 1985), pp. 133–36.

38. Lacan, "Signification," p. 288.

39. Garber, *Vested Interests*,p. 343.

40. Lacan, "Signification," p. 289.

41. Dinshaw, *Chaucer's Sexual Poetics*, pp. 160–68, pp. 176–77.

42. Lacan, "Signification," p. 290.

43. Bice Benvenuto and Roger Kennedy, *The Works of Jacques Lacan: An Introduction* (New York: St. Martin's Press, 1986), pp. 132–33.

44. Lacan, "Signification," p. 288.

45. Dinshaw, *Chaucer's Sexual Poetics*, pp. 182–83.

46. See, e.g., Dinshaw, *Chaucer's Sexual Poetics*, p. 157.

47. Garber, *Vested Interests*, pp. 339–45.

48. I do not wish to imply that this constellation of details appeared in the medieval versions of Salome's story or that her story influenced Chaucer in any way: neither the Bible nor any medieval source mentions the veils or the kiss, which appear to be nineteenth-century additions. My interest lies only in comparing how these two entirely independent stories function.

49. Garber, *Vested Interests*, p. 342.

50. Benvenuto and Kennedy, *The Works of Jacques Lacan*, p. 133.

51. I wish to thank Laura Hodges, Lorraine Stock, and Jeffrey Cohen for their advice on various aspects of this essay at different stages in its composition; of course, the views expressed here are, like any remaining errors, my own.

TRANSVESTITE KNIGHTS IN MEDIEVAL LIFE AND LITERATURE

Ad Putter

Examples of cross-dressing knights exist in abundance, both in historical records and in chivalric romances. This essay examines a number of examples to discover what transvestitism meant for a medieval audience.

The transvestite is fast becoming the critics' cult-hero, and—credit where credit is due—s/he is indeed a godsend to the field of gender studies. Anyone working in this field will have felt the limitations of seeing the world starkly in terms of gender oppositions, but as in real life (where we make instant assumptions about the sexual identity of our fellow humans) so in criticism our attachment to categories may be as powerful as our sense of their constraints. Perhaps we cannot live without our categories, though literary critics and cultural historians certainly do not find it easy to live *with* them either. This discomfort explains the prodigious recent interest, shared by medievalists, in phenomena that nag away at our confidence about being able to tell the sexes apart: hermaphrodites, transsexuals, "effeminate" men, and, the subject of this essay, transvestites.[1]

Imagine, as Marjorie Garber does in her study of cross-dressing, a transvestite standing at the most uncompromising of our gender cross-roads: the public toilet. On the left is a door with a picture of someone in a dress, on the right a door with someone in a suit.[2] Which door should the transvestite choose? Our difficulty with this question sums up the transvestite's interest for students of gender: for the transvestite it is not a matter of either/or, but of both. He or she, or rather he *and* she, exist beyond the reach of classifications, revealing that all it takes to upset the certainty of our gender assignment is a different selection from the menu of cultural signifiers: dress, make-up, or gesture. And while the transvestite's choices can be rejected, they do remind us that we, too, make choices from this menu. Of this we constantly need reminding, since upbringing and routine have the opposite effect of naturalizing our daily choices until the richness of the menu that is actually available to us no longer presents itself to consciousness, until choices no longer appear as choices.[3]

Like the transvestite, we, too, perform gender roles and, while we come to forget this, our performance is not inherently more "natural" than the transvestite's. For the cultural artifacts we use to express sexual identity—blue baby clothes for a boy but pink ones for a girl, boxer shorts for a man but high heels for a woman—are only remotely connected with the facts of anatomical difference they are supposed to bear out.[4] "Maleness" and "femaleness" do not, after all, inhere in the fabric of clothes. Any "natural" associations of clothes with sexual identity are the effect of our projections, our habit of elaborating bodily differences into cultural forms that know nothing of our private parts. By scrambling our associations of cultural artifacts with sexual difference—lipstick "means" woman—the transvestite reveals the arbitrariness of the relation between our bodies, our dress, and our behavior.[5]

The transvestite's power to unsettle assumptions, status, and hierarchies readily explains part of the history of the transvestite in the Middle Ages, namely the official persecution and repudiation of the transvestite, but it also prompts questions when we face the surprising fact that cross-dressing was a regular occurrence in the world of medieval chivalry and particularly in the Arthurian tournaments and romances of the later Middle Ages, where real or fictional knights frequently cross-dressed. In this essay, I hope to document and explain that curious fact.

The presence of cross-dressing in chivalric spectacles and romances is not, I think, commonly discussed in literary criticism,[6] but it is difficult to overlook. In *Le rire et le sourire*, Philippe Ménard mentions some cross-dressers in medieval romance as examples of a medieval joke.[7] This, no doubt, is how medieval romances want us to treat knights in drag: as a joke. In the figure of the transvestite knight, medieval romance shows us not how indistinguishable men and women can sometimes be, but how different they are from each other and how preposterous, therefore, is the idea of someone trying to be both at the same time. Behind the transvestite joke thus lies a deep conservatism, for *getting* it requires our acceptance of the incompatibility of the two sexes, just as *taking* it demands the audience's profession of this fact in the form of laughter.

Philippe Ménard willingly meets the demands of the transvestite-joke, but I should like to pause briefly before laughing cross-dressing away and look in more detail at how the transvestite-joke in chivalric literature is made. For, as modern criticism has amply demonstrated, the transvestite is not *prima facie* a comic figure. Cross-dressing has not in the past (and is not now) universally met with laughter, but often provokes fear or startled disbelief. If Garber is right about the transvestite's powers of horror, we need to investigate how the transvestite is made safe for laughter. What prevents the transvestite in chivalric romance and tournament from producing "cultural anxiety?"

Before analyzing some cases of medieval knights in drag, it is worth emphasizing that medieval people, too, were not all amused by transvestitism. The Bible told them in no uncertain terms that cross-dressing was an abomination:

> Non induetur mulier veste virili nec vir utetur veste feminea; abominabilis enim apud Deum est qui facit haec. (Deuteronomy 22.5)
>
> The woman shall not wear that which pertaineth unto a man, neither shall a man put on a woman's garment: for all that do so are abominations unto the Lord thy God.[8]

The prohibition was restated in the council of Granga (before 341), and laid down as law in the Theodysian code (435) and in Burchard's *Decretals* (c. 1010).[9] At around the time that transvestites are offered up for laughter in chivalric romance and spectacle, we find condemnations of cross-dressing in Hildegard of Bingen's *Scivias* (c. 1150), and the *Summa Theologica* attributed to Alexander of Hales (c. 1240).[10]

Evidently, then, not everyone in the Middle Ages thought a transvestite was funny. Indeed, medieval writers deserve some credit for seeing the wider implications of cross-dressing well in advance of modern critics. To many medieval minds, cross-dressing meant more than blurring the distinction between men and women: they realized that once that distinction collapsed, other cultural divisions legitimized by it were likely to follow.[11] Above all, transvestitism posed a threat to the orders of clerics and laymen, whose mutual exclusiveness had been justified as an extension of the difference between the two sexes. As the eleventh-century Raoul Glaber wrote: "just as there are two sexes, so there are two orders: those of clerics, and those of laymen."[12] Thus the stakes in keeping the sexes apart were high, and medieval writers knew it. Many condemnations of cross-dressing in the Middle Ages worry, for example, that the ability of women to look like men might validate their ambitions to become clerics.[13] And as we shall soon see, in chivalric spectacles, too, knights masquerading as ladies often rub shoulders with other knights dressed as monks. One category crisis always leads to another.

It stands to reason, then, that transvestitism was classified as a mortal sin: a sin against nature.[14] Two important exceptions were made, both of which impinge on the subject of cross-dressing in tournaments and romances. The first is that of actors on stage. In most secular and religious plays, women's roles were taken by men. But, with few exceptions, cross-dressing was tolerated and made tolerable, since the context of the stage allowed transvestitism to take place in the understanding that it was not "for real."[15] A second exception was made for women *in periculo castitatis.*[16] The medieval period is rich in examples of women who escaped marriages in male disguise, and female saints who entered monasteries as monks, some growing divinely implanted beards to perfect their disguises.[17] Even in the case of women whose chastity was not at risk, medieval tolerance was higher than it was with regard to transvestite men, for the transformation of a woman into a man could at least be conceptualized as a change in the right direction. With men-become-women, the change was for the worse, which may explain why recorded instances of transvestite men are believed to be rare when compared with those of their female counterparts.[18]

***

It is now commonly accepted that male cross-dressing in the Middle Ages left few traces in surviving records, but this may well be a partial truth. Examples of men in female disguise in fact and fiction are quite numerous; it is just that they are to be found where historians have least expected them: in the lives and literature of medieval knights. In my review of these examples I shall not be concerned with ladies dressed as knights, firstly, because the many warrior-women in chivalric romance have already received their share of critical attention,[19] and secondly, because female cross-dressers are, as we have seen, a case apart, less problematic and degrading in medieval eyes than the sight of a man in woman's clothes. This is not to say that female transvestites could not equally be regarded as "gender–troublemakers." As Simon Gaunt has pointed out, *all* medieval stories involving cross-dressing—whether male or female—must at the least raise the possibility that gender and the perceptions of gender are susceptible to manipulation and distortion (even if they raise the possibility the better to refute it).[20] However, the scandalousness of female cross-dressers was always mitigated by the fact that a woman's aspiration to pass for a man was readily comprehensible to medieval people in terms of a "natural" desire for social elevation and self-improvement. With transvestite knights we move into waters that are more troubled and also muddier, for where it is easy to see what advantages women might have gained by cross-dressing, the gain for transvestite men is not, at first sight, apparent.

One initial clue, however, ought not to escape us: the first knights known to cross-dress do so in an activity where their actual masculinity is least in doubt: the joust. As is well known, from the thirteenth century onwards, tournaments began to be modeled on Arthurian romance.[21] Interestingly, in one such "Round Table" tournament—held in 1286 to mark the coronation of Henry II of Lusignan as King of Jerusalem—cross-dressing is rife. The following description is taken from Philippe de Navarre's eyewitness report:

> Et fu la feste la plus belle que l'on sache, .c. ans a, d'envissures et de behors. Et contrefirent la table reonde et la raine de Femenie, c'est saver chevaliers vestus come dames et jostent ensemble; puis firent nounains quy estoient avé moines et beordoient les uns as autres; et contrefirent Lanselot et Tristan et Pilamedes, et mout d'autres jeus biaus et delitables et plaissans.[22]

> The feast was the most beautiful one in one hundred years of feasts and tournaments, and they imitated the Round Table and the reign of Femenie, that is, knights dressed as ladies, and they jousted together. Then they played nuns that had with them monks and they jousted with each other; and they impersonated Lancelot and Tristan and Palamedes, and played many other splendid, delectable, and pleasant games.

What exactly took place in Acre remains unclear, but the festivities seem to have involved a combat between one group of knights representing the "table reonde" and an opposing group of knights pretending to be Amazonian warrior-women.[23] The tournament at Acre thus saw cross-dressing twice over, with "chevaliers vestus come dames" playing the part of women dressed as men of war ("la raine de Femenie").[24]

It might be thought strange for a knight to dress as a woman and stranger still that he should do so in the course of a tournament, when knights are generally thought to have put their masculinity on display. But machismo and transvestitism do not always stand in an antithetical relationship to one another. The career of the thirteenth-century Bavarian knight Ulrich von Lichtenstein, as narrated in Ulrich's autobiographical poem *Frauendienst*, is further evidence of this. Ruth Harvey has demonstrated Ulrich's preoccupation with *manheit*,[25] but this same Ulrich was also a master of disguise.[26] Thus Ulrich relates how he presided over one tournament in the *persona* of King Arthur himself. In another jousting tour, the so-called *Venusfahrt*, he dressed up, more originally, as Lady Venus. His example proved inspirational, for others soon joined in the masquerade, one jousting as a monk, another as a woman.[27]

Lodewijk van Velthem's continuation of the *Spiegel Historiael* (1316) furnishes a final instance of male transvestitism at a chivalric feast. Lodewijk van Velthem is known as the compiler of a Middle Dutch *Lancelot* cycle, and so it need not surprise us that in his different capacity as chronicler he spent much time describing (and no doubt inventing) details of a Round Table feast that marked the marriage of Edward I of England and Margaret of France.[28] Among many theatrical impersonations, we should note the entry of the "Loathly Lady" (inspired by Chrétien's *Perceval)*, who comes riding into the hall to deliver a message to the barons. As "she" rides out Lodewijk reveals "her" true identity:

> Als dese joncfrouwe was uter zale,
> Const si daer die pade wale.
> Si was ontslopen saen,
> Ende heeft die paruren af gedaen
> Daer si mede ontlicsent was.
> Dese joncfrouwe, daer ic af las,
> Was .i. van des coninc cnapen:
> Entie coninc had dese wapen,

Ende dit ansicht, ende dit hoeft
Heymelike doen maken, des geloeft,
So dat na een joncfrouwe sceen. (l556–66)[29]

When the damsel had left the hall, she went on her way. She had soon slipped away, and took off her disguise with which she had changed her likeness. This damsel, as I read, was one of the king's squires, and, in truth, the king had secretly ordered these accoutrements to be made, as well as the disguise, and the mask, so that he looked like a damsel.

Philippe de Navarre's *Livre*, Ulrich von Lichtenstein's *Frauendienst*, and Lodewijk van Velthem's *Spiegel* allow us fascinating glimpses of chivalric cross-dressing, and they are are all the more valuable in that they bear out the interdependence of apparently unrelated cultural categories. Far from being an isolated phenomenon, cross-dressing occurs in all three texts within a field of numerous other crossings, such as the crossing of social classes (knights become monks, and monks joust); the crossing of historical times (the present merges with the Arthurian past); and the crossing of existential modalities (the real world becomes one with the mythical world of pagan deities or Amazons). The scene of male transvestitism is dense with other identifications and associations.

The evident fondness for cross-dressing in actual tournaments may have provided the inspiration for a more famous scene of travesty and cross-dressing in medieval literature: the Tournament of Surluse. The episode of the Tournament of Surluse originally formed part of the fourteenth-century *Prophécies de Merlin*,[30] but it also found its way into versions of the Prose *Tristan*. Malory, who adapted the Prose *Tristan* into English as the *Book of Sir Tristram de Lyones*, probably came across the episode in a manuscript which contained an expanded version of the Prose *Tristan*.[31]

The butt of the transvestite joke in the Tournament of Surluse is Sir Dinadan, "a grete skoffer and a gaper, and the meryste knyght amonge felyshyp that was that tyme lyvynge" (665.7–9). On the seventh day of the tournament of Surluse, Dinadan's mischievousness rebounds on him. Lancelot has been called many names by Dinadan (such as "olde shrew" [665.24]), and takes revenge by giving Dinadan a taste of his own medicine. Disguised as a maiden, Lancelot is led onto the field as if he were a prize to be fought over but is soon seen galloping towards Dinadan, who is easily defeated by the "maiden":

> So sir Dynadan departed and toke his horse, and mette with many knyghtes and ded passyngly well. And as he was departed, sir Launcelot disgyred hymselff and put uppon his armour a maydyns garmente freysshely attyred. Than sir Launcelot made sir Galyhodyn to lede hym thorow the raunge, and all men had wondir what damesell was that. And so as sir Dynadan cam into the raunge, sir Launcelot, that was in the damsels aray, gate sir Galyhodyns speare and ran unto sir Dynadan.
>
> And allwayes he loked up thereas sir Launcelot was, and than he sawe one sytte in the stede of Sir Launcelot armed. But whan sir Dynadan saw a maner of a damesell, he dradde perylles lest hit scholde be sir Launcelot disgysed. But sir Launcelot cam on hym so faste that he smote sir Dynadan over his horse croupe. (669.15–29)

After being unhorsed, Dinadan is dragged off by some practical jokers, forced into a lady's dress, and so released to make an undignified *rentrée* at court.

The episode of the Tournament of Surluse helps to bring the paradox of transvestitism into sharper focus. On the one hand, wearing a woman's dress means degradation or symbolizes defeat.[32] Being unhorsed by "a maner of a damesell" is bad enough, but Dinadan has to suffer the further humiliation of returning to the hall in a "womans garmente" (669.31). On the other hand, knights who *voluntarily* dress up as a woman, like Lancelot (or Ulrich von Lichtenstein) are not feminized. Quite the opposite, the "damsels aray" provides Lancelot with a means of proving that he is in fact no damsel at all, but something far better: a man capable of outfighting other men. As Lancelot proves his mettle against Dinadan, it becomes evident that one reason for him wearing women's clothes might be that it permits the conspicuous demonstration that they do not fit.

That the tournament should provide the setting for many scenes of cross-dressing is no coincidence. Firstly, the tournament, with its fixed rules, places, and duration, creates what anthropologists call a "play-world": a world in which actions take place at one remove from reality and have a certain license, because the play-world frames them as unreal or unserious.[33] The tournament defuses the transvestite's subversive potential not only because of the *a priori* assurance that all its active participants are male anyway (women either watch from a distance or are fought over), but also because it encodes cross-dressing as "play," where actions "do not denote what these actions for which they stand would denote."[34] Like the stage (another setting where cross-dressing was permitted) the tournament can *represent* men dressed as women without *presenting* them as a reality. Inevitably, once the play is over, the disguise will be dropped, and life will return to normal. On stage and in the tournament, the transvestite is domesticated by virtue of being placed in a "progress narrative" (the phrase is Garber's), in which the confusion of gender must necessarily make way for clarification.

In the second place, the tournament thrives on disguise, and cross-dressing is only one of many forms which this disguise can take. Knights changing the color of their arms to avoid identification; knights fighting in another knight's armor: these are the commonplaces of the medieval tournament in fact and fiction. Louise Fradenburg has written suggestively about the function of the *incognito* in the tournament, relating it to the cult of honor that asks that knights must be *seen* in order to be, must capture attention and fascination. A knight in disguise creates that fascination around himself by means of a striptease that turns his potential rivals for attention into voyeurs. "Who am I?" he asks, and the momentary withholding of the answer serves to fix public attention on the dramatic moment when his identity is unveiled: "It is me!" Behind the disguise stands the principle of deferred gratification, the principle that the sum total of received recognition will be greater the longer recognition is refused. In Fradenburg's words, "the desire of knight and king, in romance and in tournament, to efface identity, is produced by the desire to prove the incontestability of identity."[35] The extra advantage that cross-dressing offers over other types of disguise is that it makes masculinity an inseparable part of that incontestable identity.

But the knight's desire to prove the "incontestability" of his gender, his desire to re-encode his body's masculinity in rituals of dressing and undressing, also exposes just how fragile and incomplete his sense of masculinity actually is. The need to exorcise femininity by stripping the body of women's clothing betrays an awareness of the body's constant vulnerability to effeminization. To defend against this awareness, male transvestitism creates the powerful illusion that the masculinity it manufactures (by assuming and dropping the female disguise) could always have been taken for granted. Put slightly differently, cross-dressing knights disarm questions about their masculinity by asking (and answering) the question—am I really female?—themselves. The efficacy of this strategy is apparent from the difference between the humiliation of knights like Dinadan, who passively endure effeminization, and the triumph of knights like Lancelot or Ulrich von Lichtenstein, who master potential humiliation by turning it into an active process.

The case I am proposing is paradoxical: that in chivalric romance and tournament knights show they are not women, by pretending to be women. In a discussion of drag-artists, Adam Phillips points out the strange logic that is at work here:

> It is indeed curious...that I am confirmed in not being a woman if I can pretend, or enjoy others pretending, to be one; that what I really am is what I am unable to imitate. My true identity becomes something which, by definition, I cannot perform.[36]

This logic, Adam Phillips suggests, lies behind the astounding popularity of male transvestite acts with fiercely homophobic audiences. The impersonation of a woman protects the fantasy of an authentic masculine essence by associating womanhood (its opposite) with performance, with cosmetics, and with superficiality. The imitation of femininity aims, in other words, to persuade us of the *inimitability* of male identity.

That the pretense of being a woman can indeed be used to heighten our consciousness of the knight's masculinity is confirmed by a burlesque scene of cross-dressing in Raoul de Houdenc's Arthurian romance *Meraugis de Portlesguez* (c. 1220). Meraugis and Gawain are imprisoned by a lady on a small island. They have no means of reaching the mainland, but every day a small boat of trusted servants arrives to supply the lady with food and drink. Meraugis plans an escape: taking the lady and her household by surprise, he locks them up, and disguises himself as the lady of the house. Then he goes to welcome the sailors who soon arrive to replenish the lady's stock of provisions:

> Et que fist il?— parfoi, il prist
> Trestote la robe a la dame,
> Et lors dou tot come une fame
> Se vest et lace et empopine
> Plus acesmez qu'une popine.
> Descent aval de cel chastel,
> S'espee desoz son mantel.
> Que vos diroie? Au havre vint

Einsi vestuz; mout li avint,
Car il estoit bien fez et genz.
De l'autre part virent les genz
Meraugis qui par l'isle aloit
Et de sa main les assenoit
Einsi com la dame sieut fere. (3335–48)[37]

And what did he do? By may faith, he took the lady's garment and with it he dresses and laces himself just like a woman, and he tarts himself up more prettily than a little doll. He goes down from the castle, with his sword under his mantle. What should I say? He came to the harbour dressed like this; and it suited him well since he was well-proportioned and handsome. From the other side, the people saw Meraugis, who walked about the isle, and with his hand he gestured to them to come, just as the lady used to do.

The sailors are taken in by Meraugis's impersonation until Meraugis jumps on board and the planks creak under his weight. When the sailors sense something is wrong, Meraugis takes the opportunity to improve the joke with a verbal travesty. Drawing the sword hidden under his mantel, he points to it and announces to the sailors that their mistress has arrived:

Desoz le mantel a porfil
Tret Meraugis l'espee nue
Si dit: "Vostre dame est venue."
"Ou est"— "Vez la ci en ma main."
Por li mostrer abat son frain
Et dit as mariniers: "Par m'ame,
Ceste espee, c'est vostre dame
Dont vos avrez dampnatïon."(3357–64)

From underneath his embroidered mantle, Meraugis pulls out the naked sword and says: "Your lady has come." "Where is she?"—"Look, here she is in my hand." To show them he takes off the belt and says to the sailors: "By my soul; this sword is your lady, from which you shall have perdition."

For a brief moment, the sailors have been made to believe in a world where men are women and swords are ladies. Now, the sight of the sword dangling before their eyes breaks the spell, and the sailors promptly surrender to Meraugis.

This episode from Raoul de Houdenc's *Meraugis* takes us further away from the realities of the medieval tournament than Malory's *Book of Sir Tristram*, but it demonstrates more graphically that a woman's dress can serve precisely to draw attention to the hard core of masculinity underneath, a core that is accentuated in *Meraugis* by the motif of the "sword under the mantle." One important reason why Meraugis's cross-dressing can be relished and enjoyed by an audience is that the sword wards off any risk of effeminization that looking and behaving like a woman might otherwise involve. For the sword in medieval culture effectively guarantees the masculinity of the bearer. Hence the sailors need no further evidence apart from Meraugis's sword that the person whom they took to be their lady cannot be a woman after all. Ladies, after all, do not hold swords; or rather (since they can, of course, help to arm the knight) they do not hold *naked* swords. Note, for instance, King Anguin's words in the Prose *Tristan*, when he sees his wife clutching a "naked sword":

> A ce cri vient li rois Anguins toz esbahiz por ce qu'il voit que la roïne tient l'espee *tote nue*.... "Or me baillié, fait il, ceste espee, qu'il n'est pas droez que dame teigne espee *en tel maniere*." (1: 176; my italics)[38]
>
> Hearing these cries King Anguin arrives all amazed because he sees that the queen holds the *totally naked* sword.... "Now hand the sword to me, he says, because it is not right that a lady should hold a sword *in this way*."

The naked sword is (or should be) the exclusive property of men. The phallic connotations of swords can be relied upon by Raoul de Houdenc to place the issue of Meraugis's maleness beyond dispute. Of course, the readers of *Meraugis* are never left in doubt of his masculinity anyway—we are told, for one thing, that he has "s'espee desoz son mantel"—but the sailors' rude awakening comes only after the hero's cry: "here's your mistress in my hand." With this punning verbal travesty, Meraugis exposes the travesty of his dress and adds insult to injury by suggesting that mistaking Meraugis for a woman is as stupid as confusing ladies with swords. As in Malory's *Book of Sir Tristram*, the drama of veiling and unveiling, recognition and non-recognition, permits a climactic staging of "manhood." Scratch a transvestite knight and you are likely to find an exhibitionist, gleefully awaiting the moment when the signs of masculinity can be disclosed in triumph.

The psychoanalyst Robert Stoller observed the connection between cross-dressing and exhibitionism in some of his patients. The male transvestite, he observed, "is constantly aware of the penis under his woman's clothes...and gets great pleasure in revealing he is a male-woman."[39] That this link between cross-dressing and flashing is not anachronistic is illustrated by the *fabliau Trubert*, written by Douin de Lavesne in the thirteenth century. In this *fabliau*, the joker Trubert wreaks havoc in the Duke of Burgundy's household in transvestite disguise. Pretending to be his own sister, he takes on female identity, and under the assumed name "Couillebaude" (Happy-Balls) he is appointed lady-in-waiting to the Duke's daughter Rosette. Rosette is promptly deflowered, and Trubert proceeds to shock the Duke's priest by lifting his skirt during confession. His private parts exposed in their full glory, Trubert challenges the priest to match him for size:

> Trubert si a fors trait le vit,
> Si que li chapelains le vit:
> "Sire prestes," ce dit Trubert,
> "Vos öes ont eles teus bes?"
> Quant li prestre vit le vit grant,
> Cent foiz se seigne en un tenant. (2693–8)[40]
>
> And so Trubert pulls out his dick so that the chaplain sees it. "Sir priest," says Trubert, "do your flock have beaks like this?" When the priest saw the large dick he crossed himself a hundred times in one go.

Trubert usefully lays bare the connections between transvestitism and exhibitionism. And without claiming for chivalric romance the same degree of explicitness, I would suggest that cross-dressing in Raoul de Houdenc's *Meraugis de Portlesguez* and Malory's *Book of Sir Tristram* holds some of the same attractions as it does in *Trubert.* For what Lancelot and Meraugis seek by dressing up as women is the opportunity to dress down and so to convert the castration symbolized by a woman's dress into a demonstration of undisguised manhood.

I do not wish to deny that Raoul de Houdenc and Malory intended their depictions of knights disguised as maidens to excite risibility rather than critical analysis. Yet the resisting reader will notice that the "laughability" of cross-dressed knights depends on the text's ideological labor of rendering their female clothing *transparent* to the reader. Unpersuasive acting is therefore of the essence in the transvestite joke in medieval romance: Lancelot bursts through his role as maiden when he smites Dinadan "over his horse croupe." Meraugis fails to reckon with his body-weight when he lands on the planks of the ship and reaches instinctively for his sword. As these examples suggest, transvestitism is funny only when it does not become too convincing.

***

The importance of that condition cannot be overstated, as it accounts for the other conventional context (besides the tournament) in which cross-dressing frequently occurs. This context is the "get-the-girl" scenario, in which female disguise is a means of gaining access to the lady. This kind of cross-dressing scenario is commonplace in the comic literature of the Middle Ages, which abounds in scabrous tales of men who penetrate convents and nuns in female disguise; of men who are admitted to the beds of their lovers in the disguise of a pregnant woman, or who insinuate themselves as playmates of their objects of desire by acting like an innocent girl.[41]

Chivalric literature plays many variations on this tune. Thus, in the Vulgate *Merlin*, Merlin exposes twelve "handmaidens" of the empress of Rome, who turn out to be her toyboys in disguise:

> & sachies de fi que che ne sont mie femes ains sont homme comme autre . & faites les desuestir si saures se ce est uoirs ou non . et sachies ke toutes les fois que vous ales fors de la uile se fait ele seruir en ses cambres.[42]
>
> And you should know in truth that they are not women but men like others. Have them undressed and you will know whether this is the truth or not. And you should know that whenever you are out of town she has herself serviced by them in her room.

The *Roman de Silence* by Heldris of Cornwall has, instead of twelve cross-dressed servants, one "nun" whom Merlin exposes as Queen Eufeme's lover in disguise.[43]

Into the "get-the-girl" category also falls a more interesting episode from the Prose *Tristan* where the great hero himself pretends to be a "demoiselle." When Mark holds Yseult captive in a tower, Yseult hits upon a way of ending her enforced separation from Tristan: her lover is to cross-dress and pass himself off as Yseult's messenger.[44] Brangain is asked to deal with the practicalities:

> Si fait querre maintenant la robe d'une demoiselle et la baille Tristan, si qu'il n'a home leanz qui le sache fors solement Gorvenal. Cil l'apareille...(*Roman de Tristan*, 2:141)
>
> She immediately orders a woman's robe to be fetched and gives it to Tristan in such a way that there was no man who knew of it apart from Gorvenal. He makes Tristan ready....

Dolled up as a girl, Tristan slips past Mark and the guards unnoticed and takes his pleasure with Yseult for three days on end.

Like the earlier scenes of cross-dressing tournament, the "get-the-girl" scenario in the *Tristan* frames the transvestite as a comic figure, but again the joke works precisely because his libido places his manhood beyond controversy. Underneath the "robe d'une demoiselle," Tristan has the phallus, and once again, the motif of the "sword under the mantle" reinforces the assurance of masculinity on which the transvestite joke depends:

> Atant s'en vet Tristanz apareilliez de vesteüre de demoiselle, mes totevoies por ce qu' il soit plus asseür porte il s'espee desoz son mantel. (*Roman de Tristan*, 2:141)
>
> And so Tristan goes decked out in a girl's clothing, but, to be on the safe side, he carries his sword under his mantle anyway.

What has been said of Lancelot and Meraugis thus proves to be true of Tristan as well: he becomes a woman in order to prove he is a man.

One final aspect of this assurance of normality, which the Prose *Tristan* has begun to bring to light, is that transvestitism in chivalric romance is never seen to distort the "straightness" of male desire. The nightmare of medieval theologians, who tended to lump transvestitism and sodomy together as sins against nature, was that it could. The *Summa Theologica* (4: 772) attributed to Alexander of Hales warns us that "a woman's dress greatly excites male desire" ("magna enim provocatio libidinis viris est vestitus muliebris"). Could not, then, a man in woman's dress tempt a man to sexual intercourse as if he really *were* a woman?

The facts of life in the later Middle Ages did not always allow this question to rest at the hypothetical level. This is shown by the surviving record of an interrogation of a male transvestite prostitute by the mayor and aldermen of London, which has recently been edited by David Boyd and Ruth Karras.[45] From an entry in the Plea and Memoranda Rolls, we learn that in December 1394 a certain John Brithby was arrested in a lane off Cheapside for having intercourse with John Rykener, a transvestite prostitute known to her friends and clients as "Eleanor." John Brithby confessed to the "unspeakable" vice of sodomy, but claimed that he had paid John Rykener thinking he was a woman ("ipsum mulierem fore suspicantem"). Among John Rykener's other clients, some men (and women) seem to have been under no illusion about "Eleanor's" real sex. Other men—such as the three "unsuspecting scholars" (*scholares ignotos*) which the Plea Roll names—were apparently led astray by Eleanor and first took "her" on without knowing what they were letting themselves in for.

It was not beyond the capacity of medieval romancers to conceive of the possibility that confusions of sexual identity might result in same-sex intercourse, but they raise the possibility in order the more forcefully to rebuff it. The chance to set homosexuality up in order to knock it down came to them in the form of a classic twist often found in scenes of transvestitism: that of the transvestite knight who is only minding his own business when he is sexually harassed by a man who cannot see through his disguise. One romance that adds this comic complication to an episode of transvestitism is the thirteenth-century *Witasse le Moine*, in which the hero Eustache wages a war of wiles against the count of Boulogne, in the course of which he dresses up as a woman:

> Wistasces qui molt sot de gile
> Entra apriés lui [the count] en la vile;
> Les dras vesti a une dame,
> A grant merveille sambla fame.
> D'une muelekin fu afublés,
> Molt par fu bien enmuselés,
> A son coste ot sa kenoulle. (1188–94)[46]
>
> Eustace, who knew everything about trickery, entered the town after the count, dressed in the clothes of a lady. He looked astonishingly much like a woman. He was wearing a linen dress, and was well covered under a veil. By his side he had his distaff.

Eustace finds a fervent admirer in a hot-blooded sergeant, who guards the count's horses, but who permits the "lady" a ride on one of the horses in the hope of repayment in kind. Lusting after "her," the sergeant follows Eustace to his hide-out in the forest, where Eustace crushes the sergeant's expectation of sex by revealing his male identity. And yet, just in case Eustace's clothes had set *us* wondering about the hero's masculine credentials as well, the text emphasizes that Eustace "is not a pervert, or an arse-fucker, or a sodomite" ("N'est pas herites / Ne fout-en-cul ne sodomites" [1268–9]).

A comparable development occurs in the late thirteenth-century Arthurian romance of *Claris et Laris*, in which the unfortunate Calogrenant is changed by enchantment into a "pucele," to live and dress as a girl until he has found the two best knights of the world:

Claris and Gawain. Strictly speaking Calogrenant is not a transvestite; yet he, too, retains his male ego after his appearance has changed, and this ego protests loudly when Mordred, mistaking him for a woman, takes a fancy to him:

> Kalogrenanz con damoisele
> Salue, puis li dist: "Pucele,
> Dites moi, de quel pars venez?
> Par la grant foi, que me devez,
> Deduisonnez nos .i. petit!" (26304–8)
>
> He greeted Calogrenant as one greets a damsel and then said: "Maiden, tell me, where do you come from? By that great faith, which you owe me, let us amuse ourselves a bit."

After a wrestling match, Calogrenant succeeds in escaping from Mordred's clutches. Fleeing on Mordred's horse (with Mordred in hot pursuit), Calogrenant finally catches up with Claris and Gawain and resumes his original form:

> ... Quant voit Claris
> Et Gauvain, de grant jois a ris,
> Car a son point est revenuz;
> Ore est diversement vestuz,
> Car il est vestuz con pucele
> Si li convient robe nouvele. (26352–7)
>
> When he saw Claris and Gawain he laughed with joy, because he has returned to his point of departure. But he is still differently dressed, because he is dressed as a girl. So he needs new clothing.

Transvestitism often raises the specter of homosexuality.[47] But, as *Witasse le Moine* and *Claris et Laris* suggest, chivalric romance flirts with the possibility of homoeroticism only for the fun of shrugging it off. And it can do so all the more persuasively for having already reduced homosexuality to a matter of benighted men who mistake men for women, to a silly confusion of gender identity, which a bit of muscle power can easily clear up.

Malory's *Tale of Sir Launcelot* contains a comparable moment of homophobia: in the course of a quest, Lancelot goes to sleep in an empty pavilion; in the dark the owner of the pavilion returns and joins Lancelot in the bed where he expects his *amie* to be:

> He wente that his lemman had layne in that bed, and so he leyde hym adowne by sir Launcelot and toke hym in his armys and began

> to kysse hym. And whan sir Launcelot felte a rough berde kyssyng hym he sterte oute of the bedde lyghtly, and the other knyght after hym. (259.29–33)

Shocked and appalled by this "treson" (260.9), Lancelot pursues the knight (Sir Belleus) and nearly kills him in a fight, relenting only when the knight explains his kiss as a misunderstanding. Here, as in *Witasse* or *Claris et Laris*, homosexuality is presented as an elementary mistake that nobody really intends. Its suppression by force and the subsequent process of enlightenment re-produces heterosexuality as the only safe and sensible option.

***

Sir Philip Sidney caught the spirit of the medieval transvestite joke well when, in his *Defence of Poetry*, he commented that male cross-dressing in classical literature "breedeth both delight and laughter":

> For as in Alexander's picture well set out we delight without laughter, and in twenty mad antics we laugh without delight; so in Hercules, painted with his great beard and furious countenance, in a woman's attire, spinning at Omphale's commandment, it breedeth both delight and laughter: for the representing of so strange a power in love procureth delight, and the scornfulness of the action stirreth laughter.[48]

But when cross-dressing threatens to spill over into "deviant" sexual object choice (as in *Wistasse le Moine* and *Claris et Laris*) it also breeds violence—a useful reminder that male transvestitism is funny only if kept within the bounds of heterosexuality and incredibility. The funny medieval transvestite must be as straight and unconvincing as Sidney's Hercules. Within these boundaries the transvestite joke has to work; beyond them the joke would go too far. It is only by steering close to these boundaries but then safely backing away from them, that the transvestite knight raises his laughs.

In his theory of the joke, Freud explained the phenomenon of laughter as a release of energy that suddenly becomes available when it is freed from a psychical task to which it was previously tied ("cathected"), such as the task to keep up resistances or the need to maintain defensive inhibitions. The energy that has thus been "economized" becomes superfluous and is discharged in laughter:

> The hearer of the joke laughs with the quota of psychical energy which has become free through the lifting of the inhibitory cathexis; we might say that he laughs this quota off.[49]

The laughter of relief works in this way: liberated from the mental strain of fearing the worst, "psychical energy" finds an outlet in laughter, the intensity of which is proportionate to the anxiety that previously consumed this energy.

This way of seeing laughter enables us to see the kinship in the two faces that the medieval transvestite wears: one face (visible in chivalric romance and tournament) is laughable, the other (visible in ecclesiastical prohibitions) is abominable and horrifying. At times in this essay it may have seemed that the transvestite knight of the Middle Ages, a comic and assuredly masculine figure, bears no relation at all to the subversive transvestite as imagined in modern theory and medieval church writings: a dangerous outlaw, who blurs the difference between the sexes and so threatens to bring down all cultural edifices constructed on its slender foundations. What has this outlaw to do with the transvestite joke in Arthurian literature—especially when that joke is so plainly amuring that Guinevere, for one, bursts out laughing when she sees a knight in drag?

> And than was sir Dynadan brought in amonge them all, and whan quene Gwenyver saw sir Dynadan ibrought in so amonge them all, than she lowghe, that she fell down; and so dede all that there was. (669.35–36, 670.1–2)

But there is, in the case of the transvestite joke, too, not only the question of what is being laughed at (Dinadan in female dress) but also the question of what is being "laughed off," the question of what kind of economy has created the surplus of energy that laughter discharges. If the transvestite joke makes us laugh (and if Freud is right), then it must in some way have economized our expenditure of psychical energy. Perhaps chivalric literature makes that saving by obviating the confusion of gender which the transvestite ordinarily generates.

As I have argued, chivalric romance makes transvestitism laughable because it allows us to see through it. By dis-mantling the transvestite on our behalf, it liberates us from the need to endure the transvestite's challenge to perceptual tolerance. It might thus be suggested that, so far from being immune from the "cultural anxiety" produced by the transvestite, the joke of the knight in drag *saves* us this anxiety by reassuring us that transvestitism cannot fool us for long. The relation between the jocular transvestite knight in romance and his subversive counterpart in modern theory and medieval law could then be put as follows: the one laughs the other off.

NOTES

1. For some discussions of these topics in the medieval period see Vern L. Bullough, "Transvestites in the Middle Ages," *American Journal of Sociology* 79 (1974): 1381–94, repr. (with slight modifications) as "Transvestitism in the Middle Ages," in *Sexual Practices and the Medieval Church*, Vern L. Bullough and James Brundage, eds. (Buffalo, NY: Prometheus Books, 1982), pp. 43–54; Michèle Perret, "Travesties et transsexuelles: Yde, Silence, Grisandole, Blanchandine," *Romance Notes* 3 (1985): 328–40; Miri Rubin, "The Person in the Form: Medieval Challenges to Bodily Order," in *Framing Medieval Bodies*, Sarah Kay and Miri Rubin, eds. (Manchester: Manchester University Press, 1994), pp. 100–23 (on hermaphrodites); Ad Putter, "Arthurian Literature and the Rhetoric of Effeminacy," in *Arthurian Romance and Gender*, Friedrich Wolfzettel, ed. (Amsterdam: Rodopi, 1995), pp. 34–49.

2. Marjorie Garber, *Vested Interests: Cross-dressing and Cultural Anxiety* (London: Routledge, 1992), pp. 13–15. A full bibliography of modern writings on transvestitism is beyond the scope of this essay, but I should like to record my indebtedness to the following: Sandra M. Gilbert, "Costumes of the Mind: Transvestitism as Metaphor in Modern Literature," in *Writing and Sexual Difference*, Elizabeth Abel, ed. (Chicago: University of Chicago Press, 1980), pp. 193–220; Stephen Greenblatt, "Fiction and Friction," in *Shakespearean Negotiations* (Oxford: Clarendon Press, 1990), pp. 55–93; and Adam Phillips, "Cross-dressing," in *On Flirtation* (London: Faber, 1994), pp. 122–30.

3. Anthony Giddens, *The Constitution of Society* (Cambridge: Polity Press, 1984), pp. 60–64.

4. "In every known society," Margaret Mead observes, "mankind has elaborated the biological division of labour into forms often very remotely related to the original biological differences that provided the original clues": *Male and Female* (Harmondsworth: Penguin, 1962), p. 30.

5. See Judith Butler on drag in *Gender Trouble* (London: Routledge, 1990), pp. 128–9.

6. An important exception is Louise Olga Fradenburg's insightful analysis of chivalric cross-dressing in *City, Marriage, Tournament: Arts of Rule in Late Medieval Scotland* (Madison: University of Wisconsin Press, 1991), pp. 212–16.

7. Philippe Ménard, *Le rire et le sourire dans le roman courtois* (Geneva: Droz, 1969), p. 351.

8. Quoted from the Latin Vulgate, with the translation from the Authorized Version.

9. The position of the early medieval church on transvestitism is discussed by James Brundage, *Law, Sex, and Christian Society in Medieval Europe* (Chicago: University of Chicago Press, 1981), p. 108; and John Anson, "The Female Transvestite in Early Monasticism," *Viator* 5 (1974): 1–33. For the prohibition in Burchard's *Decretum*, see PL 140: 805.

10. Hildegard of Bingen, *Scivias*, ed. A. Führkötter, *Corpus Christianorum Continuatio Mediaevalis* 43–43A, 2: 291; Alexander of Hales, *Summa Theologica*, V. Doucet et al., eds. (Quaracchi: Bibliotheca Francescana Scholastica Medii Aevi, 1924–79), 3: 477–8 and 4: 772.

11. The "strict separation of male-female indicators" was necessary in order to "strengthen symbolically the social differences within Christian communities": Gábor Klaniczay, *The Uses of Supernatural Power*, Karen Margolis, eds. and Susan Singerman, trans. (Cambridge: Polity Press, 1990), pp. 54–55.

12. Quoted in Georges Duby, *The Three Orders: Feudal Society Imagined*, Arthur Goldhammer, trans. (Chicago: University of Chicago Press, 1980), p. 194.

13. In Hildegard of Bingen's *Scivias* the prohibition against cross-dressing is preceded by a chapter barring women from priesthood (*Scivias* 2:290–1); cf. Anson, "The Female Transvestite" and Gerhoh of Reichersberg's nightmarish evocation of cross-dressing quoted in n. 15.

14. "Contra naturam est" are the words repeated in medieval commentaries on Deuteronomy 22.5. See Rabanus Maurus, *In Deuteronomium* (PL 108: 923); *Glossa Ordinaria* (PL 113: 475); and Alexander of Hales, *Summa Theologica* 3: 478.

15. In *The Drama of the Medieval Church*, 3rd ed. (Oxford: Clarendon Press, 1967), Karl Young records some stage directions calling for actors to be dressed as women (2: 402); Young also prints Gerhoh of Reichersberg's unusual attack on transvestitism on stage. I translate from Gerhoh's *De Investigatione Antichristi* (2: 525): "But the godhead and the wise face of the church abhor theatrical spectacles in which men lower themselves to become women, as if they were ashamed to be men, and in which clerics become knights, and men are transfigured into demonic specters." On cross-dressing in Middle English mystery plays, see Meg Twycross, "'Transvestitism' in the Mystery Plays," *Medieval English Theatre* 5 (1983): 123–80.

16. Hildegard of Bingen, *Scivias* 2: 291, and Alexander of Hales, *Summa Theologica* 3: 477. According to James Brundage, Stephen of Tournai also "distinguished between respectable women who adopted male dress to

avoid threats to their chastity, and loose women" (*Law, Sex, and Christian Society*, p. 314).

17. See Bullough, "Transvestites"; Anson, "The Female Transvestite"; and Evelyne Patlagean, "L'histoire de la femme déguiseé en moine et l'évolution de la sainteté féminine," *Studi medievali* 17 (1976): 597–623.

18. A point made by Bullough, "Transvestites," and Caroline Walker Bynum, *Fragmentation and Redemption: Essays on Gender and the Human Body in Medieval Religion* (New York: Zone Books, 1991), pp. 170–71.

19. See Lewis Thorpe, "Trois guerrières Arthuriennes; Maligne, Avenable et Silence," *BBSIA* 3 (1951): 104; Perret, "Travesties"; and with specific reference to Grisandole and Silence: Lucy A. Paton, "The Story of Grisandole," *PMLA* 22 (1907): 234–76; Joan Ferrante, "Public Postures, Private Maneuvers: Roles Medieval Women Play," in *Women and Power in the Middle Ages*, Mary Erler and Maryanne Kowaleski, eds. (Athens: University of Georgia Press, 1988), pp. 213–29; and Simon Gaunt, "The Significance of Silence," *Paragraph* 13 (1990): 202–16. To the list of women disguised as knights in Arthurian literature can be added the three "knights" defeated by the Handsome Coward in *Claris et Laris*, J. Alton, ed. (Tubingen: Bibliothek des literarischen Vereins in Stuttgart, 1884), ll. 27664ff.

20. Simon Gaunt, *Gender and Genre in Medieval French Literature* (Cambridge: Cambridge University Press, 1995), pp. 242–56.

21. Roger Sherman Loomis, "Arthurian Literature on Sport and Spectacle," in *Arthurian Literature in the Middle Ages*, Loomis, ed. (Oxford: Clarendon Press, 1959), pp. 553–9; Ursula Peters, *Frauendienst: Untersuchungen zu Ulrich von Lichtenstein* (Göppingen: Kümmerle, 1971), pp. 173–205; and Maurice Keen, *Chivalry* (New Haven: Yale University Press, 1984), pp. 90–95.

22. *Livre de Philippe de Navarre*, in *Recueils des historiens des croisades: Documents Arméniens*, A. Beugnot, ed. (Paris: Imprimerie Nationale, 1906), 2: 793.

23. A slightly different reconstruction of events is given by David Jacoby, "La littérature française dans les états latins de la Méditerranée orientale á l'époque des croisades," in *Essor et fortune de la chanson de geste* (Modena: Mucchi Editore, 1982), pp. 617–46; repr. in Jacoby, *Studies on the Crusader States and on Venetian Expansion* (Northhampton: Variorum, 1989). The tournament at Chauvency, which took place one year before the feasts at Acre, saw similarly elaborate scenes of cross-dressing and disguise: Keen, *Chivalry*, pp. 93–94.

24. The chivalric fascination with the "realm of Femenie" has recently been explored by Susan Crane, *Gender and Romance in Chaucer's Canterbury Tales* (Princeton, NJ: Princeton University Press, 1994), pp. 76–84.

25. Ruth Harvey, *Morîz von Craûn and the Chivalric World* (Oxford: Clarendon Press, 1961), pp. 160–62.

26. Fradenburg, *City, Marriage, Tournament*, p. 215.

27. Peters, *Frauendienst*, p. 195.

28. This episode in Lodewijk's chronicle is summarized in Roger Sherman Loomis, "Edward I, Arthurian Enthusiast," *Speculum* 33 (1958): 242–55.

29. *Lodewijk van Velthem's Voortzetting van den Spiegel Historiael*, Hans van de Linden and Willem de Vreese, eds. (Brussels: Hayez, 1906), 1: 318.

30. *Les prophécies de Merlin*, Lucy A. Paton, ed. (London: Oxford University Press, 1926), 1: 385–6.

31. I rely on the editorial notes to *Sir Thomas Malory Works*, Eugène Vinaver, ed., rev. P.J.C. Field, 3rd ed. (Oxford: Clarendon Press, 1990), 3: 1504. All subsequent citations from Malory are from this edition.

32. Female dress was also used to humiliate men in the ritual of the "Skimmington Ride," in which henpecked husbands were led through town, dressed as women and seated backwards on a horse or a mule: Natalie Zemon Davis, *Society and Culture in Early Modern France* (Stanford: Stanford University Press, 1975), pp. 124–52. Examples of the backwards ride date from the eighth century: Ruth Melinkoff, "Riding Backwards: Theme of Humiliation and Evil," *Viator* 4 (1973): 153–76.

33. On the medieval tournament as "play" see Michel Stanesco, *Jeux d'errance du chevalier médiéval* (Leiden: Brill, 1988).

34. I am quoting Gregory Bateson's formulation of the difference between a real bite and a playful bite: "A Theory of Play and Fantasy," in *Play: Its Role in Evolution and Development*, J.S. Bruner, A. Jolly, and K. Sylva, eds. (Harmondsworth: Penguin, 1976), pp. 119–29, at p. 120.

35. Fradenburg, *City, Marriage, Tournament*, pp. 207–8.

36. Phillips, "Cross-dressing," p. 128.

37. Ed. M. Friedwagner (Halle: Niemeyer, 1897).

38. *Le Roman de Tristan en Prose*, Renée Curtis, ed., 3 vols. Woodbridge: Boydell and Brewer, 1985). Subsequent quotations from the Prose *Tristan* are from this edition.

39. Robert Stoller, *Sex and Gender*, International Psycho-Analytic Library 81 (London: Hogarth Press, 1968), p. 177.

40. *Trubert, fabliau du XIIIe siècle*, Guy Raynaud de Lage, ed., Textes littéraires français (Geneva: Droz, 1974). For pertinent discussions, see Kathryn Gravdal, *Vilain and Courtois: transgressive parody in French literature of the twelfth and thirteenth centuries* (Lincoln: University of Nebraska Press, 1989), pp. 114–40; and Gaunt, *Gender and Genre*, pp. 248–51.

41. See D.P. Rotunda, *Motif-Index for the Italian Novella in Prose* (New York: Haskell House, 1973), p. 104, and Stith Thompson, *Motif-Index of Folk Literature*, 2nd ed. (Bloomington: Indiana University Press, 1966), s. K1321.

42. Oskar Sommer, ed., *The Vulgate Version of the Arthurian Romances*, 7 vols. (Washington, D.C.: Carnegie Institution, 1908–16), 2: 288.

43. Heldris of Cornwall, *Roman de Silence*, Sarah Roche-Mahdi, ed. and trans. (East Lansing: Colleagues Press, 1992), ll. 6531–40.

44. Being a messenger is a female privilege in Arthurian romance. Male strangers with messages are usually cast in a hostile structural role. One can formulate the general rule that while female visitors at court are messengers, male visitors are challengers (or prisoners). This pattern explains why many knights are described as dressing as messenger girls: the squire in Lodewijk van Velthem's *Spiegel Historiael* dresses up as a woman to play the role of messenger; Tristan cross-dresses as a messenger; and in *Guiron le Courtois*, Morholt of Ireland comes to deliver a message to Arthur disguised as a damsel: E. Loseth, *Le roman en prose de Tristan, Le roman de Palamede, et la compilation de Rusticien de Pise* (1881; repr. New York: Burt Franklin, 1970), p. 440. Female disguise permits men to be accepted as messengers rather than challengers.

45. David Boyd and Ruth Mazo Karras, eds., "The Interrogation of a Male Transvestite Prostitute in Fourteenth-Century London," *GLQ* 1 (1995): 479–85.

46. *Li romans de Witasse le moine, roman de treizième siècle*, Denis J. Conlon, ed. (Chapel Hill: University of North Carolina Press, 1972).

47. Cf. Simon Gaunt's analysis of the lives of female transvestite saints, who similarly struggle to repel unwanted women suitors: "Straight Minds/'Queer' Wishes in Old French Hagiography: *La Vie de Sainte Euphrosine*," *GLQ* 1 (1994): 439–57.

48. Sir Philip Sidney, *A Defence of Poetry*, in *Miscellaneous Prose of Sir Philip Sidney*, Katherine Duncan Jones and Jan van Dorsten, eds. (Oxford: Clarendon Press, 1973), p. 115.

49. Freud, *Jokes and Their Relation to the Unconscious*, J. Strachey, trans. (London: Routledge, 1960), p. 149.

THE VICIOUS GUISE: EFFEMINACY, SODOMY, AND *Mankind*

Garrett P.J. Epp

While Mankind *ostensibly condemns effeminacy and sodomy, this essay suggests that dramatic performance of this allegorical play allows for more positive construction of male homosexual desire.*

> Thys ys to me a lamentable story
> To se my flesche of my soull to haue
> gouernance.
> Wher þe goodewyfe ys master, þe goodeman
> may be sory. (*Mankind*)[1]

> But eventually I sort of thought, 'Maybe I'm like *that*, too.'...And I just left my husband and...uh...sort of took on a new life. (*Forbidden Love*)[2]

Caroline Bynum has recently lamented modern critical tendencies both to allow the body to disappear into discourse and to assume "that medieval thinkers essentialized body as matter or essentialized either body or matter as feminine."[3] Such tendencies might seem difficult to resist in dealing with a work such as *Mankind*, a late fifteenth-century English moral interlude which repeatedly draws parallels between women and the body, as well as between words and flesh, and between words, flesh, and excrement. It is all too easy to read the play's infamous, excessive physicality as pure metaphor—this is, after all, a personification allegory, in which abstractions such as Mischief engage in verbal duelling with Mercy and the devil corrupts Mankind by whispering in his ear. However, resistence is indeed crucial. Unlike poetic allegories in which bodies both represent and are represented by discourse, *Mankind* is a play, and as such requires the physical involvement of actual bodies.

Moreover, all of these bodies are explicitly male. Whereas a majority of moral interludes include a female character, usually signifying Lechery, *Mankind* attributes lechery primarily to men, and in a mostly homoerotic context. Women are frequently referred to but always absent; the flesh we see is ultimately figured less as feminine than as effeminate. This distinction is important, if slippery. Effeminacy crosses and confuses both male/female and masculine/feminine binaries, sliding into a categorization more closely akin to sexuality than to sex or gender.

As Jonathan Goldberg and others have stressed, counter to common modern assumptions, when the English term itself becomes more common in sixteenth-century England, "effeminacy was more easily associated with, and was a charge more often made about, men who displayed excessive attention to women than taken as an indication of same-sex attraction."[4] But same-sex attraction cannot ever entirely be ruled out, given its explicit link with effeminacy in sources as various as John Marston's 1598 satire, *The Scourge of Villanie* and the condemnation by Ordericus Vitalis of the twelfth-century court of William Rufus.[5] Both these works also invoke the name of Sodom, with all its notoriously unstable but always sexual connotations. This linkage of sodomy and effeminacy is hardly uncommon and seems to increase over the intervening centuries. In the sixteenth-century antitheatrical criticism of Phillip Stubbes, for instance, "sodomy" and "effeminacy" are virtually interchangeable. Where the late fourteenth-century Wycliffite Bible translates the Vulgate's "effeminati" (in 1 Kings 14.24) as "men maad wymmenysch," the Geneva Bible of 1560, like the King James Bible after it, substitutes "sodomites."[6] The phrase "men maad wymmenysch" might be read as implying the loss of an essential masculine identity, but not in exchange for any other identity. Substantives such as "effeminati" and "sodomites," on the other hand, impose an identity, albeit one that little resembles a modern sexual self-identity.[7] As Bruce Smith has pointed out, sixteenth- and seventeenth-century English satire invoked the sodomite as a character type, "giving homosexual desire a recognizable body and a distinctive voice, but...in terms that are useless to a man who feels that desire himself."[8] This is ostensibly the aim of *Mankind*, as well, in its characterization of the effeminate male as vice figure: effeminacy is personified in order to condemn it as vicious; a personal identity is created in an attempt to render it useless, or unavailable, to actual persons. However, allegory is itself a notoriously slippery medium, particularly in the theatre. The static identity that is imposed on bodies, threatening to turn them into a discourse of pure vice and virtue, is inhabited by an actual body that is not so easily defined or contained. Moreover, once something akin to a sexual identity has been suggested, and a category of identity thus established, however contingently, other versions of that identity likewise become possible and available.

Availability of any given subject-identity relies on recognition. In *Forbidden Love*, a film that documents the lives of Canadian lesbians in the 1950s, Reva Hutkin describes how, when she was in her early twenties, a friend lent her a series of lesbian novels:

> And at some point she sort of confessed and said 'Well, I think I'm like that.' And I totally freaked out and said 'Oh, no! Not like *that*!' Whatever 'that' was—because it was all kind of a new experience for me. But eventually I sort of thought 'Maybe I'm like *that*, too.' Ultimately we got it together, and I just left my husband and…took on a new life.

The novels generally ended in the death or separation of their lesbian characters, ostensibly condemning homosexual relationships as vicious and untenable. Still, they rendered homosexual desire visible to their audience. Reva Hutkin and her new lover dressed up in their very best butch and femme outfits and went to Greenwich Village "to look for the lesbians" since that is where the novels said they were, and how they were dressed. Unfortunately, as she says, "They just weren't there, or we couldn't find them. Or we didn't recognize them, because they weren't wearing butch and femme things." However, they themselves had found an identity and, in the metonymic signifier of gendered (and cross-gendered) clothing, a visible means of claiming it.

Personification allegory, too, makes visible what usually is not, if very differently from these novels, externalizing and reifying abstract qualities and inner desires. And again one of its methods, particularly in drama, involves clothing. Throughout early English drama, clothing functions to identify not only a character but also certain changes that the character might experience.[9] Such use of clothing has particular force and relevance here, since effeminacy is closely associated with fashion—an association that still remains common despite radical changes in both. Long before and long after *Mankind* was written, fashionable or extravagant clothing on men was also specifically associated with lechery and sexual enticement. Chaucer's Parson, speaking of the sin of pride, denounces clothing "that thurgh hire shortnesse ne covere nat the shameful membres of man, to wikked entente";[10] nearly two centuries later, Phillip Stubbes will rail against all English men as "wicked, & licentious in all their wayes, which easily appeareth by their apparell, & new fangled fashions euery day inuented…for no cause so much as to delight the eyes of their harlots withall, and to inamoure the mindes of their fleshly paramours"—a passage which follows a summary of biblical punishments for pride, including the destruction of "Sodoma and Gomorra."[11]

In *Mankind*, the very source of corruption is effeminate fashion, as represented by three characters—New Guise, Nowadays, and Nought. On behalf of the dominant vice, Mischief, and aided by the devil, Titivillus, this vicious trio draws the protagonist, Mankind, away from productive work and prayer, ultimately bringing him to the brink of suicidal despair. While the playtext does not indicate what any of these characters actually wears, it is clear that costume alone would clearly distinguish the farmer Mankind from the distinctively urban company of vices. Immediately after he first joins their company, the vices alter his long "syde gown"—twice—into a fashionably short "jakett."[12] Their efforts at corrupting him are not immediately or easily successful, however, in part because Mankind is warned against them, and against "þe superfluouse gyse" (239) that they both wear and represent, by the play's sole representative of virtue, Mercy. For his part, Mercy is characterized as a priest or, more likely, a Dominican friar—early in the play, New Guise takes leave of Mercy with an apparent pun: "Gode brynge yow, master, and blyssyd Mary / To þe number of þe demonycall frayry!" (152-53).[13] What the modern reader can only presume, Mercy's costume would have made evident to the play's medieval audience.

Clothes do indeed seem to make the man here, but the effeminate man is also a bodily presence with bodily functions. The play of *Mankind* is most infamous for its preoccupation with excretion—a preoccupation that increases as the play proceeds. Unlike countless other devils and vice figures, Mankind's vices do more than merely talk about excrement. Late in the play, Nowadays mocks the recently departed Mercy, then states, "My bolte ys schett." Nought's response indicates that this "bolte" is not—or not merely—verbal:

> I am doynge of my nedyngys; be ware how ȝe schott!
> Fy, fy, fy! I haue fowll arayde my fote.
> Be wyse for schotynge wyth yowr takyllys, for Gode wott
> My fote ys fowly ouerschett. (783-86)

Still, even this physicality has tended to disappear in critical discourse, given the association within the play between words and excrement: lack of physical control parallels a vicious lack of proper verbal control. Midway through the play Mankind is said to have been "sent...forth to schyte lesynges" (568)—that is, lies—but the issue of verbal control is evident much earlier, if less explicitly so, in the sheer volume of empty or inappropriate verbiage that the vices utter. This ranges from Mischief's initial parody of Mercy's latinate diction to the scurrilous "Crystemes songe" they make the audience sing, and from scattered expletives to repetitious nonsense, all increasing as the play proceeds.

This is precisely the sort of language that, along with excessive use of rhetorical ornament, is generally characterized in rhetorical manuals from Quintilian onward as feminine or effeminate. It is not masculine, precisely because it lacks, and should be under, reasoned masculine control. This same conjunction of uncontrolled word and flesh is also specifically associated with sodomy in works such as Matthew of Vendôme's twelfth-century *Ars versificatoria* and in Alan of Lille's contemporary but more influential *De planctu Naturae*, where sodomy is characterized as the ultimate rhetorical error.[14] When New Guise, whose name is virtually synonymous with sartorial extravagance, first mentions "the new guise," he refers not to clothing, but to speech. Asked by Mercy to speak but "Few wordys, few and well sett"—the "masculine" style—New Guise answers:

> Ser, yt ys þe new gyse and þe new jett.
> Many wordys and schortely sett,
> Thys ys þe new gyse, euery-dele. (103-05)

Like fleshly matter, verbal matter is not always and everywhere in the Middle Ages deemed essentially feminine, although it often is. Still, masculinity is strongly associated with control. According to Isidore of Seville, "Man [*vir*] is so named, because there is greater force in him than in women [*feminis*]...or, he is so named because he controls women [*feminam*] forcefully." He also adds "there is the greatest strength [*virtus*] in man [*viri*], and less in woman [*mulieris*] so that she might be forebearing to man; otherwise, if women were to repel them, sexual desire might compel men to desire something else or rush off to another sex..."—implying that whatever else is sufficiently forebearing and unforceful might also prove attractive to men.[15] That which is properly masculine always masters and controls whatever is not, be it one's own words or flesh, or other human beings of any sex. New Guise and his fellows are masters of nothing and therefore effeminate men.

New Guise, in particular, also represents not merely a lack of mastery but overmastered male flesh. In his first major altercation with the vices, Mankind lashes out with his spade, the archetypal masculine tool from Adam onward. Nowadays is beaten over the head, and Nought is hurt on the arm, but New Guise sustains injury to his "jewellys" (381). The trio then runs for comfort to the dominant vice of the play, Mischief. New Guise is the first to complain: "Alasse, master, alasse, my privyte!" To this Mischief answers, "A, wher? alake! fayer babe ba [kiss] me!" He then adds "Abyde! to son I xall yt se" (429-31). Here "yt" can only mean one thing, which New Guise, apparently fumbling with his codpiece, is about to reveal. Mischief stops him from doing so, but in the process suggests both an onstage action with homosexual overtones, and an offstage history—a past and a future—of similar actions.

These lines also indicate that Mischief, the dominant vice, is also the dominant sexual partner. The others all refer to him as "master," while he calls them his "fayer babys" (427), which is allegorically appropriate: mischief is certainly older than any current fashion; in *Mankind* it is the origin of all that is fashionable. All three subordinate vices are also simply that—subordinate—and thus "boys" in a master/servant relation to Mischief. However, New Guise at least would appear to play "boy" to this master in a specifically sexual way. Bruce R. Smith has demonstrated how various meanings of the word "boy" in early modern England—"boy" as "servant" and as "rogue," but also as term of endearment—coalesce in regard to what he calls the "Master and Minion" model of homosexual relations, a model that is built upon a class-related power differential.[16] And as Alan Bray has noted, more egalitarian homoerotic bonding, such as those which Smith outlines in his chapter entitled "Combatants and Comrades," would normally have been read, perhaps even by loving comrades themselves, not as sodomy but as friendship.[17] To be read as such, sodomy requires difference. That difference is often, but not always, expressed in gendered terms: the "boy" takes the "female" role, plays the "woman's part." Yet even in such cases, the subordinate male is less regendered than unsexed—his biological maleness is simply irrelevant. Mischief certainly does not limit himself to male sexual partners: in the midst of a dramatic escape from prison, Mischief pauses to embrace and kiss the wife of the jailer he has just killed (644-46). In stating that he does not want to but will soon see New Guise's wounded genitals, Mischief suggests that, like the "master-mistress" of Shakespeare's infamous Sonnet 20, New Guise has been "pricked...out" with "one thing to [Mischief's] purpose nothing."[18] As boy or minion in this relationship, New Guise may value his own "jewellys," but the only portion of his "privyte" that matters to his master is the ring of his anus.

Yet New Guise is still male, if not properly masculine, and his genitals do matter in regard to another relationship in which he is not master, namely, his marriage. Just prior to his first encounter with Mankind, having interrupted Mercy's monologue on the theme "Mesure ys tresure," New Guise mockingly commends Mercy's advice:

> Ȝe sey trew, ser, ȝe are no faytour [liar].
> I haue fede my wyff so well tyll sche ys my master.
> I haue a grett wonde on my hede, lo! and þeron leyth a
> playster,
> Ande anoþer þer I pysse my peson. (245–48)

Both his head and his penis have been wounded by his wife, presumably before he ever appears onstage—a double metonymy of wounded masculine authority. Thus, quite aside from his name and the effeminately fashionable clothing it implies, New Guise is easily and immediately identifiable as an effeminate male. Yet his wife remains an absence, and any sexual desire he might feel toward her remains unrepresented. When his "peson"[19] is further injured, further damaging his chances to gain or regain his masculinity, New Guise immediately cries out, "Alas, my jewellys! I xall be schent of my wyff!" (381) However, he goes for consolation to his other master, Mischief, who neither requires nor desires that which has been lost, yet does desire him.

Mischief himself is never characterized as effeminate, at least not explicitly, in the text. He dominates even the virtuous Mercy in their onstage encounters, until Mercy's final entrance, armed with a manly *baleis* or rod (ll. 811–12) to chase away the vices, who are about to help Mankind hang himself. In that same encounter, New Guise, demonstrating the use of the gallows, is himself very nearly hung; Mischief, as always, escapes unharmed. The difference between the two figures suggests something akin to the dominant understanding of sexuality in modern Mexico and Latin America—"a configuration of gender/sex/power that is articulated along the active/passive axis and organized through the scripted sexual role one plays."[20] As Tomás Almaguer notes, within this system "it is primarily the anal-passive individual…who is stigmatized for playing the subservient, feminine role"[21] in a homosexual coupling. Unlike the active partner within this system, Mischief hardly escapes censure—he is, after all, a vice figure—but his masculinity as such does not seem to be questioned. He is the indomitable but vicious male, the masculine "top" to the effeminate "bottom" of New Guise.

On the other hand, this does not mean an equation between effeminacy and any particular sexual role or orientation.[22] Effeminacy implies less any particular attraction or desire as such than acting upon it; it is the doing, more than whom you do it with—where "it" is always but never only sexual in implication. Moderate, controlled desire for the company of women is not effeminate, but the company of women—or too much of it—does "effeminate," to borrow Stephen Gosson's term. And the effeminate man seeks effeminate pleasures, which cause further degeneracy precisely through the forfeiture of masculine control over the body. *Mankind* treats sodomy as the end to which effeminacy leads, in what Laura Levine, in reference to Gosson's *Playes Confuted*, calls "a kind of 'domino theory' of the self."[23] Levine, however, elides the differences between "effeminate" and "feminine" and even "female" in her analysis of this and other antitheatrical tracts. She claims, for instance, that Gosson's explicit accusation that theatre both is effeminate and effeminates the mind "implies that things that are like women are likely to turn into women."[24] Gosson states, rather, that too close an association with what is effeminate (such as the theatre, or indeed actors themselves)—not merely with what is feminine (that is, women)—effeminates men, causing or increasing their treasonous abandonment of masculine control and restraint. Men remain male but effeminate when they take too great a pleasure in theatre, or in fashionable clothing, or in women, or in playing the "woman's role" sexually, or in all of these—and each of these passive pleasures will lead one on to another, to further and greater indulgence.

Levine's article examines notions of the self inherent in sixteenth-century antitheatrical tracts. Yet the only "essential" self assumed by the likes of Gosson and Stubbes would seem to be, as for previous centuries, a God-likeness available to men and women alike. Given the assumed masculinity of God, this self—a self that is sometimes but not always identified with the soul—is also, likewise, assumed to be in some generic sense masculine but not male. Christ, being all things to all humanity, may be physically feminized in medieval art, the wound in his side depicted as being like a vulva or a female breast,[25] but an effeminate Christ is unimaginable within orthodox Christianity. A "virile" woman is generally deemed worthy of praise, where a woman in men's clothing is subject only to derision; the first in and through her self-control properly imitates a masculine God, but the second falsely and improperly imitates men, taking on false appearance of masculinity and none of the strength [*vis*] considered proper to it.[26] However, it is also generally assumed that virile women are the exception, that most women will be "feminine" in the various abject senses of that descriptor, due to their already overdetermined association with ornamentation, flesh, and sexuality—not in the sense of orientation, but of inclination. For women, the dominoes have always already fallen. Men have a greater chance—and duty—of keeping the dominoes from falling, of remaining properly masculine.

In keeping with the didactic purpose of the moral interlude, *Mankind* gives its audience an early glimpse of the potential sodomitical end of degenerative effeminacy. The very first lines that New Guise addresses to Mankind, well before the spade starts swinging, have homoerotic overtones:

> The wether ys colde, Gode sende ws goode ferys!
> 'Cum sancto sanctus eris et cum peruerso peruerteris.'
> 'Ecce quam bonum et quam jocundum,' quod þe Deull to
> þe frerys,
> 'Habitare fratres in vnum.' (323–26)

Editors regularly gloss "ferys" as "fires,"[27] but the lines that follow (quoting Psalms 18.25–26 and 133.1) indicate that New Guise has in mind another method for keeping warm—"feris" in the more common sense of "mates," here with conjugal implication. His misappropriation of Psalm 133—"behold how good and how pleasant it is for brothers to dwell in unity"—in this context gives the phrase "habitare fratres in unum" a distinctly sexual turn, particularly given the interpolated reference to the devil and friars, a reference that recalls other antifraternal satire, in particular the twenty thousand friars living closely and warmly together in "the develes ers" in the Prologue of Chaucer's Summoner (3.1705).

More immediately, though, it recalls New Guise's own, still earlier farewell to Mercy: "Gode brynge yow, master, and blyssyd Mary / To þe number of þe demonycall frayry" (153).[28] While this earlier line indicates that Mercy is not yet among that number, the later one implies otherwise. Between these lines come the introduction of *Mankind*, several long didactic speeches by Mercy with offstage commentary by the vices, and a kiss. That kiss, between Mercy and Mankind, could on its own be construed as entirely orthodox, but its context constructs it otherwise. The comments by New Guise regarding the devil and friars are only one part of the immediate context. The line that directly precedes the kiss refers to Mischief being "redy to brace yow in hys brydyll" (306). This line suggests both a literal riding as presented in later interludes such as *Like Will to Like* (1568), where the vice Nicholas Newfangle makes his final exit on the devil's back,[29] and also a sexual embrace or "riding"—a meaning reinforced by the apparent pun on "brydyll" as "bridal" or "wedding." Mercy then offers his own embrace, his kiss, as a substitute, but the substitution serves to show the similarity. So, too, does the wording of his offer or rather his order: "Kysse me now, my dere darlynge" (307)—a line echoed just over a hundred lines later, when Mischief asks a kiss of New Guise, then turns to the wounded Nowadays and addresses him as "sely darlynge" (433). Nor does Mankind's response to Mercy's kiss work effectively against this, despite its invocation of a soul/flesh binary: "Now blyssyd be Jhesu! my soull ys well sacyatt / Wyth þe mellyfluose doctryne of þis worschyppfull man. / The rebellyn of my flesch now yt ys superatt…" (311-13). The allegorical point, of course, is that good Christian doctrine conquers rebellious flesh and satisfies the soul, but what the audience sees is a satisfying fleshly kiss between two men. Mercy's proper and masculine authority has already been undercut by the antifraternal satire of New Guise; here it is refigured as yet another eroticised homosocial power differential.

Antifraternal satire in the mouth of a vice figure should logically cancel itself—praise from a vice should damn. However, the invocation of an entirely homosocial institution in conjunction with a supposed condemnation of homoeroticism allows each to collapse into the other. The similarity between ostensibly virtuous and vicious kisses only furthers this collapse. So, too, does the fact that the performers themselves, including the actor playing Mercy, constitute part of a larger homosocial institution likewise regularly accused of all manner of vice, including effeminacy and sodomy, from at least Tertullian onward through to Gosson and Stubbes. Moreover, the actor playing Mercy also plays Titivillus, the devil—the only doubling possible in this play. The difference between good and evil itself, as between effeminacy and proper masculinity, is in several senses a matter of performance and of one's understanding of that performance. Conscious recognition of the performance as performance makes it available for critique, denaturalizing differences.

This is what Jonathan Dollimore calls the perverse dynamic—the revelation of radical proximity where radical difference has been assumed and depended on.[30] Vice is dangerous precisely because it is so similar to, so inseparable from virtue. In this play they too often seem to be the same thing or at least too often occupy the same ground along the continuum of masculinity and effeminacy, where they should occupy opposing ends. Virtuous company perversely proves no more masculine than vicious company; the same company performs both and in much the same way. In his discussion of the problematic relationship between "the sodomite" and "the masculine friend," Alan Bray writes, "The signs of the one were indeed sometimes the signs of the other, but the conventions of friendship were set a world away from the wild sin of Sodom by the placid orderliness of the relationships they expressed."[31] Here, too, some signs prove indistinguishable from one another, and all ultimately depend upon the understanding that the audience brings to the performance. If one is inclined to sympathize with, or even recognize, antifraternal satire and understands Latin, one will be unable to avoid making the same association between Mercy and homoeroticism that New Guise makes; the parallel between the Mercy/Mankind and Mischief/New Guise couplings will be more obvious. If one is also conscious of the common associations between actors, effeminacy, and vice in general, the moral distinction between these couplings collapses entirely. In Dollimore's terms, each role, each institution is transgressively reinscribed over the other: the vicious, effeminate actor inhabits the role of masculine virtue; Titivillus is Mercy in disguise; the good friars are sodomites.

In part this is inevitable, a problem with the medium. Allegory, as a mode of "meaning otherwise," is notoriously unstable. Moral interludes, more than nondramatic allegories, invoke the complex world outside that of the allegory, proper, in their representation of abstract vice and virtue as individual human beings. In doing so, they must always compromise the radical simplicity and supposed universality of those abstractions and reveal the instability and constructedness of their personified subjects. *Mankind*, more than most dramatic allegories, seems to flaunt this effect, as if attempting to prove Judith Butler's assertion that "the performance constitutes the appearance of a 'subject' as its effect...."[32] It does so both through self-conscious theatricality and through its personification of effeminacy, a vice that is necessarily relative and—like the concept of "sodomy"—always unstable. Like fashion, the "new guise" that is its visible metonymic signifier, effeminacy is not only subject to change, but itself virtually signifies change. As do actors, with their protean skills. When Mercy cries out to the absent, corrupted Mankind, "I dyscomende and dysalow þin oftyn mutabylyte" (746), it is all too easy for the audience to remember that the actor speaking this line has himself just changed roles and costumes. The line itself closely echoes an earlier statement by Mercy to the audience:

> The goode new gyse nowadays I wyll not dysalow.
> I dyscomende þe vycyouse gyse; I prey haue me excusyde,
> I nede not to speke of yt, yowr reson wyll tell it yow.

By allowing for, but not describing or representing, this "goode new gyse," the play allows too much free play to its audience, to read it as they will.

Virtue generally gets the last word in moral interludes; in *Mankind*, Mercy gives a rousingly virtuous epilogue. Here as always, however, it is the vices that we as audience best remember—it is the vices who, like the actors that represent them, exercise a masculine control over the plot and over our imaginations. They even make us both pay and sing for their perversity; vice plays with us. Thus we as audience, both as participants in the vices' game and as observers of Mankind's corruption and redemption, are made subject to the effeminate pleasure of a passive surrender to the will of others who are themselves defined, on a variety of levels, as effeminate. That much seems allegorically and didactically appropriate: the audience occupies fairly much the same position in relation to the vices as does Mankind, who represents them. Phillip Stubbes, for one, thought that the story would rarely end there:

> Than these goodly pageants being done, euery mate sorts to his mate, euery one bringes another homeward of their way verye freendly, and in their secret conclaues (couertly) they play *the Sodomits*, or worse. And these be the fruits of Playes and Enterludes, for the most part.[33]

Whether Stubbes here refers to homosexual activity as most modern critics assume, or, as seems more likely, to illicit heterosexual couplings,[34] is largely irrelevant. His explicit fear is that one "will learn to playe the vice"[35]—that one might imitate in life the vice one sees enacted onstage—yet he does not explicitly identify those on stage as playing "*Sodomits*, or worse." He thus implies what Gosson proposes outright, namely, that one version of effeminacy generally leads to another and that the theatre audience is always necessarily effeminated by the experience of playgoing. *Mankind*, a full century earlier, proposes the first, and, in performance, proves the second.

Stubbes's fear of imitation on the part of the audience has further implications here. In its inclusion of a character that personifies sodomitical effeminacy itself, *Mankind* gives homoerotic desire visible representation—a name, and a costume. Much like the lesbian novels of the 1950s, mentioned earlier, the play condemns what it represents. However, once the possibility of desiring otherwise has been admitted, it becomes difficult to shut down, at least for some, under some conditions. The performance would certainly make a difference—we cannot know, now, how New Guise was actually played, or what the actor or his costume looked like. More crucially, we cannot know whether the body under that costume was considered desirable; we cannot know the desires of the audience, or whether they recognized them, or—if they did—whether and how they acted upon these. We can know only the possibilities that the playtext itself allows or encourages. Men in the medieval audience may have recognized in themselves a desire for the body under the new guise of sartorial extravagance rather than for—or in addition to—the extravagance itself. And, both despite and because of the playtext, they may not have read that desire as effeminate. If Mischief can desire the effeminate New Guise yet remain masculine, one version at least of homoerotic desire may be read as masculine. New Guise may desire sexual domination by another male body, but his attempt to dominate Mercy and Mankind may be read as the desire for a measure of masculine control; his desire for "good ferys" may be read as the desire for sexual reciprocity.

In her 1984 article, "Thinking Sex," Gayle Rubin explains the difference between the "sodomite" and the modern "homosexual" through reference to the 1631 trial and execution for sodomy of the Earl of Castlehaven:

> The earl did not slip into his tightest doublet and waltz down to the nearest gay tavern to mingle with his fellow sodomists. He stayed at home and buggered his servants. Gay awareness, gay pubs, the sense of group commonality, and even the term homosexual were not part of the earl's universe.[36]

Jonathan Dollimore, however, has since suggested that

> in early modern England the sodomite, although not an identity in the modern sense, could and did denote subject positions or types; 'he' precisely *characterized* deviant subject positions as well as denoting the behaviour of individuals.[37]

Much like those women in the 1950s who imitated literary types by dressing butch and femme and then headed off "to look for the lesbians," the Earl of Castlehaven might well have read Stubbes, put on his most effeminate fashions, and headed off to the theatre to "play the sodomite," but found none to play with because the other sodomites were not dressed effeminately or were of the same class as himself and thus not recognizable to him as potential sexual partners. Or perhaps he found what he sought, within his class, but the lack of a power distinction made those relationships unrecognizable to the outsiders who eventually prosecuted him. We simply cannot know. We can know that, at the time, some persons at least thought they knew what sodomites looked like and what they did. A century and a half earlier, audiences watching *Mankind* were shown the personification of sodomitical effeminacy, and were told to reject this "vicious guise." We cannot know whether they did so, or whether the performance of this new guise, or the desirability of the body that performed it, led any of the men in the audience to realize that maybe they, too, were in some way "like *that.*"

NOTES

1. *Mankind* (c. 1470), ll. 198–200, in Mark Eccles, ed., *The Macro Plays*, Early English Text Society OS 262 (London: Oxford University Press, 1969); this edition is cited hereafter in the body of this paper by line number.

2. *Forbidden Love: The Unashamed Stories of Lesbian Lives*, dir. Aerlyn Weissman and Lynne Fernie, National Film Board of Canada / Studio D, 1992.

3. Caroline Bynum, "Why All the Fuss about the Body? A Medievalist's Perspective," *Critical Inquiry* 22 (Autumn 1995): 4, 17.

4. Jonathan Goldberg, *Sodometries: Renaissance Text, Modern Sexualities* (Stanford CA, Stanford University Press, 1992), p. 111. I have framed my own discussion largely around works from or concerning sixteenth-century England, in part due to a more explicit interest in the connections between effeminacy and sodomy and theatre, on the part of contemporary writers and modern scholars alike, than can generally be found in regard to writers from or concerned with the fifteenth century. I have also done so partly in order to disperse the impression one often gets from the modern scholars that these issues, and the connections between them, were themselves invented, or at least reinvented, in the sixteenth century.

5. Quoted and discussed in Bruce R. Smith, *Homosexual Desire in Shakespeare's England: A Cultural Poetics*, (Chicago, University of Chicago Press, 1991), p. 180, and John Boswell, *Christianity, Social Tolerance, and Homosexuality: Gay People in Western Europe from the Beginning of the Christian Era to the Fourteenth Century*, (Chicago; London, University of Chicago Press, 1980), pp. 229–230, respectively.

6. See also 1 Kings 15.12, 22.46/7, and 2 Kings 23.7, in *MS Bodley 959: Genesis-Baruch 3.20 in the Earlier Version of the Wycliffite Bible*, ed. Conrad Lindberg, vol. 3 (Stockholm: Almqvist & Wiksell, 1959), and *The Geneva Bible: A Facsimile of the 1560 Edition* (Madison: University of Wisconsin Press, 1969).

7. This is, more or less, what Arnold Davidson, using similar linguistic criteria, has argued did not happen until the nineteenth century. Davidson, "Sex and the Emergence of Sexuality," in *Forms of Desire: Sexual Orientation and the Social Constructionist Controversy*, Edward Stein, ed. (New York and London: Garland, 1990), pp. 89–132. See especially p. 122, on the doctrine of "dynamic nominalism," and p. 127, on sexual perversion as dealt with by Augustine and Aquinas.

8. Smith, p. 185.

9. See Jean MacIntyre and Garrett Epp, "'Cloathes Worth All the Rest': Costumes and Properties in English Theatre to 1642," *The New History of Early English Drama*, John D. Cox and David Scott Kastan, eds. (New York: Columbia University Press, forthcoming).

10. *The Canterbury Tales,* X.421, in *The Riverside Chaucer*, 3rd ed., Larry D. Benson, gen. ed. (Boston: Houghton Mifflin, 1987).

11. Phillip Stubbes, *The Anatomie of Abuses* (London, 1583; rpt. Amsterdam: Theatrum Orbis Terrarum, 1972), G7r, G6r.

12. See ll. 671–76, 695–700, 718. The costume is taken offstage first, appropriately, by New Guise, who comes in with something shorter. Naught deems this alteration insufficient and takes it offstage again, coming back with something presumably more reflective of his own name—that is, so short as to be worthless as clothing.

13. See Eccles, p. 218.

14. See Jan Ziolkowski, *Alan of Lille's Grammar of Sex: the Meaning of Grammar to a Twelfth-Century Intellectual* (Cambridge MA: Medieval Academy of America, 1985), and Garrett Epp, "Learning to Write with Venus's Pen: Sexual Regulation in Matthew of Vendôme's *Ars versificatoria*," in *Desire and Discipline: Sex and Sexuality in the Premodern West*, Jacqueline Murray and Konrad Eisenbichler, eds., (Toronto: University of Toronto Press, forthcoming).

15. *Etymologiae* XI.ii.17, trans. Alcuin Blamires, *Woman Defamed and Woman Defended: An Anthology of Medieval Texts*, Alcuin Blamires, ed. (Oxford: Clarendon Press, 1992), p. 43.

16. Smith, pp. 193–196.

17. Alan Bray, "Homosexuality and the Signs of Male Friendship in Elizabethan England," in *Queering the Renaissance*, Jonathan Goldberg, ed. (Durham NC: Duke University Press, 1994), pp. 40–61.

18. Sonnet 20.13,12. The "master-mistress" sonnet itself remains controversial. Among the more useful analyses of its homoerotic implications are those of Joseph Pequigney, *Such Is My Love* (Chicago: University of Chicago Press, 1985), pp. 30–41, and Gregory W. Bredbeck, *Sodomy and Interpretation: Marlowe to Milton* (Ithaca: Cornell University Press, 1991), pp. 175–78. It might be noted here that even the ambiguous epithet of "master-mistress" suggests a level of masculine control that New Guise lacks.

19. The gloss on line 248 offered in Eccles' standard edition of *Mankind* and repeated in more recent editions defines "peson" as a synonym to "pease," which has little to do with pissing; according to the OED, a "peson" is a balance, a weighing device with balls hung on the end of a staff—that is, figuratively, a penis.

20. Tomás Almaguer, "Chicano Men: A Cartography of Homosexual Identity and Behavior," in *The Gay and Lesbian Studies Reader*, Henry Abelove, Michèle Aina Barale, and David M. Halperin, eds. (New York and London: Routledge, 1993), p. 257.

21. Almaguer, p. 257.

22. Alan Sinfield has asserted that such an equation emerged in English culture only with the trial of Oscar Wilde. See Sinfield, *Cultural Politics—Queer Reading* (Philadelphia: University of Pennsylvania Press, 1994), pp. 14–18. However, Sinfield sees no connection between homoeroticism and effeminacy prior to the late nineteenth century; I see a strong connection, even in some of the examples Sinfield cites, but no precise equation.

23. Laura Levine, "Men in Women's Clothing: Anti-theatricality and Effeminization from 1579 to 1642," *Criticism* 28.2 (Spring 1986): 126.

24. Levine, p. 131; see Gosson's *Playes Confuted* (London, 1582), G4r, and *The School of Abuse* (London 1579), B3r, in *Markets of Bawdrie: The Dramatic Criticism of Stephen Gosson*, ed. Arthur F. Kinney (Salzburg: Institut für Englische Sprache und Literatur, 1974). The word "effeminization" in the title of Levine's essay similarly conflates "effeminate" (Gosson's usual verb, and one I use here) and "feminize," the usual modern term but one that itself encourages the elision of effeminacy, femininity, and femaleness, which I see as occupying three separate, if often similar or overlapping, categories.

25. See Caroline Walker Bynum, *Jesus as Mother: Studies in the Spirituality of the High Middle Ages* (Berkeley, Los Angeles, and London: University of California Press, 1982).

26. Phillip Stubbes, for instance, states "to weare the Apparel of another sex, is to participate with the same, and to adulterate the veritie of his owne kinde. Wherefore these Women may not improperly be called *Hermaphrodita*, that is, Monsters of bothe kindes, half women, half men" (*Apologie*, F5v). Levine repeatedly cites this passage as referring to actors wearing women's clothing (pp. 121, 130), although Stubbes—surprisingly—has nothing explicit to say on that particular topic.

27. In addition to Eccles, see J.A.B. Somerset, ed. *Four Tudor Interludes* (London: Athlone Press, 1974), p. 167, and David Bevington, ed. *Medieval Drama* (Boston: Houghton Mifflin, 1975), p. 914.

28. These lines are discussed earlier in this paper. It is perhaps not coincidental that the Dominicans were closely associated with

antisodomitical activity—see Boswell, pp. 283, 294–95. Such an association would reinforce any perceived reference to antifraternal satire.

29. There are other variations on this action: in Wager's *Enough Is as Good as a Feast* (c. 1570), the devil carries the dead protagonist Worldly Man away on his back. However, the riding of the devil in *Like Will to Like* does suggest sexual domination in much the same sense as the ride, discussed and illustrated in a variety of medieval sources, of Phyllis on the back of Aristotle, on which see Blamires, pp. 180–81, 194, and Plate 5. The longer example given here, by Jehan Le Fèvre, deems Aristotle guilty of "solecism" (Blamires, p. 180), the same rhetorical metaphor that Alan of Lille uses to describe sodomy—see Ziolkowski, pp. 35–39, 55–59.

30. Jonathan Dollimore, *Sexual Dissidence: Augustine to Wilde, Freud to Foucault* (Oxford: Clarendon Press, 1991); see especially pp. 228–230.

31. Bray, p. 47.

32. Judith Butler, "Imitation and Gender Insubordination," in *The Gay and Lesbian Studies Reader*, p. 315.

33. Stubbes, L8v.

34. Stubbes refers one other time in this same work to a couple "playing the vile *Sodomits*" (H6v), and then it is explicitly a heterosexual couple.

35. Stubbes, L8v.

36. Gayle Rubin, "Thinking Sex: Notes for a Radical Theory of the Politics of Sexuality," in *The Gay and Lesbian Studies Reader*, p. 17.

37. Dollimore, p. 239.

OUTLAW MASCULINITIES: DRAG, BLACKFACE, AND LATE MEDIEVAL LABORING-CLASS FESTIVITIES

Claire Sponsler

This essay explores the laboring-class masculinities produced in late medieval England by the wearing of drag and blackface in mummings and morris dances.

My purpose in this essay is to explore the production and performance of laboring-class masculinity in late medieval England by examining a cluster of seldom-scrutinized theatrical practices: the wearing of drag and blackface in the men's seasonal ceremonials known as mummings and morris dances. This is a slippery topic, I have discovered in the course of researching and writing this essay, made elusive not only by the scarcity and ambiguity of archival evidence about these theatrical practices but also by a lack of critical reflection about the potential meanings of these practices for the men who engaged in them and the spectators who watched. My goal is thus in part simply to make these theatrical practices visible and to call attention to their formative role in producing laboring-class masculine subjects—subjects who themselves are often not easy to discern given their limited influence over written accounts and other forms of cultural transmission.

Some things are known. Archival records make it clear that in theatrical performances of all kinds face painting, including "blacking" of the face, and the wearing of female costume by men were exceedingly frequent performance practices.[1] Men almost invariably played all roles, both male and female, in nearly every form of medieval dramatic activity including public processions, pageants, masquerades, morris dances, and mummings; the one exception appears to have been court maskings and disguisings in which women were allowed to participate. Male transvestism thus has to be seen as the theatrical norm, an ordinary and conventional occurrence within dramatic and festive performances. Blackface also appears to have been a fairly widespread theatrical convention, though its use is hard to pin down with any precision since in archival records it is not always easy to distinguish blackface from related practices such as the wearing of masks and visors or face gilding (gilded faces were common for actors playing the character of God). The Smiths' Accounts at Coventry in 1548, for instance, record payments "to the paynter for payntyng the players facys," without further specifying which characters had their faces painted and whether it involved blackface or gilding or something else.[2] Numerous other references describe the "heads" or masks made for actors playing such roles as giants, demons, fools, Herod, and Jesus. Documents do, however, also repeatedly mention the blackface worn by many unspecified characters as well as by "blakke soulys" and devils, who traditionally appeared with their faces blackened.[3]

Though these theatrical practices are known to historians of medieval drama, their cultural implications—especially for questions of subjectivity—have not been examined. Instead, the use of blackface and female costume by male performers has usually been understood either as a matter of theatrical tradition (in the case of dramas such as the Corpus Christi plays or the moralities) or as simple "disguise" meant to conceal the performer's identity (in the case of carnivals, mummings, morris dances, and other seasonal festivities)—interpretations that render these practices unproblematic and unremarkable. But such a perspective works to preclude full consideration of the issues of race, gender, status, and performative subjectivity raised by these theatrical practices. It also fails to do justice to their deviance and transgressiveness. When seen just as conventions of costuming and make-up,[4] rather than as drag and blackface, these theatrical practices are defused and denatured, removed from the realm of social and cultural struggle into the safe space of stage history where they can be viewed as theatrical devices, hence customary and inconsequential. Though my arguments will necessarily be somewhat speculative and preliminary, I want to take a different tack, insisting on the dangerousness of the use of drag and blackface in late medieval festivities like mummings and morris dances and calling attention to the centrality of racial and gender difference in their performance of a laboring-class masculinity.

In so doing, I seek to explore how discourses of blackness and femaleness, embodied in drag and blackface, might have operated to construct and deconstruct the performative maleness enacted in mummings and morris dances, festivities that themselves were socially menacing, straddling as they did the borders of theatricality and criminality. In these seasonal festivities, which brought together large groups of men licensed by the performance context to engage in such quasi-criminal acts as ritual trespass, robbery, and riot, the limits of cultural definitions of laboring-class manhood were tested and protested. For the almost exclusively male participants, I wish to suggest, the use of drag and blackface represented elaborate play with outlaw masculinities, theatrical experimentation with structures of laboring-class maleness not allowed and indeed often feared by hegemony. It is possible, then, to see in these performances the acting out of a complicated drama of othering and identification, of fear and desire, that was tied to a contest between normative or hegemonically sanctioned and outlaw or self-created laboring-class masculinities.

Early mummings and morris dances were important constitutive discourses of the plebeian male body, responsible for producing and displaying laboring-class masculinity. They also represent one of the best places for us to glimpse that otherwise often hidden masculinity being shaped. The perhaps surprising and unexpected use of drag and blackface in these festivities no doubt had a range of possible functions and meanings but derived at least part of its power from a conjuring up of the overlapping discourses of femininity and blackness—discourses that were for medieval European males profoundly other. What was the cultural work of such signs of otherness worn on the bodies of the less than fully enfranchised men who were the principal participants in these festivities? What did it mean for a man to inhabit, even if only temporarily, a body so radically othered? And how did those with other ideas about how laboring-class masculinity ought to be performed look on these transformative practices?

***

Although it is not my intention to attempt to unravel the complex and confusing history of medieval mummings and morris dances, a brief sketch of their salient features would no doubt be useful here. Information about these festivities has to be patched together from a sparse historical record and inference from later performances. Though they might well have begun earlier, morris dances in England start to show up in written records in the middle of the fifteenth century.

The first reference to morris dancing in England comes in 1466 in a household account book in Cornwall and the first performance of a morris dance was recorded by the Drapers in London in 1477.[5] Records suggest that in the early sixteenth century morris dancing spread over the Thames valley; performances are recorded at Kingston in 1507, Reading in 1513, and Abingdon in 1560. By 1550 morris dancing was apparently common throughout all parts of England. According to the Early Morris Project, an archive and database that attempts to list all references to morris dancing in England up to 1750, morris dancing fell into four overlapping types: royal morris, which involved a mime or dramatic narrative; guild/urban morris, which was processional in form; village morris; and private-house morris.[6] Although this picture may be somewhat distorted, since elite performances tend to be over-represented in the historical record, what it implies is that morris dancing was popular across a broad social spectrum, though perhaps for varying reasons in different cultural contexts.

Like morris dances, mummings were performed in a variety of settings by a wide range of participants, typically as part of seasonal festivities, especially those associated with Christmas and New Year's.[7] E. K. Chambers has described the widespread celebration of the New Year with processions of skin-clad mummers led by a cervulus or hobby-horse and Joseph Strutt's *Sports and Pastimes of the People of England* reproduces late medieval drawings showing mummers processing through the streets disguised with animal heads.[8] Mummings seem to have begun as village and urban street processions that included house-to-house visits featuring dice games or, later, the performance of a short play that ended with a *quête* or demand for food or money.[9] The city accounts from London in 1334, 1393, and 1405, for example, forbid citizens to go masked or disguised through the streets and to enter houses; in 1417 "mummyng" is specifically mentioned in a similar prohibition.[10] Many mumming plays have been identified (usually some variant of the Wooing Ceremony, the Sword Dance, or the Hero-Combat Play), all having in common some form of ritual violence and regeneration that would make sense at New Year's festivities.[11]

Whether courtly or plebeian, urban or rural, mummings and morris dancing almost invariably were located within a nexus of community-based festive behavior—whatever that community might have been—that included music, drama, dance, feasting and drinking, processions, and ritual behaviors such as rough humor, social and gender role reversals, and other carnivalesque acts that usually accompanied seasonal ceremonies.[12] There is good reason, however, to think of morris dances and mummings as definitively laboring-class performances. Despite a record of aristocratic and elite involvement and indeed co-optation,[13] mummings and morris dances remain firmly identified with the laboring classes from the late Middle Ages up to the present. Much of the early morris dancing seems to have been associated chiefly with landless countrymen and between 1660 and 1900, a period for which there are ample records, the dancers were drawn almost entirely from the lowest social rungs.[14] Similarly, late medieval mumming was popular among the rural and urban laboring classes and the participants in later versions such as the Philadelphia Mummers' parade, the Newfoundland mummers, and the various village mumming groups still performing in England at the end of the nineteenth century have all been almost exclusively working class.[15] So although they were available for use by other social groups, mummings and morris dances as cultural activities were largely the province of laboring-class males.

I identify these men as laboring-class rather than as plebeian, as they are more often described by historians of popular culture, not because there is any hard and fast distinction between the terms but in order to point to the formative role of work in shaping the meaning of these performances and hence the masculine identities linked to them. To think of them as laboring-class performances is to envision them not as timeless and universal rituals of the folk or the people but as historically-defined activities that take place within specific socioeconomic orders determined, in the case of late medieval England, by labor and the control of labor. Although I do not have the space here for the full discussion this issue deserves, one crucial way that late medieval mummings and morris dances can be understood is as carefully structured antidotes to and protests against the everyday world of often ill-paid and unrewarding labor. In these festivities many of the aspects of masculinity valued by those who profited from and controlled the work of laboring men—such as physical strength, energy, obedience to authority, and collective effort—were put to the ends of voluntary festivity rather than coerced labor.[16] It is worth noting in this regard that official attempts to suppress these festivities, which I discuss a bit later, often seem to turn precisely on their troublingly subversive and inverted resemblance to work, a concern that seems also to underwrite puritan attacks on them as inappropriate ways to spend the (non-working) Sabbath day.

The point I wish to stress about how morris dances and mummings re-invent and resist the hegemonic terms of labor is that these performances are in fact connected with the most extreme and overt inversion of normative patterns of work: outlawry. This certainly seems to have been the view of officialdom. Indeed, much of our information about these festivities comes from accounts that point specifically to their dangerousness and that vilify, try to rein in, or outright ban them. From the sixteenth century up to the present, the participants in these festivities have been widely perceived by more prosperous observers to be lazy, criminal, drunken, and violent.[17] This should not be surprising since by their very nature these were transgressive performances that threatened boundaries of all kinds. Knowingly or not, participants in these festivities overthrew spatial parameters (by invading, penetrating, and trespassing), social status norms (through role reversals and play with stranger-householder relations), gender constructs (through cross-dressing and sexual inversion), and racial divisions (with the use of blackface). Even the category of "human" was questioned through the putting on of animal disguises. Through these symbolic transgressions, mummings and morris dances effectively opened up space for other forms of outlawry, including revolt and rebellion.

The relation between seasonal festivity and rebellion has recently been investigated by a number of scholars.[18] Their findings show that in a surprising number of instances popular festivity provided a cover for and even inspired rebellious behavior. Demands for increased wages could be couched as a collection or *quête*, rebellions were hatched in ale-houses (as were festivals), the mock king of a church ale could become a rebel leader, and both revelers and outlaws used distinctive livery or "disguise" to join together in brotherhoods or gangs.[19] Popular celebrations on Palm Sunday, May Day, and Midsummer Day licensed crimes "against the vert," allowing people to trespass and steal flowers, timber, and trees from forests and parks.[20] The disturbances at Essex that triggered the revolt of 1381 started at Whitsun, a feast associated with morris dances, ales, summer kings and queens, Robin Hood plays, and other folk dramas.[21] In 1414 Sir John Oldcastle and his Lollards were accused of using a mumming as cover for sedition.[22] And in 1443 the mayor and citizens of Norwich challenged Henry VI's authority through a mumming procession featuring a mock king; the mayor and aldermen tried to cover up their actions by claiming that the "disguising" was part of a traditional Shrove Tuesday festivity and hence entailed no threat to Henry.[23]

Late medieval officials, both church and secular, were well aware of the potential for disorder associated with popular festivities and tried where possible to avert or contain it. A London order of 1334 forbade mummers (or night walkers) to go to homes disguised with false faces; the order was repeated in 1393, 1405, and 1418.[24] A parliamentary act of 1511 similarly proscribed visits of disguised mummers to great houses.[25] Where not forbidden outright, festivity was often carefully circumscribed: the Coventry Leet Book, to cite just one example, contains an entry for 1421 urging that better order could be kept at Midsummer's Eve by appointing wardens to keep tabs on each ward so as to avoid "grett debate and man slaughter and othure perels and synnes yat myght fall and late haue fallen."[26] By the late sixteenth century, puritan attitudes toward public behavior increasingly clashed with the noisy, drunken, licentious, festive plebeian and populist culture that the morris dance and mummings had come to represent. As a result, in the seventeenth century there was increasing church legislation against such performances, followed by secular legislation.[27] Morris dance, in particular, came to stand as a vivid sign of the pagan, heathenish, and profane pleasures despised by puritans. As if in recognition of the subversive content and rebellious tendencies of such popular festivities, puritan reformers attacked them for encouraging the disobedience of "the common vulgar against the magistrate and minister, servants against their masters, children against their parents, and wanton wives against their husbands."[28] In 1614 the House of Commons, spurred by puritan sentiments, passed an act suppressing the performance of morris dancing and bear baiting on the Sabbath.[29] What this brief sketch should add up to is an impression of mummings, morris dances, and other related festivities as ritual performances that made available a range of symbols and practices that could be employed for rebellious acts of all kinds—occasionally even by elites, though much more commonly by men from the laboring classes, who found in these performances mechanisms not only for social protest but also for identity production.

***

When viewed as constituent features of such transgressive and rebellious festivities, the costuming practices of morris dancers and mummers take on increased significance. Given that the costumes for these festivities apparently varied and were often probably improvised or hastily thrown together, the fact that they consistently employed some form of drag and blackface seems telling. In the morris dance, drag was used when a male performer dressed as a woman in the role of Maid Marion. In mummings, men dressed as women in the procession and in the role of the Betty, or man-woman, who also appears in a number of mummers' plays.[30] Blackface seems to have been at times adopted by all of the performers in morris dances and mummings and at times reserved just for one character such as the fool or, in later periods, the Sambo or Turkish knight figure.[31] The charged link between drag and blackface—forms of masquerade that on the face of it might not seem to have much in common—is suggested not only by the fact that they appear in the same kinds of performances but also because cross-dressing is attacked in the same Decretals and legal proclamations that proscribe masks and blackface.[32] In the eyes of those with a vested interest in maintaining social order, drag and blackface appear to have been taken as similar kinds of performative acts requiring similar kinds of restriction.

Late medieval attempts to ban drag and blackface might be interpreted as having to do with fears of crime and disorder. Since disguises could provide a cover for criminal acts or, on a festive occasion, prevent identification of rioters, regulations forbidding men to disguise themselves in these ways would presumably make it harder for them to perpetrate crimes or to evade detection and apprehension. In this view, face blacking and cross-dressing are seen as gestures of invisibility, ways of warding off surveillance, hiding from authority's eyes, and thereby escaping recognition. This would seem to point to festive disguise as being primarily a means of concealing identity, which is how an act of 1511 views it. The preamble to this act against disguising and the wearing of visors complains that "lately wythin this realmd dyvers persons have disgysed and appareld theym...in such manner that they sholde nott be knowen and divers of theym in a Companye togeder namyng them selfe Mummers have commyn to the dwellyng place of divers men of honor and other substanciall persones; and so departed unknowen."[33] It seems clear that disguise is linked here with a hiding of identity that permits potentially disturbing social trespassing, allowing inferiors to masquerade as the equal of their superiors and so enter unrecognized into their homes.

But the function of disguise in popular festivities is too complex to be limited to one meaning. In some instances, such as in court disguisings or in the Newfoundland mummings, which continue today, the concealing of identity is the central feature of the festivities, and a final unmasking is an essential part of the ritual. Yet on other occasions disguise may work in exactly the opposite way, not to conceal the self but rather to call attention to and enhance the identity of the performer, as is the case in some recent English folk dramas.[34] I would like to pursue this line of thinking in relation to mummings and morris dances in order to propose that the drag and blackface used in them could work not just to conceal identity but also to display and flaunt it. Moreover, concealing identity and displaying it need not be seen as opposed or mutually exclusive behaviors but rather can be understood as aspects of the same fluid process of the production of the laboring-class male body and through it a certain kind of subjectivity. Perhaps, then, we can say that part of what was being restricted by those seeking to regulate drag and blackface was a laboring-class masculinity that alternately veiled and unveiled itself, employing the discourses of femaleness and blackness to produce itself according to its own (outlawed) terms. It need not seem odd that this display of an outlaw masculinity also and necessarily involved the stealthy hiding of identificatory signs by which hegemony might recognize and punish it. In this way subterfuge and flamboyance can be taken as related moves in the same game of identity construction. As one identity is put on display, another is shunted aside and hidden.

The use of drag and blackface in these festive performances offered access to important signs of alterity that could be creatively incorporated into this double-sided process of the concealing and displaying, the erasing and producing, of masculine selves. What is central to both is that they represent stark otherness in gender and racial terms. And it is this potent otherness that makes them so valuable in their work of laboring-class male identity construction. Natalie Zemon Davis has amply described the transgressive power of "femaleness" that male cross-dressers invoked when they put on women's clothing in a festive or rebellious context. Given medieval European assumptions of female inferiority and woman's association with disorder, the wearing of female clothing allowed men to tap into a powerful symbolics of sexual inversion and to descend into a netherworld of de-masculinized behavior. Davis recounts a notable number of rebellions from the sixteenth through nineteenth centuries that involved men dressed as women (and wearing blackface, too, though Davis does not consider what meanings that usage might have had). In part, Davis argues, these disguises were a form of "practical concealment" that were "readily at hand in households rarely filled with fancy wardrobes." But Davis also makes clear that impersonating a woman was a useful tactic for a man interested in resisting authority: cross-dressing freed men from full responsibility for their deeds while also allowing them to draw on the sexual power of the unruly woman, thereby sanctioning riot and civil disobedience.[35] In a festive context, it was thus not only permissible but even empowering for men to dress as women. Becoming female could effectively remake males into powerful new selves, man-woman figures that evaded normal binary gender distinctions and hence resisted forces that had traditionally evolved to conscript and contain each separate sex.

An important issue that Davis does not address, however, is what happens to status when men cross-dress as women. In medieval Europe a woman who wore men's clothing was not considered abnormal since it was assumed that by dressing like a man she wished to become more manly and hence "better" herself. Tolerance of female cross-dressing thus depended on notions of male superiority and female inferiority that were common in medieval scientific and philosophical discourse.[36] A woman's status was enhanced when she "became" a man. But for men to dress as women was quite another matter. Since it entailed an implicit status reversal, a descent into the abnormal that came from a deliberate choosing of inferior female status, cross-dressing men looked distinctly strange. Men who cross-dressed as women were in fact often stigmatized, and their behavior was associated with status loss.[37]

Cross-dressed men in mummings and morris dances exploited this association of femaleness with inferiority, not just in Davis' sense that they used it to evade full responsibility for their actions but as a means of overdetermining and hence highlighting their own (inferior) status. From this perspective, drag can be seen as a performative gesture that calls attention to rather than conceals the status of the men who wear it. In this way tropes of gender positioning were used to frame challenges to status positions. Becoming a woman, even if only temporarily, could thus work within the festive context to bring masculine status issues to the foreground. One way in which the act of wearing drag in mummings and morris dances functioned, then, was to make visible the underlying logic of the larger social and economic order in which laboring-class men looked more like women than like (upper-class) men. Less powerful, less free, less fully in charge of the labor of their own bodies, laboring-class men were subjected to the demands of elite males in a way that was analogous to the general female-to-male relationship. It is perhaps worth noting in this context that civic prohibitions and other forms of social regulation such as sermons repeatedly link women and apprentices together in one category, a linkage that appears to express hegemonic male attitudes towards them as a similar set of unruly subjects. Drag could thus become a flamboyant gesture—a sign of excess, unruliness, and the grotesque—that protested the predicament of laboring-class males—look at us, we're like women—while also licensing momentary rebellion against the social strictures that encircled them.[38]

This collapsing of gender and status difference is made apparent in sixteenth-century attacks on theatrical cross-dressing, which have been thoroughly interpreted in terms of their meaning for the sex-gender system but have not been examined for their relevance to status.[39] In this rather typical passage from Stephen Gosson's *Playes Confuted in Five Actions* (1582), however, gender and status deviance are clearly connected: "in Stage Playes for a boy to put one the attyre, the gesture, the passions of a woman; for a meane person to take vpon him the title of Prince with counterfeit porte, and traine, is by outwarde signes to shewe them selues otherwise then they are, and so with in the compasse of a lye."[40] Whether it involves a boy dressed as a woman or a plebeian as a prince, the transgression of gender and status lines is understood as deceptive, a masking of true identity, a social lie. Perhaps something similar is implied in fourteenth-century documents from Beverley that carefully encourage the male actor to "represent" rather than "be" the female character he plays, thereby avoiding the chance of falling into a similar act of identity shifting and social deception.[41]

The use of drag in morris dances and mummings could thus work to hide the male performer's identity, in effect protecting him from the consequences of his actions and therefore, somewhat paradoxically, allowing him more fully to act out his image of himself—as man-woman, as outsider, as other, as outlaw. Wearing drag could free the male performer from the confines of his usual social position, making room for the re-imagining of an alternate laboring-class masculinity.

Though similar in its workings, blackface in medieval festivities is a more ambiguous performance practice and representational category than drag. It is also more elusive for us, in part because any racial valence to it has been consistently downplayed or rejected by scholars. In their defense, it does seem clear that blackface had more than just a racial force. In fact a range of meanings were available in the Middle Ages for interpreting the act of face blacking within a festive or theatrical context. It could be understood as impersonation of the dead, as it seems to have been understood by early maskers. It could be taken as *sordidatio...faciei*, or a mark of dirtiness, as it was often taken to be by the church or in the folk play character of "Dirty Bet." It could signify devils or Satan, who in medieval iconography were usually depicted with blackened faces. It could represent wickedness and evil or identify souls damned to hell.[42]

When employed in plebeian festivities like mummings and morris dances, blackface is often rather benignly assumed to have been a form of convenient disguise that used burnt cork or shoe-polish as readily-available masking devices, or in the view of many folklorists, a traditional village custom deriving from primitive fertility rites.[43] Evidence also suggests, however, that "blackness"—and hence blackface—could be understood in explicitly racial terms. Most relevant is the frequent association of geographic, ethnic, and racial labels with blackness. The term "ethiope"—referring to a distinct racial group from a specific geographic region—was frequently used to describe devils and Satan, who were charred when they fell from heaven. Hoccleve, for instance, has a dying man see fiends, whom he describes as "blake-faced ethiopiens," lying in wait for his soul.[44] References from the sixteenth century make it clear that the English equated "Moors" with African "blacks"; [45] the commonly used term "blackamoor" witnesses to this synthesis. Blackface could thus be used to depict Africans or Moors, such as the *Moreskoes* of court masquings. On Shrove Tuesday in 1510, for example, Henry VIII and two ladies dressed in "turkish manner" with faces and arms blackened so that they seemed to be "nygrost or blacke Mores."[46] When Queen Anne commissioned Ben Jonson to write her first court masque, she asked specifically for something that would allow her and her ladies to dress as "Blackamoors"; Jonson obliged with *The Masque of Blackness* (1605).[47] This courtly conceit of blackness was nothing new, historians say, but was instead part of a long-standing interest in impersonating black characters.[48] This fascination with blackness points to an awareness of racial difference as well as to an interest in appropriating and playing with those exotic signs of otherness.

Morris dancing is specifically linked with these discourses of blackness through its name, though the derivation of both the name and the dance it identifies remains unclear. In the early eighteenth century there seems to have been a general belief that morris dance, also called the *morisco*, was a moorish dance imported from Spain. Even though no concrete evidence of the morris-moorish connection exists, it might possibly be true, Keith Chandler claims, given early ties between the English and Spanish courts.[49] E. K. Chambers, however, hypothesized just the reverse: that morris dancers' faces "were not blackened, because the dancers represented Moors, but rather the dancers were thought to represent Moors, because their faces were blackened."[40] Whichever way around it was, a link in the popular imagination between morris dancing and blackness understood as racial difference seems to have been established from a fairly early period.

In the case of mummings, the only direct evidence I am aware of that indicates a racial understanding for the use of blackface comes from eighteenth and nineteenth-century mummers' plays, which usually feature a Sambo or Turkish knight character who wears blackface. Whether those characters derive from earlier performance conventions is difficult to say. In other nineteenth-century mumming groups, all of the performers wear blackface, which is presumably closer to the late medieval practice but once again a racial meaning cannot be identified with certainty. Given the connection of mummings with morris dances, however, and the morris association with racial otherness, it seems not too far-fetched to assume that a similar sense of racial difference informed at least in part the practice of face blacking in mummings as well as in morris dances.

Like drag, blackface—with or without an explicitly racial meaning—was associated with inferiority, unruliness, excess, and the grotesque. Just as drag could conjure up images of female unruliness, blackface could invoke the imaginative unruliness and excess broadly associated with the notion of "blackness." Like femaleness, blackness was seen as a form of excess that revealed itself in outlandish bodily movements, noisy music, boisterousness, lavish drinking and eating, and unbridled sexual appetite. Frequently, the power of "blackness" centered on bodily display and on manliness and involved themes of vulgarity and grotesqueness. Though they do not explicitly mention blackface, early modern commentators in fact insisted on viewing the morris dance as "grotesque," describing it as an outlandish series of contortions, leaps, kicks, and capers.[51] Perhaps the blackface of the morris dancers, their "diffourmyd or colourid visages," as one commentator put it,[52] intensified for these observers the sense that they were watching grotesque and unnatural behavior. Meg Twycross and Sarah Carpenter argue that while God, devils, and damned souls in mystery plays could wear masks or painted faces, on ordinary characters these features of costuming were always seen as grotesque and denoted evil or disfigurement.[53] If ordinary characters in mystery plays could not wear face paint and remain "normal," then what about the performers in morris dances and mummings? Did they, too, become grotesque by wearing blackface?[54] If they did, then their grotesqueness might have signified the rebellious power of bodily excess of the sort identified by Mikhail Bakhtin, an uncontrollable vitality that refuses to be subdued or show obedience to authority.

Blackness was also associated with other kinds of bodily excess. As Edward Said has pointed out, Mohammed has been a sign for sexual and moral depravity since the Middle Ages.[55] The blackamoors that were being imitated by Henry VIII and Queen Anne were thus likely opening up the way to a certain amount of aristocratic sex play, licensing erotic behavior that might otherwise have been forbidden. By James I's time, the excesses of the court had in fact become widely perceived as "oriental" and were explicitly linked to the racial otherness of blackness.[56] Thus tropes of "Eastern" disorder and abandon mingled with the discourse of blackness as grotesque excess to create possibilities for deviant forms of behavior or to give a name to licentious acts.

Blackness in late medieval England was also a sign of lower status, hence normally intransigent and needing to be subdued by an order grounded on (white) male, aristocratic privilege. Like femaleness, blackness could be seen as a mark of innate inferiority, whether in racialized terms or as a sign of dirtiness, corruption, and evil.[57] In romances like *Aucassin et Nicolette* and the *Roman de Silence*, the aristocratic heroines cross-dress as men and blacken their faces in order to disguise themselves by inverting the visible signs of gender and status difference. In the case of Nicolette and Silence, wearing blackface helped them fabricate a lower status, thus aiding their masquerades and providing them with a temporary escape from their social positions, which enabled them to satisfy their desires. In the case of laboring-class mummers and morris dancers, blackface might like drag have signaled the men's status, calling attention to rather than hiding their inferior socioeconomic position. In this way blackface could have served double duty: presenting the mummers and morris dancers to themselves as they really were—socially and economically marginalized—and to their more prosperous observers as they imagined them to be—dirty, miserable, and inferior.

Through all of these associations, blackface seems to have expressed a fascination with alien difference, representing an opportunity to put on an alien (and alienating) identity. Putting on an identity marked by the sign of blackness, blackfaced mummers, and morris dancers would have been tapping into a powerful set of alternate identities produced by blackness' associations with excess, the grotesque, and inferiority. The cultural meanings of blackface thus seem to overlap considerably with the meanings of femaleness: both are powerful signs of radical alterity that for laboring-class men could mask as well as flaunt their identity.

It is also important for discerning the masculinity produced in mummings and morris dances that blackface and drag were privileged terms for a specifically criminal or outlaw masculinity tied to poaching. Poaching has in fact more than a little significance for the outlaw masculinities performed in mummings and morris dances. Barbara Hanawalt has demonstrated the role of poaching in reinforcing male gender identity. Like lawful hunting, poaching contributed to male bonding, forging masculine social ties and strengthening local alliances and loyalties.[58] Hunting also had an explicitly sexual meaning that poachers could invoke and play with, as in the case of poachers who stole foresters' horns and, in one instance, cut off a buck's head and left it with a spindle in its mouth, a sexual insult drawing on gender inversion and using the quintessential sign for femininity—the spindle.[59] Poaching gangs or fraternities were popular social organizations and involvement in them could spill over from other leisure pastimes, such as drinking.[60] Poaching was also widely associated with other forms of criminal activity, especially among the lower classes. In the first Game Law of 1389-90, Richard II's government forbade hunting by servants and artificers because it was assumed to be for them a cover for conspiracies and an encouragement of disorder.[61] More importantly, poaching could be an elaborate performance, enacted on the stage of the woodlands and forests, that allowed its participants to make a statement that was often more spectacular than criminal. As theater, it could serve as a stand-in for duels and the settling of personal affronts or supply a place for protest against unpopular political or economic policies.

If poaching, like hunting, can be seen as political theater that provided a chance to display power,[62] then the use of drag and blackface in it become privileged theatrical gestures. Drag and blackface were in fact key aspects of poaching activities. Records of the County of Kent in the late fourteenth century refer to the practice of poachers "blacking" their faces and by 1485 deer hunting while disguised or at night was made a felony.[63] So widespread was the practice of blackface that poachers became known as "Blacks," their faceblacking made a capital offense in the eighteenth-century Black Act.[64] Female dress was also sometimes used by poachers. In 1523–24 John Turner, underkeeper of the Royal Park of Quernmore, complained that the deer stealers hired men "disguised in women's apparel" to ambush and murder him.[65] Given that venison was associated with feasting and incidents of deer poaching thus increased before Christmas, Easter, and Whitsuntide,[66] one wonders how much slippage there was between the use of drag and blackface by the mummers and morris dancers who would have taken part in those seasonal festivities and by poachers seeking venison for the same festivities. They might well have often been the same men. As Alexander Barclay claimed in the early sixteenth century when he attacked the practice of masking, people disguise themselves as (black) devils in order to do the devil's work at Christmas, Easter, or Whitsuntide—and certainly from the point of view of someone like Barclay the devil's work could encompass mumming and morris dancing as readily as poaching.[67]

Once again, I wish to stress that the drag and blackface used by poachers should not be taken just as disguises but rather as performative acts that made and unmade criminal identity, enabling the men who started off drinking in the village ale-house and then joined in a poaching raid on a nearby forest to reshape their identities from law-abiding citizens to criminals and back again. Like the drag and blackface of seasonal festivities, poachers' theatrical disguises were not just masking devices that worked to conceal identity, though they might well have done that in part; instead, they were also deliberate gestures that announced a powerfully altered masculine identity.[68] As such, drag and blackface were meant *to be looked at.* They were purposefully intended to call attention to the men who wore them, to make those men visible. It is suggestive that when blackface apparently became too common or ordinary for both poachers and mummers, they responded by painting their faces not black but white, as did the eighteenth-century gang led by a poacher called King John, or black and white, as did the Luddite mummers in the nineteenth century.[69] The substitution of white for black face-paint strongly insinuates that blackface was a recognizable performance act, one that signified a kind of threatening and flamboyant masculinity but that if overused or watered down by imitators could lose its dramatic impact.

Part of what the use of blackface and drag by poachers indicates is a desire for an exoticized, otherized, "black" masculinity that, like femaleness, is specifically designed to be looked at, to attract attention, and to become the object of the gaze. A number of recent film studies have explored masculinity as spectacle, adopting and to some extent reversing the terms set by Laura Mulvey's influential essay on male spectators and female objects, asking how the issues of identification, looking, and spectacle that she poses apply not just to images of women but to images of men and to the male spectator.[70]

What happens, these critics ask, when not just femininity but also masculinity becomes a spectacle? One result, they claim, is that masculinity comes to be seen not as a fixed essence but as always and necessarily a masquerade that involves the putting on and off of costumes and roles. Desire and identification as a consequence become multiple and fluid, taking many forms and transgressing fixed social and gender roles. The upshot is a continual confusion of subject and object that denies neat patterns of either identification or voyeurism along gender, racial, or status lines and so destabilizes subjectivity; most films, however, work to contain those fractured identifications within socially acceptable frames.[71] In the case of medieval mummings and morris dances, masculinity was similarly shown to be a masquerade, a choice of costumes and roles that were, however, heavily regulated and controlled by the performance context; hence, a self-constructed laboring-class masculinity remained relegated to the more or less acceptable space of seasonal play.

However circumscribed, the spectacular masculinity of mummings and morris dancing nonetheless succeeded in directing attention to otherwise unnoticed male bodies, using the discourses of femaleness and blackness to raise laboring-class male bodies to the level of visibility while also reformulating the terms under which hegemony liked to see those bodies. No longer malleable, docile, obedient, and lawfully hard-working but now irrepressible, disruptive, and engaged in quasi-unlawful actions, the laboring-class male body produced in seasonal festivities effectively escaped the boundaries set for it. As Richard Dyer has argued, the body is always problematic for capitalist societies, since to recognize embodiment fully means recognizing that capitalism is fueled by exploitive labor performed by bodies. As a consequence, the body has to be culturally contained, for instance, reduced to the purely sexual or dispersed into discrete parts by medical discourse.[72] In mummings and morris dances, male bodies resisted forces of containment, adopting powerful symbols to display themselves while also hiding the signs of their everyday identities in order to avoid recognition and punishment. Thus questions of identification and "knowing" were at the heart of the drag and blackface used in mummings and morris dances. In these performances a "new" masculine identity was produced, displayed, and "known" in contrast to the docile laboring body produced on a daily basis by late medieval social and economic structures.

In a discussion of blackface minstrelsy, Eric Lott has argued that "blackness" has been necessary to the process of constructing white American manhood, which "simply could not exist without a racial other against which it defines itself and which to a very great extent it takes up into itself as one of its own constituent elements."[73] Although in rather altered ways and within a different cultural context, late medieval males employed blackness to construct their own identity. As Davis has observed, for a man to cross-dress as a woman was literally, for a time, to become female, to put on the antithetical (non-rational, grotesque, sexually voracious) qualities that were understood by males to constitute femaleness. Blackface provided access to similar tropes of cultural otherness and deviance. Morris dances and mummings reveal how late medieval laboring-class men "lived" their maleness, producing it through and on their bodies. In these male rituals of violence, quasi-criminality, and demonstrations of bodily vigor, which employed plots (such as courtship or combat) based on male mastery over the bodies of women and of other men, laboring-class men performed their self-created and deviant identities in the face of the cultural presence of class superiors who sought to restrict these expressions of transgressive masculinity. The racial and gender parodies of morris and mumming with their purloining of tropes of femaleness and blackness aided this process of identity production.

Can we also imagine that in these performances interracial and intergender solidarity was briefly achieved? Perhaps so. As Kobena Mercer has argued in an analysis of Robert Mapplethorpe's photography of black males, the fetishization of racial difference can be a potential deconstruction of whiteness.[74] In this way the fetishizing of femaleness and blackness in mummings and morris dances might also have worked to break down a monolithic white-European masculinity. But drag and blackface in late medieval seasonal festivities also must have worked to exercise control over subversive cultural forms (women and blackamoors) while also invoking the power associated with such forms. In order to contain the dangerously transgressive power they called forth, such performances also had to make femaleness and blackness "disappear," to direct attention away from the real subjects whose signifiers men were borrowing. Put simply, male fantasies of women (and black men) undergird the subject positions men occupy and the subterranean qualities that give maleness its shape constantly require policing. Morris and mumming thus must have reinstituted the gap between male and female, white and black, while also briefly closing it in order to exploit it. Drag and blackface were raced and gendered practices that sought to internalize the imagined attributes of cultural others, but devices to control the threat of female and black bodies included the return to a normative order at the end of the festive occasion.

It has become something of a cliché to say that identity is performative. But clichés can be true. If, as Judith Butler has said, "there is no performer prior to the performed," then one lesson of mummings and morris dances is that they did not just feature laboring-class men, they *produced* them.[75] In that production, I have been arguing, drag and blackface played crucial roles, providing access to powerful sites of cultural alterity. What mummings and morris dances also teach us is that, to quote Butler once again, identity always "runs the risk of becoming *de*-instituted at every interval."[76] It is easy to see why these festivities, repeated with ritualistic regularity season after season, were perceived as assaults on the docile masculinity favored by hegemonic forces, always threatening to de-institute it and replace it with a wilder masculinity. Perhaps the ultimate threat of these festivities, however, was that they foregrounded the performative nature of subjectivity, reminding even hegemony that its preferred version of laboring-class masculinity was itself at best a counterfeit, a performance, a disguise.

NOTES

1. For a discussion of theatrical cross-dressing, see Meg Twycross, "'Transvestism' in the Mystery Plays," *Medieval English Theatre* 52 (1983): 123–80; for a discussion of face-painting, see Meg Twycross and Sarah Carpenter, "Masks in Medieval English Theatre: The Mystery Plays 2," *Medieval English Theatre* 3 (1981): 69–113, esp. 89–90, on the use of blackface.

2. *Coventry: Records of Early English Drama*, R.W. Ingram, ed. (Toronto: University of Toronto Press, 1981), p. 181.

3. See the Drapers' Accounts of 1572, *Coventry: REED*, p. 259. Twycross and Carpenter, "Masks," 71, note that devils' faces were traditionally black. For the costuming of souls, see Meg Twycross, "More Black and White Souls," *Medieval English Theatre* 13 (1991): 52–63.

4. In the *Records of Early English Drama* volumes, information about blackface is indexed under "Make-up"; references to cross-dressing have to be sought under "Costume."

5. See H. L. Douch, "Household Accounts at Lanherne," *Journal of the Royal Institution of Cornwall*, n.s. 2 (1953), 27–29. A bit later, a will dated 1458 refers to a cup "sculptos cum moreys daunce"; see PRO, Prerogative Court of Canterbury, Stokton 24–25 (1458), cited in Keith Chandler, *'Ribbons, Bells and Squeaking Fiddles': The Social History of Morris Dancing in the English South Midlands, 1660–1900* (London: Hisarlik Press for the Folklore Society, 1993), p. 42.

6. John Forrest and Michael Heaney, "Charting Early Morris," *Folk Music Journal* 6 (1991): 169–86; as Forrest and Heaney note, these phases should be seen as highly speculative, given the scarcity of historical references for the earliest periods.

7. The word mumming is said to derive fom the Dutch momme and Danish mumme, meaning "disguise oneself with a mask," but the performance was also known by many other names; see Alan Brody, *The English Mummers and Their Plays* (London: Routledge, 1970), p. 4. For the different names given the folk performance known as mumming, see E.K. Chambers, *The English Folk-Play* (Oxford: Clarendon Press, 1933), 4–5. For a discussion of aristocratic (indoor) mummings, see Glynne Wickham, *Early English Stages, 1300 to 1660*, 2nd ed. (London: Routledge and Kegan Paul, 1980), pp. 191–228.

8. E.K. Chambers, *The Mediaeval Stage* (Oxford: Oxford University Press, 1803), 1:249–73; Joseph Strutt, *Sports and Pastimes of the People of England* (London: Chatto and Windus, 1876), pp. 238–39.

9. See Brody, *English Mummers*, pp. 14–16.

10. See Chambers, *Mediaeval Stage*, pp. 393–99.

11. See the plays collected in the early years of the twentieth century by R.J.E. Tiddy, *The Mummers' Play* (Oxford: Clarendon Press, 1923) and the analysis of the three broad types nf mummers' plays in Brody, *English*

Mummers. The T.F. Ordish collection (housed in the English Folk Lore Society Library at the University of London) contains over 600 versions of the mumming plays. Charles R. Baskervill, "Dramatic Aspects of Medieval Folk Festivals in England," *Studies in Philology* 17 (1920): 19–87, sees beheadings in sword dances and St. George plays as end of old and welcome of new year rituals (34).

12. An engraving after a picture by Pieter Brueghel, depicting a village *Kirmess*, shows how a whole complex of festive activities, including dancing, eating and drinking, wrestling, a Sword Dance, and a St. George play, could overlap on one occasion; the engraving is reproduced following p. 204 in Chambers, *English Folk-Play.*

13. In 1377, for example, disguised mummers (identified by John Stow as 130 men from the "Comons of London") rode on horseback to pay a Christmas visit to Richard II, playing a game of dice with him (rigged so that Richard would win), drinking, dancing, and then returning to London; see John Stow, *A Survey of London*, ed. William J. Thoms (London: Chatto and Windus, 1876), p. 37. See also the mummings written by John Lydgate to be performed either for the king or for the mayor of London, in *The Minor Poems of John Lydgate*, Henry N. MacCracken, ed., EETS os 192 (London: Oxford University Press, 1934). In the seventeenth century, the monarchy underwrote a whole program of co-optation of "traditional" festivities for political purposes; see, for example, James I's *Book of Sport*, popularly known as the "morris book," which tried to revive the old games.

14. See Chandler, *'Ribbons, Bells and Squeaking Fiddles,'* pp. 42–47.

15. For a history of the Philadelphia mummers, see Charles E. Welch, *Oh! Dem Golden Slippers* (New York: Thomas Nelson, 1970). Susan G. Davis, *Parades and Power: Street Theatre in Nineteenth-Century Philadelphia* (Philadelphia: Temple University Press, 1986), pp. 113–53, describes the role of parades and ceremonies in working-class Philadelphia. For discussions of the Newfoundland mummers, see the essays in *Christmas Mumming in Newfoundland: Essays in Anthropology, Folklore, and History*, Herbert Halpert and G. M. Story, eds. (Toronto: University of Toronto Press, 1969).

16. For an analysis of the way twentieth-century Italian-American *feste* operated as alternatives to the world of ill-paid and dangerous immigrant labor, see Robert Orsi, *The Madonna of 115th Street: Faith and Community in Italian Harlem, 1880–1950* (New Haven: Yale University Press, 1985). Orsi's arguments are useful for considering late medieval performances.

17. See Chandler, *'Ribbons, Bells and Squeaking Fiddles,'* p. 115.

18. For instance, Yves-Marie Bercé, *Fête et révolte: Des mentalités populaires du xvie au xviie siècle* (Paris: Hachette, 1976); Sandra Billington, *Mock Kings in Medieval Society and Renaissance Drama* (Oxford: Clarendon Press, 1991); Natalie Zemon Davis, *Society and Culture in Early Modern France* (Stanford: Stanford University Press, 1975); and Emmanuel le Roy

Ladurie, *Carnival in Romans: A People's Uprising at Romans, 1579–80*, Mary Feeney, trans. (New York: G. Braziller, 1979). With specific regard to mummings, see Tom Pettitt, "'Here Comes I, Jack Straw': English Folk Drama and Social Revolt," *Folklore* 95 (1984): 3–20; and Norman Simms, "Ned Ludd's Mummers Play," *Folklore* 89 (1978): 166–78, which discusses the Luddite riots of the early nineteenth century, and his earlier "Nero and Jack Straw in Chaucer's *Nun's Priest's Tale*," *Parergon* 8 (1974): 2–12, which considers the relationship between folk drama and the uprising of 1381.

19. See Billington, *Mock Kings*, p. 15.

20. See Charles Phythian-Adams, *Desolation of a City: Coventry and the Urban Crisis of the Late Middle Ages* (Cambridge: Cambridge University Press, 1979), p. 176.

21. See the discussion of this and other English festive rebellions in Pettitt, "'Here Comes I,'" 3–8.

22. *The Historical Collections of a Citizen of London*, James Gairdner, ed., Camden Society, n.s. 17 (Westminster: Printed for the Camden Society, 1876), 108; quoted in Chambers, *Mediaeval Stage*, 1:395–96.

23. *Selected Records of the City of Norwich*, W. Hudson and U.J.C. Tingay, eds. (Norwich, 1906), 1:340; discussed in Billington, *Mock Kings*, 18–20.

24. *Memorials of London and London Life: A Series of Extracts from the Archives of the City of London, 1276–1419*, H. T. Riley, trans. and ed. (London: Longmans, Green, 1868), pp. 193, 534, 561, 669; also see Chambers, *Mediaeval Stage*, 1:393–94.

25. 3 Henry VIII, c.9; cited in Chambers, *Mediaeval Stage*, 1:396.

26. *Coventry: REED*, p. 8.

27. See Heaney and Forrest, "Charting Early Morris," 172–74.

28. Henry Burton, *Divine Tragedie*, 29; quoted in David Underdown, *Revel, Riot, and Rebellion: Popular Politics and Culture in England, 1603–1660* (Oxford: Clarendon Press, 1985), p. 67. Phillip Stubbes, *The Anatomie of Abuses*, 4th ed. (London: Richard Jones, 1595), describing plays and festivities, similarly complains: "Was there ever less obedience in youth of all sorts, both menkind and womenkind, towards their superiors, parents, masters, and governors?" (pp. 109–10). Underdown interprets these attacks as part of a widening gap between the prosperous and the poor; the Injunctions of 1559, for example, limited Rogationtide processions to property owners, whose circumambulation of parish boundaries could be seen as affirming—not challenging—property rights (*Revel*, pp. 47–8).

29. Michael Heaney, "Kingston to Kenilworth: Early Plebeian Morris," *Folklore* 100 (1989): 88–104 and 248–49. Around this time, morris dance was increasingly described as "grotesque"; not until the revaluing of folk culture that began around 1870 was the word "grotesque" replaced by "quaint" in commentaries; see Chandler, '*Ribbons, Bells and Squeaking Fiddles*,' p. 209.

30. The popularity of the Maid Marion character seems to have developed after 1510; it is unclear whether or not earlier morris dances featured a female character. The early seventeenth-century painting of morris dancers on the banks of the Thames at Richmond by the Flemish artist David Vinckeboons shows one dancer dressed as a woman; see the description in Chandler, *'Ribbons, Bells and Squeaking Fiddles,'* p. 6. The female characters are known by various names in the surviving mummings: Besom Bet, Molly Tinker, Bessie Brownbags. A female character also plays a role in most of the Sword Dance and Wooing Ceremony plays; see the discussion in Brody, *English Mummers*, pp. 99–104 and Tiddy, *Mummers' Play*, pp. 76–77.

31. Tiddy argues that the morris fool, the Doctor's man, Beelzebub, the fool of the mummers' plays, the clown of the sword dance, and the devils and vices of moralities and Interludes "are all, by dint of their mischief or their black faces or their fooling, ultimately one and the same" (*Mummers' Play*, p. 113). Brody describes nineteenth-century mumming costumes as varied: some include men dressed as women, and a blackface Sambo character (at Minehead, Somerset); the Marshfield Paper Boys wear shredded paper in a wild man costume—which Richard Southern, *The Seven Ages of the Theatre* (New York: Hill and Wang, 1961), p. 38, compares to an African medicine man. Brody argues that the traditional costumes' purpose seems to be "the simple purpose of disguise" (*English Mummers*, p. 24). In the mummers' play from Longborough, Gloucestershire, acted as late as 1905 or 1906, all the performers blacked their faces, while in the version from Burghclere, Hampshire, only the Turkish knight blacked his face; see Tiddy, *Mummers' Play*, pp. 180, 185.

32. See Chambers, *Mediaeval Stage*, "Winter Prohibitions," 2:290–305. Drag and blackface are also linked in modern mummings and morris dances, most prominently in the Philadelphia Mummers' parade (where blackface was finally banned in the 1960s). A photograph from the early years of the twentieth century shows four Philadelphia mummers in female dress and blackface; reproduced in Welch, *Oh! Dem Golden Slippers*, p. 64.

33. 3 Henry VIII, c.9; cited in Chambers, *Mediaeval Stage*, 1:396.

34. See the discussion in Pettitt, "'Here Comes I,'" 14.

35. Zemon Davis, "Women on Top," *Society and Culture*: 124–51; the quotations are from 149–50.

36. See the discussion of this issue in Vern L. Bullough and Bonnie Bullough, *Crossdressing, Sex, and Gender* (Philadelphia: University of Pennsylvania Press, 1993), pp. 46–51.

37. Bullough and Bullough, *Crossdressing*, pp. 60–61.

38. In this context, see the discussion of insurrections involving "masterless men" and "apprentices" (a term that included not just apprentices but also servants, vagrants, discharged soldiers and sailors, and boys) in Roger B. Manning, *Village Revolts: Social Protest and Popular*

Disturbances in England, 1509–1640 (Oxford: Clarendon Press, 1988), pp. 157–219. Apprentice rioting was associated with Shrovetide (during the years 1606–41) and Midsummer; see Manning, *Village Revolts*, p. 192.

39. For a concise summary of these interpretations, see Jean E. Howard, *The Stage and Social Struggle in Early Modern England* (London: Routledge, 1994), pp. 159–60, n. 2.

40. Stephen Gosson, *Playes Confuted in Five Actions* (London, 1582; New York: Garland Facsimile Reprint, 1972), sig E 5r.

41. Quoted in Twycross, "'Transvestism' in the Mystery Plays," 152.

42. See Twycross and Carpenter, "Masks," 89–90.

43. Or, in the words of E. K. Chambers, *Mediaeval Stage*, 1:199, "the primitive custom of smearing the face with the beneficent ashes of the festival fire."

44. *Hoccleve's Works: The Minor Poems*, F. J. Furnivall and I. Gollancz, eds., revised J. Mitchell and A. I. Doyle, EETS es 61, 73 (London: Oxford University Press, 1970), pp. 671–9; quoted in Twycross and Carpenter, "Masks," 71.

45. See William Torbert Leonard, *Masquerade in Black* (Metuchen, N.J.: Scarecrow Press, 1986), pp. 127–28. Leonard's book provides a history of theatrical blackface in England and America, beginning with Shakespeare's *Titus Andronicus and Othello.*

46. Edward Hall, *Hall's Chronicle* (London: Printed for J. Johnson, 1809), pp. 513–14.

47. Chambers, *The Elizabethan Stage* (Oxford: Clarendon Press, 1923), 1:196, cites an unnamed contemporary writer who judged the blackface and blackened arms of this performance to be an "ugly sight."

48. See Anthony Gerard Barthelemy, *Black Face, Maligned Race: The Representation of Blacks in English Drama from Shakespeare to Southerne* (Baton Rouge: Louisiana State University Press, 1987), p. 20. Kim F. Hall reads Jonson's masque as a sign of "a renewed fascination with racial and cultural differences and their entanglements with the evolving ideology of the state"; see her "Sexual Politics and Cultural Identity in *The Masque of Blackness: The Performance of Power: Theatrical Discourse and Politics*, Sue-Ellen Case and Janelle Reinelt, eds. (Iowa City: University of Iowa Press, 1991), p. 3.

49. See Chandler, *'Ribbons, Bells and Squeaking Fiddles,'* p. 10.

50. Chambers, *Mediaeval Stage*, 1:199.

51. These descriptions are eerily close to what early nineteenth–century commentators in the United States said about the dances of blackface minstrels; see Eric Lott, "'The Seeming Counterfeit': Racial Politics and Early Blackface Minstrelsy," *American Quarterly* 43 (1991), 230.

52. *Memorials of London*, 669; quoted in Chambers, *Mediaeval Stage*, 1:394 n. 3.

53. Twycross and Carpenter, "Masks," 96.

54. Suggesting that there was an explicit link between blackface and the grotesque, Chambers observed that there is reason to believe that the morris was a form of grotesque court mask; see Chambers, *Elizabethan Stage*, 1:194–95:

55. Edward Said, *Orientalism* (New York: Random House, 1979), p. 62.

56. Kim Hall, "Sexual Politics," p. 13.

57. See Winthrop Jordan, *White over Black: American Attitudes toward the Negro, 1550–1812* (Chapel Hill: University of North Carolina Press, 1968), pp. 11–20.

58. Barbara A. Hanawalt, "Men's Games, King's Deer: Poaching in Medieval England," *Journal of Medieval and Renaissance Studies* 18 (1988): 175–93.

59. Described in Hanawalt, "Men's Games," 190–91.

60. Roger B. Manning, *Hunters and Poachers: A Social and Cultural History of Unlawful Hunting in England, 1485–1640* (Oxford: Clarendon Press, 1993), 160–62. Also see his "Poaching as a Symbolic Substitute for War in Tudor and Early Stuart England," *Journal of Medieval and Renaissance Studies* 22 (1992): 185–210.

61. 13 Richard II, st. 1, c.13.

62. As Manning argues in *Hunters*, pp. 54–55.

63. *Kent Records: Documents Illustrative of Medieval Kentish Society*, F. R. H. du Bouley, ed. (Kent: Kent Archaeological Society, 1964), p. 217, pp. 254–55; see the Game Act of 1485 (1 Henry VII, c.7).

64. The Black Act is reproduced in Appendix I of E. P. Thompson, *Whigs and Hunters: The Origin of the Black Act* (New York: Pantheon, 1975), pp. 270–77; Thompson points out that the Act treats "blacking" itself as a capital offence.

65. Manning, *Hunters*, p. 51. See also the cross-dressed turnpike rioters at Ledbury in 1735, discussed in Thompson, *Whigs and Hunters*, pp. 256–57.

66. See Hanawalt, "Men's Games," 180, and Tiddy, *Mummers' Play*, p. 21. Tiddy claims that at a mumming at Leafield a licensed deer hunt was also held.

67. *Shyp of folys* (London: Richard Pynson, 1509), f. ccxlv^{r}; cited in Twycross and Carpenter, "Masks," 80.

68. See the similar argument about the Luddites in Simms, "Ned Ludd's Mummers Play," 172.

69. For the first example, see Thompson, *Whigs and Hunters*, p. 145; for the second, see Simms, "Ned Ludd's Mummers Play," 171.

70. See, for example, Steve Neale, "Masculinity as Spectacle: Reflections on Men and Mainstream Cinema," *Screening the Male: Exploring Masculinities in Hollywood Cinema*, ed. Steven Cohan and Ina

Rae Hark (London: Routledge, 1993). Laura Mulvey's essay "Visual Pleasure and Narrative Cinema" first appeared in *Screen* in 1975.

71. See Carol Clover, "Her Body, Himself: Gender in the Slasher Film," *Representations* 20 (1987): 187–228. John Ellis, *Visible Fictions* (London: Routledge and Kegan Paul, 1982), p. 43, argues that the viewer identifies with all the available subject positions—villain, hero, heroine, bit player, etc.

72. Richard Dyer, *Heavenly Bodies: Film Stars and Society* (New York: Macmillan, 1986), esp. p. 138.

73. Eric Lott, "White Like Me: Racial Cross-Dressing and the Construction of American Whiteness," *Cultures of United States Imperialism*, Amy Kaplan and Donald Pease, eds. (Durham: Duke University Press, 1993), p. 476. See also Natalie Zemon Davis, "Women on Top," *Society and Culture*: 124–51.

74. Kobena Mercer, "Skin Head Sex Thing: Racial Difference and the Homoerotic Imaginary," *New Formations* 16 (1992): 1–23, esp. 12.

75. Judith Butler, "Imitation and Gender Insubordination," *Inside/Out: Lesbian Theories, Gay Theories*, Diana Fuss, ed. (New York: Routledge, 1991), p. 24.

76. Butler, "Imitation and Gender Insubordination," p. 24.

NORMATIVE HETEROSEXUALITY IN HISTORY AND THEORY: THE CASE OF SIR DAVID LINDSAY OF THE MOUNT

R. James Goldstein

Goldstein argues that a historicist reading of Judith Butler helps us map the poetic career of Sir David Lindsay in terms of early modern constructions of heteronormative masculinity.

Sir David Lindsay of the Mount (c. 1486–1555), the most important vernacular poet of the decades leading to the Scottish Reformation, offers a unique glimpse of a world in transition. His career unfolded during a period of unprecedented trauma as medieval ideologies and institutions were losing their political grip and cultural authority in sixteenth-century Scotland. Although previous scholars have examined his work in the context of the political and theological conflicts of his time, they have paid little attention to the relations among power, gender, and sexuality that pervade his work. Yet from his earliest court poetry to the three major works of his final years Lindsay is conspicuously preoccupied by proper definitions of gender and the regulation of sexual desire.[1]

The following account of Lindsay's career seeks to exploit the tense relation between psychoanalytic and historicist theories of the construction of sexuality and gender; here Judith Butler's two recent books provide the main theoretical reference point.[2] Before turning to Lindsay's writing, I briefly sketch Butler's complex and challenging theoretical work, focusing on the relatively undeveloped but nonetheless important historicist dimensions of her argument.[3]

Both *Gender Trouble* and *Bodies That Matter* share the assumption that psychoanalytic theory offers the most sophisticated account available of how bodies assume the status of subjects, an assumption that I also wish to entertain here (*GT,* 28; *BM,* 24). The more recent book, however, thoroughly revises her earlier concept of gender as performance in an effort to avoid the voluntaristic implications that troubled many critics of her earlier work. In *Bodies That Matter*, she retains the Foucauldian thesis that power is *productive* of sexuality rather than that which simply *represses* it.[4] But now Butler recognizes the need for a more rigorous definition of "performativity," which she partially derives from Derrida's notion of iterability, or the instability and endless repeatability of a citation without an original (*BM*, 13, 95). Performativity can no longer be mistaken for an individual "act" analogous to an actor's donning a mask or performing a role, though it "acquires an act-like status in the present" by concealing "the conventions of which it is a repetition." Butler thematizes Derrida's iterability in Lacanian terms, moreover, to reveal the non-singular or sedimented nature of a given "act." The foreclosed status of performativity implies that the theatrical analogy is misleading because the "apparent theatricality [of performativity] is produced to the extent that its historicity remains dissimulated (and, conversely, its theatricality gains a certain inevitability given the impossibility of a full disclosure of its historicity)."[5]

To explain how the regulatory fictions of heterosexual norms reproduce themselves over time, Butler stresses the necessarily phantasmatic mirroring involved in identity formation.[6] In Butler's revised notion, gender is not an ontological essence but a continuously unfolding citational practice through which the materialization of the sexed body takes place; the failure of a body to assume its "proper" gender marks its exclusion from cultural intelligibility within the terms defined by hegemonic regulatory schemas. Yet if the pathways by which gender is produced, if the ways in which sex is "materialized" through the forced reiteration of gender norms, are not fully determined in advance (*BM*, 95), we may wonder to what extent the morphology of the sexed and gendered body is subject to historical contingency and variation.

A close reading of both *Gender Trouble* and *Bodies That Matter* suggests that Butler by no means assumes that the subject's assumption of gender is unvarying throughout all of history. Yet if Butler assumes the historicity of the processes that differentiate "bodies that matter" from those that are repudiated, abjected, or unliveable, the space she allows to historical change, I suggest, is not capacious enough to perform the theoretical work that she appears to assign it, though her more recent book insistently moves further in that direction.

Gender Trouble hints at the "historical variability" of the symbolic law that fixes "the phantasmatic content of identity" in the unconscious:

> As opposed to the founding Law of the Symbolic that fixes identity in advance, we might reconsider the history of constitutive identifications without the presupposition of a fixed and founding Law....It seems important to consider that the *meaning* that the law sustains in any given historical context is less univocal and less deterministically efficacious than the Lacanian account appears to acknowledge. (*GT,* 66–67)

Yet Butler's gesture toward the cultural and historical variability of the strictures of the law and the multiple identity formations it puts into play may leave us with more questions than it resolves. What are the limits of its variability? What counts as significant historical change from this psychoanalytic perspective? In her discussion of Gayle Rubin's "The Traffic in Women," Butler observes: "That systems of compulsory heterosexuality may alter, and indeed have changed...seems clear" (*GT,* 75). Her acknowledgement of an unspecified plurality of heteronormativities should leave a historicist reader with a series of further questions: How many "systems" have there been in the history of the West? Have multiple systems coincided at a given moment? Can a single body be the site of a multiplicity of heteronormative systems whose "proper" origins are historically differentiated?

If Butler occasionally delineates a theoretical space for historical variability in the earlier work, such questions occupy even more of her attention in *Bodies That Matter*. The "regulatory schemas" at work in producing the identifications of the bodily ego "are not timeless structures but historically revisable criteria of intelligibility" (*BM,* 14). Anticipating the objections of an imagined historicist interlocutor, she stresses that her analysis of a variety of discourses from Plato to the film *Paris Is Burning* should not be misinterpreted: "The historical range of materials is not meant to suggest that a single heterosexualizing imperative persists in each of these contexts" (*BM,* 16). The ability of language to fix stable, sexed positions for the bodily ego in the way that Lacan presumes, she suggests, "depends upon the permanence and fixity of the symbolic domain itself" (*BM,*

138). At this point Butler cites an allied theorist for an argument against the common interpretation of "the Lacanian symbolic as static and immutable."[7] Whatever we wish to make of Brennan's complex and learned thesis, for the present purpose it is worth stressing that Butler's citational practice reserves the marginal space of a note for her most detailed consideration of the historicity of the symbolic.

In the chapter that pays the closest attention to the vicissitudes of history, "Arguing with the Real," Butler distinguishes her theory of performativity from the voluntarist versions with which it is sometimes confused: "the reading of 'performativity' as willful and arbitrary choice misses the point that the historicity of discourse and, in particular, the historicity of norms...constitute the power of discourse to enact what it names" (*BM,* 186). She thus attributes a significant role to the historicity of prescriptive norms, the historically contingent nature of the productive function of power. Yet she does not subject the historical variability of norms to further investigation for reasons we might describe as our current disciplinary regimes of knowledge. (In a later note, Butler will defend philosophical abstraction from accusations of "presentism" when she renders illicit any move toward "prescribing that all philosophy become history"[*BM,* 282, n. 8]). Butler emphasizes the importance of not viewing "the law or regulatory mechanisms of foreclosure" by which we emerge as coherent subjects "as ahistorical and universalistic" lest we imagine that "the law" somehow might be "exempted from the discursive and social rearticulations that it initiates" (*BM,* 190). If the law were to enjoy such an exemption, she claims, what are only "*contingent* regulatory mechanisms of subject-production may be reified as universal laws, exempted from the very process of discursive rearticulation that they occasion" (*BM,* 191; my emphasis). Butler thus insists that there is no "preideological 'law,' a prediscursive 'law' that works invariantly throughout all history" (*BM,* 206). In short, she insists on the *historicity* of the phantasmatic identifications through which sex and gender construct themselves to appear stable and fixed instead of revealing themselves as a non-teleological series of reiterations.[8] Yet if her politics depend on admitting historicity to her argument, her theory postpones a more rigorous definition of *significant* historical contingency, one with real consequences to how bodies that matter have been materialized in the past or might be materialized differently in the future. That is, Butler only gestures toward history as an endlessly expanding theoretical horizon but one that in the end risks being nearly devoid of specific content.[9] Or perhaps it would be fairer to say: she has, as it were, handed her readers an indispensable theoretical map, pointed us to the terrain of history, and invited us to discover what paths we may.

***

To the general question, then, posed by this volume: What were the historical contingencies of becoming male in the Middle Ages? For Sir David Lindsay, there can be no doubt that *the body that matters most is the body of the king*, which in the phantasmatic identifications of the medieval and early modern periods assumed the double morphology of the king's two bodies. Of all the catastrophes that Scotland endured during Lindsay's career—decades of intermittent war, plague, famine, political and religious upheaval—perhaps none is harder for us to imagine than the trauma of living for twenty-eight years without an adult sovereign. Indeed, a recent book identifies the precariousness of Stewart succession as the most formative influence on Lindsay's political outlook.[10] Drawing on Edington's valuable work, I wish to rethink her traditional analysis of power in terms of heteronormative sexuality and gender and the patriarchal regimes such a regulatory matrix enables even, or most especially, when its operation seems nearly invisible because it is everywhere taken for granted.

We might begin with Lindsay's later recollection of his intimate contact with the young body of the future James V. Shortly after Lindsay enters the surviving historical record in service at the royal court (probably as early as 1508) he appears as usher to the infant heir apparent in 1512.[11] He seems to have retained the position after the death of James IV at Flodden the following year. As usher Lindsay thus had a special relationship with the body natural of the king. Surviving records from 1517 to 1523 describe him variously as Keeper of the King's Grace, Usher, Master Usher, Gentleman of the Bedchamber of the King.[12]

Lindsay remained active in the administrative and ceremonial office of Master Usher until his dismissal late in 1524 when a new struggle for control of the government began.[13] After the death of

James IV the governorship fell to John, Duke of Albany, who despite being a resident of France had become heir presumptive to the throne with the accession of James V. Margaret Tudor, the dowager queen and sister of Henry VIII, was excluded from the government, ostensibly for undertaking a disastrous brief marriage with Archibald Douglas, sixth earl of Angus, less than a year after James IV left her a widow.[14] By July 1524, however, Margaret Tudor was allied with James Hamilton, Earl of Arran, who seized power from the Albany government. In the factional struggles that tore apart a highly dysfunctional royal family, possession of the body of the adolescent king functioned as a unique signifier of legitimate rule.[15] Within a few months the possession of the king's person and control of the government passed to the Douglas faction led by Archibald Douglas, Earl of Angus, Margaret's estranged second husband. But in 1528 the sixteen-year-old monarch finally escaped captivity and declared himself fully sovereign.

Once again Lindsay returned to his activities at court. His earliest surviving poetry dates from the first years after James's rise to power and seeks to contribute to the education of the young king. Although Edington usefully places Lindsay's writing in the context of medieval kingship literature, she is uninterested in how *The Dreme* and *The Complaynt* place special emphasis on the regulation of heterosexual desire or the proper gendering of the royal body and the regime of power it enables.[16] Yet these topics remained a constant concern not only in his early court poetry but in his more nationally directed works of the 1550s written during the minority of the absent Queen Mary.

The special nature of Lindsay's service as royal usher created an intensely personal relationship that included a physical intimacy between the adult male and the infant king to which *The Complaynt*, written about 1529–30, directly alludes. Writing shortly after his return from his exile from court, the poet looks back nostalgically to his early physical and emotional bond with the young sovereign, reminding the newly empowered adolescent monarch of their previous happiness. The loyal servant hopes for reward, recalling the former period "Quhen I lay nychtlie be thy cheik" (80). His idealization of James's childhood as a time of innocent play—I am tempted to say *jouissance*, but *whose* enjoyment seems less certain—suggests how the poem performs the work of mourning by incorporating the lost object of an imaginary object relation: "I bure thy grace vpon my bak, / And, sumtymes, strydlingis on my nek, / Dansand with mony bend and bek [dip and jump]" (*Complaynt*, 88–90). This remarkable scene seems to present a chiastic mirroring: the body mystic of the sovereign offers an ego-ideal for the identity formation of subject (in both the political and psychoanalytic senses of that word) while the adult offers an ego-ideal to the body natural of the child-king. It is worth noting that Lindsay was later crowned Lyon King of Arms, the highest heraldic office in Scotland, and may have participated symbolically in "a quasi-royal aura."[17]

Among the crossings the remembered scene of childhood presents, however, we might pause momentarily before the spectacle of a small boy's legs astraddle the neck of a grown man who bounces him rhythmically in play. Let me hasten to make it clear: I am not suggesting that there is anything overtly sexual in this description of innocent horsing around. Yet such an insistence on reading these body pleasures as "innocent" only confirms Butler's point that normative heterosexuality is necessarily constructed on or rather through the prior prohibition against homosexual desire.[18]

When Lindsay plays the role of surrogate father to the royal infant, then, it is more than a literary fiction; it is also a lived one. As one of only a handful of adult male figures in close proximity to the fatherless boy, the royal usher was symbolically possessed of the phallic signifier during the boy's identity formation. Thus Lindsay places himself at the scene of the king's first speech act, claiming that the syllables of his own name stand in for the Name of the Father: "The first sillabis that thow did mute / Was *pa, Da Lyn*" (88–92).

In Butler's revisionary reading of Lacan, the symbolic sexes the subject by exerting pressure and defining limits through "a series of demands, taboos, sanctions, injunctions, prohibitions, impossible idealizations, and threats—performative speech acts, as it were, that wield the power to produce the field of culturally viable sexual subjects" (*BM*, 106). The continued force of these prohibitions depends on the iterability of the constitutive norms of psychic development, which have no ontological status apart from a series of repetitions or citations. Butler thus argues that Lacan's account of the incest prohibition, which is supposedly put into place and reenforced by an imaginary threat of castration, depends on what for Lacan remain unexamined heterosexual norms but which for Butler need not be mistaken for a fixed universal law.

In short, unless we are prepared to believe that psychoanalysis describes a historically invariable process, we cannot predict in advance whether the assumption of a sexed position in the royal court of sixteenth-century Scotland must follow the same trajectory it would in a modern bourgeois household. Even had his father survived his infancy (the boy was under two years old at the time of his father's death), surely the child-rearing practices of the late-medieval household would limit the role James's real father might play in his identity formations. If the cultural work performed by Lindsay's *Complaynt* is to cite and interpret "the law" in the ways Butler describes, we should locate within the Stewart court itself the specific nexus of familial and political power which dictated to James V the heteronormativity he was compelled to reiterate as sovereign.

In the elaborately organized hierarchy of the royal household, symbolic authority was necessarily distributed along multiple pathways. The poem thus reenacts a struggle over who may exercise authority over the pre-adolescent king. Lindsay describes the "suddand cheange" (126) that took place in 1524 when the new government effectively kidnapped the twelve-year-old king. *The Complaynt* focuses on the threat this crisis posed to the training of the young king's virtue when his new guardians remove him "frome the sculis, / Quhare he, vnder Obedience, / Was lernand vertew and science" (132–34). They prematurely place "the gouernance of all Scotland" in his incapable young hands (136). Interrupting his formal education, the guardians offer dangerous sports and frivolous pastimes instead (175–85). Lindsay expresses particular concern for the adolescent king's sexuality in a vividly imagined dialogue among the king's guardians, who try to outdo one another in their offers of sexual enticement to his young majesty. One man offers a lusty Fife lass; another knows of a much fairer one in Linlithgow (which the audience recognizes as the site of a royal palace). Language itself begins to break down in this phantasmatic imagining of moral dissolution: "Now trittyll, trattyll, trolylow" (245), says the third man, who offers a lass of Stirling (another locus of royal power). But the fourth man outbids the rest: "'Schir,' quod the fourt, 'tak my counsall, / And go, all, to the hie boirdall. / Thare may we lope [i.e., copulate] at lybertie, / Withouttin ony grauitie'" (249–52). Lindsay, the young man's legitimate figure of authority, can do nothing to prevent the king's moral dissolution because the royal usher is no longer welcome at court, finding himself "trampit doun in to the douste" (256). Yet by the time Lindsay composes his *Complaynt*, these threats to sovereign virtue have nearly subsided as the poet celebrates the king's successful government now that "thow to no man art subiectit" (377).

The moral corruptions that threatened the young king in *The Complaynt* should remind us that in the highly theologized discourse of sexuality in pre-Reformation Scotland, not all practices of heterosexuality qualify as "normative." The vision of hell presented in a slightly earlier poem known as *The Dreme of Schir Dauid Lyndesay* makes this point even more graphically, as the persona observes kings who failed to cite heterosexuality properly and are damned "for publict adultrye and incest" (249). Women are condemned to eternal punishment for their "adultrye" (272), "lychorye" (278), and "prouocatyue impudicitie" (279). Given this context, it is important to recognize that Lindsay's closing exhortation to the king, which reiterates the need to cultivate the cardinal virtues, takes for granted the successful installation of heterosexual desire but with the insistence that it must be practiced within the bounds of lawful marriage if the Stewart lineage is to be preserved without contamination: "keip thy body clene," he implores the unmarried sovereign, "tyll that thow get ane lusty, plesand Quene: / Than tak thy plesour, with my benesoun" (1095–96). The stanza links the king's sexuality with the health of the body politic by tracing the destruction of the Roman kingship to Tarquin's rape of Lucretia.

Concern for the proper governance of bodily pleasures, for the dangers posed by unconstrained sexuality, forms an ongoing concern in Lindsay's work. In his humorous reply to the king's lost flyting (c. 1535–36) he urges his sovereign's moral reformation by pointing to the self-destructive nature of the king's notorious sexual adventures. James continues "waistand" his "corps," running "royatouslie lyke ane rude rubeatour [libertine], / Ay fukkand lyke ane furious fornicatour" (46–49). Thus the excesses of improperly cited heterosexuality risk the destruction of the royal body and the failure to produce a legitimate heir for the nation.

The rhetorical climax of the poem narrates a sexual one, a memorable escapade when the king "caist ane quene [whore] ouerthort ane stinking troch [malting vat]" (53). This is not the kind of "queen" the poet had in mind when he composed *The Dream*! The sexual adventure turns into a mock infernal scene when the trough overturns, dousing the couple in the foul dregs as they are reduced to lying "swetterand [wallowing] lyke twa swyne" (58). Lindsay thanks God for preserving the king "from gut & frome grandgore" [venereal disease] (63), and warns him about too much "lawbouring of ȝour lance" (67).[19] The comic exposure that makes up the central narrative of the flyting, Lindsay's warning about improperly wielding phallic power, and his jokes about his own loss of sexual power ("I was better artailȝeit ['artilleried'] / Nor [than] I am now" [31-2]): all these provide a thinly veiled threat of castration by the surrogate father figure, whose chief concern is for James to produce a legitimate heir. This desire for legitimate offspring of the royal body was soon to be thwarted, as Lindsay records in his solemn *Deploratioun of the Deith of Quene Magdalene* (1537), when James's first wife, the sixteen-year-old daughter of the French king Francis I, died before she could even reach Scotland, before "we some fruct had of hir bodie sene" (28). The two sons by his second wife, Mary of Guise-Lorraine, died in their infancy. When James died in 1542, his one-week-old daughter Mary survived as the only legitimate heir.[20] For the rest of his life, Lindsay was to be haunted by the absence of a king.

***

By the time *Ane Satyre of the Thrie Estaitis* was first performed in 1552, the king had been dead for almost ten years. The play as a whole is concerned with the moral reformation of the individual and the body politic of the kingdom. The central figure of Rex Humanitas or King Humanitie is young and easily misled: his loose-living courtiers encourage his corruption by the voluptuous Dame Sensualitie and her ladies. When the King retires to his chamber with his lady and their followers, Gude Counsall appears, promising to wait until the King is ready for his guidance. The moral nadir of part one occurs when Sensualitie and Dissait [Deceit] place Veritie and Chastitie in the stocks.

Lindsay incorporates low comedy in many scenes of the play. The coarser moments present the materiality of the body in Rabelaisian excesses of eating, drinking, fucking (1371), shitting (4009), pissing (1926), and farting (2182). A dialogue between Diligence and Foly near the end of the play provides an especially powerful image of the grotesque female body when Foly describes how he left his wife at home "neir deid" (4372). Although too long to quote in full, Foly's phantasmatic account of his wife giving birth deserves our attention:

> Scho stumblit and stutterit with sic stends
> That scho recantit at baith the ends.
> Sik dismell drogs fra hir scho schot
> Quhill scho maid all the fluir on flot;
> Of hir hurdies scho had na hauld
> Quhill scho had tumed hir monyfauld! (4388-93)

She stumbled and stuttered with such leaps that she recanted from both ends. She shot such dismal excrement that she flooded the entire floor; she had no control over her buttocks until she had repeatedly vacated herself.

The passage graphically illustrates the experience of abjection, or (to quote Butler's memorable paraphrase of Kristeva) "the mode by which Others become shit" (*GT* 134). With his wife in a sorry state, Foly takes on the role of the good mother; according to the stage direction, "*Heir sal the bairns cry 'keck' lyke ane ke [jackdaw], and he sal put meat in thair mouth*" (4426). Within a few lines, however, Foly reminds the spectators that he is the possessor of the phallus, though it proves unruly when it springs to life after he notices an attractive lass in the audience:

> Me think my pillok will nocht ly doun— [penis
> Hald doun your head, ye lurdon loun! [stupid rascal
> Yon fair las with the sating goun [satin
> Gars yow thus bek and bend. (4438-41) [makes; bow and leap

As Butler argues, if the privilege of the phallic signifier is only gained through its reiteration, "there is nevertheless in the very force of repetition…the possibility of deprivileging that signifier" (*BM,* 89).

If the poet deploys an "exclusionary matrix" to produce "a domain of abject beings…who form the constitutive outside to the domain of the subject" (*BM,* 3), however, he positions himself ambiguously in relation to the law, which he reiterates even as he voices his defiance. On the one hand, Lindsay's obsession with the grotesque female body seems excessive even by the standards of medieval misogyny. On the other hand, these marginalized carnival elements represent comic inversions of the more serious subversions of authority in the play, at least some of which Lindsay finds attractive. *The Thrie Estaitis*, that is, calls for a thorough reformation of the church at a time when to violate certain taboos was to risk loss of liberty, property, even life. Although the Scottish parliament had legalized possession and use of vernacular Bibles in 1543, traditionalists found such reforms extremely threatening. The politics of vernacular literacy and education thus form an important theme in the play.[21] Flatterie, allied with the spiritual estate, identifies Ladie Veritie's possession of the New Testament "in Englisch toung, and prentit in England!" as "herisie" and calls for a fire (1152-55). A clerical figure specifically identifies Veritie as a Lutheran (1126) and warns that the spiritual estate "will burne yow, flesche and bones" (1143; cf. 2779–9; 2995–3000).

The immediacy of the topical allusions to recent executions of Protestants would not have been lost on the Cupar audience in 1552, who viewed the play only a few miles from the ecclesiastical court at St. Andrews that presided over heresy trials.[22] In short, the playwright reminds his audience that the subversive bodies on stage and in the audience are liable to burning by order of the church or hanging by the state in spectacular rituals of discipline and punishment. At the same time, the theatrical performance also dramatizes that every body is constrained to be a properly gendered one. Lindsay reiterates the masculine heterosexual norm that constructs the grotesque female body as abject in such figures as Sensualitie, the Sowtar's wife, and even the women in the audience who "list to pisch" [wish to piss] (1926).

Yet Lindsay's satire to some extent unconsciously enacts the limits of its own gender normitivity in ways that are at least potentially subversive, since it would appear from the available evidence that the female characters were actually played by male actors in drag. Although not all the surviving records have yet been collected or interpreted, no evidence for women actors taking substantial roles in urban (as opposed to court) dramatic productions has so far come to light for sixteenth-century Scotland.[23] If my assumption that the female characters were played by men or boys in drag is valid, then what Butler writes of the drag-queens in the 1991 documentary *Paris Is Burning* may have some bearing on Lindsay's patently misogynistic citations of early modern gender: "the queen will out-woman women, and in the process confuse and seduce an audience...who, through the hyperbolic staging of the scene, will be drawn into the abjection it wants both to resist and to overcome" (*BM,* 132).

The subversion of stable binary gender oppositions that drag represents, however, is ambiguous at best, as Butler suggests by recalling the murder of the film's transvestite star. If Lindsay's play suggests that gender performativity was more fluid, less fully under control than he imagined, the female body in sixteenth-century Scotland, subjected to masculine authority in domestic and private spaces, also tended to be a subjugated one.[24] Lindsay's play thus both predicts and helps secure a historic shift by which the aristocratic, bourgeois, and peasant classes of Scotland were to act in concert to regulate the patriarchal household, fully complicit with the political order of the Stewart absolutist state, once the structures of authority under the old church were finally replaced by Protestant ones.[25]

No study of Lindsay's citations of masculine heteronormativity would be complete without at least a brief glance at his long historical work, *Ane Dialog betuix Experience and ane Courteour*. In associating "laik of faith," "ydolatrye," "fornicatioun," and "adultrye" (67-68) as the cause of contemporary wars, plagues, famines, and the disruptions of a kingless monarchy, the poem assumes that politics, religion, and sexuality are mutually implicated. Here I will focus on the threat posed by the violation of sexual taboos.

In the account of the Fall, the Courtier asks why the serpent was punished if "beistis can no way syn at all" (1031); the reply is symptomatic of Lindsay's forcible reiteration of normative heterosexuality and its connection with the law: the serpent was Satan's instrument and was punished just as in the common law, when "ane man conuickit for bewgrye [buggery], / The beist is brynt [burned] als weill as he, / Quhowbeit the beist be innocent" (1043–45). With a phantasmatic slippage that may well be unprecedented, Lindsay takes the time to endorse burning sodomites in a discussion of the Garden of Eden! Although the first statute making "buggery" a felony in English law dates from 1533, sodomy never seems to have been criminalized by statute in Scotland. The most likely interpretation is that the canon law against sodomy and bestiality continued in force in the Scottish courts after the 1560 Reformation but was administered in secular courts.[26] Lindsay does not appear to have any specific case of sodomy in mind, however, because the earliest known prosecution (and execution) for sodomy in Scotland took place in Edinburgh in 1570.[27] In short, if the famous English anti-sodomy statute of 1533 was enacted as part of the larger political project of Henrician reform, which included the dissolution of the monasteries, the imbrication of sexuality and power would have been substantially different in Scotland during Lindsay's lifetime.

Lindsay traces the invention of sexual debauchery to before the Flood. When he attributes the corruption of blood that occurred when the sons of Seth mingle with the "ladyis of Caynnis kyn," taking them "in to mariage" (1221–1227), it is clear that not all sexual practices within heterosexual marriage are proper citations of heteronormativity. He leaves the specific acts vague because the truth is "abhominabyll" (1235). Men and women "abusit thame selfis vnnaturallye" in "vncouthe fornicatioun" (1236–38). Lindsay's use of preterition, the speaking while pretending not to speak, calls to mind Sedgwick's discussion of this homophobic trope.[28] Yet at least in part Lindsay is conspicuously refusing to mention abominable *heterosexual* practices. We must therefore revise Bray's claim that Lindsay here describes homosexuality, or that he holds it responsible for the Flood.[29] The "luste abhominabyll" (1322) that leads to the Deluge is a category without clear limits. Indeed, throughout the poem it remains unclear exactly what he means by (to recall Foucault's classic formula) "Sodomy: that utterly confused category."[30] Eventually the poem will fold idolatry into the category of illicit sexuality by linking "fornicatioun and idolatrye" (2669) in Old Testament fashion, though in the context of reformist propaganda "idolatry" includes many of the devotional practices endorsed by the Catholic church.[31]

Lindsay first introduces the "s" word in his account of the destruction of Sodom and Gomorrah, whose people "Unnaturally abusit thare kyndis, / By fylthie stynkand lychorie, / And most abhominabyll sodomie" (3399-3401). God's destruction of the cities on the plain recalls the previous act of divine vengeance against the general population, when God destroyed the world: "For that self syn of sodomye, / And most abhominabyll bewgrye. / That vyce at lenth for tyll declare, / I thynk it is nocht necessare (3472-75). Since sodomy had not yet become narrowly associated in the popular imagination with "the homosexual" as a distinct identity or orientation, the problem with sodomy for Lindsay is that anyone, at any time, may be seduced by its pleasures, as his prayer reveals: "Gret God preserue ws, in our tyme, / That we commit nocht sic ane cryme" (3528-29). Lindsay thus offers (to adopt Sedgwick's useful formulation) a universalizing view of homo/heterosexual definition when he implicates both himself and his audience in sodomitic possibilities.

At a time before sodomy became restricted to narrow definitions of same-sex genital behaviors in hegemonic phantasmatic identifications, even so homophobic a writer as Lindsay might add specific texture to the suggestive but underdeveloped historicist dimensions of Butler's theory. If the symbolic law of heteronormativity is not a universal one, a rereading of this culturally pivotal writer should help us understand that to become a (masculine) body that mattered in the early modern era was to cite the force of prohibitions and taboos that were not identical to those we must work through today.

NOTES

1. I quote from *The Works of Sir David Lindsay of the Mount, 1490–1555*, Douglas Hamer, ed., 4 vols., Scottish Text Society (Edinburgh and London: Blackwood & Sons, 1931–36) except for *Ane Satyre of the Thrie Estaitis*, Roderick Lyall, ed. (Edinburgh: Canongate Publishing, 1989); all citations appear parenthetically in the text by line number; I silently amend Hamer's punctuation and capitalization.

2. Judith Butler, *Gender Trouble: Feminism and the Subversion of Identity* (New York and London: Routledge, 1990) [abbreviated as *GT* in the text]; *Bodies That Matter: On the Discursive Limits of 'Sex'* (New York and London: Routledge, 1993) [abbreviated as *BM*].

3. My reading of Butler differs substantially from Caroline Bynum's in "Why All the Fuss about the Body? A Medievalist's Perspective," *Critical Inquiry* 22 (Autumn 1995): 1–33; see 27–31.

4. See *Gender Trouble*, pp. 2, 65, on Foucault's distinction between the juridical and productive models of power; cf. *Bodies That Matter*, p. 244, n. 6.

5. *Bodies That Matter*, pp. 12–13. See *Bodies That Matter*, p. 234 on Butler's distinction between performativity and performance.

6. See chapter 3 of *Bodies That Matter*, "Phantasmatic Identification and the Assumption of Sex," pp. 93–120.

7. *Bodies That Matter*, p. 271, n. 8, citing Teresa Brennan, *History after Lacan* (New York and London: Routledge, 1993).

8. Cf. Butler's note on Žižek (*Bodies That Matter*, p. 278, n. 5). In short, she wants to theorize the possibility of "arguing with the real" (as her chapter title formulates it).

9. Butler describes the task of considering "the full domain of constraints on sex and sexuality" as "limitless" (*Bodies That Matter*, p. 96).

10. Carol Edington, *Court and Culture in Renaissance Scotland: Sir David Lindsay of the Mount*, Massachusetts Studies in Early Modern Culture (Amherst: University of Massachusetts Press, 1994), p. 70.

11. Edington, *Court and Culture*, pp. 13–14.

12. Edington, *Court and Culture*, p. 17 and sources cited.

13. Edington, *Court and Culture*, pp. 21–22.

14. Edington, *Court and Culture*, p. 20.

15. Cf. Slavoj Žižek, *For They Know Not What They Do: Enjoyment as a Political Factor* (London and New York: Verso, 1991), pp. 19–20 on the king as *point de capiton*.

16. Edington, *Court and Culture*, pp. 71–88.

17. Edington, *Court and Culture*, p. 41.

18. See *Bodies That Matter*, pp. 98, 103, 109, 112–13. For a similar account of innocent man-on-boy bodily pleasures, see *The Dreme*, lines 8-11 in Lindsay, *Works*.

19. James V is recorded as fathering no fewer than nine illegitimate sons on his various mistresses; see Michael Lynch, *Scotland: A New History* (London: Century, 1991), p. 164.

20. Lynch, *New History of Scotland*, p. 164–65.

21. Lindsay calls for a vernacular Bible in *Ane Dialog betuix Experience and ane Courteour*, lines 538–684 in Lindsay, *Works*.

22. See Margaret H. B. Sanderson, *Cardinal of Scotland: David Beaton, c. 1494–1546* (Edinburgh: John Donald, 1986).

23. I am grateful to John J. McGavin of the University of Southampton for sharing his knowledge of the documentary evidence; cf. Edington, *Court and Culture*, pp. 65–66.

24. Cf. Lindsay's address in *Ane Dialog* (2693–2700), urging married men to prevent their wives and daughters from risking their virtue on pilgrimages.

25. In *Ane Dialog* Lindsay expresses his conviction that "all women, in thare degre, / Suld to thare men subiectit be" (1069–70).

26. I am grateful to Hector MacQueen, Professor of Private Law, Edinburgh University, for providing the information on Scots law in the above paragraph. For definitions of *ius commune* (common law), see Hector

MacQueen, *Common Law and Feudal Society in Medieval Scotland* (Edinburgh: Edinburgh University Press, 1993), pp. 2–3.

27. For a partial transcription of the record, see Robert Pitcairn, *Ancient Criminal Trials in Scotland* (Edinburgh: Bannatyne Club, 1833), vol. II, p. 491 n. 2, cited Alan Bray, *Homosexuality in Renaissance England* (London: Gay Men's Press, 1982), p. 124, n. 40 (citing incorrect volume). Professor MacQueen informs me that the only other recorded sodomy prosecution before the nineteenth century is from 1630, though prosecution of bestiality was more frequent. Pitcairn, *Ancient Criminal Trials*, II, p. 491, records one such case from 1605, describing a sentence that parallels the one Lindsay mentions for "bewgrye."

28. Eve Kosofsky Sedgwick, *Epistemology of the Closet* (Berkeley and Los Angeles: University of California Press, 1990), p. 202. Sedgwick (citing Bray) uses a different passage from the poem to illustrate the history of this homophobic trope.

29. Bray, *Homosexuality*, p. 26. Unfortunately his discussion of Lindsay's poem ignores his own caveat that homosexual acts by no means exhaust the meanings of the terms "sodomy" and "buggery" in the early modern period (p. 14). Cf. Sedgwick's sensible discussion of definitional issues (*Epistemology*, p. 155).

30. Michel Foucault, *The History of Sexuality: An Introduction,* trans. Robert Hurley (New York: Pantheon Books, 1978), p. 101.

31. Cf. the description of Rome as a "systerne full of sodomye" (4950). Bray, *Homosexuality*, p. 29 overestimates the centrality of antipapal rhetoric to the design of the poem; cf. Edington, *Court and Culture*, pp. 194–96.

ON BECOMING-MALE

Michael Uebel

Uebel offers a synthesis of the essays as they relate to the theme of spatialized identity: spaces actually offer men diverse possibilities for recomposing their existential corporeality and their social identity.

We all know the old conundrum: under what conditions, if any, can two bodies occupy the same space? But what is involved in imagining this possibility, other than its reverse, viz., the conditions under which two spaces can occupy (especially in the sense of "to maintain control over") the same body? The latter question seems to me the one motivating the present collection of essays. Together, the essays look at the various ways social, political, religious, sexual, linguistic, and economic spaces intersect to suspend momentarily the single (and singular) male body. Of course the masculine body in the Middle Ages never remains suspended, precisely because the spaces it inhabits are less the territories in which it resides than the fields through which it moves. Nor does the male body remain single or unitary. If the general psychoanalytic principle that humans are objects—just bodies—before they are subjects has any validity, then the "becoming-subject" of identity, which *takes place* as agency is acquired and autonomy discovered, offers the key to understanding how one person, some body, can be simultaneously the product of multiple and conflictive sites of meaning.

I draw attention in the previous sentence to the expression *takes place* in order to highlight the concept of space as highly mobile. It is chiefly through perceiving, manipulating, and symbolizing space that self-creation can take place—as in *happen*, *occur*, or *become*. Thus the poet Mallarmé's observation that "Nothing shall have taken place but place"[1] seems to exhaust those dimensions of space that become the necessary expressions of historical subject positions. We begin to trace how identities come into being only when we grasp the spaces in which identities circulate. The process of identities formation amounts to nothing less than a process of spatialization. "Identity," as Jacques Rancière has put it, "is not a matter of physical or moral features, it is a question of space."[2] But can such a formula contain the often-contradictory multiplicity of medieval ideas about medicine, natural philosophy, theosophy, and geography? I want to suggest that it might, if we consider the spatial contexts where male embodiment is represented, both inside and outside the body and in the very processes those spaces contain. Without claiming historical expertise in the areas of medieval learning I just enumerated, I intend to make two general points about how we might approach the notion of *becoming-male* in terms of its spatial characteristics.

The claim that subjectivity is solely the function of space may at first seem historically inaccurate, given, for example, the emphasis in medieval medical theory on physical attributes (complexion, physiological temperament, and shape) and on moral traits (embodied in the expected roles and behavior patterns corresponding to physical characteristics) as determinants of sex and gender identity.[3] Yet the belief that who you are is tied to where you live was dominant among late-medieval scientific scholastics. Thus, for example, Roger Bacon's statement on the intrinsic relation of geography to natural characteristics, which summarizes a long tradition of Western and Eastern views on the significance of place: "If [the latitude and longitude of every location] were known, man would be able to know the characteristics of all things in the world and their natures and qualities which they contract from the force of this location."[4] Circulating in a scientific tradition founded in Aristotle, extending through Pliny and Ptolemy, to Isidore of Seville and the Arabic scientist Mesue, and achieving its most acute articulation in the late-medieval scientists Bacon and Albertus Magnus, the belief that geography was destiny maintained a prominent place in thinking about identity, especially the identity of cultural "others." Bacon labeled place "the beginning of our existence"[5] because he felt location vigorously determined character and influenced appearance. As in Pliny and his Aristotelian sources, the "other" residing at the place of extremes—especially extreme temperature and humidity or vulnerability to astral influences—

was not only markedly different from but was culturally inferior to the medial or temperate.[6] Indeed, distance from the moral center of things placed such implicitly "masculine" attributes as bravery in battle and unflinching asceticism inevitably in question.[7]

In her reading of Rimbaud's early lyric "Rêve pour l'hiver" in terms of its promotion of "nonpassive spatiality," Kristin Ross conceives of the poem as a "true *invitation au voyage*," an appeal to reconceptualize space radically as movement, as becoming. The poem works, she argues, through an "invitation to conceive of space not as a static reality but as active, generative, to experience space as created by an interaction, as something our bodies reactivate, and that through this reactivation, in turn modifies and transforms us."[8] I find Ross's formulation necessary for rethinking the embodiment of subjectivity, that is, how we might imagine identity in a constant condition of material process or becoming rather than spatial rootedness, or how we might determine the social consequence of the very context in which the body is constantly re-creating itself. However, I would want to go a bit further to suggest that the interaction taking place between embodied subjects and spaces is not only an external, often overtly political one. Indeed, what Paul Schilder pointed out over sixty years ago, with respect to psychoanalytic considerations of the spatial dimensions of identity, applies just as well to current historical and theoretical considerations: namely, that researchers "have not given sufficient attention to the fact that there is not only a space outside of the body but also a space which is filled up by the body."[9]

In the first part of what follows I want to take a look at that part of space that is filled by the medieval male body, emphasizing how the motility of the human body itself establishes gender identity as a dynamic process, a *becoming-male* that is radically contingent and, as I will urge, quintessentially, if only fleetingly, private. In the second part, I glance at the spaces, several of which are thoughtfully examined in this collection, that confer upon medieval men a public orientation, an interanimating relation with the ideological spaces they inhabit.

SPACES WITHIN

> The *self* of the other is already within the 'same' that is not itself. It trembles through the 'same,' shudders through it so that all at once the 'same' gives way and finds itself determined. The other *transits*, or *entrances*, the 'same' and makes it come to pass.
>
> Jean-Luc Nancy[10]

As theoretically useful as the distinction between a private and a public male body may be, the division is in fact, historically speaking, somewhat problematic. For, as feminist inquiry reminds us, such a division has been ruthlessly pressed into the service of antifeminism, to legitimize a split between genders rather than a distinction between men. I refer to the multi-layered dichotomy of nature/culture, body/soul, madness/rationality, insufficiency/completeness, change/stasis, fragility/solidity, and so on. But such a set of familiar binarisms, we must remind ourselves, is more the legacy of the Enlightenment than of the Middle Ages. In an essay on the current critical interest in the body and its implications for medievalism, Caroline Bynum stresses that medieval thinking, art, and literature are not the dualistic practices and structures they are often taken to be, that in fact the body/soul split was neither strictly binaristic nor always reified in terms of an isometric gender division.[11] It would seem then that the Middle Ages offers us a particularly rich field in which to begin to explore the manifold meanings of embodied identity and the fluidity of subjectivity and difference that lie beyond polarity.

In my own focus on the medieval male body—a body that is, at least momentarily, private, given my concern with its interior processes prior to socialization—I mean to highlight a corpus recognizable as the "original space of human activity." Original, in the sense that the body contains, and sometimes fails to contain, the source of its sexual and social identity: all of the desires, motions, flows, and shifting humidities and temperatures (the mix of humors constituting a body's "complexion") that determine what a person will be like, what *he* will become. The norm for medieval personhood was defined—needless to say—as masculine: femininity was construed as imperfection, incompleteness, passivity, childishness, failure.[12] Considered as a discursive community, writers on the body—medieval academics, scientists, doctors, philosophers, theologians—focused almost exclusively on the male body and the movements of its desires. What often appeared to be discussions of the feminine, or even the more general human, condition turned out to be instead discussions of the masculine condition.[13] Yet in illuminating the differences between the sexes, later medieval writers found at their disposal a not fully coherent system of thought: Hippocratic, Aristotelian, Soranic, Galenic, Avicennic ideas were variously influential, often incompatible, but nevertheless possessed a certain degree of conceptual unity. This unity we might characterize as the belief that the body is the site for the production of its unique social (gendered) identity. The medieval body is not a passive entity shaped by a dominant seat of mind or reason but an ensemble of generative, even machinic, components creating and re-creating a particular social existence.

Medieval accounts of the body as a productive and creative one refocus our interest in gendered identities by underscoring the degree to which those identities are dependent upon the character of the body itself. If, as Jeffrey Cohen has written, "the personal body is a text across which is written a cultural narrative"[14]—and I believe in the Foucauldian sense it is—we must nevertheless work to correct the view that the body is only, even primarily, that which is written upon, inscribed, shaped and unshaped by dominant cultural codes. Social identity in the Middle Ages cannot only be related to nature, culture, or soul, but rather to an understanding of the possibilities of an individual's condition in its corporeal state.

Medieval men, despite the repeated assertion of their superiority and transcendence in learned texts (especially in terms of activity or force [L. *vis*; etymon of *vir*]), nevertheless were, like women, subject to categorical assumptions constraining the range of their corporeal activities. Indeed, the passive living of one's own political, social, or gendered identity is nothing short of an impossibility since thinking itself is dependent for its activity upon the state of one's corporeality.[15] We might begin, then, to investigate in medieval texts modalities of cognition that are gendered by virtue of their being embodied.

An example from fiction that illustrates how, and the extent to which, notions of what it means to be masculine are deeply imbricated with bodily productions is Chaucer's *Nuns' Priest's Tale*.[16] In the tale, Chauntecleer, our hypermasculine bird-hero, lord of his harem of "sevene hennes for to doon al his plesaunce" (2866), awakes one early morning from a frightful dream in which he sees a fox seize hold of him. When the rooster begins to groan rather than crow, Pertelote, his chief paramour, immediately berates him at some length for his cowardice:

"Avoy!" quod she, "fy on yow, hertelees!
Allas!" quod she, "for, by that God above,
Now han ye lost myn herte and al my love.
I kan nat love a coward, by my feith! (2908–11)
. . .
How dorste ye seyn, for shame, unto youre love
That any thyng myghte make yow aferd?
Have ye no mannes herte, and han a berd?
Allas! and konne ye been agast of swevenys? [*dreams*
Nothyng, God woot, but vanitee in sweven is.
Swevenes engendren of replecciouns [*arise from overeating*
And ofte of fume and of complecciouns, [*vapor from the stomach; mixture of humors*
Whan humours been to habundant in a wight.
Certes this dreem, which ye han met to-nyght,
Cometh of the greete superfluytee
Of youre rede colera, pardee.(2918–28)

Pertelote continues in this vein, skeptical that Chauntecleer's dream could be anything more than the result of his humoral condition, before prescribing for him a regimen of digestives and laxatives designed to purge his excessive cholera. Pertelote's diagnosis of Chauntecleer's "sickness" implies that cholera and masculinity are somehow inversely proportional. However, that Chauntecleer should be both hypermasculine and excessively choleric was considered perfectly natural.[17] Bartholomew the Englishman described the cock as a "ful bolde and hardy" fighter, naturally hot and dry of complexion.[18] The choleric body is an especially dynamic one, vigorously masculine in activity, "in miȝt and in lordschippe," the antithesis of the feminine phlegmatic body—cold, moist, and sedentary.[19]

But only the most fully masculine body is elusive: it cannot be known definitively since over time it is never identical to itself. Chauntecleer's humoral body, "ful coleryk of compleccioun" (2955), resists treatment, as Pertelote's manic overprescription of herbs (which would unhappily *increase* the cock's choleric condition) suggests, precisely because such a body invites a perverse kind of empiricism, one confusing "the distinction between diagnostics and intervention."[20] Pertelote's diagnosis and aggressive treatment elide the possibility that male "sickness" could be "an original and, in a certain sense, 'true' self-expression of the 'subject.'"[21] The cock's humoral condition is his definitive attribute: defining him as at once warlike, uxorious, jealous, regal, proud, valorous—together the qualities that make him truly "the barnyard epitome of the typical hero of epic and romance."[22] Indeed, on the one hand, Pertelote implicitly ridicules the idea that Chauntecleer's "greete superfluytee" of choler is anything but the momentary expression of his individual masculine comportment.[23] Yet, on the other, her knowledge of dream theory and natural science compels her to see only an "excessive" body, one therefore less masculine, in need of regulation and temperance.[24]

Bird or man, or bird-man, Chaucer's cock reminds us that medieval male bodies are spaces wherein particular social meanings are produced before they are given public expression. The cock's crow neatly symbolizes the subject's capacity to *body forth* an identity beyond its own bodily limits. From bodies are produced social scripts, narratives that harbor the potential to form relations and to convey identities: "My joly body schal a tale tell" (1185), announces Chaucer's Shipman in the endlink of *The Man of Law's Tale*.[25] Always noteworthy, the movement from the somatic to the social is, nevertheless, not always untroubled or ideal. As Vance Smith argues in his contribution, male bodies are intricately bound up with certain historical productivities, the avoidance or shortcircuiting of which constitutes treason against the natural body itself. In Smith's reading, both usury and sodomy are shown to be linked in dissolving the vital association of body and world, in stripping the outside world of its meaning, a meaning derived from the mechanics of the masculine *corpus* itself. Men create (in) the world because they are condemned to (Adam's curse), because their own materiality forms the necessary starting point for world-creativity.

Although a crucial starting point for becoming-male, the self-fashioning body can also be the reception point of processes well beyond its control. Perhaps there is no more graphic example of this subjection of the male body to the world, in this case its violent unmaking, than the mid-fifteenth-century "wound man" (see figure 1).[26] Here the lugubrious male body is depicted in the process of its undoing. Penetrated, lacerated, ulcerated, this un-becoming male body, like its oddly jubilant brother the "illness man" (see figure 2),

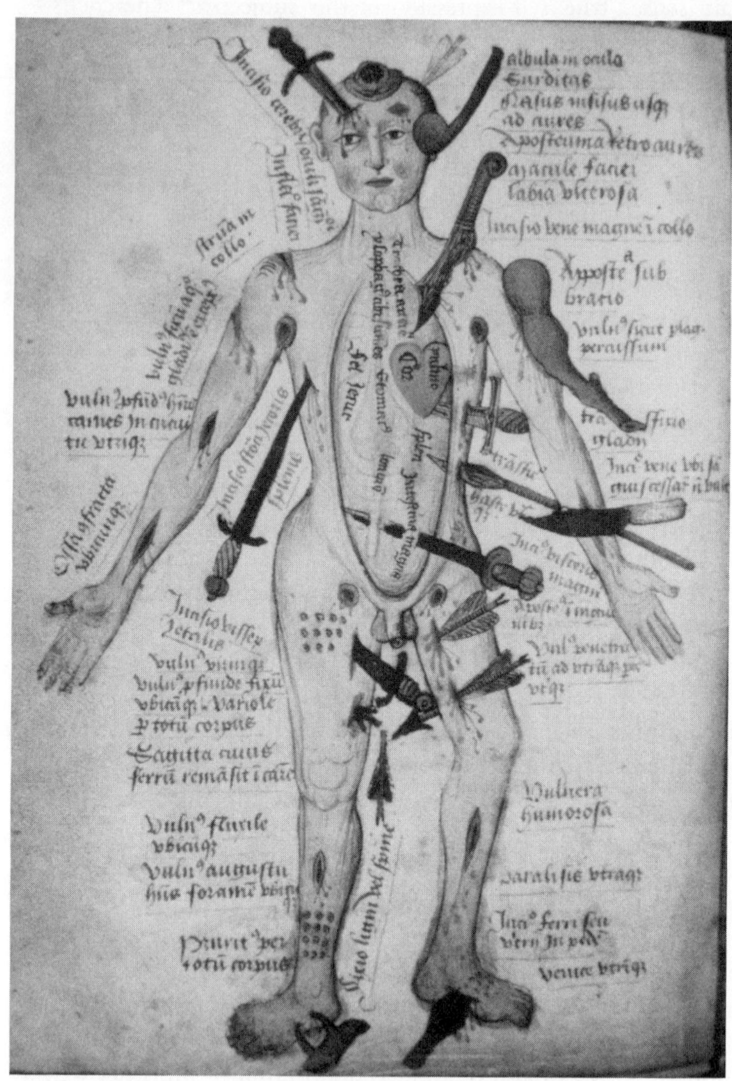

Figure 1. "Wound Man," Western MS 290, f. 53v (By permission of the Wellcome Institute Library, London).

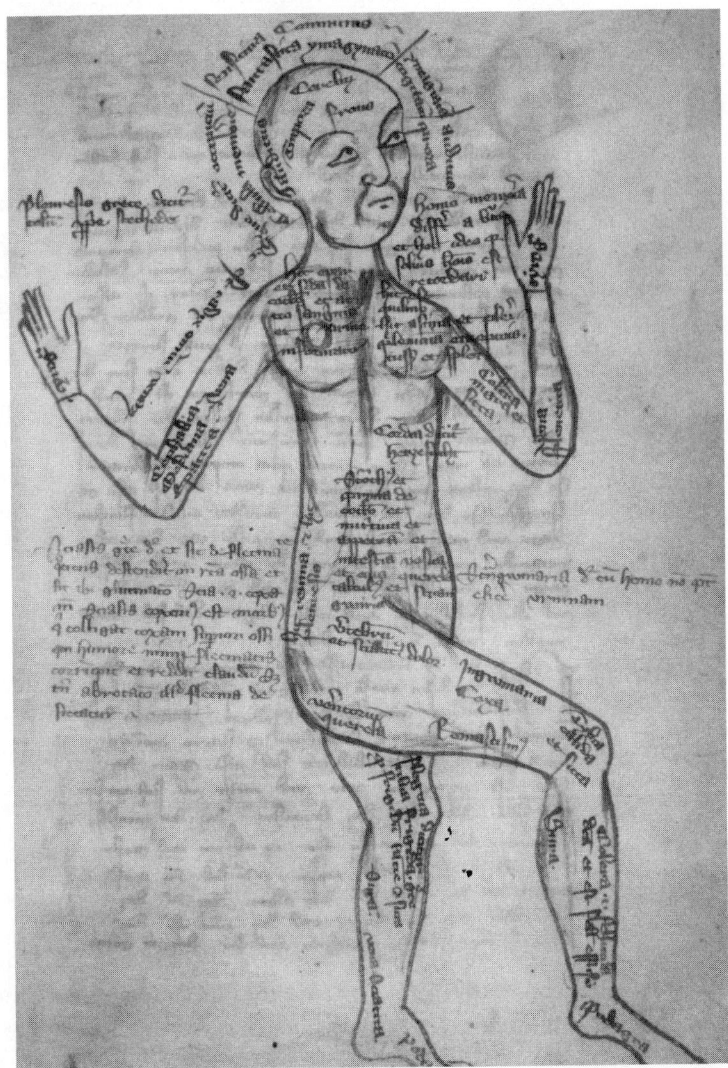

Figure 2. "Dancing Illness Man," Arundel MS 251, f. 37 (By permission of the British Library, London).

maps pain and disease across a bodily landscape, emphasizing not only the body's decomposition into local sites of (potential) agony but the body's systematic, integrative functioning. Male bodies are assemblages of dynamic parts, the proper preservation and ordering of which ensure a body's claim to dominance in the social sphere.

Indeed, the human body served as the ultimate guarantee of hierarchically organized society, from Plato's notion of the state as an organism (*Republic* 5.462d) through St. Paul's idea of the Christian community resembling a body to poetic expressions of "sacred anatomy" such as the Old English *The Ruin*, Grosseteste's *Le Chasteau d'Amour*, the *Sawles Warde* homily, and Passus IX of *Piers Plowman* (B text).[27] Given their profound link to the collective body, individual male bodies could be punished as sources of social disruption, as contributor Glenn Burger shows in his reading of Chaucer's *Miller's Tale*. Bodies in need of humoral rebalancing, Absolon's and Nicholas's are subject to a kind of "erotic discipline," a sadistic project aimed at restoring control over/in their bodies. However, the tale also constructs its own masochistic project, one that acknowledges the intractability of the bodily, its pleasurable mutability and liberatory heterogeneity.

If there is a body that is absolutely private, it is impossible to locate historically. For we are always reminded in our investigation of the specific meanings of "becoming-male" that bodies are never sealed microcosms, however much they are represented and represent themselves as such, but instead they open directly onto the changing cultural field. If the line between the somatic and the social is fuzzy, it is particularly so in the Middle Ages, a period of intermediacy, as Cohen and Wheeler suggest in their Introduction, in which body and *socius* come together to subsist in the course of their animation, their becoming. By invoking Jean-Luc Nancy at the beginning of this section, I wish to signal the difficulty of specifying the space that is uniquely a body's own. For into that space something other is incessantly fluttering, and though inherently nomadic it is arrested momentarily by the historian's fixative gaze (and hence marked in this collection as queer, boyish, non-Christian, animal, ironic, and so on). But it is the movement of alterity, the translation of other spaces (of gender, sexualities, religion, politics, commerce, animality), into the space of the subject that conditions identity as a state of continual becoming.

WITHIN SPACES

> Space does not become comprehensible to the subject by its being the space of movement; rather, it becomes space through movement, and as such, it acquires specific properties from the subject's constitutive functioning in it.
>
> Elizabeth Grosz[28]

Space and somatic subjectivity are mutually transformative and invigorating. Their interanimation means that neither bodies nor spaces can be passive for long, that stable subjectivity issues from switching back and forth between ideological perspectives: "It is our positioning within space, both as the point of perspectival access to space, and also as an object for others in space, that gives the subject a coherent identity."[29] Yet such stable positioning is never a given. Indeed, the essays in this collection suggest that the difficulties of placing oneself at the center of one's own space recur throughout the medieval literary tradition. Coherent identities, it would seem, were hard won. Never more so than for fringe elements of medieval society, those who were (out)cast as "objects for others in space": non-Christians, usurers, crossdressers, sodomites, eunuchs, animal-men, and so on. Such categories, we know, interpenetrate, so that, for example, religious alterity was construed on the basis of gender difference. Feminized in Western discourse, Jewish and Muslim men represented a threat to Christian virility, an assault upon the masculine "body-politic" of religious community. However, integration of these others, through conversion, into the Christian body-politic only served, as Steven Kruger argues, to exacerbate the "gender trouble" they originally represented. Despite the effects of religious realignment, Jewish and Islamic male bodies retained their essential alterity. That becoming Christian did not necessarily entail becoming properly male also suggests that notions of teleology, of a becoming male that must also become X or Y, do not apply to medieval bodies.

It is probably no surprise that discussions of the non-teleologically constructed body, a body both unified (an entity within space) and fragmented (possessing multiple spaces within), circulate most notably around questions of gender and sexuality. The contributors to this collection see conceptualizing male identities in their state of becoming as a compelling way to dismantle the conventional linkage of the categories sex and gender. Committed to freeing up moribund readings of medieval texts and culture, the collection offers fresh readings of medieval sexuality and gender as dissociated and in dynamic relation to one another. By opening up the space between sex and gender in her investigation of male drag and blackface performance in late medieval theater, Claire Sponsler shows an array of desires and cultural tensions both shaping and unshaping working-class male subjectivities. Furthermore, her essay on "outlaw masculinities" finds, in the interplay of normal and deviant masculinities, a space wherein subjectivity is rearticulated and reconfigured.

This space, I would suggest, is precisely the arena of all becoming, a "space of play"[30] belonging neither to the individual nor to the world but serving to keep those areas distinct. Here identity is ceaselessly negotiated, revised in relation to external reality and, more crucially, to other possible identities. A space of transition, of crossover, it envelopes the subject's own psyche and the immediate "contact zone" of his interpersonal existence. In other words, this zone of play delimits the subject by conditioning his perception of the porous boundary between inner and outer worlds, while effectively marking the outer (outlaw) spaces in which he plays at being a man. The contributors to this volume view their critical intervention as a reminder that the expression "space of subjectivity" is never only a convenient metaphor: different subjectivities possess different forms at different times.

The life of Abelard is a dramatic illustration of the symbolic labor involved in coming to terms with a new bodily form and its effect upon social subjectivity. Though the essays of Martin Irvine and Bonnie Wheeler clash on the notion of whether or not Abelard was engaged in a project of remasculinization, both reveal the castrate's deep investments in dialectic and disputation—discursive forms allowing for the rehearsal and performance of masculinity in a space where such forms assume a full "phallic exchange value" (language *as* phallus).[31] Opened up through language, Abelard's space of play enables a (fetishistic) relation to the lost object and its equivalent in language that effectively wards off the menace of castration.

Attention to the forces that shaped male-becoming allows us not only to see multiple bodies in their specificity, but also the body as itself multiple, composed of generative forces and flows. The attention this collection pays to instances of monstrous becoming (becoming-dog and becoming-wolf) reorients us to a medieval male body that is highly mobile, resistant to coding by one transcendental signifier. Analyses of radical becoming, like those of Cohen and Dunton-Downer, show how male identity operates across independent, but always interconnected, economies: humanness and maleness, Oedipalness and non-Oedipalness. Nevertheless, there is something inveterately nomadic about masculine bodily identity, an inherent fluidity or plasticity, that impels its own regulation. Institutionally sanctioned authority inevitably constrains the trajectories for refiguring subjectivity. Despite the liberatory possibilities for recomposing one's existential corporeality and social identity, cultural forces such as the Church or court worked to direct lines of flight or becoming. The identity plots wherein Gowther becomes a saint and Bisclavret becomes human by losing his maleness dramatize the different ways bodily identity is organized along specific lines of flight within a historically defined social field.

The point to underscore is that there are several organizing lines. The Early-Modern sexed body reveals, as James Goldstein shows, that however much the body is subject to the heavy pressures of the symbolic order, that order is anything but historically immutable. Indeed, a plurality of sexed body-positions were taken up in relation to metaphysical abstractions such as the Phallus (Sturges's essay) or Adult Sexuality (Frantzen's essay) and to the regime of heterosexuality (the essays of Burger and Epp). The lines along which medieval male bodies moved through social space were untried passageways of escape as well as deeply worn tracks of necessity. This collection offers one map of those byways.

A critically informed study of masculinity in the Middle Ages ought not merely to regard men as memorial objects, inert correlatives of knowledge-power systems, for such treatment elides the degree to which historicity and memory themselves entail desire for the new—desire, as Deleuze and Guattari teach us, that implies the ceaseless fabrication of desiring/becoming subjects.[32] What is at stake in the study of medieval masculinities, the contributors agree, is nothing less than emphasizing the historical formation of men's desire to become. This is an intervention that involves stressing men's ontological desire, their unique predisposition toward being. It leaves behind the familiar historical questioning of men ("What ever became of them?") in order to begin to pursue another, more crucial line of questioning: In what ways did they come to be? What are the forms of masculine subjectivity considered from the viewpoint of their production?

NOTES

1. Quoted in George Poulet, *The Interior Distance* (Baltimore: Johns Hopkins UP, 1959), p. 281.

2. Jacques Rancière, "Discovering New Worlds: Politics of Travel and Metaphors of Space," in *Travellers' Tales: Narratives of Home and Displacement,* George Robertson, Melinda Mash, Lisa Tickner, Jon Bird, Barry Curtis, and Tim Putnam, eds. (New York: Routledge, 1994), p. 33.

3. See Danielle Jacquart and Claude Thomasset, *Sexuality and Medicine in the Middle Ages*, Matthew Adamson, trans. (Princeton: Princeton UP, 1988), and Joan Cadden, *Meanings of Sex Difference in the Middle Ages: Medicine, Science, Culture* (Cambridge: Cambridge UP, 1993).

4. Roger Bacon, *The Opus majus of Roger Bacon,* Robert Belle Burke, trans., 2 vols. (Philadelphia: U of Pennsylvania P, 1928) 1: 320. Compare statements in Pliny the Elder, *Naturalis historia* 2.80.189–91, in *Natural History*, H. Rackham, trans., 10 vols. (Cambridge: Harvard UP, 1949), and Albertus Magnus, *De natura loci*, tract. 1 cap. 2, in *De natura loci/De causis proprietatum elementorum/De generatione et corruptione*, ed. Paul Hossfeld, vol. 5, pt. 2 of *Opera omnia* (Aschendorff: Monasterii Westfalorum, 1980), pp. 3–4.

5. Bacon, *Opus majus*, p. 159.

6. Thus Albertus Magnus, in *De natura loci*, distinguishes among the seven habitable zones:

> Propter quod iam quartum clima et vicinum sibi quintum laudabilia sunt, quae media sunt inter istas excellentias, habentia laudabiles utriusque gentis proprietates medias, secundum quod unicuique facile indagare, qui scit medium constitui ab extremis; est enim aetas istorum longa et operationes tam naturales quam animales laudabilissimae et mores boni et studia laudabilia, nisi ex consuetudine inducantur ad prava. Mores autem aquilonarium lupini sunt propter cordium eorum calorem. Leves autem nimis sunt meridionales. Medii autem inter hos facile colunt iustitiam et fidem servant et pacem amplectuntur et hominum diligunt societatem. (tract. 2 cap. 3, p. 27)

The same kind of cultural superiority is expressed in Aristotle's *Politics* 7.6 (see *Politics*, H. Rackham, trans. [Cambridge: Harvard UP, 1967], p. 567). The middle regions of the world, here the fourth and fifth climates, were naturally conducive to the benefits of golden moderation: justice, faith, peace, and respect for the society of men. The "others" at the edge, strangers to such benefits, became the victims of a science that rooted them in place, thus subject to the influences of climate, and of a morality that fixed their abject relation to the virtuous center.

7. William of Malmesbury, for example, attributed to Pope Urban the theory that climate determines physique, which in turn determines national character. Such climate theory was used to explain why Turks refuse to close with their enemies, preferring to fire their arrows from a distance. See William of Malmesbury, *De gestis regum*, William Stubbs, ed. (Rolls Series, 90) 2: 393ff. More commonly, climate theory explained the bestiality of eastern peoples living in the hot regions. Jacque de Vitry, for instance, held that "in partibus Orientis, et maxime in calidis regionibus bruti et luxuriosi homines, quibus austeritas Christiane religionis intolerabilis et importabilis videbatur,...viam que ducit ad mortem, facile sunt ingressi" (*Libro duo, quorum prior orientalis, sive Hierosolymitanae: alter, occidentalis historiae nomine inscribitur* [Douay, 1597], vol. 1, cap. 6: 25–26).

8. Kristin Ross, *The Emergence of Social Space: Rimbaud and the Paris Commune* (Minneapolis: U of Minnesota P, 1988), p. 35.

9. Paul Schilder, "Psycho-Analysis of Space," *International Journal of Psycho-Analysis* 16 (1935): 274. Indeed, contemporary readings of the spatial metaphorics of identity tend to focus almost exclusively on the intersubjective, political space outside the body. See, for instance, Kathleen M. Kirby, *Indifferent Boundaries: Spatial Concepts of Human Subjectivity* (New York: Guilford, 1996); *Sexuality and Space*, Beatriz Colomina, ed. (New York: Princeton Architectural Press, 1992); and Doreen Massey, *Space, Place, and Gender* (Minneapolis: U of Minnesota P, 1994).

10. Jean-Luc Nancy, "Identity and Trembling," in *The Birth to Presence*, Brian Holmes, trans. (Stanford: Stanford UP, 1993), p. 30.

11. See Caroline Bynum, "Why All the Fuss about the Body? A Medievalist's Perspective," *Critical Inquiry* 2 (1995): 12–18.

12. See Cadden, *Meaning of Sex*, pp. 169–227.

13. See, for example, Cadden, *Meaning of Sex*, pp. 180–81.

14. Jeffrey Jerome Cohen and the Members of Interscripta, "Medieval Masculinities: Heroism, Sanctity, and Gender," http://www.georgetown.edu/labyrinth/e-center/interscripta/mm.html.

15. For studies of how thinking is embodied and how bodies constitute the limit of discourses of knowledge, see *Thinking Bodies*, Juliet Flower MacCannell and Laura Zakarin, eds. (Stanford: Stanford UP, 1994), and Elizabeth Grosz, *Volatile Bodies: Toward a Corporeal Feminism* (Bloomington: Indiana UP, 1994), pp. 27–111.

16. All quotations are from *The Riverside Chaucer*, 3rd ed., Larry D. Benson, gen. ed. (Boston: Houghton Mifflin, 1987); hereafter cited in text by line number.

17. On the characteristic traits of *gallus domesticus*, see John M. Steadman, "Chauntecleer and Medieval Natural History," *Isis* 50 (1959): 236–44.

18. Bartholomaeus Angelicus, *De proprietatibus rerum* (London, 1601; rpt. 1964) 12.17, trans. as *On the Properties of Things: John Trevisa's Translation of Bartholomaeus Angelicus'* De proprietatibus rerum*: A Critical Text*, M. C. Seymour et al., eds. (Oxford: Clarendon P, 1975) 1: 627.

19. Bartholomew the Englishman contrasts the sexes this way: "The male passiþ þe femel in parfite complexion [and wirkyng, in wiþ and discrecioun, in miȝt and in lordschippe: in parfit complexioun] for in comparisoun to þe femel þe male is hoot and drie, and þe femel aȝgenward. In the male beþ vertues formal and of schapinge and werchinge, and in þe femel material, suffringe, and passiue" (Bartholomaeus Angelicus, *On the Properties of Things* 6. 12; 1: 306).

20. Peter Sloterdijk, *Critique of Cynical Reason*, Michael Eldred, trans. (Minneapolis: U of Minnesota P, 1987), p. 343. See pp. 343–346 for a development of the notion of "black empiricism" in medical approaches to the body.

21. Sloterdijk, *Critique*, p. 345.

22. Steadman, "Chauntecleer," 241. Princely and warrior-like, the cock became, as Steadman points out, the very model for knightly conduct in Jean de Condé's *Li Dis du koc.*

23. The choleric body is subject to the timely movements of its own production of humoral material. Albertus Magnus explained that choler moves chiefly in intervals of three (at every third year, month, and so on), and in the case of the cock, every third hour is the time at which he sings most strongly because then choler is produced in the gall-bladder and transferred to the heart. Such "fumositates cholericae" compel the cock to flap his wings before crowing, and, compared to the less-choleric hen, the cock's voice is especially shrill. See Albertus Magnus, *Quaestiones super De animalibus*, Ephrem Filthaut, ed. (Aschendorff, 1955), vol. 12 of *Alberti Magni opera omnia,* Bernhard Geyer, gen. ed. (Aschendorff, 1951–), pp. 201–2.

24. The contradictions in Pertelote's intervention are manifold: she misdiagnoses the cause of Chauntecleer's dream as excessive choler while also displaying a deep knowledge of masculine bird physiology; she takes his groaning to be at once a sign of his unmanliness and a symptom of his excessive choler, and urges upon him purgatives aimed at reducing the very heat and dryness vital to his masculinity (as signified in hearty crowing).

25. Thirty-five MSS contain *The Man of Law's Epilogue*, and of those, 28 attribute the statement to the Squire, 6 to the Summoner, and one to the Shipman, though it is to the latter editors usually attribute the statement. And although medieval scribes and modern editors unanimously attribute the statement to a male, since the *Epilogue* was probably designed to introduce *The Shipman's Tale*, a tale most likely assigned to The Wife of

Bath or another female speaker, the phrase *my joly body* (echoed by the wyf of *ShipT* at line 423) does itself suggest a female speaker. Despite the chain of probabilities here, the fact remains that medieval readers had no trouble in seeing the phrase as exemplifying a masculine mode of production.

26. Indeed, Melanie Klein's descriptions of the space of the body in fragments suggest that the unitary body is an impossible structure. See, especially, Melanie Klein, "Notes on Some Schizoid Mechanisms," in *The Selected Melanie Klein*, Juliet Mitchell, ed. (New York: Free Press, 1986), pp. 175–200. Compare Lacan's picture of this space: "We must turn to the works of Hieronymous Bosch for an atlas of all the aggressive images that torment mankind" ("Aggressivity in Psychoanalysis," in *Ecrits: A Selection*, Alan Sheridan, trans. [New York: Norton, 1977], p. 11). For the premodern body in fragments, see Piero Camporesi, *The Incorruptible Flesh: Bodily Mutation and Mortification in Religion and Folklore,* Tania Croft-Murray and Helen Elsom, trans. (Cambridge: Cambridge UP, 1988); *Juice of Life: The Symbolic and Magic Significance of Blood*, Robert R. Barr, trans. (New York: Continuum, 1995); and Jonathan Sawday, *The Body Emblazoned: Dissection and the Human Body in Renaissance Culture* (New York: Routledge, 1995). For a stimulating account of mutilation as cultural and psychological practice, see Armando R. Favazza, *Bodies under Siege: Self-Mutilation in Culture and Psychiatry* (Baltimore: Johns Hopkins UP, 1987).

27. Conceptions of the social body (world, political community) and architectural structures (house, hall, church, temple) as analogous to the human body are not only ancient but found in nonwestern traditions. See, for example, A. K. Coomaraswamy, "An Indian Temple: The Kamdarya Mahedo," in *Coomaraswamy: Selected Papers*, R. Lipsey, ed. (Princeton: Princeton UP, 1977). For more on body metaphorics, see Archie Taylor, "A Metaphor of the Human Body in Literature and Tradition," in *Corona: Studies in Celebration of the Eightieth Birthday of Samuel Singer*, Arno Schirokauer and Wolfgang Paulsen, eds. (Durham: Duke UP, 1941); and Elizabeth Grosz, "Bodies-Cities," in *Space, Time, and Perversion: Essays on the Politics of Bodies* (New York: Routledge, 1995), pp. 103–110.

28. Grosz, "Space, Time, and Bodies," in *Space, Time, and Perversion*, p. 92.

29. Grosz, "Space, Time, and Bodies," p. 92.

30. See D.W. Winnicott, *Playing and Reality* (New York: Basic Books, 1971).

31. In Jean Baudrillard's terms, bodies only assume their "phallic exchange value" within the logics of perversion. The female, or castrated, body sets up an "erotic return" where, for example, through the erotic self-gratification of striptease, narcissism protects the subject from the threat of castration and the death drive. See the chapter "The Body, or the Mass Grave of Signs," in his *Symbolic Exchange and Death*, Iain Hamilton Grant, trans. (London: Sage, 1993), pp. 101–24.

32. See Gilles Deleuze and Félix Guattari, *A Thousand Plateaus: Capitalism and Schizophrenia*, Brian Massumi, trans. (Minneapolis: U of Minnesota P, 1987). See also Félix Guattari, "On the Production of Subjectivity," in *Chaosmosis: An Ethico-Aesthetic Paradigm*, Paul Bains and Julian Pefanis, trans. (Bloomington: Indiana UP, 1995), pp. 1–32. Or the badly translated essay "Becoming a Woman," in Félix Guattari, *Molecular Revolution: Psychiatry and Politics*, Rosemary Sheed, trans. (New York: Penguin, 1984), pp. 233–35.

CONTRIBUTORS

Glenn Burger is Associate Professor of English at the University of Alberta. He has published on gender and sexuality in Chaucerian texts. He is currently working on *Queer Chaucer*, a queer deconstruction of Chaucerian canonicity and gendered representation in *The Canterbury Tales.*

Jeffrey Jerome Cohen is Assistant Professor of English and Associate Director of the Program in Human Sciences at George Washington University. He has edited a collection of essays on the intersection of teratology and identity theory, *Monster Theory: Reading Culture,* and is working on *Sex, Monsters, and the Middle Ages.*

Leslie Dunton-Downer, currently a Junior Fellow at the Harvard Society of Fellows, studies poetic language.

Garrett P.J. Epp is an Associate Professor of English at the University of Alberta. He works on issues of gender, sexuality, and performance in early English drama. His 1994 production of *Mankind* offended audiences in Toronto and Edmonton.

Yves Ferroul is a psychoanalyst and cultural historian on the faculty of the University of Lille III. His most recent book is *Heloise et Abélard, lettres et vies* (1996).

Allen J. Frantzen teaches Old and Middle English at Loyola University, Chicago. He is working on a hypertext edition of the Anglo-Saxon penitentials and *Straightforward*, a book on same-sex relations in early medieval England.

R. James Goldstein, Associate Professor of English at Auburn University, is the author of *The Matter of Scotland: Historical Narrative in Medieval Scotland.* He has recently completed an essay for the *Cambridge History of Medieval English Literature.*

Martin Irvine is Associate Professor of English and Director of the Communication, Culture, and Technology Program at Georgetown University. He is the author of *The Making of Textual Culture* and the co-director of the Labyrinth, a Website for medieval studies. He is currently at work on a book on the letters of Abelard and Heloise.

Ruth Mazo Karras is Professor of History at Temple University. She is the author of *Common Women: Prostitution and Sexuality in Medieval England* and numerous articles on aspects of gender and sexuality in medieval Europe.

Steven F. Kruger teaches queer studies and medieval studies at Queens College and CUNY. He is author of several books, such as *Dreaming in the Middle Ages*. His next book project is a study of medieval identity categories and conversion experience.

Ad Putter is Lecturer in English at the University of Bristol, England. He is the author of *Sir Gawain and the Green Knight and French Arthurian Romance* (1995). His *An Introduction to the Gawain-Poet* is in press.

D. Vance Smith is an Assistant Professor of English at Princeton University. He holds a Ph.D. from the University of Virginia, and was a Fulbright Scholar at King's College, London, and Magdalen College, Oxford. He has also taught at West Virginia University.

Claire Sponsler teaches at the University of Iowa, is the author of *Disciplines of Identity: Bodies, Goods, and Theatricality in Late Medieval England*, and is writing a book about medieval drama in America.

Robert S. Sturges is Professor of English at the University of New Orleans. He is the author of *Medieval Interpretation* and of numerous essays on medieval literature. He is working on a book about Chaucer's Pardoner and theories of gender.

David Townsend is Associate Professor of Medieval Studies and English at the University of Toronto. He has published extensively on medieval Latin texts and their interpretation. His verse translation of Walter of Châtillon's *Alexandreis* is forthcoming.

Michael Uebel teaches at the University of Virginia, where he recently finished a Ph.D. in medieval literature. He is the editor of *Race and the Subject of Masculinities* (Duke University Press, 1997).

Bonnie Wheeler is Director of the Medieval Studies Program at Southern Methodist University. She writes about late medieval literature and culture, and is the editor of the quarterly *Arthuriana*. She is the editor of *The New Middle Ages* series for which she has recently co-edited *Fresh Verdicts on Joan of Arc* and *Medieval Mothering*.

Elliot R. Wolfson is Professor of Hebrew and Judaic Studies and Director of Religious Studies at NYU. Author of a number of monographs and essays on the history of Jewish mysticism, principally in the High Middle Ages, he is currently working on a book on *eros* and the construction of gender in Jewish mysticism.